OXFORD HISTORICAL MONOGRAPHS

The Theatre of Nation

Irish Drama and Cultural Nationalism
1890–1916

BEN LEVITAS

CLARENDON PRESS · OXFORD

OXFORD
UNIVERSITY PRESS

Great Clarendon Street, Oxford OX2 6DP

Oxford University Press is a department of the University of Oxford.
It furthers the University's objective of excellence in research, scholarship,
and education by publishing worldwide in

Oxford New York

Auckland Bangkok Buenos Aires Cape Town Chennai
Dar es Salaam Delhi Hong Kong Istanbul Karachi Kolkata
Kuala Lumpur Madrid Melbourne Mexico City Mumbai Nairobi
São Paulo Shanghai Taipei Tokyo Toronto

Oxford is a registered trade mark of Oxford University Press
in the UK and in certain other countries

Published in the United States
by Oxford University Press Inc., New York

British Library Cataloguing in Publication Data

Data available

Library of Congress Cataloging in Publication Data

Data available

ISBN 0-19-925343-9

1 3 5 7 9 10 8 6 4 2

Typeset in Ehrhardt by
Cambrian Typesetters, Frimley, Surrey
Printed in Great Britain
on acid-free paper by
Biddles Ltd,
Guildford and King's Lynn

For my mother,

JACKIE LITHERLAND

and in memory of my father,

MAURICE LEVITAS

PREFACE

What role did the theatre of the Irish literary revival play in the politics of identity so avidly debated in pre-revolutionary Ireland? Conversely, how far did that debate influence the development of the theatre? This book is an examination of the vexed dialectic of such questions through an integrated study of the nationalist debate 1890–1916. In part it was the very necessity of forcing together two areas of apparently distinct concern that first attracted me to tackle the material at issue. The spheres of political history and literary examination are too often estranged in existing scholarship, but their combination is essential to this subject. Tackling the political debates and the controversial drama of this unusually creative era, the theatre is here revealed as a focal point for the culturally charged controversies of the period.

Those controversies are also revealed as far from static, and far from limited to the most obvious issue of Irish independence. Concerns about class, race, gender, regional and generational difference were no less central during what was recognized as a period of cultural flux. Nor were such considerations limited to Ireland, but extended to Ireland's situation in the Empire and, particularly, to its European status. It is in this reaction to European as well as imperial modernity that the theatre's role in inspiring insurrectionary logics is concluded.

To plot the course of this discourse through the turns and twists of its expression, from the disgrace of Parnell to the crisis of *The Playboy* 'riots' and the denouement of the Easter Rising, requires a diverse range of materials. The Abbey Theatre and its directors, W. B. Yeats, Lady Gregory, and J. M. Synge performed a central part in the processes outlined here, but beyond the Abbey were the equally crucial popular, propagandist, and the regional theatres. The theatre movement is discussed here in its splendid variety, drawing upon a much wider array of dramatic talent than is allowed for by the existing canon. Such talent was evident in the plays of the period, in performances, in criticism both public and private, and in the organizational skill of impresarios. The cultural and political dispute which surrounded and included this movement likewise found its form through newspapers, personal correspondence, through private and public debate. This book employs the full range of media, often considering new material and familiar text in unfamiliar context. What pleasure was derived from its construction may in no small part be ascribed to the quality of these discussions and their unpredictable energy.

My most pressing acknowledgement is to Roy Foster. As supervisor to the D.Phil. thesis upon which this book is based, and as sub-editor to the completed work, he has been unstinting in advice, and without his encouragement and care it would never have come to pass. I would also like to thank for their consideration and comments Terry Eagleton, Adrian Frazier, and Philip Waller.

My study for the doctorate at Oxford University was funded by the British Academy. Wadham College, my academic home during those years, provided a stimulating and supportive base from which to explore the wealth of Oxford's learning. The conversion of thesis into book was largely completed while lecturing at Queen's University, Belfast, and to everyone at the School of Politics my gratitude for making my time there so conducive. My thanks too for the generous support of my current colleagues at the Drama Department, Goldsmiths.

The staff and librarians of the following institutions made my research pleasant as well as feasible: the Archives Department, University College, Dublin; the National Library of Ireland, Dublin; the British Library, including Colindale Newspaper Library, London; the Bodleian Library, Oxford; the Linen Hall Library, Belfast; the Queen's University Library, Belfast; the Henry W. and Albert A. Berg Collection, New York Public Library.

Many thanks are due Oxford University Press: to Anne Gelling, Dorothy McCarthy, Ruth Parr, and Kay Rogers for so expertly facilitating the publication of this book; and to Rowena Anketell for the excellence of her copy-editing. The following people also deserve, whether for their hospitality, kindness, or formative influence, special mention: Scott Ashley, Michael Ayton, Dave Bell, Nicola Gordon Bowe, Sean Bulmer, Fergus Campbell, Stephen Cummins, Angela Darnell, Simon Doubleday, Peter Hart, Alan Finlayson, Jane Garnett, Alex Gefter, Charles and Natasha Grigg, Jessica Grigg, John Kelly, Jim Martin, Patrick Maume, Sharon McClenaghan, Francesca Morris, Roo O'Driscoll, Jim O'Hanlon, Manus O'Riordan, Eileen Reilly, Robin Whitaker, and Neal White. Double salutations go to Ronan McDonald and Ray Ryan for their friendship and disputatiousness, both crucial; to my sister Rachel for her unswerving support; and to my wider family. The dedication is merely a small recognition of all my parents have done for me; my mother Jackie Litherland also offered key improvements to the text, for which extra thanks. To Jennifer Grigg, my wife, I owe a debt deeper than can be expressed here. And finally, to our son Samuel, who has helped to make me a morning person.

B.L.

CONTENTS

Abbreviations   x

Introduction   1

1. The Quintessence of Parnellism: The Search for an Irish
   Theatre, 1890–1897   9

2. 'A Mesh of Error': Dramatic Alliances, 1898–1902   37

3. The Union of Sceptics, 1903–1906   75

4. The Room of Mirrors: The debut of *The Playboy of the
   Western World*   115

5. 'The Loy in Irish Politics', 1907–1909   137

6. *Ghosts* and Spectres: Theatres of War, 1910–1916   178

Conclusion: Mahon and the Echo   227

Bibliography   243

Index   259

ABBREVIATIONS

ACS	*An Claidheamh Soluis*
AOH	Ancient Order of Hibernians
Berg	The Henry W. and Albert A. Berg Collection, New York Public Library
BL	British Library
CDS	Cork Dramatic Society
CLS	Celtic Literary Society
DMP	Dublin Metropolitan Police
GAA	Gaelic Athletic Association
ILS	Irish Literary Society
ILT	Irish Literary Theatre
INA	Irish National Alliance
INDC	Irish National Dramatic Company
INTS	Irish National Theatre Society
IPP	Irish Parliamentary Party
IRB	Irish Republican Brotherhood
ISRP	Irish Socialist and Republican Party
ITGWU	Irish Transport and General Workers' Union
IWFL	Irish Women's Franchise League
NLI	National Library of Ireland
NLS	National Literary Society
NTS	National Theatre Society
RIC	Royal Irish Constabulary
TCD	Trinity College Dublin
UIL	United Irish League
ULT	Ulster Literary Theatre
UCD	University College Dublin
Yeats, *VP*	*The Variorum Edition of the Plays of W. B. Yeats*, ed. Russell K. Alspach, assisted by Catherine C. Alspach (London, 1966)

Says the Eastern Proverb—'A man is more like his own time than his own father.' The dramatist is the child of his time and his locality.

Padraic Colum
Evening Telegraph, 20 May 1911

Introduction

Curtain up at the Opera House in Cork, September 1907. In the theatre for the first time since childhood, Risteard Ó Crúca had little idea what to expect. Frankly unschooled in the ways of drama criticism, he somehow found himself reporting on the National Theatre Society's—the Abbey Theatre's—first trip to his native city. He was overwhelmed:

> I had hazy impressions of visits in days gone by to plays like 'Robert Emmet,' 'Conn the Shaughraun,' and the 'Colleen Bawn,' as staged by such strolling Barnstormers as chanced to our little town . . . With the rise of the curtain, I forgot Cork and its incongruities. In a moment I knew I would not be disappointed. My boyish illusions were replaced by realities sweeter than the illusions. Here I saw men and women that I knew, and heard talk that was not strange to me . . . Here I saw before me the life of my own people, and it was not caricatured nor demeaned to a laughing-stock. I was at home, and felt delighted and happy. And ever since I've been seeing plays in the streets and the market places, where formerly I passed with unseeing eyes.[1]

Ó Crúca's rapture was comprehensive. But despite celebrating his 'great joy', praising actors, play, and playwrights, he finally felt unequal to the task. Of *Cathleen ni Houlihan* he admitted, 'I am no more able to express the exquisite pleasure it gave me than the man who reads and appreciates a beautiful poem can write one'; and of *Riders to the Sea* confessed, 'I feel how inadequate must be anything that I can say. No tragedy that I ever read affected me like this.'[2]

The budding critic had another problem. He was reporting for the *Leader*, the satirically scathing organ of Catholic cultural nationalism, and a severe critic of the Abbey—particularly that year, the year of J. M. Synge's riot-inducing play *The Playboy of the Western World*. The paper's editor D. P. Moran published the piece, but naïve wonderment was out of place, and thus Ó Crúca blessed his pages only once, in the smallest bit part of the Irish literary revival.

For today's critic, for the historian of that revival, the uninformed enthusiasm of that report is nevertheless a salutary encounter. The honest excitement of a sensitive viewer seeing for the first time an attempt to

---

[1] 'The National Theatre Society in Cork,' *Leader*, 7 Sept. 1907.
[2] Ibid.

produce a self-consciously national drama, winning through to create a
new perception of the dynamism of that shared community, is palpable.
Yet so are the questions that remain unanswered, or for Ó Crúca, un-
answerable. What had taken place on Ireland's stages to account for the
change from the melodramatic 'strolling Barnstormers' he remembered
from his youth, to the farm-centred productions he now witnessed? Were
these plays typical of the Abbey's output? If their attempt to treat a
national subject was so successful, what had made the National Theatre
Society (NTS) such a controversial outfit? What place did their performances have in the aspirations of Irish nationalists to reassert a native
culture or to establish Ireland's political independence? In other words,
what role did the national Drama have in the National drama?

W. B. Yeats provided an answer which for a long time became orthodoxy. The key, he famously suggested, was the fall of Charles Stuart
Parnell in 1890, after which a 'disillusioned Ireland turned from politics'[3]
to cultural nationalism, and from thence to physical resistance. And there
is potency in this theory. Nationalist politics in Ireland appeared to be
gathering force and gaining cohesion toward the end of the nineteenth
century. The 1870s and 1880s saw a coming together of constitutional and
physical-force nationalists behind organizations which included a popular Land League movement and a disciplined Nationalist Party. Reforms
that eroded the power of the Protestant Ascendancy elite had been
conceded by the imperial parliament at Westminster, and if the crucial
repeal of the Act of Union had yet to be achieved, the advent of Home
Rule was eyed with confident anticipation. There was inevitably a loss of
that momentum when the Party learned of Parnell's adultery and split
over the issue of whether to follow a leader whose credibility had been
broken along with his reputation. How could another failed Home Rule
Bill in 1893 not have sealed disillusion and sent Ireland's mind elsewhere?
And once engaged in redefining its own sense of identity, would it not
lead, naturally, to a more vigorous drive for independence?

This idea of a linear progression made from political to cultural to
military nationalism by a homogeneous 'people' has been ably undermined by both historians and literary critics. The imposingly versatile
scholar Joep Leerssen has demonstrated at length the centrality of
cultural discourse to national identity in Ireland, tracing its development
across the eighteenth and nineteenth centuries, thereby scotching any

---

[3] *Autobiographies* (London, 1955), 559; repr. from his Nobel lecture to the Royal
Academy of Sweden in 1923.

notion that the phenomenon of cultural nationalism appeared magically with the fall of Parnell;[4] and John Hutchinson's able analysis also carefully records the momentum of the revival prior to his departure.[5] Likewise it has been persuasively argued that political nationalism did not make way for its cultural cousin, but was an ever-present element of the cultural milieu that formed the context for the literary revival.

F. S. L. Lyons once complained that the two decades after 1890 had often been 'dismissed by historians as a kind of political vacuum',[6] while William Irwin Thompson, whose elaboration on the Yeatsian model, *The Imagination of an Insurrection*, evidently influenced Lyons, had mused that 'we can only hope . . . we will be able to see the integrity of the curve without spending a lifetime inking in a thousand points'.[7] A generation later, as Patrick Maume has observed, scholarly coverage of the period is still 'patchy'.[8] But much has been done to ink in the vectors of Ireland's development. A diversity of identities, notions of class interest, generational revolt, and gender difference have been allowed to trouble the easy oppositions which previously prevailed. Tom Garvin has investigated the 'protean' nature of nationalist ideology; Paul Bew and Roy Foster have sought out the missing politics of the period in mainstream nationalism and marginal cultural operatives; Dermot Keogh and C. D. Greaves have forced the issue of trade-unionism; the rise of feminism has begun to be traced by Rosemary Cullen Owens and Cliona Murphy, and new studies of aspirational middle-class politics have been produced by Senia Paseta and Patrick Maume.[9]

[4] *Mere Irish and Fíor-Ghael: Studies in the Idea of Irish Nationality, its Development and Literary Expression prior to the Nineteenth Century* (2nd edn., Cork, 1996), and *Remembrance and Imagination: Patterns in the Historical and Literary Representation of Ireland in the Nineteenth Century* (Cork, 1996).

[5] *The Dynamics of Cultural Nationalism: The Gaelic Revival and the Creation of the Irish Nation State* (London, 1987).

[6] *Ireland since the Famine* (London, 1971), 202.

[7] *The Imagination of an Insurrection—Dublin, Easter 1916: A Study of an Ideological Movement* (Oxford, 1967), 232.

[8] *The Long Gestation: Irish National Life 1891–1918* (Dublin, 1999), 1.

[9] Garvin, *Nationalist Revolutionaries in Ireland 1858–1928* (Oxford, 1988); Bew, *Conflict and Conciliation in Ireland 1890–1910: Parnellites and Radical Agrarians* (Oxford, 1987) and *Ideology and the Irish Question: Ulster Unionism and Irish Nationalism 1912–1916* (Oxford, 1994); R. F. Foster, *Modern Ireland 1600–1972* (London, 1988) and *Paddy and Mr Punch: Connections in Irish and English History* (London, 1993); Dermot Keogh, *The Rise of the Irish Working Class: The Dublin Trade Union Movement and Labour Leadership 1890–1914* (Belfast, 1982); C. D. Greaves, *The Irish Transport and General Workers' Union: The Formative Years 1909–1923* (Dublin, 1988); Rosemary Cullen Owen, *Smashing Times: A History of the Irish Women's Suffrage Movement 1889–1922* (Dublin, 1982); Cliona Murphy, *The Women's Movement and Irish Society in the Early Twentieth Century* (Hemel Hempstead,

This is a period, moreover, in which literary history has proven a powerful engine of enquiry. Such was the frenzy of activity during the literary revival and so insistent has been the literature generated out of it, that it is investigation into this literature, and the manner of its relation with politics, that has driven much historical research. When examining a period in which it was de rigueur to add one's weight to the wheel of Irish cultural identity, the role of literary historian becomes one of unusual significance. An understanding of politics is necessary as literary insight to a biographer of the period, as has been recently demonstrated in Adrian Frazier's *George Moore*, W. J. McCormack's *J. M. Synge*, and Foster's *W. B. Yeats*, volume i.[10] The Yeats industry in particular has become an international mining operation, excavating enough detail of the poet's life and works to fuel adjacent engines of enquiry for some time to come. The *Yeats Annual* edited by Warwick Gould and Deirdre Toomey has become essential reading, and the scholarship in John Kelly's early editions of the collected Yeats letters has set the standard. Complementing this counter-offensive by literary history against the tendency of literary criticism to colonize other areas of the academy, has been the application of post-colonial theory to the Irish experience. Despite controversies that have occasionally misconstrued political difference as methodological incompatibility, this approach has supported rather than undermined historical revision with sophisticated expansions upon an already complex dialectic. David Cairns and Shaun Richards, Seamus Deane and Declan Kiberd are merely the foremost in a small army of critics whose elaborate placings of Irish literature into a colonial model have combined broad overviews with the close reading of texts and a good deal of comparative work, aligning Ireland with other colonized cultures.[11]

Edward Said, gearing up for a radical revision of Yeats as a decolonizing poet, posited a wary approach to nationalism (adopted from Fanon via Partha Chatterjee):

Successful anti-imperialist nationalism has a history of evasion and avoidance . . .

1989); Senia Paseta, *Before the Revolution: Nationalism, Social Change and Ireland's Catholic Élite 1897–1922* (Cork, 1999); Maume, *Long Gestation*.

[10] Frazier, *George Moore, 1852–1933* (New Haven, 2000); McCormack, *Fool of the Family: A Life of J. M. Synge* (London, 2000); R. F. Foster, *W. B. Yeats, A Life*, i. *The Apprentice Mage, 1865–1914* (Oxford, 1997).

[11] Cairns and Richards, *Writing Ireland: Colonialism, Nationalism and Culture* (Manchester, 1988); Deane, *Celtic Revivals: Essays in Modern Irish Literature, 1880–1980* (London, 1985) and *Strange Country: Modernity and Nationhood in Irish Writing since 1790* (Oxford, 1997); Kiberd, *Inventing Ireland* (London, 1995) and *Irish Classics* (London, 2000).

Nationalism can become a panacea for not dealing with economic disparities, social injustice, and the capture of the newly independent state by a nationalist elite . . . culture's contribution to statism is often the result of a separatist, even chauvinist and authoritarian conception of nationalism.[12]

Against this, Said was anxious to add, the wide spectrum of nation-alisms has to be taken into account; the self-critical elements as well as the polemical. The object is—while viewing the process under observation as generally one of liberation—to recognize the need to ground literary and cultural evaluation in historically situated power relations, internal and external. Even a cultural critic as hostile as David Lloyd to the suppos-edly statist emphasis of empiricism has called for the 're-envisioning' of modernization to provide 'new and supplementary histories of what has been left out of Irish history'.[13]

My intention with this book is to provide an integrated reading of the development of the national theatre in Ireland, alert both to political complexity and the literary nuance essential to its apprehension. Despite the range and quality of the scholarship already available, disciplinary barriers in the academy have tended to preserve the false divisions of Yeatsian orthodoxy, limiting the impact of each set of revisions one upon the other. To the breadth of this task may be ascribed the temporal para-meters of this book, which returns to the clichéd dates of 1890 and 1916 without apology. If literary, cultural, and political nationalism were contin-ually evolving and interacting, the conditions of their development must be followed with equal diligence, demanding the integration, and widen-ing, of existing scholarship. Apart from the irony that historical revision must often observe the parameters of orthodoxy, there is a distinct need for a manageable time span. Boundaries, while always suspect, necessarily help throw up the shapes as well as fluidities of change.

In attempting to follow this relationship between literature and poli-tics, there is perhaps no form more appropriate for investigation than drama and its performance. The theatre provides a plethora of images for those describing the political process and is, after all, an arena where one may also perform exploratory surgery or watch gladiatorial contests. Drama is a public art which shares the immediate benefits and inevitable risks of speaking directly with its constituency, the audience.[14] Because of

---

[12] *Culture and Imperialism* (London, 1993), 262.

[13] *Ireland after History* (Cork, 1999), 37.

[14] Raymond Williams, *The Long Revolution* (London, 1961) and *Modern Tragedy* (London, 1966); see also Michael Hays, 'Theatrical Texts and Social Context', *Theater* (Winter 1983); Maria Shevtsova, *Theatre and Cultural Interaction* (Sydney, 1993).

this ability to generate a shared response (which can then be more easily historicized), a play's performance is a surer model for tracing literary-political interaction than the printing of a poem, although the latter has been more frequently used in judging the mindset of Irish revolutionaries.

The dramatic and cultural critic Raymond Williams once reflected that, because of its role in the national struggle, Irish theatre had been neglected as a subject of integrated study. 'I can now see', he commented, 'that an interesting essay could be written analysing precisely the phases of the national movement in terms of the evolution of dramatic forms.'[15] Yet while the huge array of work on or about Irish theatre, particularly the Abbey Theatre, has benefited from incisive and varied treatments, it continues to suffer from a tendency to use a hastily painted backdrop of political life, against which more sophisticated discussions centring on the text may be played out. Every scholar in the field is indebted to the multi-volume *A History of Modern Irish Drama* compiled by Robert Hogan, James Kilroy, and others,[16] and to Cheryl Herr and Stephen Watt for bringing melodrama back into the equation.[17] Critics such as Christopher Murray, Nicholas Grene, Robert Welch, and Christopher Morash have pushed beyond canonical restrictions,[18] and a range of new studies (unhappily too new to have informed this project) from Morash, Lionel Pilkington, and Mary Trotter have widened again the ambit of enquiry.[19] but a still larger dramatis personae is required; and without developing the political background into a three-dimensional space in which to perform, their actions and motivations cannot be properly appreciated.

One of the principal devices in orchestrating this literary and political dialogue is allowing the advanced and cultural nationalist press room to

[15] *Politics and Letters: Interviews with New Left Review* (London, 1979), 200.

[16] Robert Hogan et al., *A History of Modern Irish Drama*, vols. i–vi, (Dublin, 1970–84).

[17] Herr, *For the Land They Loved: Irish Political Melodramas 1890–1925* (Syracuse, 1991); Watt, *Joyce, O'Casey, and Irish Popular Theater* (Syracuse, 1991).

[18] Murray, *Twentieth-Century Irish Drama: Mirror up to Nation* (Manchester, 1997); Grene, *The Politics of Irish Drama: Plays in Context from Boucicault to Friel* (Cambridge, 1999); Welch, *The Abbey Theatre 1899–1999: Form and Pressure* (Oxford, 1999); Morash, '"Something's Missing": Theatre and the Republic of Ireland Act', in Ray Ryan (ed.), *Writing in the Irish Republic: Literature, Culture, Politics 1949–1999* (London, 2000), 64–81.

[19] Morash, *A History of Irish Theatre, 1601–2000* (Cambridge, 2002); Pilkington, *Theatre and the State in Twentieth-Century Ireland: Cultivating the People* (London, 2001); Trotter, *Ireland's National Theaters: Political Performance and the Origins of the Irish Dramatic Movement* (Syracuse, 2001). See also the essays collected in Stephen Watt, Eileen Morgan, and Shakir Mustafa (eds.), *A Century of Irish Drama: Widening the State* (Bloomington, Ind., 2000).

speak. In doing so I have sought to establish a structure in which the contemporary evaluation of the national theatre project is seen in the light of more general ideological positions. Voices other than the strictly dramatic must be heard in order to expand toward a wider drama of national becoming. The inclusiveness of *The Field Day Anthology of Irish Writing* has gone no small distance in allowing the journalism of this period to stake its own claim to renaissance,[20] and I hope this study will reinforce that claim. Whether one is considering the pugnacious work of Arthur Griffith, the corrosive wit of D. P. Moran, or the polemics of the master controversialist W. B. Yeats, there can be little doubt of the quality of this neglected genre.

Ireland's is a unique position, an example both of (almost) post-colonial liberation and of (semi-) successful European nationalism, located at the interface between Eurocentric nationalist ambition and a struggle against British imperialism.[21] The history of the political movements involved in these processes is therefore inevitably complex, and benefits from as much historical 'inking-in' as possible. Without this, assessing the relationship of the literary renaissance to the culture of politics becomes inevitably reductive or ceases altogether. As W. J. McCormack put it: 'behind most of the Theory erected on or about the material of Irish literature, one discovers the discarded dust jackets of someone else's empirical research'.[22] However, if my reading sacrifices theory to an emphasis on situation, it is not my intention to dismiss the processes of conceptual analysis, which I hope would be stimulated by this study.

As this study has indeed been stimulated by more theoretically centred work. When the relationship between nationalism and imperialism, or between artist and state (*in situ* or in waiting), or religious sectarianism is under consideration, it is necessary to disturb expectations with other issues. Generation, gender, and class, these three; but the greatest of these is class. Two more writers notable for the negotiation of such paradigms manifest in the Ireland under scrutiny here are Terry Eagleton, particularly those essays in *Heathcliff and the Great Hunger* which consider the hegemonics of literary production; and Adrian Frazier, whose *Behind the Scenes: Yeats, Horniman and the Struggle for the Abbey* tackles the role of the cash nexus in the mode of production of a self-professed national

---

[20] Esp. the section edited by Seamus Deane, 'Political Writings and Speeches 1900–1988', *The Field Day Anthology of Irish Writing*, iii (Derry, 1991), 681–808.

[21] Stephen Howe, *Ireland and Empire* (Oxford, 2000), 232–3.

[22] *From Burke to Beckett: Ascendancy, Tradition and Betrayal in Literary History* (Cork, 1994), 23.

theatre.[23] My intention has thus been to engage in a conjunctural study, both in the familiar sense of the term, and in Antonio Gramsci's usage as 'an intermediate field of opposition, often personal in nature, through which politics is conducted while the society is in deep crisis; and revolution immanent'.[24]

My argument thus takes shape, rather than being abstractly postulated. Through emphasizing the varieties of nationalist response to drama, those elements of the theatre which tested convention do not appear doomed to an inevitable rejection by a homogeneous, conservative nationalist audience. Nor were they necessarily trapped by tribal cultural divisions which predetermined their reception. I have sought to replace such assumptions with a model which stresses regional difference and the impact of class, gender, and generational rebellion on public perception of artistic norms.

In my opening chapter, I have linked closely the names of Ibsen and Parnell as figures whose very controversiality becomes part of the glamour of their reputation. It is in tracking the progress of such reputations that the metaphors which link politics and theatre so insistently become ever more telling. For those of a revolutionary inclination, the result of watching the progress of the theatre was to construe the lasting legacy of any given event as dependent, not on the immediate audience response, but on future judgement. Describing this process in the Irish context has led me to suggest that the very concept of theatrical unconventionality informed the awareness of audience dynamics apparent in the act of insurrection.

---

[23] Eagleton, *Heathcliff and the Great Hunger: Studies in Irish Culture* (London, 1995); Frazier, *Behind the Scenes: Yeats, Horniman and the Struggle for the Abbey* (Berkeley and Los Angeles, 1990).

[24] 'The Modern Prince', in *Selections from the Prison Notebooks*, (London, 1971), 177–8.

The Quintessence of Parnellism: The Search for an Irish Theatre, 1890–1897

Displaying the collective hubris that gave Parnell's eventual demise the status of tragedy, the *Freeman's Journal* confidently beckoned in the final decade of the nineteenth century. Attempts to link the nationalist leader to political murder had been exposed as forgery, the Chief was newly vindicated, and all was set fair for the future. 'What a scatter has been made of his defamers!', the editorial proclaimed:

Ireland today has greater faith, if possible, in him—greater belief in his star than ever. And we are sure that the expressions of that faith and of that belief shall pour in upon him at this juncture, and make him proud and strong in the security of the nation's alliance, and unshakeable, unalterable, and unswerving fealty of all Ireland, at home and abroad, to him and the holy cause to which he is guiding with honour to victory.[1]

A year on, such certainty appeared to belong to another age. Parnell's fall from grace and power to martyrdom ushered in a decade of infighting for the Irish Parliamentary Party (IPP). It was an unsightly mêlée soon seen by Parnellite apologists as the hinge upon which cultural consciousness turned, opening the door to release a literary renaissance, a language movement, and a militarily useful heroic mythology. The theory later became orthodoxy when W. B. Yeats's *Autobiographies* established a causal link between it and the next epochal occurrence, the Easter Rising. 'Troubled by that event's long gestation',[2] disillusioned Ireland in mourning sickness spewed culture, in culture found identity and in identity independence.

That was a trick of the political light. Parnell's well-made destiny was already set on its disastrous course; the sub-plot of Irish cultural confidence

---

[1] *Freeman's Journal*, 4 Jan. 1890.
[2] *Autobiographies* (London, 1955), 559, repr. from his Nobel lecture to the Royal Academy of Sweden in 1923.

already ripe.[3] The *Freeman's* statement came not from another age—just from the ominous third act of one of Ibsen's recently notorious studies in the unstable chemistry of public and private morality. When the denouement arrived—with the divorce court revelations of the long-term liaison with Katherine O'Shea, the inevitably shocked response of the moral majority (Catholic and Nonconformist), Gladstone's ultimatum, and the IPP's rancorous split—the wonder is that no one predicted Parnell's death as a necessary dramatic conclusion. 'Life is Art's best, Art's only pupil', postulated Oscar Wilde in 1889,[4] the same year that Ibsen first caught the imagination of London.[5] When, in 1891, the West End debut of *Ghosts* provoked a rancorous public row reminiscent of that already begun in Ireland, Ibsen and Parnell both appeared as Dr Stockmann, enemies of the people forced on to the back foot of righteous unpopularity. 'You have a faction (of another kind) raging in Ireland just now,' commented the *Freeman's* London correspondent omnisciently. 'You know what sort of things men *will* say about each other when they have got it badly.'[6]

George Bernard Shaw, then in the process of establishing himself in London's socialist and literary circles, had been fulminating on the importance of Ibsen when the Parnell scandal ignited. He found his conclusions confirmed. Published in 1891, *The Quintessence of Ibsenism* marked a juncture of rejection, in which the double cause célèbre had exposed the false idealism of bourgeois society no less ably than one of

[3] For the more recent counter-emphasis on continuity, see Malcolm Brown, *The Politics of Irish Literature, from Davis to W. B. Yeats* (London, 1972); John Hutchinson, *The Dynamics of Cultural Nationalism: The Gaelic Revival and Creation of the Nation State* (London, 1987); R. F. Foster, *Modern Ireland 1600–1972* (London, 1988) and 'Thinking from Hand to Mouth: Anglo-Irish Literature, Gaelic Nationalism and Irish Politics in the 1890s', in *Paddy and Mr Punch: Connections in Irish and English History* (London, 1993); Joep Leerssen, *Remembrance and Imagination: Patterns in the Historical and Literary Representation of Ireland in the Nineteenth Century* (Cork, 1996).

[4] 'The Decay of Lying', in *De Profundis and Other Writings* (London, 1954), 75.

[5] Ibsen had been adopted by socialist theatre groups in London (organized by G. B. Shaw and Eleanor Marx Aveling) in the mid-1880s, but only achieved wider recognition when a shilling edition of translations of *An Enemy of the People*, *The Pillars of Society*, and *Ghosts* (by William Archer and Marx Aveling) was published in 1888. The sales were boosted by excitement over first productions—*A Doll's House* in 1889, then *Ghosts* in 1891—and went on to sell 14,000 copies in five years. Tracy C. Davis, *George Bernard Shaw and the Socialist Theatre* (Westport, Conn., 1994), 28–32. See also Ian Donaldson, 'A Transplanted Doll's House: Ibsenism, Feminism and Socialism in Late-Victorian and Edwardian England', in Donaldson (ed.), *Transformations in Modern Irish Drama* (London, 1983).

[6] *Freeman's Journal*, 30 Apr. 1891.

the maestro's plays.[7] Irish politics operated in tandem with European theatre. But if Parnell provided Shaw with the impulse to publish his treatise, Ibsen was its subject, and literary conscience its priority. The playwright pushed the play to the front of social change, hailing the modern era in drama, insisting that the politics of the age would follow in the theatre's wake. It was a signal of Shaw's own priorities; but *The Quintessence of Ibsenism* was also a splinter of the fractures that produced it. In one sense Parnell's trouble could be seen as ushering Ireland into an era of social trauma that was international rather than particular, and thus be amply accommodated in Shaw's arch generalities. For those more intent on observing the specifics of Ireland's condition, it also made evident the obverse revelation: that the apparent unity of purpose Parnell had brought to Ireland's struggle for liberation was no less composed of suppressed contradiction than was troubled Europe.

The synchronicity given form by Shaw was scarcely recognized by his contemporaries. When W. B. Yeats and his fellow poets met to form the Irish Literary Society (ILS) in Bedford Park, London, their attention was commanded neither by Parnell's departure nor Ibsen's notoriety.[8] Their impetus came less from fracture than from the continuity offered by earlier attempts at distinctively Irish hubs of literary activity—ranging from the *Dublin University Magazine* to the Dublin Young Ireland Society of the 1880s to the ILS's immediate predecessor, the Southwark Literary Society.[9] Nevertheless, Parnell's position as he led the rump of his party into battle established a certain political criterion which lent his cause a new identity, one which would soon command their interest, and one which chimed with Shavian observation: that of the modern.

Taking on the anti-Parnellites, who were under the nominal leadership of Justin McCarthy but driven by the moral vituperation of Timothy Healy, meant a scrabble for allies. Although one of the erstwhile leader's gambits was to appeal to more extreme nationalists, ribbon-Fenians and 'mountainy-men' who took a dim view of over-dependence on Liberal opinion, it was an essential element of the Parnellite cause that alternative as well as established political considerations should be taken into account. New elements previously overshadowed by the self-assurance of predestination could emerge. Parnell's inclination to advance political

---

[7] Michael Holroyd, *George Bernard Shaw*, i. *1856–1898, The Search for Love* (London, 1988), 198.

[8] W. P. Ryan, *The Irish Literary Revival* (London, 1894), 34.

[9] Ibid. 11–25. Also R. F. Foster, *W. B. Yeats: A Life*, i. *The Apprentice Mage* (London, 1997), 39–44, 115–20.

issues before land reform and his new-found status as anathema both contributed to his power base being Dublin, where the Church was weaker and his cult stronger.[10] Dublin also offered other nascent forces to which drastically weakened Parnellites, made radical through accident and opportunism, could turn.[11] One was urban labour, another cultural nationalism. Harbouring such elements bespoke the necessity for the broadest coalition available—but it also supplied the possibility of emphasizing insecurity, unpredictability, and change as terms in a debate where Parnell's reputation for calm pragmatism was an essential aspect of his leadership credentials.

Parnell's first move in asserting control in Dublin was the forcible recapture of his flagship weekly, *United Ireland*, which took place the morning after his return to Ireland on 9 December 1890. With Parnell was the MP for North-East Cork, Edmund Leamy, who resumed editorship of the paper. Leamy, already involved in the revival—his *Irish Fairy Tales* had appeared earlier in the year—consolidated his literary-minded approach by taking on as sub-editor John McGrath, a contemporary of Yeats who had been a casualty of the *Freeman's Journal*'s change in stance. Early in 1891, McGrath pressed the need to expand the paper's literary role on his willing editor.[12] Thus recruited into a political battle against the odds, the very marginality of the burgeoning literati became for its allies a badge of integrity and vision, rather than evidence of subordination. The war cry of the Parnellite few ' "Hurrah for the Cause Never Lost" ' ('Don't in your charge stop to number their host')[13] revealed them as more confident of vindication by 'the coming generation'[14] than the moral majority presently guided by the Bishops and the 'McCarthyites'. Just as Parnell had proclaimed, from the balcony of the *United Ireland* offices, 'I rely on Dublin. Dublin is true. What Dublin says today Ireland will say tomorrow',[15] so the paper's pages drew on the nascent literary movement for new, different, and individual talent to break tradition and advance to a future consensus:[16] in effect, to modernize Irish opinion and bring it behind the knowing cosmopolitan capital. ' "Whoso would be a

---

[10] Robert Kee, *The Laurel and the Ivy: The Story of Charles Stewart Parnell and Irish Nationalism* (London, 1993), 586–7.

[11] Frank Callanan, *The Parnellite Split 1890–1891* (Cork, 1992), 240–1, 292.

[12] Ryan, *Irish Literary Revival*, 126.

[13] Thomas S. Cleary, 'The Cause Never Lost', *United Ireland*, 3 Jan. 1891.

[14] *United Ireland*, 10 Jan. 1891.   [15] Kee, *The Laurel and the Ivy*, 588.

[16] For John McGrath's account, see 'W. B. Yeats and Ireland', *Westminster Review* (July 1911), 3–4.

man," says Emerson, "must be a non-conformist. Absolve you to your-self, and you shall have the suffrage of the world." Such is the lesson we must learn. We must be true to our own instincts.'[17]

Parnellite pragmatics mobilized the literary column, rather than creat-ing it. But the readiness to give young writers space and status did stoke the momentum of the revival.[18] In a mechanistic way, it provided an outlet; and in an ideological sense, it prioritized the cultural in a self-consciously counter-hegemonic effort. Each of Parnell's three by-election failures to recapture majority support underscored his Party's need to imagine Ireland differently—not least for reasons of morale. This dynamic could only be intensified when Parnell went to an early grave 'Heart-broken at the ingratitude of the people',[19] an intensification coupled by a stiffening of cultural criticism. *United Ireland* had quickly championed the ILS set up by Yeats, D. J. O'Donoghue, and T. W. Rolleston in London. But the deficiencies of that group, which used an Irish spin to advance careers in the imperial capital as much as to satisfy idealism, were soon brought to book. To be consistent with the aims and ambitions of politically motivated enthusiasts, the movement would have to move back to Ireland, following Parnell's latter-day example of shifting emphasis from Westminster to College Green. Only from Dublin could a literary revival fulfil its transformative function, encouraging a future Ireland to become incapable of present betrayals—evidence if any were needed that cultural corruption was already thorough:

We believe that an Irish Parliament is only one means to the end we have in view; we are convinced that, in comparison with literature and art—and especially liter-ature—its influence would be small in creating the sturdy *Irishism* amongst our people which will be the ultimate guardian of our National liberties.[20]

After contemplating this brief debate—'The Irish Literary Capital: Where is It?'—Yeats speedily aligned himself with the *United Ireland*-sponsored move to set up in Dublin the National Literary Society (NLS) in the summer of 1892. Under its auspices the president of the new organ-ization, Douglas Hyde, began to advance the argument for prioritizing the Irish language, culminating on 25 November in his seminal speech 'On

---

[17] *United Ireland*, 14 Feb. 1891.
[18] For the recognition and elaboration of this dynamic, see John S. Kelly, 'The Political, Intellectual and Social Background to the Irish Literary Revival to 1901', Ph.D. thesis (Cambridge, 1972) and subsequent essay 'The Fall of Parnell and the Rise of Irish Literature: An Investigation', *Anglo-Irish Studies*, 2 (1976).
[19] 'He is Dead!', *United Ireland*, 10 Oct. 1891.   [20] *United Ireland*, 2 Apr. 1892.

the Necessity for De-Anglicising the Irish People'.[21] The following year saw the founding of the Gaelic League.

The split between those committed to regenerating the Anglo-Irish literary tradition and those who wanted to 'maintain and promote the use of Gaelic as a spoken language in Ireland'[22] would be a source of continuing friction. Yeats's attempt to sideline the language issue for 'longing to recall . . . the snows of yesteryear'[23] quickly brought rebuke from *United Ireland* correspondents enthused by the clarity of Hyde's argument for cultural renewal. The paper itself indicated early support by introducing an Irish-language column in May 1893.

As cultural nationalism gained strength, the League would increase its input. For the moment, however, the most apparent division in the literary revival lay in the direction of its guiding aesthetic. The Celticist movement, influenced as it was by the decadent movement dominant in London, pressed for a contemporary voice, expressed in English but informed by the Gaelic tradition; attempting to find a specifically Irish tone without ignoring the stringencies of contemporary critical thought.[24] Most influential were, of course, Yeats, composing the works due to comprise *The Rose*, and Hyde, whose *Love Songs of Connacht* appeared in the same year of 1893. Yeats argued that identifying twilit verse as Anglicized was merely a mistake arising from crepuscular confusion: 'we have the limitations of dawn. They have the limitations of sunset.'[25] Nevertheless it was this unique sense of being sandwiched between Irish renascence and global apocalypse that forged the dynamics of *The Countess Cathleen*.

Six years on, the performance of that play would inaugurate a new theatrical dynasty. But the advent of the Irish Literary Theatre (ILT) did not inaugurate Irish theatre per se. Just as the demise of Parnell was no year zero in a new Irish calendar, but did make existing anomalies in the Irish polity more apparent, the ILT emerged out of a rather longer series

[21] J. E. Dunleavy and G. W. Dunleavy, *Douglas Hyde: A Maker of Modern Ireland* (Berkeley and Los Angeles, 1991), 182. Douglas Hyde, 'The Necessity for De-Anglicising Ireland', in *The Revival of Irish Literature: Addresses by Sir Charles Gavan Duffy, KCMG, Dr George Sigerson, and Dr Douglas Hyde* (London, 1894).

[22] John [Eoin] MacNeill, in a printed letter to potential Leaguers, 12 June 1893, quoted in Dunleavy and Dunleavy, *Douglas Hyde*, 189.

[23] *United Ireland*, 17 Dec. 1892; repr. in *Uncollected Prose by W. B. Yeats*, ed. John P. Frayne and Colton Johnston, i (London, 1970), 255–6.

[24] Stephen Regan, 'W. B. Yeats and Irish Cultural Politics in the 1890s', *in* Sally Ledger and Scott McCracken (eds.), *Cultural Politics at the Fin de Siècle* (Cambridge, 1995), 70.

[25] 'Hopes and Fears for Irish Literature', *United Ireland*, 15 Oct. 1892; repr. in *Uncollected Prose*, i. 247–50.

of searches and debates. Alternatives, suddenly of more central concern in the opened-out disputes of the 1890s, were offered up. And inevitably the form of those alternatives to some degree followed the political function contemporary circumstances dictated.

In 1891, when *United Ireland* first took up the cudgels for literary endeavour, only three theatres in Dublin were licensed to produce drama: the Theatre Royal, the Gaiety Theatre, and the Queen's Royal Theatre.[26] The Theatre Royal had been lost to fire in 1880, and until it reopened in 1897 the latter two exerted easy dominance over the several smaller variety halls. They guarded their monopoly jealously, operating concertedly to stifle even amateur competition.[27] The Gaiety of the 1890s operated as an important but provincial theatre, playing host to touring companies from London. Regular doses of Shakespeare by companies such as the Bensons (a different play each night for ten nights) were offset by substantial offerings of opera, with productions of Wagner, Berlioz, Verdi, and Bizet to the fore; Gilbert and Sullivan was also much in evidence. Established repertoire including Sheridan, Goldsmith, and Boucicault was available, along with the more modern offerings of Pinero and Wilde, mixed with farce and lesser light romantic (often musical) comedies.[28] The Queen's Royal Theatre offered a different diet, leavening as it did the staple of imported comedy with a distinctively home-grown ingredient. Although the theatre's proprietor and in-house playwright James W. Whitbread was English, he had adopted with relish the tradition of nationalist melodrama established by Dion Boucicault and developed by Hubert O'Grady.

Parnellites had to look away from the literary and theatrical establishment, identified as it was with its Nationalist Party opponents—a dynamic which became particularly evident in the split over the NLS's promotion of a 'national library'. The series of proposed editions swiftly degenerated into a battle over whether the library should be typified by reprints or new writing. Despite Yeats's reputation as a committed

[26] In Dublin an Act of the Irish Parliament dating from 1786 was still in force (Statute 20th George III., chap. 57), which restricted dramatic performance to the three theatres granted patents from the Crown.

[27] The solicitor Francis R. Wolfe wrote an influential pamphlet on this theme on behalf of the Amateur Dramatic Defence Association, following further threats by the Patentees of the Gaiety Theatre, Theatre Royal, and Queen's Royal Theatre to proceed against infringement 'for the penalty of £300'. 'They . . . have persistently', he complained, 'opposed every scheme for every new theatre and every scheme of reform proposed to regulate the theatres of Dublin to the direct injury of the city and county.' Francis R. Wolfe, *Theatres in Ireland* (Dublin, 1898), 37.

[28] Joseph Holloway Papers, NLI MSS 12069–72, 73.

nationalist, many doubted the rejuvenating potential of his fey tonalities. The canonical verse of Thomas Davis seemed a more obvious choice for heightening national sentiment, and the reputation of Young Ireland as a radical school was distant enough for its rhetoric to seem safely familiar to more mainstream voices. When Yeats found the forward march of his generation halted by a jealous guardian of that tradition, Gavan Duffy, he seemed thwarted. But though Duffy deftly outmanoeuvred his callow opponent, to informed onlookers Yeats's bid to assert that it was youth that fuelled Young Ireland held true, particularly since the veteran Duffy had once been roundly abused for timidity by John Mitchel in his *Jail Journal.*[29] *United Ireland* stood by what McGrath called the 'Dantonesque audacity'[30] of its young champion:

The Irish literary movement is no more aesthetic crusade, no mere bookish propaganda with some finnicking literary principle to carry it on for a month or two to an early grave; it is the natural and inevitable birth of a new generation of Irish intellect seeking its true field of work.[31]

A revival theory which reflected continuity served an anti-Parnellite majority far more than the theory of departure, post-Parnell, which Leamy and McGrath had publicized. Similarly, any note of disquiet or self-criticism sat ill with McCarthyite reassurances prior to the pending Home Rule Bill. Thus William O'Brien, one of the more moderate anti-Parnellite leaders, took the opportunity (in an introduction to a Land League romance by the young journalist William Patrick Ryan) to emphasize the momentum of the 1880s rather than the sudden shock with which that decade ended:

The revolution of the last twelve years has supplied in extraordinary richness two prime conditions of a national literature—novel and dramatic elements of a national life wherewithal to fill Irish books, and a public to buy and read them . . . The man who would aid in the creation of an Irish national literature must begin by sympathising with the people as they live and move, by recognising the new forces that have come into play in Irish life, and by addressing himself not to the sceptical, despairful, and ineffectual elements of the national character, but to all that is strenuous, generous, and buoyant, alive to our country's astonishing successes, and panting for greater things to come.[32]

[29] Elizabeth Butler Cullingford, *Yeats, Ireland and Fascism* (London, 1981), 35–6.

[30] *Westminster Review*, July 1911, 4.

[31] *United Irishman*, 24 June 1893. The paper maintained this support. See McGrath again, 18 Aug. 1894: 'Mr Yeats's criticisms are amply justified'.

[32] W. P. Ryan, *The Heart of Tipperary* (London, 1893), 5. Ryan's title indicated his intention to update the insights of Charles Kickham's best-seller *Knocknagow, or The Homes of Tipperary* (1873).

In this argument may be detected the degree to which the national library brought literary issues into political debate. O'Brien placed the roots of the revival in the advances of the 1880s, emphasizing the role of confidence. Whatever 'new forces' the artist might apprehend, they should take care to select for examination only those that would serve to bolster well-being. In other words, to concentrate on the momentum of unified nationalism rather than the recent schisms that had put Parnellism's 'astonishing successes' on hold. As the *Freeman's Journal* put it, 'progressive spirits believe that the best way to nourish Irish national-ity is to break with Ireland's past . . . but old Ireland is old Ireland yet'.[33]

At first the *United Irishman*, indulging the London Irish, eagerly supported any playwright with the most tenuous claims on its interest. Commenting on *A Sicilian Idyll*, John Todhunter's camp-arcadian verse play,[34] John McGrath generously suggested that 'Irish drama (in its widest sense) is . . . in a somewhat rosy condition'.[35] Elsewhere in the paper, Boucicault's non-Irish repertoire was taken, along with produc-tions of O'Keefe and Sheridan, as evidence of 'the supremacy of Irishmen in the English drama'.[36] Even before Wilde and Shaw began in earnest what Yeats quickly understood (in September 1891) as being their 'extravagant crusade against Anglo-Saxon stupidity',[37] drama could be seen as one of the only elements of literary endeavour where the Irish had exerted a tangible, continuing influence on the very culture from which Hyde would recommend detachment.

Once the focus began to shift towards a more demanding cultural nationalism, the project of the literary renaissance could not afford to be so generous. Irish drama had to be considered in its less than 'widest sense'. Yeats swiftly sought to define the terms of the debate, adopting the Celticist criteria of Irish lore plus decadence to remove both Todhunter and Whitbread from the equation. Contemplating his friend's *The Poison Flower*, a Baudelarian verse play of macabre black magic whose sexual connotation required some censorial trimming,[38] Yeats was under-standably impressed. Nevertheless he used the opportunity to introduce the idea of a more thoroughgoing Irish theatre as an essential element of the revival.

---

[33] 'The New Spirit of the Nation', *Freeman's Journal*, 30 Jan. 1894.

[34] *A Sicilian Idyll* (London, 1890).

[35] *United Ireland*, 13 June 1891. [36] Ibid., 23 May 1891.

[37] 'Oscar Wilde's Last Book', ibid., 26 Sept. 1891; repr. in *Uncollected Prose*, i. 203–5.

[38] John Todhunter, *The Poison Flower*, BL MS 53476K. Censors' marks against Todhunter's text include the lines 'his philtres, | His sperms, his germs, elixirs masculine | And balsams feminine, have wrought they say | Strange Cures', 14.

When our political passions have died out in the fulfilment of their aim shall we, I wonder, have a fine native drama of our own? It is very likely . . . We love the dramatic side of events and have too much imagination to think plays which advertise 'a real locomotive engine' or a 'real fire engine' as the chief attraction to be a better form of drama than the heroic passions and noble diction of the great ages of the theatre. We have never been fairly tested. Our playwrights have been poor men who were forced to write for an English public in the very last stages of dramatic decadence. I should very much like to see what Dr. Todhunter could do with an Irish theme written and acted for an Irish audience.[39]

The unstated ambition to fulfil this aim himself was, as ever with Yeats, part of the subtext—*The Countess Cathleen* was after all in its final stages at the time of writing. But his neat polarization of theatrical forms into empty show and profound spectacle was no less sincere for the element of self-interest. The tired conventions of the melodramatic form provoked him just as sub-Davisite verse did. And he had pointed out the cultural materialities behind one central dichotomy: the business side of theatre kept those with literary pretensions on the wrong side of the water, while Whitbread's company at the Queen's produced theatre which was Irish in aspect and audience, but was cripplingly unversatile. Once again, Yeats's argument was one made in the context of a political situation that invited dialectics. As such, rather than having the quality of reaching a new consensus, his position reached out to a new controversy. But at least that meant existing theatre traditions were no longer wholly taken for granted.

The valorization of the 'stage Irishman' had been a process in train from degraded nemesis to sentimental hero throughout the eighteenth century, and in the mid-nineteenth, Dion Boucicault wrought another departure in making Irish nationalism a stock virtue rather than an accusation.[40] O'Grady and Whitbread's entertainments followed suit, and the result was unsurprisingly popular. Just as the battle over control of the national library indicated the force of cultural impetus, the theatrical establishment was considerably more robust than the young pretenders of the revival supposed. The commercial imperatives upon which theatre companies operated underlined the unlikelihood of any immediate challenge on Irish soil. As John Augustus O'Shea, a veteran of the London

---

[39] 'Plays by an Irish Poet', *United Ireland*, 11 July 1891; repr. in *Uncollected Prose*, i. 181–2.

[40] Joep Leerssen, *Mere Irish and Fíor-Ghael: Studies in the Idea of Irish Nationality, its Development and Literary Expression prior to the Nineteenth Century* (2nd edn., Cork, 1996), 77–150; *Remembrance and Imagination*, 171–3.

literary scene, proclaimed: 'I would sooner risk my money on the production of the "Colleen Bawn", "Arrah na Pogue", "The Shaughraun" or the rest of his [Boucicault's] Irish plays than on the mathematical monstrosities of Ibsen, the hysterical balderdash of Maeterlinck or the crude absurdities of the Independent Theatre.'[41]

Boucicault's popularity, won in the 1860s and 1870s, continued unabated not least because his capacity for generating a romantic whiff of Fenian charm while securing a comedic restoration of social strata maintained a broad appeal, successful in New York, London, and Dublin.[42] His hits *The Colleen Bawn*, *Arrah-na-Pogue*, and *The Shaughraun* also supplied the basic structures of Irish melodrama to his successors, O'Grady, Whitbread, and P. J. Bourke. Hubert O'Grady, a native of Limerick, had found fame acting Boucicault leads in Dublin, and had first tried his hand at writing with the imitative *The Gossock* in 1877.[43] However he soon adapted and developed these structures for topical political comment during the 1879–82 Land War and consequent radicalization of the IPP. In a long defence of his friend in the *New Ireland Review*, James Scanlan brought this fact to critics' attention.

O'Grady has produced at each crisis in our later history a work, which in a way, harmonised with the times. Thus, while our people were emigrating in thousands he wrote 'Emigration', which showed up the manner in which they were treated on the voyage over. When the 'battering ram' was doing its fell work with the little country homesteads he produced 'The Eviction'; and he took us back to the terrible trials of '48 when he gave us 'The Famine', the prologue to which is as heartrending as any pathetic scene that has yet been presented on the stage.[44]

The first point was a good one: O'Grady's work had harmonized with the times. That said, dramatic convention and political timing also conspired to make his 'treatments' of crisis happier affairs than Scanlan implied. O'Grady's first major piece, *The Eviction* (1879), characteristically cast two middlemen as the blackguards of the piece—Mark Downey a corn merchant plotting to grasp Lord Hardiman's land (and his beautiful daughter, Lady Eveleen); Nat Rooney a bailiff he needs to execute the plan to remove her beau Dr Chessman. Rooney, however, also has an

---

[41] O'Shea made this interjection in response to a lecture by Lionel Johnson to the NLS on 'The Irishman of Fiction'. When listing Irish dramatists, Johnson, like many since, simply left out Boucicault and his successors. *United Ireland*, 13 May 1893.

[42] Nicholas Grene, *The Politics of Irish Drama: Plays in Context from Boucicault to Friel* (Cambridge, 1999), 17.

[43] Stephen Watt, *Joyce, O'Casey and the Irish Popular Theater* (Syracuse, 1991), 57.

[44] 'Irish Drama: A Symposium', *New Ireland Review*, 3/2 (Apr. 1895), 112.

obstacle to his object of desire (the spirited Molly O'Hara), one Dermot McMahon. In exchange for helping Downey, Rooney demands the removal of McMahon—hence the eviction. Lacing his dialogue with Land League reasoning ('I'd rather have a lase wid the worst landlord— than no lase wid the best landlord'[45] declares Dermot), O'Grady managed to use the apparent irrelevance of romance to highlight the precarious insecurity of the tenant farmer. Act I closes with a brutal (though characteristically over-egged) eviction scene in which the McMahon family are put out of their 'Irish cabin' on a winter night, despite eloquent pleas and physical resistance.

The Eviction was a two-act play, however, and in the end O'Grady gave in to a more comic impulse. Dermot McMahon's parents have died as a result of Lord Hardiman's order of eviction, and he falls into a company of 'wild boys' who resolve to take revenge. But at their head is Rooney, reappearing as an agent provocateur intent on having his rival imprisoned rather than just homeless. The world of arbitrary romance begins to draw the drama away from further discussion of social conflict toward reassuring resolution. As the form demands, the separate villains operate in separate tiers of a socially segregated world; for them to be foiled, each tryst must happily conclude, leaving that structure undisturbed.

A wildly improbable reconciliation is required and duly provided. In the course of the assassination attempt, Dermot cottons on to Rooney, and they start a gun battle. Dermot wounds Rooney who in turn accidentally wounds Lord Hardiman; Rooney is arrested and Dermot restored to favour. Then, unexpectedly, Dermot throws himself on the mercy of his oppressor, with equally unexpected results:

DERMOT. Lord Hardiman I meant to shoot ye tonight but I winged that blackguard instead! Ordher me arrest if you plaze.

LORD HARDIMAN. Poor fellow I would I could repair the wrongs which I have wrought upon you . . . I have a neat cottage which you may occupy for the remainder of your life rent-free.[46]

To cap it all Lady Eveleen presents the parents (not dead!) who unknown to all she has been nursing back to health at Hardiman Castle.

Naturally the audience would have enjoyed the flamboyant unlikeliness of this comic closure. But it also flattered everyone that things would only get better, and in a rather personal and undemanding manner. Hardiman extends largesse rather than tenant rights, and at most

---

[45] *The Eviction*, BL Add. MS 53226D, 7.   [46] Ibid. 16.

promises to 'practice that best of virtues liberality'.[47] The Land War was a period of violent conflict and of burgeoning belief in the application of popular will to political ends.[48] O'Grady's happy resolution managed to 'harmonize' with this war while offending none of its combatants (or paying public), which was in itself rather hopeful. If the first act is tragic, its second is ironically idyllic—relegating conflict to the past in anticipation of a future that will overlook the fudge at the end of the play.

Emigration (1880), O'Grady's next piece, rather than being a study of the maltreatment aboard coffin ships, was categorized more accurately as a 'nautical comedy'.[49] But *The Famine* (1886) is a more substantial play that remained an enduring favourite with Queen's audiences, and here the mood of the day wrought an even greater disjuncture. A powerful starvation scene, which acts as a prologue, has little bearing on the subsequent action. In this pre-play, Lumley Sackville, an overseer of relief, withholds food from the O'Connor family in revenge for the political activism of the father and its effects on his father's estate. The substantive story takes place 'fifteen years' later when Sackville corrupts the daughter Nelly O'Connor and reneges on a promise of marriage. John O'Connor, Nelly's brother, returns from the army to find her the victim of a conspiracy to have her committed to a lunatic asylum, but foils the plot with the help of the government inspector Sir Richard Raymond and his daughter Lady Alice (people of the highest scruple upon whom Sackville has been preying).[50]

Just as in *The Eviction*, O'Grady was drawn by the dramatic possibilities of portraying death and deprivation, of introducing social commentary to the reliable format, only to be overwhelmed by the same format's resistance to such tragic and serious themes. Famine could only be introduced in a prologue because the romance and adventure of the central story precluded it. Then again, it should be noted that 'The Famine' portrayed was not the Famine of 1848, but a later episode historically fixed by Sackville's reference to his enemy Vincent O'Connor's crime—mustering tenants to the 'No Rent Manifesto'. In effect the prologue is

---

[47] Ibid.

[48] Charles Townshend, *Political Violence in Ireland: Government and Resistance since 1848* (Oxford, 1983), 125.

[49] As Joseph Holloway described it, 'A Dublin Playgoer's Impressions', NLI, Joseph Holloway Papers, MS 1798. The text of *Emigration* at the BL (Add. MS 53236), ed. Stephen Watt, *Journal of Irish Literature*, 14/1 (Jan. 1985), is incomplete. Watt identifies it as a one-act drama, but Holloway reported it as being three.

[50] *The Famine*, ed. Stephen Watt, *Journal of Irish Literature*, 14/1 (Jan. 1985), 25–49.

recent past, and the main play near future.[51] Thus, despite the grim opening to this drama, the sense is of an accelerated retribution made plausible by socially pervasive political confidence. This aura of progress permits the happier conclusion to take place. The 'No Rent Manifesto' was now history, and soon O'Grady's difficult task of troubling melodrama with social concerns would be too. As Father Barry says to the famished O'Connors: 'Keep up your hearts; brighter days are in store and hope for our country. And I hope we may live to see her with her own parliament controlling her domestic affairs and "Eviction", "Famine" and "Emigration" banished forever from our native land.'[52] O'Grady's plays remained popular fare at the Queen's, a popularity which reflects the allegiance of the vast majority of Irish supporters who remained loyal to their local champion in the IPP: still convinced by Father Barry's words of consolation.

J. W. Whitbread continued that popularity and made it pay, owning as he did the Queen's Royal Theatre. Coming to the fore in the years of high Parnellism, however, Whitbread's early work was more conservative than his predecessor's. *Shoulder to Shoulder* (1886), *The Irishman* (1889), and *The Nationalist* (1891) owed more to Boucicault. Romance and heroism in high society was mirrored by loyalty and bravery among a brogue-bearing servant class who often came to the rescue. While his titles suggested a more radical spirit, these plays used nationalist politics largely as a device labelling the hero as a noble soul. And as befitted the contemporary rhetoric of the 'union of hearts', even greater care was taken not to offend establishment sensibilities. The plots were unhindered by social commentary. The villains were not landowners, but malevolent, deceiving agents out for their own advantage—Felix Blake's fiendish blackmail in *The Irishman*,[53] for instance, or Matt Sheehan's plot to disinherit his young master in *The Nationalist*. What Whitbread did share with O'Grady was his faith in the future. These plays had customarily happy conclusions,

---

[51] Watt, 'The Plays of Hubert O'Grady', *Journal of Irish Literature*, 14/1 (Jan. 1985), 12. For an alternative view, see Christopher Morash, 'Sinking Down into the Dark: The Famine on Stage', *Bullán*, 3/1 (Spring 1997), 78, who regards the reference to *the* famine as indicating a conflation of the 1840s and 1880s. Though the title must have piqued expectation for the audience, as well as O'Grady's friend Scanlan, the reiteration of the title at the close of the play was pure convention (and self-advertisement) rather than the emphatic dramaturgy Morash suggests.

[52] *The Famine*, ed. Watt, 27. O'Grady's advance did indeed stop there: as Watt points out (10), he accurately described his final play *The Fenian* (1888) to the British censor as 'a romantic Irish Love Story and . . . nothing to do with *Patriotic*, *Political* or *Social* evils'.

[53] *The Irishman*, BL Add. MS 53437.

reflecting political optimism. As the priest advises the couple at the end of *The Nationalist*: 'Ye'll live, both of ye, to see our beloved country prosperous once more, her children flourishing and contented, her name revered among nations, and yourselves the happiest of the happy!'[54]

Performed at the end of the troubled year of 1891, this sentiment carried a different connotation than it would have a year earlier. The popularity of such plays was unabated, but in a divided Ireland that criterion was open to question. Whitbread's success was predicated on providing entertainment to a nationalist movement tied to Liberal ambitions for Home Rule, but that policy had been thrown into doubt by Parnellite defection. Their emphasis on independence from the British party system as a central tenet of opposition involved accusations of co-option, of compromise and corruption inspired by the power and wealth of the imperial capital. In this process the commercial and political imperatives to which melodrama responded could also be implicated. The necessity for de-Anglicization was nowhere more obvious than in Dublin's theatres, dominated as they were by the touring companies who came to Dublin as they would to any provincial city. With public taste no longer a guarantee of national well-being, the artistic limitations and unambitiousness of melodramatic theatre could then be linked to a complacency no longer affordable. Post-Parnell, dissentients required a self-image of greater resolution. Reviewing *The Nationalist* (Whitbread's 'New Irish Play') in January 1892, *United Ireland* awarded the company 'all honour . . . for the efforts it has made to give us some semblance of modern Irish drama', but went on to assert that the genre 'distorts and misrepresents . . . while it takes the most extraordinary liberties with Irish history and Irish character'. The popularity of the plays was no defence:

Mr. Whitbread will perhaps say that his Dublin audiences like it. Then, I say, should come in the Dublin critics to correct their taste, and point out to them that false and boisterous representatives of their countrymen should not alone be offensive to their sense of national dignity, but that if they were rightly-minded they would prove much less interesting, indeed, than a true characterization of the events and social and political life of the country.[55]

The clubs of Dublin gratefully took on this mantle of advanced opinion. In 1893 the young radical William Rooney founded the Celtic Literary Society (CLS), at the time one of many fledgling groups then emerging, but which came to provide a focus for a new, literary, nationalist militancy.

54 *The Nationalist* (Dublin, 1892), 87.
55 'An Irishman', *United Ireland*, 16 Jan. 1892.

Within a month of the inaugural meeting Rooney debated the question 'Is the Stage Irishman True to Life?' and argued to discard positive as well as negative caricature.[56] 'The character is so full of bravado and dare-devilry', he complained, 'that it only creates ridicule.'[57]

The anti-commercial experimentation in Paris and London, of the Théâtre Libre and the Independent Theatre Society, established in 1887 and 1891 respectively, suggested that more demanding, less compromised models were available. When Paul Fort founded the Théâtre d'Art in 1890 (to become Lugné-Poë's Théâtre de l'Œuvre in 1893), adding a symbolist alternative, possibilities for the stage appeared to be multiplying. Ibsen and Wagner had already demonstrated the possibility of incorporating national myth and legend into theatrical works; a ploy which might satisfy the criteria of those who demanded literature have a demonstrable political use after all. Alice Milligan put the question:

Should men of culture and taste, for the sake of developing Irish literature, leave the noisy field of political warfare, and attempt to develop their art in some paradise apart, or should they bring to the conflict the keen intellectual weapons which can do good service there, though the edge will be blunted and the lustre dimmed by hacking of coarser opposing blades?[58]

Milligan's metaphorical choice was an early indication of her own conviction that the modern battles had greater force when fought in a mythic form that happily combined the apparently separate categories of culture and politics. But new modes of theatre had far from won the field as yet. One 'T.F.G.' answered Milligan's query by accepting that a radical change had to be made in subject matter, demonstrating the advances made in the claims of literature as a political weapon and the Celticist quest for untainted source material. More than that, the most effective use of this matter would be made in the theatre. Under the heading 'Wanted—A National Drama', the correspondent declared:

I hold most emphatically that the Irish stage could be made one of the surest and readiest means of instilling a vigorous nationality in the bosoms of the people, and exorcising there from every odious thought and impulse that smacks of West Britonism . . . Suppose it could be possible to produce, say, a drama dealing with the Danish Invasion, and Irish resistance to their encroachments, with Brian Boru

---

[56] CLS Minutes, 25 Oct. 1893, NLI MS 200.

[57] *Evening Herald*, 27 Oct. 1893.

[58] Milligan ('Iris Olkyrn'), letter written in reponse to a paper, 'The Celt—the Silent Sister', given by Ashe King to the NLS. *United Ireland*, 16 Dec. 1893.

as hero . . . what would be the effect on the audience, supposing them to have only a modicum of national sentiment? Why it would be revolutionary.[59]

However, T.F.G. was not diverted by the pretensions of the Bedford Park crowd. In 1894, a year that showcased all the alternatives available, what interested him more was the latest melodrama by Whitbread, *Lord Edward, or '98.*

I am inclined to call it a National Work, as any work deserves to be called which, as far as its influence extends and intensifies and strengthens National sentiment . . . I can myself testify to seeing a few prominent Government officials who outside the theatre would not betray a spark of national sentiment for a crown of glory clap their hands in a veritable frenzy of enthusiasm.[60]

In Irish melodrama the project of reclaiming the stage Irishman generally insisted on victorious and confident final scenes. Whitbread's new work instead followed the example of Boucicault's lesser-known last Irish play *Robert Emmet*, first produced in Chicago ten years earlier. Boucicault had there recast his formula to the subject of Emmet's martyrdom, but the sombre conclusion sat ill with audiences and the play was not a success. Whitbread now attempted the same, intelligently choosing for his subject the romantic figure of Lord Edward Fitzgerald. The first of many taking 1798 as a subject, the play prefigured the centennial excitement and restoration of the United Irishmen as role models by some four years. In doing so Whitbread forced Fitzgerald through the formulaic twists that were his stock in trade, but with a difference. Lord Edward stepped into this caste-ridden world with a dramatis personae of historical figures, insisting on a tragic ending as he left it. History stretched the boundaries of melodramatic convention, injecting a degree of realism that suggested to some the seed of a new Irish drama.

But there was a limit to the innovation. After *Lord Edward*, Whitbread lapsed back into less demanding work. Cashing in on the very centennial celebrations he had pre-empted, his 1898 play *Wolfe Tone* dealt exclusively with that United Irishman's adventures in the French Army, where he could safely deal with picturesque depictions of Tone's attempts to persuade Napoleon to invade Ireland. He did return to the tragic format, and later oscillated between these two poles of tragic historicism—such as *The Ulster Hero* (McCracken)—and comic exoticism—like *The Irish Dragoon* (again set in the French army).[61] But like O'Grady he remained

[59] *United Ireland*, 14 Apr. 1894.   [60] Ibid.

[61] Watt, *Joyce, O'Casey and Irish Popular Theater* 80–1.

a prisoner of his craft. His work absorbed the impact of a more reflective Ireland, now not only post-Parnell but post- the predictably doomed 1893 Home Rule Bill, yet did so without any fundamental change. The plays' characters, still locked into crude opposition and stilted exchanges, demonstrated that the melodramatic form still held. Compared with the rising currency of republicanism such drama grew increasingly to resemble the safe rhetoric of parliamentarians, happy to play to nationalist sentiment without intending too literal an interpretation. T.F.G.'s observation about the Government officials' 'frenzy of enthusiasm' only underscored the point.

For those less convinced of a parliamentary road to success, established norms of art and entertainment were implicated, along with establishment politics, in the assimilation of Irish culture. As the contemporary debates indicate, this was not a simple case of a political-cultural switch. *The Lyceum*, established in 1887 as the voice of Catholic revivalism emergent from University College, Dublin, in 1894 altered its name to the *New Ireland Review*.[62] The change of title was justified by alluding to a shift in cultural priorities wrought not by political crisis but by social change. 'New Ireland', editor and Jesuit economist Fr. Thomas Finlay observed, was no longer a peasant culture but a society experiencing a redivision of labour. New types—the farmer, the artisan, the labourer—had forced forward their identities for consideration. The 'Irishman' was

Intellectually, economically, politically . . . a new being, with new needs and aspirations, striving for new ends with new capacities and powers . . . At such time when new ideas must necessarily take shape, and a deeper examination of current problems must necessarily be brought about, it is important that outward expression should be given to the notions that are abroad, and temperate discussion bestowed on the questions with which the public occupies itself.[63]

Contemporaries were alert to the effects of the sequence of reforms that had begun with the Ashbourne Act of 1885 and continued with the Land Acts of 1891 and 1896. Signs also apparently confirmed Parnell's prediction that 'The Labour question will be after the Irish question, the great question of the future'.[64] In 1894 tentative working-class organization culminated in the establishment of the independent Irish Trades

[62] Hutchinson, *Dynamics of Cultural Nationalism*, 138.
[63] Fr. Thomas Finlay ('The Editors'), 'New Ireland', *New Ireland Review*, 1/1 (Mar. 1894), 2–3.
[64] *Freeman's Journal*, July 1891. Quoted by Callanan, *Parnellite Split*, 297.

Union Congress.[65] The idea of a 'New Ireland' heightened the image of the revival as a 'young' movement demanding more sophisticated equipment for the interpretation of their surroundings.[66] William G. Fay, seven years before his ground-breaking production of Douglas Hyde's *Cásadh an tSúgáin* (Twisting of the Rope) for the ILT had his first introduction to the opportunities becoming available. In 1894, at the age of 22, Fay was already an experienced actor, having served his apprenticeship touring Whitbread's plays (particularly *The Irishman*) in Ireland and Britain. He and his brother Frank, then establishing their own amateur dramatic company, were anxious to judge for themselves the modern theatrical idiom advertised by recent controversies. 'With only newspaper reports and articles to help us we could not really find out how the new plays differed from the old', he later recalled.[67] But evidence was at hand. On 28 September they attended the first showing of an Ibsen play in Ireland—Herbert Beerbohm Tree's production of *An Enemy of the People* at the Gaiety Theatre. 'I have never seen, before or since, an intelligent audience so completely flabbergasted . . . But Frank and I were delighted . . . We saw that Ibsen had discerned the dramatic possibilities of every class in the community.'[68]

The experience prompted both Fays to a more rigorous approach to stagecraft; their understanding of the gap between the subtle diversity available to a writer like Ibsen and the blunt instrument of melodrama was most easily articulated when comparing the possibilities in each for interpreting complex social dynamics.[69] The impulse to become proficient in the 'new' drama combined a youthful drive to champion iconoclasm with a sense that drama flexible enough to accommodate complex politics was becoming increasingly necessary.

---

[65] Dermot Keogh, *The Rise of the Irish Working Class: The Dublin Trade Union Movement and Labour Leadership 1890–1914* (Belfast, 1982), 42.

[66] Ireland's theatrical response could thus be considered a late example of what George Lukács understood in 1909 as 'the increased [social] complexity which determines dramatic character'. Lukács, 'The Sociology of Modern Drama', in Eric Bentley (ed.), *The Theory of the Modern Stage* (rev. edn., London, 1976), 427.

[67] W. G. Fay and Catherine Carswell, *The Fays of the Abbey Theatre: An Autobiographical Record* (London, 1935), 108.

[68] Ibid.

[69] 'The melodramatist's libels on human nature are quite outside my sympathy', wrote Frank Fay in 1899. 'I positively loathe the virtuous persons of melodrama, and would have their blood were it not that between us, intervenes that horrible instrument of torture, the orchestra of the Queen's theatre.' *United Irishman*, 9 Sept. 1899. Also Frank J. Fay, *Towards a National Theatre: The Dramatic Criticism of Frank J. Fay*, ed. Robert Hogan (Dublin, 1970), 29.

W. P. Ryan noted the mood. His first attempt at a novel had been occasion for William O'Brien to assert that the revival was longer in the tooth than the young guard gave it credit. Ryan now, not for the last time, exhibited a keen reading of the Zeitgeist. His topical 'record of Irish literary awakenings', *The Irish Literary Revival*, noted a warning delivered by an unnamed 'able young Irishman' to the newly founded ILS: ' "I see one danger, and one danger only before the Society. It is old fogeyism. Trample on it, crush it at every turn!" The words were the index of a very prevalent feeling.'[70]

That was a view from one side of the argument, given in the context of tactful support for Yeats in the row with Duffy. It cut little ice for those in the IPP, however, for whom new departures were new distractions, and this division was reflected in the emphasis each side gave to events of theatrical moment. During April 1894 the *Freeman's Journal* followed with enthusiasm the fortunes of *Lord Edward*, remarking with approval that 'The romantic interests with which the dramatist has so cleverly invested the historic incidents treated considerably moved the audience.'[71] Meanwhile Parnellite papers *United Ireland* and the *Irish Daily Independent* found space to report an event unrecorded by their rival: the London debut of Yeats, second on the bill initially to Todhunter, then to George Bernard Shaw. The *Independent* found in Yeats's 'distinctly Celtic' *The Land of Heart's Desire* 'evidence of considerable promise'.[72] *United Ireland* first greeted Yeats's play—which eclipsed Todhunter's main billing *Comedy of Sighs*—then reported the partnering of Yeats's play with Shaw's *Arms and the Man* a week later with the question 'Are we on the eve of another epoch of Irish dramatists?'[73]

Epochal though it may have been, the opening bout between WBY and GBS underscored unsolved problems. 'Certainly there is promise of an Irish National drama', Yeats and Todhunters' reviewer had pondered; 'But what of the Irish National stage?'[74] W. P. Ryan's overview noted the obvious—that Irish drama required stage and audience, not just Irish playwrights or even subject matter.

As the Irish revival expands in new directions, will not some take heart and attempt something for Irish dramatic literature? The real Irish drama is a thing unknown . . . surely the materials for the national drama are wasting in profusion before us. We may see in our day in Dublin genuine Irish plays, of truth and

---

[70] *Irish Literary Revival*, 61.   [71] *Freeman's Journal*, 3 Apr. 1894.
[72] *Irish Daily Independent*, 1 Apr. 1894.
[73] *United Ireland*, 28 Apr. 1894.   [74] Ibid., 21 Apr. 1894.

talent, written for the people, moving and moulding the people. Otherwise I fear that the city will not half deserve to be the capital of a nation.[75]

It was a charge that neatly reversed the rationale behind the establishment of the NLS: if Dublin failed to produce a revival theatre, how could it claim to be the intellectual capital of anywhere? The potential evident in such productions was tantalizing for those who (long before Lady Gregory had adopted Yeats and combined with her Connaught neighbour Martyn to form the ILT) were searching for an Irish national theatre sophisticated enough to provide an alternative to melodrama. But for the present, London's charms and opportunities maintained the pull of its literary sphere.

Shaw's success also touched on the problem of definition. *Arms and the Man* may have proved that melodrama could be forced into self-satire with a punishing dramatic construction and philosophical panache. In terms of theatrical and critical success it may have dished Yeats. But it was set, rather scrupulously, in Bulgaria. Shaw's Irishness was not enough to earn comment on works such as *Widower's Houses*; likewise, Oscar Wilde's triumphs of the early nineties merited no inclusion in the new debate. They had acclimatized too well, it seemed, to the London stage. But Yeats's *The Land of Heart's Desire* left no doubt that the land of which it spoke was Ireland.

To those for whom the arrival of Ibsen brought the possibility of treating Irish concerns with fresh complexity, Shaw's offering may have been closer to the ideal. But it was Yeats's play that drew spiritual and stylistic choices distinctly Irish in aspect. Already in *The Countess Cathleen*, he had found parallels between politics and art on the one hand and realism and symbolism on the other. *The Land of Heart's Desire* continued to obtrude into a humble peasant setting fantastic and poetic elements. Verse form from the first intimated that this was a world in which art was in the ascendant over quotidian life, even before Maurteen Bruin had enquired of her errant daughter-in-law Mary, 'Colleen, what is the wonder in that book | That you must leave the bread to cool?'[76] Through the gate of incantation steps the summoned child-faery, who after tricking the visiting priest Father Hart into removing a protecting crucifix, steals the body and soul of Mary away 'Where beauty has no ebb, decay no flood'. More potent than the imprecations of the priest, comes the litany of Irish mythology:

---

[75] *Irish Literary Revival*, 181.
[76] *The Land of Heart's Desire*, in *VP*, 183.

> White armed Nuala, Aengus of the Birds
> Fiachra of the hurtling foam, and him
> Who is the ruler of the Western Host,
> Finvara, and their Land of Heart's Desire[77]

This was a signal not only of Yeats's growing assurance as a playwright, but of the force in Irish culture of the very elements which prove victorious in the play. If the monks had had the upper hand in his earlier short story 'The Crucifixion of the Outcast', here a combination of folklore, myth, and verse prove stronger. The land of faery, the land of Ireland, the land of the play *The Land of Heart's Desire* are lands contained in poetry's power to conjure an altered state: the land desired invoked, not merely wished for.

Yeats's next dramatic project was to disdain realism more overtly, inspired by the literary atmosphere of the 1890s and his exposure to symbolist experimentation in Paris, where he absorbed the cloudy influence of Maurice Maeterlinck and witnessed first hand the (five-hour) mystical extravagance of Villers de l'Isle Adam's *Axël*.[78] Ever-unresolved, *The Shadowy Waters* apparently led him, like its hero Forgael, further from the coastline of identifiably political concerns. But the trip to the Continent had also opened a new axis of influences. Drinking from the fount of bohemianism at source newly validated his aesthetics as independent of English influence, with French militant literariness sending reinforcement to Ireland's cultural resistance. His Parisian excursions certainly fed such confluence, being part literary safari (coffee with Verlaine, watching riots greet Jarry's *Ubu Roi*), part link-up with Fenians in exile, courtesy of Maud Gonne.[79] And one prize of these travels was his friendship with John Millington Synge, whom he encouraged to invert the dynamic by departing Paris for the Aran Islands.

Yeats's confidence *vis-à-vis* clerical power was also part of a literary-political coalescence. His patron in republicanism, John O'Leary, had already warned him of the hostility between the Church and the Irish Republican Brotherhood (IRB).[80] Given the importance of the pulpit to the rural vote, Parnell's vilification had made it an issue for his supporters too. In parallel with the release of literary energies, the liberalization

---

[77] *The Land of Heart's Desire*, in *VP*, 205.

[78] For symbolist, esp. Maeterlinck's, influence, see Katherine Worth, *The Irish Drama of Europe from Yeats to Beckett* (London, 1978), 12–47, 78–98.

[79] Foster, *W. B. Yeats*, i. 138–40, 173.

[80] Yeats, *Autobiographies*, 209. ' "In this country," he had said, "a man must have upon his side the Church or the Fenians, and you will never have the Church." '

of social debate became an issue. 'The days of wholesale clerical intimidation are numbered', asserted John Redmond. 'In an Irish parliament
perfect freedom of political thought and action would be speedily established and jealously guarded.'[81] In 1895 the trial of Oscar Wilde carried
the sexual charge of Parnell's disgrace to a new level, another detonation
at the heart of Victorian morality. A number of Irish men of letters
offered support, via Yeats calling in to Lady Wilde between trials, agree-
ing to recommend her son fight rather than flee to French exile himself;[82]
Dublin and Paris again cohering as notional anti-Londons. In this heightened atmosphere the Parnellite-Republican combination kept options
open. While such a political dynamic was in operation nationalist
Protestant writers anxious to promote an inclusive 'post-sectarian' ethos
of the Gael (Hyde as well as Yeats) could keep favour and friends inside a
Catholic constituency. Further occasion for combination was provided by
a longer-term phenomenon: the tendency for class issues to produce
increasing tension between conservative and progressive Catholic opinion.

Religious issues were an indication of how cultural questions could
float across party affiliation, as evident in the issue of anti-Semitism. The
champion of rural radicalism Michael Davitt, editor of *Labour World*
1890–1 and an anti-Parnellite, became a champion of Jewish rights in
Ireland, against the advice of the influential clerical journal *Lyceum*.[83]
Frank Hugh O'Donnell, a regular correspondent for *United Ireland*, used
his regular slot on the 'Foreign Situation' to preach ultramontanism and
a theory of Jewish-Protestant conspiracy 'reinforced by all the floating
scum of infidelity and free-thinking arrayed under the banners of the
Masonic Brotherhood'.[84] Nevertheless O'Donnell's invective sat ill with
the generally liberal tenor of the newspaper. When the *Lyceum* became
the *New Ireland Review*, its editors declared an ambit of discussion closed
to anything that might 'attack the religious convictions or the National
character of our people'.[85] *United Ireland* in turn questioned whether it

[81] *United Ireland*, 8 July 1893.

[82] Richard Ellmann, *Oscar Wilde* (London, 1987), 441–2.

[83] See Davitt, *Freeman's Journal*, 13 July 1893, and *Lyceum*, 6/70 (July 1893) ('The Jew
in Ireland' edn.). See also *Lyceum*, 6/72 (Sept. 1893).

[84] *United Ireland*, 3 Mar. 1894. See also his allegations of a Jewish white slave trade, ibid.,
19 May 1894: 'One of the most awful illustrations of the Jewish lust for gold at any risk is
afforded by their connection with the International Brothel System. Wherever misery
strikes a working population there a Jew Syndicate is on the watch to seduce it or trap starving girls for the service of the houses which have been established by Jew capital throughout the world.'

[85] *United Ireland*, 17 Feb. 1894.

was not 'to be seriously held in Ireland that a little healthy criticism now and then . . . may not be useful?'[86] A cultural nationalism choosing Catholic identity as its rallying point would continue to gather strength, though its capacity for censorship and conservatism would continue to produce sceptical challengers from within as well as without. The undiscerning generosity of spirit which had blithely taken *The Countess Cathleen* on board would fall foul, first of D. P. Moran's acerbic criticism of Celticisms in the *New Ireland Review*, and then of clerical judgement on the play's debut in 1899, whipped up by the same F. H. O'Donnell. But the existence of anticlerical republicanism, of class-based concerns of the left, and of liberal Catholic opinion, would continue to protect even the most Ascendancy of dramas from being conclusively categorized according to Moran's notion of 'The Battle of Two Civilizations'.

In *The Quintessence of Ibsenism*, Shaw had heralded the modern era in drama, characterizing the playwright as a pioneer. He and Yeats could both be construed as adopting the implications of this, content with the problems of unpopularity in the knowledge that 'The pioneer is a tiny minority of the force he heads'.[87] 'The point to seize is that social progress takes effect through the replacement of old institutions by new ones; and since every institution involves the recognition of the duty of conforming to it, progress must involve the repudiation of an established duty at every step.'[88]

The problem was that, while Shaw embarked on his crusade with dazzling polemic, the social assumptions which he almost exclusively chose to assault were (as with Wilde) English. Yeats on the other hand, striking out in a very different direction, eschewed political point-making for cultural resonance. Standish O'Grady, whose mythic histories had inspired Yeats in the first place, might argue the eventual political impact of Celticism would be revolutionary; but encouraging though *The Land of Heart's Desire* might be, it could be frustrating when the possibilities of an Ibsenite format for Irish drama might be contemplated. Such misgivings were compounded by the undoubted anomaly of performing the plays in London. Absentee playwriting and Celtic rarefaction might end up being too close to George Moore's satirical glance, during a rent confrontation, at his own abstraction from Irish realities: 'After a great deal more discussion during which the poet, intensely wearied, strove to

86 *United Ireland*, 17 Feb. 1894.
87 *The Quintessence of Ibsenism* (London, 1891), 94.
88 Ibid. 7.

recall the tercets of a sonnet by Mallarmé, a bargain was struck and the tenants agreed to take twenty-five percent.'[89]

Moore's eclectic range of literary influences was far from confined to the symbolists. In 1893, already an established novelist after the school of Zola, he had attempted to compound psychological and industrial unrest in *The Strike at Arlingford*.[90] William Archer commended the play as 'like *Widower's Houses* . . . a very remarkable dramatic experiment'[91] but like Shaw, Moore set his play in England. His friend and landowning neighbour Edward Martyn looked closer to home, and in 1895 finished *The Heather Field*, soon to be united with *The Countess Cathleen* in the inaugural season of the ILT.

However, Martyn's play was still under wraps, and as the 1894 productions receded, their impact appeared more aberration than the beginning of an exponential growth in dramaturgical options. In Dublin, among the proliferating literary clubs, what little discussion of drama there was began to return to the history of the Irish stage rather than its prospects.[92] When the issue was aired, the options remained more or less the adoption of an Ibsenite model, its competitor once again melodrama rather than Celtic drama. Frederick Ryan, a young socialist journalist who kept an equally avid eye on cultural and literary developments, at the age of 22 addressed the inaugural meeting of the Dublin Literary Society on 'The Realistic Movement in Modern Drama':

The stage could not be prevented from having an educational value, and in that case the question was whether they should have education true or false. The ordinary drama had long been a collection of impossible characters in impossible situations. The systematic teaching of a false view of life was not healthy or artistic.[93]

Ibsen's bleak drama, Ryan asserted, had been a necessary 'reaction against excessive romanticism'. Ryan's belief that a 'true' realism would be more balanced reflected the bullish progress of Dublin's literary-political clubs. By October 1896, the CLS was bringing forward young nationalists like himself, William Rooney, and Arthur Griffith, whose

[89] 'The House of an Irish Poet', in *Parnell and his Island* (London, 1887), 67.

[90] Adrian Frazier, *George Moore, 1852–1933* (New Haven, 2000), 127, 225–6. As with Shaw, Moore's contact with Ibsen was coloured by his relationship with socialists in the 1880s, esp. Edward Aveling and Eleanor Marx.

[91] *The Theatrical 'World' of 1893* (London, n.d. [1894]), 72.

[92] Such as Professor Savage Armstrong's lecture to the NLS in May 1897, 'The Irish contribution to the British Drama', which had concentrated almost entirely on 17- and 18-cent. writers.

[93] *United Ireland*, 17 Oct. 1896.

enthusiasms were already detached from the waning intensity of Parnell's demise. The last despairing cries of Parnellism had by the eve of the 1895 election taken on the timbre of melodrama:

The General Election is at hand. The hour has struck. The day has come to pronounce a verdict on this shameless tale. Will an Irish nationalist give his vote for any verdict but the one which stares the world in the face—*Betrayal?* Ay, indeed, betrayal, black, bloody, bitter. BETRAYAL, BETRAYAL![94]

No clearer signal could be given of its exhaustion. Parnellism had already released its energies into the movements on which it had originally fed, including the left-wing agenda Fred Ryan had begun pursuing (another lecture that year, this time to the CLS, was on 'The Social Side of the Irish Question').[95] In fact, staying close to the working-class concerns which continued to be distinct from a broader nationalist project, he continued to preach the progressivism of Ibsenism, later modelling his own short drama on it, and giving public lectures for the fledgling Irish Socialist Republican Party (ISRP) on the subject.[96]

The quintessence of prelapsarian Parnellism had indeed been 'excessive romanticism', and Ibsen had arrived with odd sychronicity to complement the reintroduction of irony and self-doubt into the nationalist mind. *United Ireland*, rehearsing each October its ivy-wreathed mourning, had, by sponsoring the romantic Celticism generated in the confidence of the 1880s, coloured it with suspicion of middle-class mainstream politics. Parnell had reappeared in Ireland in 1890 ready to adopt old and new marginal movements, had become the element which for Shaw typified both Ibsen and Ibsenism: a pioneer. Yeats's attraction to symbolism and hostility to realism could not disguise the ease with which long-term ideals could find short-term allies in the other branch of modern theatre. As had been evident in the defence of Ibsen, Parnell, and Wilde, the hostile moral majority wrought unity in Irish alternative theatre, defined more by a common instinct to revolt than separated by stylistic rivalry.[97] Yeats admitted that Ibsen, Shaw, and he shared the same

---

[94] *United Ireland*, 29 June 1895.
[95] CLS Minutes, NLI MS 200. See also Terry Eagleton, 'The Ryan Line', in *Crazy John and the Bishop, and Other Essays on Irish Culture* (Cork, 1998), 250.
[96] ISRP Minutes, 12 Feb. 1899: 'On the above date a public meeting was held at 87 Marlborough St when F. Ryan delivered a lecture entitled "A Word on the Democratic Drama" in the course of which he dealt with and read extracts from the plays of Isben [*sic*] and Bernard Shaw.' NLI MS 16264.
[97] See Robert Brustein, *The Theatre of Revolt* (London, 1965), for a treatment of anti-bourgeois rebellion as a factor uniting disparate stylistic strands of modern drama.

enemies; when introduced to the champions of Ibsenism Moore and Martyn, the impulse to combine was conclusive.

The lines of this alliance continued to converge, catalysed by Lady Augusta Gregory, who as a Galway neighbour of Martyn, had been introduced to Yeats in 1896. The summer of the following year brought it to fruition, aided by an altered political mood. As the political cul-de-sac of Parnellite isolationism became ever more apparent, emphasis inevitably shifted. In 1896 *United Ireland* for the first time ceased to black-border its pages on the anniversary of Parnell's death. The majority faction continued to work for party reunification, spurred on by the opportunities presented by local council elections in 1898, and when William O'Brien's United Irish League (UIL) simultaneously resurrected the land question it proved a compelling power base.[98]

At the same time, new factions began to take on clearer definition. James Connolly's arrival from Edinburgh to organize the seedling ISRP had immediate effect, galvanizing anti-Jubilee demonstrations.[99] His first statement of Marxist intent to the nationalist community had been made in the *Shan Van Vocht*,[100] Alice Milligan's Belfast-based 'National Monthly Magazine'. Milligan and Anna Johnson, having left the *Northern Patriot* in January 1896,[101] were determined to correct the 'disposition to underrate the support of newspapers in the cause of literature'.[102] The result was a journal prototypical in its anxiety to accommodate both the literary revival and republicanism: the link between *United Ireland* and the *United Irishman*. Neo-Fenianism also found inspiration to action from '98 centennial celebrations and the recent experiences of nationalists who had emigrated to South Africa. 'Let the Irish nation honour '98 by repudiating for ever above the graves of its heroes that sham miscalled "Constitutional action" ', advised 'The Irishmen of the Transvaal', signing off their open letter to the republican Irish National Alliance (INA) with the postscript 'praying God we may in our generation take part in an Irish Majuba'.[103]

---

[98] Paul Bew, *Conflict and Conciliation in Ireland 1890–1910: Parnellites and Radical Agrarians* (Oxford, 1987), 48–58; R. F. Foster, 'Thinking from Hand to Mouth', in *Paddy and Mr Punch*, 262–80.

[99] C. Desmond Greaves, *The Life and Times of James Connolly* (London, 1961), 71–2.

[100] 'Nationalism and Socialism', *Shan Van Vocht*, 2/1 (8 Jan. 1897).

[101] Milligan and Johnson (the poet Ethna Carbery) complained of the overbearing interest of Fred Allen of the *Irish Daily Independent*, who denied all. *United Ireland*, 1, 8 Feb. 1896. Allen, IRB organizer par excellence, was possibly trying to impress upon the two journalists the need to follow a given line, though this is by no means clear.

[102] *United Ireland*, 19 Dec. 1896.

[103] Ibid. 24 July 1897.

Constitutional and physical-force traditions both had to take stock of the political climate produced by the policies of 'constructive Unionism' introduced during a secure Conservative administration. Engaged though W. B. Yeats was in radical outfits like the '98 Centennial Association and Wolfe Tone Memorial Committee (apparently as a frontman for the INA), his introduction into more elevated circles through Lady Gregory brought home the possibilities of realizing long-held ambitions for an Irish theatre project. To do so would require adopting the language of political as well as artistic consensus; Yeats, alone of the potential participants, was at this stage definitely nationalist. But if the Gaelic League could blur its radical nationalist potential by adopting an apolitical policy—necessary to secure Ireland's best interests—a pressure group for a theatre project could utilize the same rhetoric.

The newly forged ILT's 1897 declaration therefore displayed a careful redefinition. Increasing the national focus meant leaving out any blurring notions of pan-Celticism offered by fellow symbolists like the Scot William Sharp; while accommodating Moore and Martyn's realism allowed Yeats to dispense with the original tag of 'Celtic Theatre' and adopt the stylistically broader but politically more effective 'Irish Literary Theatre'. Indicating this supple pragmatism, Yeats cited the common artistic objections and objectives which could unite a nationally minded movement without alienating any class of potential ally.

We will show that Ireland is not the home of buffoonery and of easy sentiment, as it had been represented, but the home of an ancient idealism, and we are confident of the support of the Irish people, who are weary of misrepresentation, in carrying out a work that is outside all the political questions that divide us.[104]

The loose coalition arrayed through necessity under the steadily declining authority of the Parnellites gradually found that shelter redundant. *United Ireland* ceased publication in 1898, and just as the ILT had to look for new agents to publicize its efforts, political attention had to fix on present, and future, rather than bygone circumstances. But 'Mr. Yeats', the figure whom John McGrath had characterized as 'the leader of an Irish literary revolution',[105] had learned through the trials of its early advocation an adaptability which was itself quintessentially Parnellite.

---

[104] Robert Hogan and James Kilroy, *A History of Modern Irish Drama*, i. *The Irish Literary Theatre, 1899–1901* (Dublin, 1975), 25.
[105] Reviewing Yeats's *Poems*, *United Ireland*, 14 Dec. 1895.

2

'A Mesh of Error': Dramatic Alliances 1898–1902

In a letter to T. P. Gill in January 1899, George Russell (AE) satirized his colleague's politics. A Nationalist MP and erstwhile leader-writer for the *Freeman's Journal*,[1] Gill was an easy target for anyone with a mind to illustrate the perils of co-option. He had drifted from his days formulating the Plan of Campaign to a desk job at the offices of the Department of Agricultural and Technical Instruction, and had recently assumed an editorial role at the hitherto solidly Unionist Dublin *Daily Express*. Often given to cartoon caricature, Russell here had Gill pictured forth as 'A Political Firebrand sowing his wild oats' (labelled 'sedition' and 'treason') but reaping an ironic harvest—'A pale and delicate flower' tagged 'National Unionism'.[2]

Russell's humorous jibe was less severe for the shared knowledge that he was lampooning not Gill alone, but a mood to which he was himself a contributor. As earnest a participant in the mystic Celticism of the 1890s as his friend Yeats, Russell had agreed to take on the more practical role of heading the Department's drive for farming reform, while editing *Irish Homestead*. Both he and Gill were men who had been brought within the ambit of the establishment by the cross-party 'constructive' initiatives emerging in the programmes of Balfour and Plunkett. Such alliances offered new political opportunities for projects like the one mooted by Yeats and friends in their proposal for the ILT.

Alongside the 'delicate flower' Russell described were other, as yet less developed, blooms growing from the seeds sown in the 1880s and 1890s. The year 1898 also saw Arthur Griffith and William Rooney return from

[1] R. A. Anderson, *With Plunkett in Ireland: The Co-Op Organiser's Story* (London, 1983), 102.

[2] George Russell to T. P. Gill, 31 Jan. 1899. T. P. Gill Papers, NLI MS 13481. The cartoon was widely circulated—Lady Gregory noted Plunkett describing it at dinner with her, Yeats, and Martyn soon afterward, saying Russell intended to publish it in the *Irish Homestead*. *Lady Gregory's Diaries, 1892–1902*, ed. James L. Pethica (Gerrards Cross, 1996), 205.

South Africa, harbingers of the imminent Boer War, D. P. Moran hone his acerbic skills in the *New Ireland Review*, and James Connolly's ISRP begin producing the *Worker's Republic*. The IRB also remained active: despite the ominous fractiousness evident amongst its organizers, preparations for the centenary of 1798 and a Tone memorial piqued popular interest and made concrete a Franco-Irish political relationship which would parallel the Parisian foil to London's literary dominance.

But these elements offered less leverage than could be supplied by the establishment, then enlisting Irish elites in its bid to assuage nationalism to death. Although Yeats accompanied Maud Gonne into the turbulence which attended the Centenary Committees (during which time he provoked the enmity of Frank Hugh O'Donnell),[3] he had hatched his plan for a new theatre at Coole Park, not the IRB (or INA) headquarters. It was in this climate of cultured rather than cultural nationalism that Yeats and Lady Gregory began casting about for support among Irish MPs and courting W. E. H. Lecky in pursuit of the means to entertain, then limited to the three licensed theatres. Their pursuit was timely. The tentative devolution of power intimated by the Recess and All Ireland Committees was at that time coming to hesitant fruition in the Local Government Bill. Lecky took the opportunity to insert an amendment loosening the law:[4] the ILT was born and the midwife was constructive Unionism.

The new political creed offered ways as well as means. One of its most influential practitioners, Sir Horace Plunkett, had given the shift to the centre added definition by taking over the management of the *Daily Express*.[5] He it was who took on Gill as editor, tacitly importing into the arena of political discourse the alliances he had built in the agrarian sphere. Gill obligingly ushered in a regime that offered cultural initiatives a central role. A literature-friendly policy akin to that of *United Ireland* provided an easy means of cementing constructive consensus—and the *Express*'s weekly 'Literary Page' offered precisely the sort of publicity the theatre project needed.

---

[3] O'Donnell's attacks on Yeats started in 1897 when as his co-delegate from the Centenary Association of England and France he had misinformed the London Committee of Yeats's plans. *The Gonne–Yeats Letters 1893–1938: Always Your Friend* ed. Anna MacBride White and A. Norman Jeffares (London, 1992).

[4] Yeats, *Collected Letters*, ii. *1896–1900*, ed. Warwick Gould et al. (Oxford, 1997), 233–4, 253–4.

[5] Bought after Plunkett had reached an apparent dead end when the Agriculture and Industries Bill was dropped in 1898. Trevor West, *Horace Plunkett: Co-Operation and Politics, An Irish Biography* (Gerrards Cross, 1986), 49–55.

The form this publicity took was a stage-managed literary brawl between Yeats and the essayist and NLI librarian William K. Magee (John Eglinton), the combatants eventually being prised apart by the referee who set them off in September 1898, George Russell. There was a personal score to settle, however, lent steel by Eglinton's proximity to the Trinity College professor Edward Dowden, whom Yeats had dismissed as a rationalist.[6] True to form, Yeats's old classmate set out the parameters of the debate with clarity and foresight. Entitled 'What Should be the Subject of a National Drama?', his first article began:

Supposing a writer of genius were to appear in this country, where would he look for the subject of a national drama? This question might serve as a test of what nationality amounts to in Ireland . . . would he look for it in the Irish legends, or in the life of the peasantry, or in life at large as reflected by his own consciousness?[7]

Eglinton's view was that this consciousness had to serve as the artist's fundamental guide: so long as it remained dependent on a folk tradition, it was doomed to remain what he disdainfully termed 'Belles Lettres'. Yeats countered that the Twilight, far from being a passive reworking of the stock of lore, was 'dreaming of things to come', revivifying perception in response to the new 'spiritual mood' abroad in Europe.[8]

Taking Russell's concluding review of the debate (and the editorial asides) as a guide, this exchange has been construed as Nationality versus Cosmopolitanism in literature.[9] Yet both combatants supported their positions with examples from the Continental scene, and argued that their adoption would be the making of a distinctively Irish drama. For both, the best way to build a national theatre was by adopting the models available in Europe: by combining this with a unique cultural wealth, Ireland could generate a world-beating literature.

Rather than being a division limited to attitudes for or against national and imperial cultures, the argument revolved around the appropriate response to conditions of modernity. John Eglinton's arguments were for individualism, populism, the glamour of the new: 'the kinematograph,

---

[6] Yeats often greeted Eglinton with the cordial tag 'the enemy', while he in turn thought Yeats 'spiteful and ungrateful' for vilifying Dowden (see e.g. 'The Academic Class', Dublin *Daily Express*, 11 Mar. 1899). E. H. Mikhail (ed.), *W. B. Yeats: Interviews and Recollections*, i. (London, 1977), 6, 32.

[7] Dublin *Daily Express*, 10 Sept. 1898.

[8] Ibid., 3 Dec. 1898.

[9] See esp. Declan Kiberd, *Inventing Ireland* (London, 1995) 155–65. Also F. S. L. Lyons, *Culture and Anarchy in Ireland, 1890–1939* (Oxford, 1979), 65–6.

the bicycle, electric tramcars, labour-saving contrivances . . . themselves the poetry . . . of a scientific age'.[10] Yeats, who had already woken in a sweat after visualizing G. B. Shaw incarnate as a sewing machine, opted for traditionalism, symbolism, and the glamour of myth. Yeats's argument however, was that his opponent's attempt at claiming Continental vogue was merely passé, 'that writers are struggling all over Europe . . . against that "externality" which a time of scientific and political thought has brought into literature'.[11] Yeats perceived such conditions as being driven by a materialism which London championed, but which was not confined to London. Similarly, his rebellion was not confined to Ireland, but insisted on a wider rebellion against the 'scientific age' that was in essence no less cosmopolitan than its target.

The division was international. Despite his curious disavowal of Ibsen (brought on by Yeats's celebrations of *Peer Gynt*) Eglinton suggested a melding of realism and poetic drama commensurate with an Ibsenite position; Russell categorized the 'cosmopolitan spirit' as investing the work of 'Goethe, Balzac, Tolstoi';[12] while Yeats championed the glimmering flame of French symbolism and Wagner's romantic use of folklore. Had they been aware of their contemporary, Chekhov, the disputants might have realized that what was most modish in the debate was the debate itself—Trepliov versus Trigorin, a contemporary stylistic confrontation held in all important European capitals.[13] In casting the split in terms of nationality, Russell carefully declared his allegiance not to nationalism only but to a type of nationalism which resonated with his idealism and with Yeats's. 'Since the mystical view of nature is . . . a national characteristic', he asserted, the realist impulse was therefore obviously cosmopolitan, 'hastily obliterating distinctions'. In defining Irishness thus, internal divisions—class, religious, and cultural—were also hastily obliterated. The broad Arnoldian brush George Russell used married well with the 'faint outlines' he and Yeats admired in French painting; but more than that, it boded well for the Anglo-Irish literary gambit and its current role in politics.

---

[10] 'Mr Yeats and Popular Poetry', Dublin *Daily Express*, 5 Nov. 1898.

[11] 'The Autumn of the Flesh', ibid., 3 Dec. 1898.

[12] 'Nationalism and Cosmopolitanism in Literature', ibid., 10 Dec. 1898.

[13] Chekhov's satire on symbolist theatre in *The Seagull* (first performed in Moscow in 1896) lends itself for comparison to this debate, a resonance noted by Thomas Kilroy in the Royal Court's 1981 production, relocated to an Anglo-Irish demesne. Chekhov, *The Seagull, in a new version by Thomas Kilroy* (London, 1981).

Nationality was never so strong in Ireland as at the present time. It is beginning to be felt less as a political force than as a spiritual force. It seems to be gathering itself together, joining men who were hostile before in a new intellectual fellowship; and if all these could unite on fundamentals it would be possible to create a national ideal in Ireland.[14]

For these Protestant disputants, making use of a Unionist paper to build up interest in a national theatre project, such a gambit had its attractions. But either way Russell was confident that the debates manifested an attempt to do something new in Ireland which respected but rejected the generations of Irishmen before, whose attempts to rouse Ireland had failed. His debate-closing couplet noted the debt to Parnellism, but (rather like Yeats's 'Mourn, and Then Onward') did so with an air of dismissal, placing 'A kiss of fire on the dim brow of failure | A crown upon her uncrowned head.'[15]

The presumption was that all responses to this 'failure' would concur. The question remained whether the 'spiritual force' to which Russell referred—the 'less political than' predicate being a cultural-nationalist hallmark—really had the unifying influence he suggested. Simultaneously, D. P. Moran made forays into the limitations and definitions of nationality in the *New Ireland Review*, which in no way offered 'intellectual fellowship' with what he considered to be a thoroughly Protestant attempt to pull the wool over Irish eyes. Nor was Moran alone in reorganizing the debate. A whole spate of new publications shared the ILT's year of genesis. Arthur Griffith and William Rooney's *United Irishman*, the Gaelic League paper *An Claidheamh Soluis*, and Standish O'Grady's *All Ireland Review* all sprang from the Beltane fires of 1899. Moran's *Leader* followed a year later. They offered different mixes of ingredients in the cultural-nationalist cocktail, but were all to a greater or lesser extent wary of the concept promoted by Yeats in the ILT's house journal, *Beltaine*, that a sacred order of artists could herald a new age, conveniently exchanging (Catholic) religion for theatre.

In the first day, it is the Art of the people; and in the second day, like the dramas enacted out of old times in the hidden places of temples, it is the preparation of a Priesthood. It may be, though the world is not old enough to show us any example, that this Priesthood will spread their religion everywhere, and make their Art the Art of the people.[16]

---

[14] 'Nationality and Cosmopolitanism in Literature', Dublin *Daily Express*, 10 Dec. 1898.
[15] Ibid.
[16] 'The Theatre', *Beltaine*, 1 (May 1899), 22.

The new theatrical adventure might expect backing from the mainstream press, sporting as it did on the cover of that first programme the
support of Nationalist and Unionist establishment figures, including
representatives of all IPP factions. On its cover listing guarantors,
Redmond, Healy, and Dillon could be found together, accompanied by
Maud Gonne. Lecky, John Mahaffy, and the Ardilauns were equally
accommodated.[17] This alone might have been enough to incur the disdain
of those new commentators who defined themselves through impatience
with that establishment. Indeed, coupled with Yeats's millenial predictions, it seemed to invite a barrage of scepticism.

In such a period of political transition, when labels were becoming
hazy, the two plays presented in that first season, *The Countess Cathleen*
and *The Heather Field*, were apt articulations of blurred allegiance. To
some extent the inclination to realism and the Catholic persuasion of
Martyn and Moore (though the latter had lapsed with a vengeance)
offered protection from impending criticism. Not so Yeats's play, singled
out for sustained attack.

The opposition to the supposed calumny against the integrity of the
Catholic peasant, so evidently vulnerable to accusations of souperism,
was led by two characters who were to prove long-standing enemies of
Yeats. Two days prior to the first night, William Martin Murphy's paper
the *Daily Nation* led with a revamped attack on the play, drawing on a
diatribe by F. H. O'Donnell. O'Donnell's pamphlet *Souls for Gold!
Pseudo-Celtic Drama in Dublin* had started as a letter to the *Freeman's
Journal* published a month earlier, before being collated with a follow-up
and liberally distributed. But, as was the case in later clashes, the virulence of the onslaught made the playwright's position easier to defend.
O'Donnell had declared: 'Mr. W. B. Yeats seems to see nothing in the
Ireland of old days but an unmanly, and impious and renegade people,
crouched in degraded awe before demons . . . just like a sordid tribe of
black devil-worshippers and fetish worshippers on the Congo or the
Niger.'[18]

Such a statement was fraught with the implications of competitive
nationalism. It accused Yeats of using racial stereotypes inherent in stage-
Irish conventions, one of which was Negricization. But O'Donnell used
a dehumanized stereotype of African tribal culture to emphasize the right
of the Celt to enter the club of superior races, and at the same time take

---

[17] Cover, *Beltaine*, 1 (May 1899).
[18] *Souls for Gold! Pseudo-Celtic Drama in Dublin* (London, 1899), 6.

a side-swipe at Protestant literati interest in paganism. Like Eglinton and Yeats, he was asserting the Irish right to be considered a 'civilized' people by way of cultural comparison. Unlike them, he was asserting that it was the religious conviction of the Irish that would afford them their place in the sun, rather than willingness to lead the field in all kinds of decadent devilry. O'Donnell stood so far outside the *Express* debate that he saw both parties as agencies of cosmopolitanism, however disguised, and as such as a threat to the true Irish destiny as exemplars of Catholic piety. As a self-styled 'Foreign Affairs' specialist, O'Donnell perceived such perils as part of the wider struggle of the Catholic Church against all subversions of European 'civility', that tide which to him was not only modern and filthy, but also Black and Jewish.

Neither Yeats's play nor O'Donnell's racism was new to the public domain: the 1890s had seen them both harboured under the protection of *United Ireland*, and they were familiar to one another as INA fellow-travellers. What was significant about this attack was not its existence but its impact. The times, and the audience, had changed. Now *The Countess Cathleen* was being scrutinized by a public which considered heightened Catholic consciousness a defining characteristic. They inevitably proved less indulgent than the anticlerical Parnellite fringe to whom the play had first been exposed. Yeats had already tried to placate Martyn's fear of religious transgression by getting affidavits for the play from clergymen in advance. Despite this, and with the help of the *Daily Nation*, the play was condemned (unseen) by Cardinal Logue. O'Donnell's pamphlet, though more sinning than sinned against, had found its mark with a main thrust of its criticism—that the play was an Ascendancy, or at least a landed, aristocratic, view of social morality which cheapened the Catholic convictions of the majority of Irish people.

The Countess Cathleen told of a time in which an aristocrat sells her soul to buy back those of the peasants who have already made their trade in return for relief. At one level it was a morality play presenting a cultural choice; whether to follow the abstract impulse of Art—to 'Go with Fergus'—or to take social responsibility and help ease distress.[19] But upon the Countess's choice depended not only her personal salvation, or by extension that of her class, but the salvation of the lower orders also. This assumption, presented through a central character with a spiritual superiority concurrent with privilege (and by implication, religious

---

[19] *The Countess Cathleen*, in *VP*, 65.

persuasion),[20] was all too evident to the audience who attacked it. As the Revd George O'Neill put it:

When one thinks what the general history of the Irish peasant has been—a history of religious and political martyrdom, of saints and rebels, of starvation with the blessing of the priest preferred to all the flesh-pots of the proselytiser—then it does seem cruel that a theatre professing to be above all things sympathetically national should at its first performance show them forth as demoralised poltroons, starvelings in soul as well as body.[21]

O'Neill, a lecturer in French and English Literature at University College, naturally published this objection in the *New Ireland Review*. As such it was as much a defence of the student body who took exception to the play as it was an attack upon the play itself. The cause célèbre introduced to Yeats an up-and-coming section of the Catholic intelligentsia: the Literary and Historical Society of University College, Dublin,[22] at the time including Tom Kettle, Francis Skeffington, Arthur Clery, and James Joyce.[23] Joyce volubly supported the ILT but several of his fellow students, led by Kettle, made their disapproval plain in a letter to the *Freeman's Journal*.[24] Their complaint added to noises of protests made at the performance itself,[25] articulations of unease all the more resonant for being voiced by youth.

Yeats defended his play both on the grounds that it was a simple morality and that as an example of symbolism it had proved too opaque for a corrupted public who mistakenly took it at face value. He had in fact developed the symbolist elements of the play since its first manifestation, introducing the character Aleel, the Countess's poet-lover, and thus emphasizing the case for verse drama. But it was political context, rather than rich poetry or plot complication which altered the response.[26]

---

[20] Adrian Frazier, *Behind the Scenes: Yeats, Horniman and the Struggle for the Abbey Theatre* (Berkeley and Los Angeles, 1990), 15–18.

[21] 'The Inauguration of the Irish Literary Theatre', *New Ireland Review*, 11/4 (June 1899), 249.

[22] Senia Paseta, *Before the Revolution: Nationalism, Social Change and Ireland's Catholic Élite, 1879–1922* (Cork, 1999), 62–75.

[23] J. B. Lyons, *The Enigma of Tom Kettle: Irish Patriot, Essayist, Poet, British Soldier, 1880–1916* (Dublin, 1983), 33–4.

[24] *Freeman's Journal*, 10 May 1899.

[25] T. W. Rolleston's defence of the protestors (ibid.), that they 'expressed their sentiments with vigour but in a perfectly gentlemanlike manner', suggests that the violence of the protests may have been exaggerated.

[26] The version of the *Countess* shown in 1899 was the third of five major revisions, which introduced and developed the role of the poet Aleel, strengthening the mystical side of the social v. personal anatagonism. See Peter Ure, *Yeats the Playwright* (London, 1963), 14–15 for an 'at a glance' table of the major changes.

In one sense, the embrace of the establishment by the ILT reflected Yeats's personal social shifting. In the early 1890s, the Countess might comfortably be considered a metaphor for the self-sacrificing nobility of Gonne; by 1899, she could equally be construed in terms of the more solid influence of Lady Gregory. This was a shift that could be seen (like the reception of the play) through the terms of the famine scares of the previous year. Yeats's initial enthusiasm for Gonne's plan to go to famine districts to provoke mass appropriation of livestock and foodstuffs met with horror when related to the landlord at Coole. However acute her opinion of Gonne, Lady Gregory's vertiginous sense of social and moral elevation overcame any awareness of her argument's irony, given Ireland's (or indeed her own family's) recent history.[27] 'We who are above the people in means & education, ought, were it a real famine, to be ready to share all we have with them, but that even supposing starvation was before them it would be for us to teach them to die with courage [rather] than to live by robbery.'[28] In the stated readiness 'to share all we have' might be perceived the distance Lady Gregory had already travelled from her class instincts, and would further go as time progressed. However, the demand that the notion of nobility was not to be abstracted from its social status by poetry or philosophy was significantly effective, appealing as it did to Yeats's ideas of cultural leadership.

The Countess Cathleen suggested complicity in an established social hierarchy, and the ILT had a political orientation which appeared to match. The platform from which the play was promoted and defended, the *Daily Express* (which now printed both *Beltaine*, with its long list of underwriters, and the collected articles in the preceding debate, *Literary Ideals in Ireland*), emphasized the cross-party nature of the initiative. After the opening night on May 1899, Plunkett threw a banquet oozing with Ascendancy luminaries and literary consensus which gave Yeats the opportunity to brush off the 'Unfair Criticism'[29] he had faced, and to bathe in the eulogies delivered by Douglas Hyde, Rolleston, and, waxing most lyrically, George Moore. The following weekend Arthur Griffith commented sarcastically of this 'Irish Literary Dinner': 'Let the Irish Nation grasp the pen of Yeats for its sword and the buckle on the churn of Plunkett and be saved! . . . Will the union of butter and Poesy endure?

---

[27] Lady Gregory's family the Persse's had been proselytizers, a practice she detested but to which she as a young woman had been complicit. George Moore would in 1914 bring the skeleton to light in *Vale*, the final section of his memoir *Hail and Farewell*.

[28] *Diaries*, 167.

[29] The title of Yeats's lecture as reported in the Dublin *Daily Express*, 8 May 1899.

Will their conjugal embraces lead to the birth of a new Irish Nation? I fear not.'[30]

Yet, curiously, the very level of controversy muted criticism. Polemicists such as Griffith and Moran were glad to welcome any project they could get their teeth into, or which would provoke debate. If wary of the form it had taken, they were attracted by the idea of theatre. The *United Irishman* even-handedly commended the gusto with which young protestors voiced their disapproval of Yeats's play, while recognizing the ILT as a new departure worthy of concerned interest.[31] Moran defended the theatre from the onslaughts of the language movement by declaring in a typically backhand way: 'Insofar as the theatre question has set people thinking whom the League could not yet hope to reach, it has done good, wrong thinking being more hopeful than our great enemy—no thinking at all.'[32] On the other hand, Edward Martyn's play *The Heather Field*, much more of a critical success than Yeats's, balanced the suspiciously Protestant-folk axis with a Catholic-realist one. With class rather than culture to the fore, however, both plays brooded on a landed interest undergoing change.

While still in the process of rejecting his murky Unionist past, the Deputy Lieutenant for Galway had (in about 1894) constructed his first—and most accomplished—drama out of the tensions and contradictions attendant on such transition.[33] Sympathy in the play is generated for a landlord who on the one hand declares the ambition of 'reclaiming every inch of space in Ireland',[34] but on the other, when faced with something akin to the Plan of Campaign, evicts his tenants because he will 'never voluntarily reduce the value of . . . property'.[35] Yet his programme of 'domestication' (suggesting constructive Unionism) is doomed to fail in its efforts to make productive the wild beauty to which the hero Tyrell

---

[30] *United Irishman*, 20 May 1899. 'The remarkable gathering of Irishmen', as the Dublin *Daily Express* called it (12 May 1899), included among others: Yeats, Martyn, Moore, Douglas Hyde, John O'Leary, Dr Sigerson, Eglinton, Max Beerbohm, and Standish O'Grady.

[31] *United Irishman*, 13 May 1899. 'We cannot find it in ourselves to condemn the warm-souled youths whom even a fancied slight to the memory of an Irish patriot [can cause to] pour out the vials of their wrath.'

[32] *ACS*, 8 July 1899.

[33] Denis Gwynn, *Edward Martyn and the Irish Revival* (London, 1930), 56. In the 80s, Martyn had been opposed to the Land League and the Nationalist Party. One of his closest friends (and a cousin) was Woulfe Flanagan, author of *The Times*'s notorious articles 'Parnellism and Crime'.

[34] Martyn, *The Heather Field and Maeve* (London, 1899), 47.

[35] Ibid. 111.

finally succumbs. It struck at a problem familiar to cultural nationalists: that a distinctively Irish unruliness, symbolized by the untameable heather, might be ploughed under in the name of progress—and yet development, though smacking of colonization, was nevertheless the hope of Ireland's aspirations. As one contributor to the *Daily Express* put it: 'To conjoin the two points of view—practical progress with spiritual integrity—is the problem which has beset us.'[36]

Those intellectuals emerging from a frustrated lower middle class emphasized the need for industrialization and land reform but still felt the strength of the romantic stereotype and its potential as a propaganda weapon. Even Moran, who suggested that 'one of the most hopeful signs in Ireland at present is the growth of pessimism',[37] operated the paradox of anti-materialism and pro-modernization, somehow reconcilable if only the true spirit of Ireland could be revived:

> The economic ills of Ireland can be traced to many diverse minor causes, but if you follow them up you arrive at the great common cause—the lack of Irish heart . . . the greasy draper rubs his hands and dilates on 'the circulation of money' and the moss on the still wheel of the village well weeps for the native heart of other days.[38]

Such an infectious nostalgia (and imagery) could not help but give grudging due to the efforts of the cooperative movement, and by 1902 Moran and Griffith could be found sitting with Russell on the Gaelic League Industrial Committee.[39]

In one sense, Martyn is playing to this gallery; yet a close identification of such 'spirituality' with madness is also stressed. Ussher, Tyrell's decadent neighbour, argues that 'It is only commonplace and unimaginative people who consider the poetic and original temperament to be a mark of madness',[40] but the two Strindbergian doctors' diagnosis is proven in the end. Onlookers, it seemed to suggest, might likewise consider Martyn's approach more sensible than the apocalyptical rantings of his associates.[41] Certainly, the clinical stagecraft and dialogue so symptomatic of Martyn's

[36] 'H.N.', 'Celtic Ideals and Irish Dangers', Dublin *Daily Express*, 29 Oct. 1898.

[37] 'Politics, Nationality and Snobs', *New Ireland Review*, Nov. 1899, 129.

[38] Ibid. 111.

[39] Shane O'Neill, 'The Politics of Culture in Ireland 1899–1910', D.Phil. thesis (Oxford, 1982), 61.

[40] *Heather Field*, 54.

[41] Strindberg's *The Father* (whose doctors Martyn's so resemble) had been available in French trans. since 1888. For an analysis of the various plays from Ibsen's catalogue detectable in *The Heather Field*, see Jan Setterquist, *Ibsen and the Beginnings of Anglo-Irish Drama*, ii. *Edward Martyn* (Uppsala, 1960).

chronic Ibsenitis was more accessible than Yeatsian verse. The impression was that it put him on the justly sceptical side of the Eglinton–Yeats debate, and on the side of a sane theatrical response to the spiritual ills of Ireland—medicinal rather than poetical.

Yeats's play drew fire away from Martyn, despite the fact that for all the attention claimed by formal emphasis and the religious traditions of their respective authors, *The Countess Cathleen* and *The Heather Field* both dwelt upon the anxieties of the Irish landed elite. The allegorical dilemmas facing Tyrell gave him little time to address the suffering of his tenants. No one pointed out that, despite his much-exercised psychology, *The Heather Field*'s hero appeared strangely akin to the father of Hubert O'Grady's villain Lumley Sackville in *The Famine*, whose ruination at the hands of land agitators had led his son to revenge. Only one satirical reviewer, noted by Lady Gregory in her *Beltaine* selection, commented 'I didn't think that any Irish landlord, that ever stood in two shoes, had the makings of such things in him. I'd bear eviction by sich [*sic*] a man with a light heart.'[42]

The question remained whether the ILT itself was a recrudescence of Celtic heatherness, or a carefully cultured hothouse relative of the flower 'National Unionism' drawn by Russell. The *United Irishman* gave benefit of its not inconsiderable doubt to Yeats, applauding the project as opposed to the productions. He was to be congratulated, declared Griffith, 'not as the artist, but as the standard raiser of revolt'.[43] Moran, like F. H. O'Donnell, preferred to direct his criticism at the notion of Celticism: 'An intelligent people are being asked to believe that the manufacture of the before mentioned "Celtic note" is a grand symbol of an Irish national intellectual awakening. This, it appears to me, is one of the most glaring frauds that the credulous Irish people ever swallowed.'[44]

If there was to be a spiritual centre that Ireland could draw upon to resist the material superiority of England, Moran insisted, it was Catholicism. And to represent this spiritual root the mainly Protestant literati had no claim. His definition of national identity resisted the whole tenor of the ILT–*Express* attempts to provide an establishment purchase on cultural nationalism for Protestant and aristocratic groups. However exclusive his own strictures on what constituted valid Irishness, Moran was quick to point out the overlap between Yeatsian notions of replacing

---

[42] *Beltaine*, 2 (Feb. 1900), 28. Quoted from 'Billy Kelly and the Irish Literary Theatre' in the *Outlook*.

[43] *United Irishman*, 13 May 1899.

[44] 'The Future of the Nation', *New Ireland Review*, Feb. 1899, 352–3.

religion with art and elision of the religious differences which he thought lay at the heart of resistance to Anglicization. That Catholics might be involved in this detestable process made little difference—the Irish were after all both an 'intelligent' and a 'credulous' people—the process bespoke a fudging of cultural opposition which divested the average Irishman of the equipment needed to establish his own identity. Yeats's position conversely militated against this marginalization, by replacing it with another—seeking to assert the artistic function over more traditional labels. Artists had a unique and essential role in the divination of cultural identity because of their super-sensitivity, a mystical access to the root of the race. The literary vanguard could provide the solution to any Irish–modern paradox through a process of cultural trickledown: 'a gradual and imperceptible flowing down, as if through orders and hierarchies'.[45]

As time went on, Yeats developed this argument into a circular critique of any opponents he had in the press by suggesting that by using the most debased form of English, journalese, they were themselves the standard-bearers for the invading spirit of Anglicization.

In Ireland . . . it may be those very men, who have made a subtle personal way of expressing themselves, instead of being content with English as it is understood in the newspapers, or who see all things reflected in their own souls, which are from the parent fountain of their race . . . who may be recognised in the future as most Irish, though their own time entangled in the surface of things may often think them lacking in everything that is Irish.[46]

What the poet could supply was the priest-like role of intermediary between the word of Gael and its modern counterpart. By implication, it was clear that critics were already too far from that spirit to recognize even its decoded form if they insisted on criticizing it using newspaper prose.

As a riposte to Moran, who had 'remigrated' after long years in Fleet Street, this might have carried some weight; but it was less effective against *An Claidheamh Soluis*. Despite Hyde's sympathy for the literary movement the Gaelic League paper conducted a bitter campaign against the ILT. The objection was made that if Irishness could be claimed for productions delivered in English, it rendered the League a non-starter. A young Patrick Pearse made the point: 'If we admit the Irish literature in

---

[45] 'John Eglinton and Spiritual Art', Dublin *Daily Express*, 29 Oct. 1899.
[46] 'Irish Language and Literature', *Leader*, 1 Sept. 1901.

English idea, then the language movement is a mistake.'[47] He recommended Yeats be 'crushed' (though he did not explain how). Nevertheless, language enthusiasts' objections differed in nature from Moran's. In their efforts to put a stop to the 'nebulous twaddle of the Celtic note',[48] a debate ensued over the question 'What is National Literature?'[49] which drew forth some of the most secular and inclusive definitions of cultural nationality.[50] Indeed, the emphasis placed on language was not dissimilar to Yeats's, however logical Pearse appeared when pointing out the incompatibility of their positions.

Against the ILT's claim to access the essence of Irishness, the objection was made, 'suppose an English writer chooses to adopt the Irish note, does he thereby become a naturalised literary Irishman?'[51] Lionel Johnson may have thought so; Leaguers thought the answer so obvious as to leave the question rhetorical. But if the logical inversion of this was, as suggested by one contributor, that 'The Old Testament in Irish is Irish, and not Hebrew, literature',[52] the League's definition became radically inclusive. Any one of the Anglo-Irish who learned Irish and wrote in it could be declared to be well and truly Irish, even, as Hyde was keen to emphasize, in spite of their political persuasion—which was one reason why he sat comfortably among guests less nationalist than he at the *Express* dinner. In the end, however, practicality proved a more decisive factor. The recognition that even the Gaelic League relied on English as a vehicle for propaganda gave the ILT and its successors a convenient opt-out clause operating on the basis of cultural jam tomorrow. Under pressure from the *United Irishman*, the *An Claidheamh Soluis* editorial conceded that 'We do not discountenance English as a means to an end; we do it ourselves in these pages.'[53] *An Claidheamh Soluis*'s criticisms of the theatre were also mitigated by the League's inclination to be viewed as a modern movement. Ibsen was viewed not with distaste, but as a role model who had succeeded in making obscure Norwegian a linguistic force

---

[47] *ACS*, 20 May 1899.   [48] Ibid., 29 Apr. 1899.

[49] Ibid., 1 July 1899. Under this title the leader-writer poured scorn on the 'pleasant little primrose paths of Anglo-Irish writing, with their dainty little bends and bowers, and their dear little gurgling rivulets of thought beside them'.

[50] This debate, sparked off by the first productions of the ILT, is also notable for an early defence of Anglo-Irish drama by the young 'Cork realist' Thomas C. Murray. The row continued from May until mid-July, when it was closed. Later issues of *ACS* referred subsequent combatants (such as Seumas MacManus in 1903) back to the position adopted by the newspaper during this debate.

[51] *ACS*, 1 July 1899.   [52] Ibid., 10 Jan. 1903.

[53] Ibid., 30 Sept. 1899.

in Europe. Gaelic Leaguers were often at pains to indicate the standing of Celtic linguists in France and Germany when putting the case against the Trinity nemeses Atkinson and Mahaffy. The currency of Celtic studies in Europe gave an added intellectual cachet and served to caricature dismissive linguists as not merely oppressive but also intellectually complacent and conservative.

The eyes of nationalists turned to events outside Ireland which bore direct relation to Irish nationality, its definition and hopes for realization. Concentration on Hoche and Humbert's excursions onto Irish soil during the Napoleonic Wars stressed the inclination to play cultural leapfrog, jumping over England and onto the Continent, particularly to join Catholic France. Part of this fascination was the knowledge that external pressure on the British meant opportunities for internal friction. And at the same time, as ex-Uitlanders Griffith and Rooney were quick to recognize, the situation in South Africa was worsening. When war broke out, it was to alter the whole balance of power between the fledgling theatre company and the new crop of advanced nationalists represented by the *United Irishman.*

The outbreak of hostilities between Britain and the Boers polarized Irish politics and in the first months of 1900, the loose consensual arrangement between constructive Unionism and cultural nationalism became unworkable.[54] The *Daily Express*, which had been under financial pressure, was restored to the ultra-Unionist fold when Lord Ardilaun bought out Plunkett as part of a campaign to oust him from his South Dublin constituency.[55] Gill was replaced forthwith, and went to join Plunkett at the Department of Agricultural and Technical Instruction. But even if the old team had stayed at the *Daily Express* offices, it is unlikely that the coalition would have remained intact.

Edward Martyn, too, severed his ties with the establishment by resigning his posts as magistrate and Deputy Lieutenant of Galway, while George Moore returned to Ireland loudly proclaiming his conversion to a

[54] For the fragility of the constructive Unionist project, see Andrew Gailey, *Ireland and the Death of Kindness: The Experience of Constructive Unionism 1890–1905* (Cork, 1987), 295–322.

[55] Ardilaun had been an enemy of the hapless Plunkett since he voted with the nationalists on an evicted tenant's bill in 1896, confirmed when the Royal Dublin Society (of which Ardilaun was president) opposed the Recess Committee. Gill and Plunkett's half-baked stance on the Boer War was the last straw: taking advantage of the desperate financial straits at the *Express* office (contibutors were left unpaid for months), Ardilaun took over via the agent Dalziel News Ltd., and turned the *Express*'s fire on its previous owner. Margaret Digby, *An Anglo-American Irishman* (Oxford, 1949), 81; West, *Horace Plunkett*. Also T. P. Gill Papers, letter to D. Dalziel, n.d. [1899], NLI MS 13481.

stunned and concerned language movement.[56] Even Lady Gregory, who was becoming ever more essential to the ILT as confidante and peacemaker, found herself falling out with Lecky over the war in South Africa.[57] Lecky finally resigned his support when, in March, the imminence of Queen Victoria's recruitment-oriented visit prompted a letter from Yeats to the press condemning in strident tone any public gesture of welcome.[58]

Yeats had made a stance of some significance, both personal and political, the kind of thing a high priest had to do to gain the confidence of his people—slaying Egyptian masters, as he put it in *Samhain*.[59] It was a position made all the more attractive for the vicinity of Maud Gonne who was also responding to the Queen's visit by dishing out invective (causing the *United Irishman* to be banned) and hosting a picnic alternative to establishment attempts to buy Irish children's affections.[60] The 'Patriotic Children's Treat Committee' in turn showed the counter-influence of the cultural project, providing the basis for the nationalist women's organization Inghinidhe na hÉireann, which (mainly owing to the influence of Alice Milligan) was tinged with literary aspirations. All these gestures confirmed a new emphasis in the political sympathies of the ILT triumvirate.

At the same time, the *United Irishman*, jockeying for position with Moran's newly arrived *Leader*, pursued a course at once hostile to the ILP and its sectarian competitor. Rooney and Griffith had from the first denounced Moran's line as divisive, complaining that 'our philosopher strives to rouse the suspicions and sympathy of the Irishman of fifty generations against the Irishman of five'.[61] Henceforth, while the *Leader* and the *United Irishman* were occupied with 'blacking each other's eye',[62] the tone of their paper regarding non-Unionist Protestants was decidedly conciliatory.

---

[56] The *United Irishman*, 3 Mar. 1900, considered that Moore's conversion, given his prodigality, 'could not fail of being sensational . . . it decidedly marks an epoch'.

[57] Lady Gregory, *Diaries*, 250 (entry 3 Mar. 1900). [58] Ibid. 264.

[59] *Samhain*, 1 (1901), 4.

[60] Successful though the counter-picnic was, Maud Gonne's claim that 30,000 children participated should be treated as an ambition rather than a reliable figure—only 31,000 registered Catholic schoolchildren existed in Dublin at the time. Senia Paseta, 'Nationalist Responses to Two Royal Visits to Ireland, 1900 and 1903', *Irish Historical Studies*, 21/124 (Nov. 1999), 494–5.

[61] *United Irishman*, 10 June 1899.

[62] An accusation made to the *United Irishman*, 24 Jan. 1903. Griffith declared the week after that '*The Leader* was founded with the object of killing the *United Irishman* and *An Claidheamh Soluis*, and becoming the official organ of the League.'

It was also a tone which reflected the impact of the Boer War. The Afrikaners' Protestantism (and their own penal laws) invited comparison with Ireland in ways less complimentary to the Irish struggle, as T. W. Rolleston observed:

The Boers are a people who . . . have taken possession of a region of immense mineral and agricultural wealth, exterminating or subduing the original inhabitants. This region is about four times the size of Ireland, and the Boer population numbers less than that of Dublin . . . The Boers are, in fact, fighting for that most objectionable thing which we in Ireland know so well under the name of 'Ascendancy'.[63]

Even if Rolleston's argument that Ireland should take her place in an 'Anglo-Celtic Empire' could be easily brushed off, his point that Irish anti-colonialism could be distinctly selective was well made. It also shed light on the way the African war hamstrung Catholic nationalist invective. Anxious to distinguish between the worthy Boer cause and examples of Protestant countries not hostile to the British, division was forced between apparently reasonable (Dutch, German, some Irish) and unreasonable (Huguenot, Ulster) Protestant cultures.[64]

Such refinement of sympathies could not be held to represent the general tenor of the *United Irishman* in the latter half of 1899, while it pursued a policy of virulent anti-Semitism in response to the Dreyfus Affair. Sympathy for the beleaguered farmers of the Transvaal was also felt for the Catholic nationalists in the French military establishment, also beleaguered, this time by the secularizing propensities of the Third Republic. The ideological connection was strengthened by more concrete ties through Maud Gonne's association with Lucien Millevoye and through him with Edouard Drumont (both elected in 1898 for the Ligue Antisémitique Française, editors of *La Patrie* and *La Libre Parole* respectively).[65] French-influenced conspiracy theories abounded: Anglo-Jewish money was dictating politics in France through the Press, bribery, Freemasonry, and Huguenot organizations, in order to undermine European opposition to the Empire while Britain had its way with the

---

[63] *Ireland, the Empire and the War* (Dublin, 1900), 14.

[64] See e.g. F. H. O'Donnell: 'The French Huguenot, unlike the patriot Protestants of Germany and Holland, still nourishes the gloomy fanaticism and the pro-English treachery of Coligny . . . the loathing of the French Nation. The Freemason is but the instrument of Downing Street and the Synagogue . . . The Besotted Orangeman is the Huguenot of Ireland.' *United Irishman*, 25 Nov. 1899.

[65] Stephen Wilson, *Ideology and Experience: Antisemitism in France at the Time of the Dreyfus Affair* (Rutherford, 1982), 17.

Boers. The very fragility of the assertion recommended it to nationalists with yearnings for the apocalypse, suggesting a polarity of good and evil forces which must inevitably give rise to the final battle. Maud Gonne predicted in 1899:

England knows that sooner or later she will have to fight a coalition of Europe. Her able diplomatists and, above all, her Jewish allies, who foment quarrels and internal strife among the different countries when her policy of grab have [sic] exasperated, may be able to stave off the day of reckoning for a time, but sooner or later it will come.[66]

The pace was set when Frank Hugh O'Donnell (the 'Foreign Secretary') resumed service as resident expert on external affairs. Unlike his stint in *United Ireland*, here O'Donnell was in step with an overtly anti-Semitic editorial policy. His virulence left the others trailing. Raging against the 'Wild, savage, filthy forms from the Yiddish ghetto' who had taken part in London's pro–Dreyfusard demonstrations, his apoplexy implicated in the conspiracy liberal and left-wing supporters who made common cause.

The Jews, who swarmed from their London Ghetto into Hyde Park . . . were the loving comrades of a whole mob of blethering English agitators, Noncomformist tubthumpers, and Radical ranters, who howled against France and the French generals with a low ferocity truly Anglo-Saxon. It was a sorry gathering. Some thirty thousand Jews and Jewesses, mostly of phenomenal ugliness and dirt, had come out of their East End dens at the summons of their Rabbis.[67]

In accordance with the separation of political affiliation on this issue, the only voice raised among nationalists came from the ISRP, which castigated the *United Irishman* and O'Donnell in particular. Connolly, despite his friendship with Gonne, had already vigorously repudiated her position in *L'Irlande Libre*. Recognition of 'even intensely conservative' nationalism as anti-imperialist and therefore broadly positive, did not imply resignation of an independently Marxist position.

The Socialist parties of France oppose the mere Republicans, without ceasing to love the Republic. In the same way the Irish Socialist Republican Party seeks the independence of the nation, whilst refusing to conform to the methods, or to employ the arguments of the Chauvinist Nationalist. As Socialists we are not imbued with national or racial hatred.[68]

Fred Ryan took up this lead, engaging Griffith in a running argument over the merits of imperialism (which the editor advocated as 'merely an

[66] *United Irishman*, 23 Sept. 1899.   [67] Ibid.
[68] 'Socialism and Irish Nationalism', repr. in English in *Worker's Republic*, 3 Sept. 1898.

exchangeable term for the advance of civilization')[69] while bringing the *United Irishman* to book over its anti-Semitism. Although the Boer War meant a heightening of what Connolly identified as the subversive accord in which nationalism functioned as an 'agent for social regeneration',[70] the ISRP maintained its hostility to O'Donnell and its distance from bourgeois nationalism. As a result neither the liberal nor Protestant enemies identified by French anti-Semitic propaganda (Drumont actually claimed 'Every Protestant . . . is half-Jewish')[71] could be pursued with impunity. Although South Africa presented an opportunity to expand conspiracy theories, its inspiration as an example to nationalists was its overriding feature.

The IPP also found that external vision could help promote the fragile internal unity which had followed the swift rise of the UIL. Opposition to the first Boer War had been a parliamentary cause that helped consolidate the early leadership of Parnell. Now the growing strength of constitutionalists in turn put pressure on more advanced elements to pool resources. Connolly's flair for organization was apparent in the Irish Transvaal Committee, which provided a common platform for the ISRP and the nationalist clubs soon to be rationalized under Griffith's organization Cummann na nGaedheal. Aside from his bitter clash with Maud Gonne, this alliance was one of the reasons why F. H. O'Donnell was forced out of his position of influence in the *United Irishman*. Connolly had been demanding his head through the *Worker's Republic* and 'in numerous private representations'.[72] Not for the last time the separate agenda of the nationalist left succeeded in mitigating the wilder excesses of right-wing associates—with no small repercussions for the emergent theatre movement. The ILT would certainly be given a more favourable hearing while Frank Fay rather than O'Donnell had the ear of its editors.

The atmosphere in which the ILT gave its second 'Beltaine season' was changed indeed from the first. The most ambitious play on offer was *The Bending of the Bough*, a rehash by George Moore of Martyn's *The*

---

[69] 'Advance by Imperialism', *United Irishman*, 17 June 1899.

[70] *Worker's Republic*, 3 Sept. 1898.

[71] Wilson, *Ideology and Experience*, 417.

[72] *Worker's Republic*, 16 Sept. 1899. See also 18 Nov. 1899: 'Since it fell into the claws of Frank Hugh O'Donnell, [the *United Irishman*] has ceased to preach any intelligible or coherent national policy', and finally, 23 June 1900: 'we observe that the current issue of our stalwart nationalist contemporary, the "United Irishman" has finally broken with . . . O'Donnell. It is well.'

Tale of a Town,[73] a satire on the attempts of nationalist 'Financial Relations' agitation to force restitution following revelations of overtaxation. It also marked, in the character of Kirwan, the advent of the sea-green cultural-nationalist visionary, in this case an idealist who cannot communicate his ideas to the people except through the distorting medium of corrupt local politics. Against this background is placed the dilemma of Jasper Dean, a natural leader too tempted by a life of matrimonial bliss to give Kirwan's ideas flesh, and champion 'Northhaven' against the exploitative enemy 'Southhaven'. The material crusade is revealed as vulnerable to debasement, and just as individual politicians are exposed as open to bribery, the public too are easily bought off.

Martyn's crude original benefited hugely from Moore's polished rewrite, which rendered the allegory more subtle and the action more taut. Dean's intended, particularly, was translated from a dull English debutante into a thoroughly modern Millicent, capable of picking on Kirwan's ideas of Celtic superiority ('I wonder if I shall become absorbed? Jasper, do you think you are equal to the task?')[74] and finally, of luring her man away from public duty. The result came out like a cross between *An Enemy of the People* and *An Ideal Husband*. Epigrammatic dialogue played across a lesser version of Ibsen's tale of righteous minority, in which Kirwan, 'the strong man who stands alone', presented both the ILT and the advanced nationalists with a clique-protecting logic that guarded against critics of the cultural and political van. While audiences debated which characters caricatured whom, Yeats warned them that 'If any person upon the stage resembles any living person, it will be because he is himself a representative of the type.'[75]

In a more coded way, the *Bough*'s themes were also present in Alice Milligan's short piece *The Last Feast of the Fianna*, put on with Martyn's *Maeve*. Looking back to Yeats's narrative poem 'The Wanderings of Oisin', and forward to *Diarmuid and Grania*, Milligan's playlet suggested the potential for Celtic theatre as a political weapon. True to her stated intention to highlight fighting talk in the Eire of legend, Milligan also posited a possible source of corruption, presented in the form of faery Niamh. In her version Niamh approaches Finn before settling for Oisin, but is rebuffed by the King, who in turn upbraids his son for desertion—

---

[73] Martyn, *The Tale of a Town and An Enchanted Sea* (London, 1902). *The Selected Plays of George Moore and Edward Martyn* ed. David B. Eakin and Michael Case (Gerrards Cross, 1995), carries both plays for easy comparison.

[74] Moore, *The Selected Plays of George Moore and Edward Martyn*, 80.

[75] *Beltaine*, 2 (Feb. 1900), 94.

'Oisin, my poet, my son, art then indeed departing from me and from the comrades the Fianna Eirinn, to whom thou art bound by a vow?'[76] Written before the Boer War, and first published in the still liberal unionist *Daily Express*, the play carried that suspicion of the distractions of Celticism while suggesting its uses. From a form of betrayal, however, withdrawal into the world of Tír na nÓg (the mythical Land of Youth) had become transported into a badge of spiritual purity, as both Kirwan and Maeve, the heroine of Martyn's play, in their own ways suggested.

Maeve, from one angle, appears a thoroughly bowdlerized version of *The Land of Heart's Desire*. Stripped of that play's priest-baiting and sinister anarchism, the theft of souls by the dream of Ireland's own utopian realm became an inoffensive reassertion of that artistic and spiritual essence known only to the Gael: 'the fairy lamp of Celtic beauty'.[77] While operating within the realms of Russell's and Yeats's mystical parlance, however, Martyn took the innovative step of declining the defensive 'once upon a time' preface used by Yeats and eschewed his own drawing-room proclivities. The action moved to the here-and-now backdrop where much of Irish drama was to remain: the tenant farmer's dwelling.

Despite these departures, *Maeve* was a poorer play than *The Heather Field*; obvious and without the redeeming angst. Nevertheless, it offset *The Bending of the Bough* by allowing the central protagonist to leave behind the English suitor to whom she was betrothed, and acted as a counterbalance to *The Last Feast*'s anti-Celtic Celticism. While those plays purveyed partial defeat, *Maeve* articulated a clear victory of de-Anglicization, offering to replace their and Yeats's nervous studies of internal friction with a simpler choice between idealism and acquiescence.

Yeats, still smarting from the barracking over *The Countess Cathleen*, chose acceptance by association with the season, through *Beltaine* making it known his interpretation of the plays was that they offered the choice between spiritual beauty and 'mere intellectual life'. But the improved reception, particularly in the *United Irishman*, was a result of a gap closing from both sides. The sea change in politics was indicated as much by the plays' more overt nationalism and emasculated paganism[78] as by the more sympathetic hearing they received.

---

[76] *The Last Feast of the Fianna* (pt. 2). Dublin *Daily Express*, 30 Sept. 1899.

[77] Martyn, *Heather Field and Maeve*, 114.

[78] The *New Ireland Review*, impressed by what it perceived of as a revival of idealism, nevertheless bid 'healthy and wholesome men and women' beware the 'literary Tir-nan-Og' [*sic*], warning that 'its attractions are slightly pagan'. 'From the Study Chair', *New Ireland Review*, 13 (Mar. 1900).

For Griffith was not merely responding to something closer to his conception of appropriate dramatic form. He had been impatient with the intellectual posturing and the establishment flavour of the first season, and considered them well suited to a literary experiment which he doubted would have any immediate consequence for anyone but the elite.

Mr Yeats' project, of course, is an attempt to produce a really high-class Anglo-Irish drama; but such plays as he meditates can never be popular. They are too far above the people's heads, and while they shall not want for an audience, they will not appeal to the multitude, for whom melodrama is for a long time yet the best field to work.[79]

Curiously, Griffith chose to ignore the existing form of nationalist melodrama regularly performed at the Queen's Royal Theatre, instead parading the literary revival assumption that Dublin drama was, with few exceptions, guilty of 'persistent caricaturing and libelling of the nation'.[80] Frank Fay had reviewed Whitbread's *Lord Edward* and *Wolfe Tone* in not wholly (but mostly) derogatory terms in the *United Irishman*, so Griffith was certainly aware of them. According to his own tenets, such plays should have been worth consideration. But the very popularity of the plays may have sullied them in his eyes. The Queen's tried and tested formulas found closer correlation with the mainstream, rank-and-file nationalism it had evolved through, than the strains of cultural nationalism now emerging. Despite being what a recent historian of the Queen's Theatre has called 'the Irish national theatre' of the period[81] Griffith (and Moran, O'Donnell, Standish O'Grady, the *Express*, and the Gaelic League) chose studiously to overlook its existence.

One other reason for this must have been that nationalist melodrama was not typical of the Queen's output. The identification of nationalist melodrama with Whitechapel farce was, no doubt, enhanced by the fact that only five or six weeks of the theatre's average year were taken up with nationalist material; the rest was more typically characterized by imported musical comedy.[82] For the new nationalists a flourishing popular theatre furnished by and large with English touring companies constituted yet more evidence of an immorality concurrent with social demoralization and cultural dependency. Although the ILT also used English actors, it was attempting something which in style and content

---

[79] *United Irishman*, 11 Mar. 1899.
[80] Ibid., 4 Mar. 1899.
[81] Seamus de Burca, *The Queen's Royal Theatre, 1829–1969* (Dublin, 1983), 1.
[82] Joseph Holloway Papers, NLI MS 12069–74.

resisted that dependency, and mirrored the unease felt about the pursuit of nationalist objectives through British institutions—particularly marked in the welcoming attitude offered to Queen Victoria by representatives newly created in elections following the Local Government Act. As the war in Africa tarnished the British reputation for invincibility, so more militant displays of nationalism exercised the fear that empowerment within the existing political structure—likewise amelioration of conditions for tenant farmers—would sap any energy Ireland possessed to follow the Boers' example. This was a dynamic that *The Bending of the Bough* had made one theme: the corruption of the ideal through personal advancement. With the play's other theme of righteous minority it dovetailed neatly into the Transvaal Committee's experience of failing to convert a successful anti-recruiting campaign (and subsequent popular clash with the police in December 1899) into political capital. In the play, newspaperman Foley asserts that the corrupt Alderman Lawerence 'has carried all but the most extreme of the people with him':[83] simultaneously, Boer War veteran John MacBride was trounced in the South Mayo elections by an alliance of the UIL and the outgoing incumbent Michael Davitt.[84]

Given the synchronicity of this event with the ILT's new offerings in February 1900, it was hardly surprising Griffith could revise his earlier judgements, to declare *The Bough* as 'undoubtedly the work of genius', and reappraise the artist's role, as he did his own, with a decidedly Yeatsian slant.

There can be but one opinion amongst those really interested in the uprise of Ireland as to the value of this year's performance of the Irish Literary Theatre. That the audiences have been small, wretchedly small, only goes to show how low and how far our people have fallen from the appreciation of true art and sympathy with Irish thought, tradition and sentiment.[85]

In keeping with the shift in political affiliation, Griffith was happy to retranslate elite as vanguard. '[S]ympathy with Irish thought' was a condition dependent not on the majority view but an as yet minority notion of Irishness as defined by Griffith. The literati's capacity to assume authority dictating the boundaries of this identity was suddenly

---

[83] *Selected Plays of George Moore and Edward Martyn*, 140.

[84] MacBride was beaten 2,401 votes to 427 by John O'Donnell, with a turnout of no more than 25 per cent. It was made all the more annoying by the fact that 'Colonel Lynch', leader of the other 'Irish Brigade' in the Transvaal, was elected in Galway as an independent Nationalist at the same time.

[85] *United Irishman*, 24 Feb. 1900.

an attractive trait, particularly to Griffith's brand of bourgeois separatism. Realist satire was obviously a handy tool for ridiculing enemies and impressing friends, while Celtic mythology, once so dubious, was recognized as a means of promoting a heroic stereotype previously considered over-refined and lacking in relevancy. The interpretation of the theatre as a device capable of inspiring social unity demonstrates the common ground Griffith and Yeats could step onto, although in time their differing perceptions of that relationship between 'true art' and 'Irish thought' would prove insuperable.

It was a position which indicated how far the emerging political scenario was shaping cultural-political alliances. The early impetus behind the Fenian revival, IRB investment in the '98 movement, was on the wane, while pro-Boer activity had failed to translate into votes. Involvement with the Irish Transvaal Committee, combined with the strengthening IPP on one hand and out-and-out Irish Irelanders like Moran on the other, put pressure on the clubs to find an identity. At the same time, as long as the newspaper equivalent to the Queen's Royal Theatre remained the *Freeman's Journal*, the *United Irishman* would be sure to keep nationalist melodrama at arm's length. Those who counted themselves advanced nationalists would be inclined to seek alliance with the literary equivalent of their new thinking, especially since the ILT writers had begun to demonstrate political correctness. It would prove a mutually beneficial alliance, offering a new platform for the burgeoning dramatic movement, compensating for the loss of the *Daily Express*. But it also helped generate creative thinking in its overtly political counterpart, evident in the creation of Cumann na nGaedheal, the manifesto of which Yeats may have helped to draft,[86] and in the shared habit of casting the nationalist mind overseas to draw comparisons for the development of Irish ambitions. The relationship was symbiotic, a combination of the anxiety to, and the anxiety of, influence:[87] that rising generation of frustrated petty bourgeoisie searching for alternatives[88] to the IPP surely included those like Yeats, who rejected Davisite literature and popular drama not only because it was overtly political or unoriginal, but because its formative force carried the taint of political failure. It may even have failed because it compromised

[86] James W. Flannery, *W. B. Yeats and the Idea of a Theatre: The Early Abbey Theatre in Theory and Practice* (Yale, 1976), 114.

[87] Harold Bloom, *The Anxiety of Influence: A Theory of Poetry* (Oxford, 1973).

[88] See R. F. Foster's portrayal of the uneasy relationship between 'Young Turks and Old Soaks' in *Modern Ireland 1600–1972* (Lonodn, 1988), and 'Thinking from Hand to Mouth', in *Paddy and Mr Punch: Connections in Irish and English History* (London, 1993), 262–80.

itself artistically. Griffith's review of Yeats's critique of Davisite literature cautiously conceded this apparent convergence of movements: 'The Old Rhetoric was bad, but the New Nationality must get more iron in its soul before it can win the people to regard it as genuine . . . Mr. Yeats hopes much for Ireland from the new writers. If they were all as good Irish Nationalists as Mr. Yeats himself we should hope so too.'[89]

The marriage of true minds in 1900 was accelerated when the impediment of O'Donnell was removed,[90] and catalysed by the exacting commentary on the ILT's progress by Frank Fay. Both he and Maud Gonne were engaged in broadening the theatre movement by recruiting amateur acting troupes: Gonne's based around the Inghinidhe na hÉireann, Fay as part of his brother William's Comedy Combination. The ILT also accommodated the Gaelic League by taking Douglas Hyde on board as resident Irish language playwright, George Moore proclaiming: 'The performance of plays in our language is part and parcel of the idea which led up to the founding of the Irish Literary Theatre . . . the restoration of the language is the nation's need.'[91] Yeats backed this up with an offer that 'the profits from the sale of *Samhain* would be donated to the Gaelic League'.[92] All seemed set for a triumphant third season with a double bill sporting a full-scale mythological epic co-written by Yeats and Moore, coupled with a playlet by Hyde.

Diarmuid and Grania and *Cásadh an tSúgáin* premiered at the Gaiety Theatre in October 1901, and were greeted enthusiastically enough by the nationalist contingent for the young critic James Joyce to make his precocious allegations of populism—that the ILT 'must now be considered the property of the rabblement'.[93] The whole air of compromise was too much for a writer who wanted to free himself from the languid effeteness of Irish mythology and concentrate on squalor as well as langour (as he

---

[89] *United Ireland*, 6 Jan. 1900.

[90] In his capacity as a Boer agent, O'Donnell was in receipt of substantial funds, a portion of which Gonne wanted to use to finance her plan to bomb British troopships. To keep her at bay he cast doubts on her trustworthiness. 'If she is not a spy, she is almost one and her bragging is more dangerous than treachery itself.' See Donal P. McCracken, *The Irish Pro-Boers, 1877–1902* (Johannesburg, 1989), 77. That O'Donnell and Gonne should have ended up enemies seems against the grain of their politics, which, Celticism aside, were rather similar. Either it was a clash of egos, or Gonne's friendship with Yeats was enough to taint her by association.

[91] 'The Irish Literary Renaissance and the Irish Language', *New Ireland Review*, 2 (Apr. 1900), 66–8.

[92] Not that this was likely to bring much into the League's coffers, *Samhain*, 1 (1901), 6.

[93] 'The Day of the Rabblement', in *The Critical Writings of James Joyce*, ed. Richard Ellman (New York, 1959), 70.

later rendered it: 'That they may dream their dreamy dreams | I carry off their filthy streams').[94] But despite what Joyce described as 'Mr. Yeats's treacherous instinct of adaptability',[95] the object of his scorn had not done enough to temper a sexual sensibility that to other critics seemed ripe from Continental salons. The *Freeman's Journal*, usually kind in reviews, expressed a generally held view when it discerned in *Diarmuid and Grania* 'the unmistakeable echo of Paris boulevards'.[96]

Where Yeats's influence stopped and Moore's began was inevitably blurred, but the play unhappily accommodated airy Celticism and a study of sexual ennui more drawing room than dun. The choice of legend—a story of fracture within the fabled warrior caste wrought by transgressive love, in which Grania, pledged to marry Finn, flees with Diarmuid only to witness his death at the tusks of a mythic boar—had potential to play on themes of sex and betrayal still lingering post-Parnell. But these were surrendered either to innuendo (as when Grania, in the first act, toys meaningfully with Diarmuid's sword)[97] or Romantic portentousness. Instead an attempt was made to heighten the dramatic tension by choosing to represent Grania as suffering from seven-year itch, tempted by Finn's authority. The magic was also fading for the co-writers who, evidently intent on different styles, required considerable mediation (particularly over the character of Grania) from Lady Gregory and Arthur Symons.[98] Any note of tragic grandeur measured out in poetic diction was negated by a dark glint of frivolous tawdriness in which audiences were quick to discern the handiwork of George Moore. And although in doing this they underestimated Yeats, when Conan makes his closing remark 'Grania makes great mourning for Diarmuid, but her welcome for Finn shall be greater',[99] one does suspect Moore, aiming a puncturing barb at the overblown Celt.

The dart hit home, and as a result, the ILT's cultural defence mechanism, its sectarian-free triumvirate, began seizing up. Martyn, whom Yeats had gone to strenuous efforts to keep in the fold during *The Countess Cathleen* controversy, was again made to feel uncomfortable by the eyebrow-raising moral laxity displayed by the heroes of the Fianna, and the criticism the ILT received for celebrating it.

---

[94] 'The Holy Office' (1904), in *The Essential James Joyce*, ed. Harry Levin (London, 1977), 459.

[95] *Critical Writings*, 71. [96] Leader, *Freeman's Journal*, 2 Nov. 1901.

[97] Yeats, *VP*, 1181.

[98] Adrian Frazier, *George Moore 1852–1922* (New Haven, 2000), 295–6.

[99] Yeats, *VP*, 1222.

This troubled reception owed as much to old-fashioned prudery as it did Catholic censure; the *All Ireland Review* was as hostile as the *Leader*, *An Claidheamh Soluis*, or the *Freeman's Journal*. O'Grady declared the play a slander on 'the great, noble and generous Finn . . . the most typical Irishman'.[100] This might not have proved a fatal blow—the authors' debt to Continental influences (particularly Moore's reputation as a practitioner of the 'French novel') could, to some extent, be humoured given their service to the language movement and the anti-recruiting effort. Nevertheless, consternation at the sexual references in the play brought strictures from cultural nationalists who felt the Celt should reflect a morality acceptable to Catholic standards rather than those (loose by any measure) of the bohemian set. *Leader* contributors came down hard on the play, declaring it 'an intolerable insult' to have corrupted something so 'pure and fresh and wholesome and clean'.[101] In the course of arguing against the performance of foreign masterpieces, Moran issued a bitter warning to those who threatened his model of cultural regeneration.

Any scheme, industrial, political, artistic or literary, for this country that is not based on the fact that this country is abnormal, abnormal to an extraordinary degree, is, we submit, fundamentally wrong. This country is a mongrel country, and it will not be normal until it be made Irish through and through. Then let the world come in and it will not and cannot provincialise us. Our drama, like our industries, will grow out of Irish Ireland.[102]

Such metaphors, suggesting as they did an equivalence between deformity and racial impurity, recalled the anti-Semitism that had infected the *United Irishman*. Articles like 'Jewman Bull and Jingo Paddy'[103] reinforced the connection. By extension, the identification of a conservative strain of Catholicism with the national ideal implicated every individual with progressive social or liberal sexual attitudes in the active subversion of Irishness, much in the same way as O'Donnell had linked the *bêtes noires* of radicalism, Protestantism, and Jewry. Yeats's use of Celtic purity to deny the claims of the majority group to define an exclusive cultural criteria had been hijacked and reversed. Moore, whose satirical style suited the *Leader*, fought a tough rearguard action on this issue, arguing that the 'brutal sensuality' in *Diarmuid and Grania* was 'an integral part

[100] *All Ireland Review*, 19 Oct. 1901. [101] 'Mac an Cuill', *Leader*, 2 Nov. 1901.
[102] Ibid., 26 Oct. 1901.
[103] Ibid., 26 July 1902. The article informs the reader that 'Bull was a rapacious and aggressive Jewman who went around the world with a great big pack upon his back bullying an frightening timid people into taking his pedlary upon the instalment principle.'

of our national history'. Not only that, but Hyde's widely heralded *Cásadh an tSúgáin* had dealt with yet another version of exclusion and denial of the artist's sexual allure, in this case Red Hanrahan being tricked out of a peasant house while trying to seduce his host's daughter—'surely very flagrant', as Moore pointed out.[104]

Meanwhile, the *United Irishman* provided covering fire for its wartime ally, an editorial remarking pointedly: 'The Irish Literary Theatre is an effort to do something for Ireland, and we have no patience with people who never attempt to do anything, and throw cold water, in the name of patriotism, on those who do.'[105] This defence also reflected the impact of Hyde's Irish play. Frank Fay, who had long considered the English troupe, the Bensons, as 'gentlemanly incompetents',[106] naturally enough protested the need for indigenous actors, carefully comparing the 'intolerable' performance of the Shakespearean specialists with the success of the Irish amateurs who carried Hyde's play. William Fay had built on his experience producing Mac Fhionnlaoich's *Eilís agus an Bhean Déirce* for the Inghinidhe earlier that summer; here his direction corralled the enthusiasts of Dublin's radical Keating Branch into a performance considered by other Leaguers as epochal.[107]

The success of the language play made it all the easier for Frank Fay to dispense with what he considered the pseudo-naïvety of the ILT's detractors: 'There is a class of person here who is deeply pained when anybody says that Irishmen and Irishwomen have passions like the rest of God's creatures. Really, it is about time we gave up pretending to believe we are sinless.'[108]

Flaunting this new-found liberality, the *United Irishman* defended the name of Oscar Wilde—'the brilliant son of a great Irishwoman'[109]—after his death in November 1901, and published a series of faux 'letters' which satirized censoriousness. These ring with irony given later events; one, from an 'angry parent', complained: 'the poem describes the doings of a young man (a pagan of course) *who ran away with another man's wife!* Sir, that was enough—I put my foot down. No more Homer for *my* boys.'[110]

---

[104] 'Mac an Cuill', *Leader*, 9 Nov. 1901.   [105] *United Irishman*, 19 Oct. 1901.

[106] Ibid., 19 May 1900. He did not conceal his opinion from Yeats: see Yeats, *Collected Letters*, ii. 93, 95.

[107] Philip O'Leary, *The Prose Literature of the Gaelic Revival 1881–1921: Ideology and Innovation* (University Park, Pa., 1995), 294, 303.

[108] *United Irishman*, 23 Nov. 1901.

[109] Ibid., 30 Nov. 1901. 'Whatever his sin,' read the statement, 'it is not for the Press or the public to judge him.'

[110] Ibid.

But Griffith had to take account of the moral climate among the more overtly political readership as well as his hot literary property. Part of the means of doing this was provided through the Gonne cult, a useful hub of radicalism. Although she resigned from the IRB (forced out by O'Donnell), Griffith stood by her with characteristic pugnacity—to the point of physically assaulting Ramsay Colles, the defaming editor of *Irish Figaro*. Maud Gonne's personal friendship with Yeats was of course entwined in his famously unrequited love for her, but also in a shared adherence to millenarian occultism and romantic Celticism that coexisted with her popularity as an orator at home and abroad, and the link she provided between pro-French and pro-Boer Irish nationalism. She had arranged the Irish delegation to France in the summer of 1900, although her reputation had been tarnished by the O'Donnell debacle. To some extent, therefore, Griffith was influenced by Gonne's personal affiliation to Yeats and her enthusiasm for the idea that he would be a literary, and she a political, avatar. In the *United Irishman*'s pantheon, as in the Gaiety Theatre, 'Ireland's greatest daughter . . . sat beside Ireland's greatest poet.'[111]

But while Yeats hoped that the ILT might remain a 'wise disturber' of whatever peace there was in 1901, the ILT split under the pressure of the moral reverberations of *Diarmuid and Grania* and the creative rivalries of its writers. Yeats and Lady Gregory went one way, Martyn another, and Moore his own inimitable path. The renaming of the magazine from *Beltaine* to *Samhain*, Yeats confessed in its pages, was more than a reference to the time of year: it was a gesture of poetic honesty, acknowledging that the project had gone to seed. Fred Ryan agreed, casually diagnosing the theatre's ills and prescribing a prescient cure:

It would be easily possible to purchase or build a small hall or theatre capable of seating five or six hundred persons, neatly, though not lavishly equipped. In this, which should become a popular theatre, there should be the opportunity for producing, on a simple and inexpensive scale, the work of young authors . . . It may now breathe the atmosphere of the demigods, and anon the atmosphere of the cottage and the market-place . . . and should let the Irish drama form itself under the influence of natural inclination.[112]

If the winter of the ILT had come, the spring of amateur acting potential lay not far behind, ready to stir the latent energies that would later realize Ryan's vision. The Fay brothers had already begun to respond to

[111] Ibid., 26 Oct. 1901.
[112] 'Has the Irish National Theatre Failed?', ibid., 9 Nov. 1901.

the lead given by the ILT, performing Alice Milligan plays for the Pan-Celtic Congress in August 1901.[113] The contact with the Inghinidhe brought new focus, and the resulting 'Irish National Dramatic Company' (INDC) was soon casting about for material that could live up to its title. By April, it had miraculously come up with George Russell's *Deirdre* and Yeats and Gregory's *Cathleen ni Houlihan.*

Any reservations felt in Cumann na nGaedheal could be put aside—the last vestige of the top-heavy cultural-political consensus manifest in the pre-war ILT had been shed. Frank Fay had allowed that 'the greatest triumph of the authors lies in their having written in English a play in which English actors are intolerable'.[114] Griffith now pronounced the conjunction of Irish writing and acting talent, heralding the auspicious moment as the birth of an artistic movement that would fulfil its destiny as the animateur of Irish pride:

a Theatre where the spirit of our country can speak straight to our souls, rouse every noble emotion and rekindle the fires of patriotism, as Mr. Yeats has done in 'Kathleen ni Houlihan'; a Theatre in which, as Mr. Yeats has said, all Ireland will walk the stage . . . We have launched the Irish National Theatre successfully, and through it shall be able to refresh ourselves, as Mr. Russell put it, at the enchanted spring of our race.[115]

Yeats, who understood the dramatic strength of using colloquial language to offset verse, had taken on Lady Gregory as Moore's replacement, and with her wrote the play that was to bring him most favour in nationalist circles. But the stylistic success of *Cathleen ni Houlihan* was also implicated in its practical demonstration of the alliance between theatres of drama and politics: a play which reinvigorated the waning reputation of Maud Gonne as a public presence and presented her as national ambition incarnate. The aisling staked the claim that the nationalist movement as defined by Gonne, Yeats, and Griffith was the natural heir to '98.

Michael Gillane is wooed by the aged Cathleen, the personification of Ireland, to the love and service of his country, to fight with the French after they land at Killala: in doing so he spurns the stable culture of marriage and material well-being offered by Delia and her father Old John Cahel. Like Mary Bruin in *The Land of Heart's Desire*, Michael Gillane also spurns the stylistic representation of that acquiescent realism

[113] R. F. Foster, *W. B. Yeats: A Life*, i. *The Apprentice Mage, 1865–1914* (Oxford, 1997), 259.
[114] *United Irishman*, 26 Oct. 1901.   [115] Ibid., 12 Apr. 1902.

to answer Cathleen's poetic invocations to sacrifice. The sacrifice demanded by the daughter of Houlihan is, however, far fiercer and overt in its nationalism, forcefully implicating drama in political ambition.

They that have red cheeks will have pale cheeks for my sake, and for all that, they will think they are well paid.

> [*She goes out; her voice is heard outside singing.*
>
> They shall be remembered for ever,
> They shall be alive for ever,
> They shall be speaking for ever,
> The people shall hear them for ever.[116]

Speaking these words, Gonne emphatically bridged the divide between theatrical representation and propagandist meeting, 'addressing', as the *All Ireland Review* put it, 'not the actors as is usual in the drama, but the audience'.[117]

Yeats naturally emphasized the importance of verse, but the input of his co-author also resonated significantly with the play's thematic complexities. Another layer had been added to the disingenuous old argument with Eglinton, since Yeats, while decrying the prosaic element of modern culture was all the time taking force from it, as he did from Gregory's dialogue.[118] The impetus to revolution came not from the faery world of legend, but from French invasion, giving notice that the inspiring power of symbolist poetry and the realism of realpolitik were tightly bound to a wider European dimension. As an astute reviewer in the *Worker's Republic* pointed out, speaking of ancient Irish myth was all very well, but what of 'the cosmopolitan ideas of liberty'? ' [Mr. Yeats] stated at the conclusion of the performance that he was warning against "those cosmopolitan ideas that had come so much into Ireland, some of them from England," and yet, what in his play Kathleen inspires us all, the phrase, "The French have landed at Killala." '[119]

Cathleen ni Houlihan offered the ability of poetry to represent the abstract and spiritual dimension of nationalism, allied with the prosaic realities of European political strength, the tradition of insurrection, and

[116] Yeats, *VP*, 229.

[117] Quoted in Foster, *W. B. Yeats*, i. 262.

[118] For details of the collaboration, see James Pethica, ' "Our Kathleen": Yeats's Collaboration with Lady Gregory in the Writing of Cathleen ni Houlihan', in Deirdre Toomey (ed.), *Yeats and Women* (2nd edn., Basingstoke, 1997), 205–21.

[119] Unsigned, but probably Fred Ryan, 'The Irish National Theatre', *Worker's Republic*, Nov. 1902 (the *Worker's Republic*, suffering from lack of funds, had been a monthly since Feb. 1900).

the paradramatic presence of Maud Gonne. Yeats and Gregory had thus engineered a propaganda not just nationalist but literary-nationalist, the expression of its own cause.[120] It was a forceful assertion that the emerging grass-roots alliance between the Fays' INDC and Cumann na nGaedheal still needed its high priests. Small wonder that Griffith's conversion should be so complete.[121] Even the mocking *Leader*, which had called for a dramatic equivalent of itself—'a few comedies in English satirising shoneen Ireland and West British Ireland'[122]—suggested Yeats had finally 'seen the light'.[123]

The revelation was mutual. Yeats, delighted unexpectedly by the Fays' company, swiftly revised his opinion of the laity too. Having complained to Lady Gregory that the audience of *Diarmuid and Grania* was 'a mob that prefers Boucicualt',[124] he now enthused that 'the audience understands'[125] and 'the audience is there'.[126] With audacious speed he asserted that *Samhain* should be used to give the company a formal launch, 'with the proper blast of trumpets';[127] and deployed a statement in the *United Irishman* grandly heralding the advent of a major theatrical force: 'The Norwegian drama, the most important in modern Europe, began at a semi-amateur theatre in Bergen, and I cannot see any reason in the nature of things why Mr. Fay's company should not do for Ireland what the little theatre of Bergen did for Europe.'[128]

The plays also marked a stylistic break between Yeats and his old mystic-in-arms George Russell, as reflected in the staging of *Deirdre*, the literary Celtic play par excellence (or as the *Leader* would have it, 'in the worst sense of the word').[129] Although Yeats publicly applauded his friend's creation, privately his praise was fainter, likening it to 'wall decoration'.[130] Yeats had had the habit of puffing Russell's work where

---

[120] For a contrary view of *Cathleen ni Houlihan* as a text radically altered from Unionist text to republican performance, see Lionel Pilkington, ' "Every Crossing Sweeper Thinks Himself a Moralist": The Critical Role of Audiences in Irish Theatre History', *Irish University Review*, 27/1 (Spring–Summer 1997).

[121] It should not be overlooked that, for added measure, *Cathleen ni Houlihan* was dedicated to the late William Rooney, whose death had hit Griffith hard.

[122] *Leader*, 26 Oct. 1901.

[123] Ibid., 12 Apr. 1902. A review by 'Chanel', emerging UCD Literary and Historical Society veteran, Arthur Cleary.

[124] Yeats to Lady Gregory, mid-Oct. 1901, in *Collected Letters of W. B. Yeats*, iii. *1901–1904*, ed. John Kelly and Ron Schuhard (Oxford, 1994), 117.

[125] Yeats to Lady Gregory, 3 Apr. 1902, ibid. 166.

[126] *United Irishman*, 12 Apr. 1902.

[127] Yeats to F. J. Fay, 12 Apr. 1902, in *Collected Letters*, iii. 173.

[128] *United Irishman*, 12 Apr. 1902.   [129] Cleary, *Leader*, 12 Apr. 1902.

[130] Yeats to Lady Gregory, in *Collected Letters*, iii. 166.

etiquette precluded pushing his own, but here Russell began to become a yardstick whereby the limitations of the Celtic movement might be measured.[131]

Russell's choice of legend fulfilled the same criteria as *Diarmuid and Grania*—a tragedy hinging on exile and betrayal, rooted in sexual behaviour and resulting in political disharmony and defeat—'the Red Branch scattered and Eri rent asunder'.[132] *Deirdre*'s resonance for the post-Parnell generation was not lost on Anglo-Irish dramatists wishing to stress cultural indispensibility, and Yeats and Synge would both produce versions of the tale. It is significant, nevertheless, that Russell's reputation as a blithe Celtic spirit was offset by a choice of legend which inevitably dwelt on the dangers of overconfident convictions.

Replying to Standish O'Grady's continuing reservations about dramatization of myth, the mystic warned that 'the wild riders' of the spirit of the ancient aristocracy, once released, could not be restrained.[133] But *Deirdre* was more ambivalent. O'Grady had long mourned the *noblesse* lack of *oblige* and berated the Ascendancy for its passivity: Russell's play implicated Celticism in the ongoing effects of 'the Great Enchantment', suggesting a spell of fatal naïvety rather than sloth.[134] In the final scene, Naisi, bewitched into believing he is drowning, spoke as if warning of the deceptions of a mysticism which left its victim defenceless against the surrounding enemy. A foil to the astringent invocations of *Cathleen ni Houlihan*, his speech made the parlance of the Twilight work dramatically, because as an illustration of a literary movement as well as an example, it spoke of that movement's power to blind rather than provide vision. 'Ildathach is lit up with its shining mountains, and the golden phantoms are leaping there in the dawn! There is a path made for us. Come, Deirdre, the god has made for us an island by the sea. [*Naisi goes through the door and falls back, smitten by a spear thrust.*]'[135]

Russell's subject matter drew on a personal struggle between a mystical, creative identity and that more practical side of his nature displayed in the Irish Agricultural Organization Society and the *Irish Homestead*;

---

[131] Compare Yeats's earlier reference to 'the delicate, obscure, mysterious song of my friend, "A. E." ' alluded to in the *Leader*, 1 Sept. 1901, with his later account of *Deirdre* in *Dramatis Personae*: 'all its male characters resembled Tennyson's King Arthur'. Peter Kuch, *Yeats and AE: 'The antagonism that unites dear friends'* (Gerrards Cross, 1986), 86.

[132] George Russell, *Deirdre* (Dublin, 1907), 52.

[133] AE, 'The Dramatic Treatment of Heroic Literature', *United Irishman*, 3 May 1902.

[134] O'Grady's article 'The Great Enchantment' had been republished in an eclectic collection of essays: Lady Gregory (ed.), *Ideals in Ireland* (London, 1901).

[135] Russell, *Deirdre*, 51.

but such dichotomies also testified to a creeping sense of crisis. Russell's role in the agencies of constructive unionism was also more exposed by the shift in political emphasis since the Boer War. It was not clear as yet whether in this more vulnerable context an Anglo-Irish paganist like himself might rue or ride the cultural nationalism Celticism fuelled. *Deirdre* expressed doubt in the currency of common cause, fearing a wide-eyed walk into cultural ambush—though it was not evident at this stage from which side it might spring.

Meanwhile, the ties between the INDC and Cumann na nGaedheal grew tighter than ever, with Griffith offering Yeats a directorship of the *United Irishman* (he declined), and Griffith himself enjoying honorary membership of the new company.[136] The *United Irishman* became the first port of call for new writers encouraged by the momentum. Of all the newspapers, Yeats informed Cornelius Weygandt in May 1902, it 'alone gives full and sympathetic accounts of all intellectual activities of a literary kind in Ireland'.[137] Just as the Gaelic League's membership flourished so vigorously in this period, the options for the theatre became dramatically widened by an influx of talent. The two consecutive seasons put on by the INDC unified the romantic and realist elements of drama with its breadth. Celtic renaissance was provided for with a repeat of Russell's *Deirdre*, along with fellow Ulsterman James Cousins's *The Sleep of the King*, who also contributed a tentative experiment in tragic realism called *The Racing Lug*.[138] As a contrast to this, another Yeats–Gregory product was aired, a flimsy piece of peasant whimsy called the *Pot of Broth* (later dubbed the 'Plot of Froth' by *Sinn Féin*). Though there was no room for a new Irish play, George Moore filled the gap by offering up his garden for a production of Hyde's *An Tinéar agus an tSídheog* (The Tinker and the Fairy). By way of contrast, Martyn published a short satire in the *Leader*, *The Placehunters*, satirizing landlord corruption.[139] The two scourges of the establishment, Daly and Mooney, bore more than a passing resemblance to Griffith and Moran, the former's stubborn resilience contrasted with the incisive fatalism of the latter.

Indications that the fever of activity was spreading outside the confines of Dublin's literary pale also began to appear. Having learned their creed at the knee of Alice Milligan (and having seen Ultonians like Russell, George Roberts, and Cousins take to the stage) the young men of

---

[136] Flannery, *W. B. Yeats and the Idea of a Theatre*, 324.

[137] *Collected Letters*, iii. 183. Weygandt, an American, later published one of the first treatments of the Irish dramatic movement, *Irish Plays and Playwrights*, in 1913.

[138] *The Racing Lug*, 5 July 1902.   [139] *Leader*, 26 July 1902.

Belfast's Protestant National Association were keen to establish a Northern branch of the movement.[140] Bulmer Hobson's one-act *Brian of Banba* appeared in the *United Irishman* in August, and following a visit to Dublin to gain support for their venture, he and David Parkhill (Lewis Purcell) established what they called the 'Ulster Branch of the Irish National Literary Theatre [*sic*]' in October. Once it was pointed out that in the event of a loss, the 'parent' company would be financially liable, the company was forced to change its name to the Ulster Literary Theatre (ULT). (After the early ULT had generated a healthy debt, it was decided to 'float' the company on a public subscription. A solitary contributor sent in five shillings.)[141] Nevertheless, that year the group succeeded in staging—Maud Gonne having overruled Yeats[142]—*Cathleen ni Houlihan* and Cousin's *The Racing Lug* with the help of two of the INTS's best actors, Maire Quinn and Dudley Digges.

Compounding the sense of consensus, Griffith eased the troubled relationship with the ISRP (which he had already soothed by supporting Connolly in the municipal elections in March) by publishing Fred Ryan's *The Laying of the Foundations*. Another reworking of *An Enemy of the People*, this time into an openly socialist format, this play was one of the few of the new crop to win sincere support from Yeats. Unlike his counterpart Kirwan in *The Bending of the Bough*, Ryan's protagonist Nolan has as his ideal not a nationalist abstraction, but one firmly rooted (as the title suggests) in the means of production. Insisting on a firm grounding in class issues, the play suggested the social contract took its strength from below. As Nolan says: 'I believe in Freedom for all and the rule of labour.'[143]

Yeats's view that the satire was 'astonishing'[144] was a response to the play's fresh ideological emphasis rather than its dramatic quality, which was slight. Ryan's critical consistency over religious and racial questions, particularly his anticlerical stance over *The Countess Cathleen*, undoubtedly chimed with Yeats's sensibilities. But the affiliation went deeper. *The Laying of the Foundations'* vision of a New Jerusalem ('the city whose

[140] Bulmer Hobson, *Ireland Yesterday and Tomorrow* (Tralee, 1968), 1, 4.

[141] Rutherford Mayne, 'The Ulster Literary Theatre', *Dublin Magazine*, NS 31 (Apr.–June 1955), 16.

[142] For Hobson's account ('Everyone was cordial and helpful except Yeats') see Sam Hanna Bell, *The Theatre in Ulster* (Dublin, 1972), 1–2.

[143] *The Laying of the Foundations* in Robert Hogan and James Kilroy (eds.), *Lost Plays of the Irish Renaissance*, i. *The Abbey Theatre* (Newark, Del., 1970). Only the second act of two remains.

[144] Yeats to Lady Gregory, 4 Oct. 1902, in *Collected Letters*, iii. 232.

foundations are laid in Liberty and Truth'),[145] also appealed to Yeats's
utopian side, which owed to William Morris the impulse to 'pull down
Tottenham Court Road, and build it nearer to the heart's desire'.[146]
Perhaps he also took note of the warning given in the *Worker's Republic*
regarding the limitations of any movement staying on sufferance in the
domain of bourgeois national ideology.

We cannot speak too highly of Mr. Fay's bright little company, and trust they will
at least receive the same measure of toleration that the I.S.R.P. have obtained in
upholding through the drama that mirror, if not to nature, at least to the people
of this unhappy island, that will allow them to see that the political Dr. Jekyll is
the industrial Mr. Hyde.[147]

That trust in a 'measure of toleration' had already come into question,
for since the Boer War had concluded at Vereeniging in May, the political
mind had begun to turn inward once more, allowing contrasting, class-
based interpretations of nationalism to find redefinition. Sure enough,
the *United Irishman* had begun to compete with, as well as contest, the
assertions of the *Leader*, to exert more stringent guidelines on the representations of heroic stereotypes. 'Achilles is a sullen savage, Ulysses a liar,
and pious Aeneas a prig. But our Irish heroes are no savages, no liars, no
prigs, but brave, highspirited, truthful, magnanimous, merry, courteous
men, loving fearless, cheerful, tender vivacious women.'[148] Yeats's appreciation of Fred Ryan's play bespoke his growing sense of rebellion at this
creeping encroachment, just as he shared Ryan's hostility to received
opinion. But the links still held. Yeats's latest play *Where There is Nothing*
was written hurriedly (with a little help from Lady Gregory and Douglas
Hyde),[149] following claims from Moore contesting the originality of the
scenario, and its publication in the *United Irishman* caught the still coherent elements of the alloy before they fractured. The tone, though not
optimistic, was defiant. In it he recalled the motif of the artist-priesthood,
following the exploits of the visionary utopian Paul Ruttledge. *Where
There is Nothing* made its gesture to *News from Nowhere*, but it was one of
departure; just as it marks the point of embrace as Yeats first came into

---

[145] Ryan, in Hogan and Kilroy (eds.), *Lost Plays of the Irish Renaissance*, 37.

[146] Yeats, *United Irishman*, 9 Nov. 1901. Another point made in the ongoing battle
between he and Eglinton; this time in a mocking response to Eglinton's declared taste for
pastoral poetry.

[147] 'The Irish National Theatre', *Worker's Republic*, Nov. 1902.

[148] *United Irishman*, 27 Sept. 1902.

[149] James L. Pethica, 'A Dialogue of Self and Service: Lady Gregory's Emergence as an
Irish Writer and Partnership with W. B. Yeats', D.Phil. thesis (Oxford, 1987), 212.

contact, through the Irish-American John Quinn, with undiluted Nietzsche.[150] Ruttledge's lines, before the people he once led in insurrection lynch him for heresy, transposes populist anti-materialism into a spiritual, nihilistic individualism: 'I have entered into the second freedom—the irresponsibility of the saints.'[151]

Having sold Griffith a modern mythology which cast the playwright as a Prospero who could rouse a tempest of Irish pride and self-knowledge, Yeats was about to dissolve the insubstantial pageant and leave not a rack behind. In the same momentous issue of the *United Irishman* (1 November 1902) which included his play and Griffith's first article in a series on the edifying Hungarian struggle for nationhood, Yeats complemented his creative offering with another declaration—'The Freedom of the Theatre'. Echoing the sentiments of his protagonist, he had quite a different Shakespearean role in mind. 'We watch Coriolanus with delight, because he had a noble and beautiful pride', he wrote, concluding pointedly that 'the reign of the moralist is the reign of the mob'.[152]

In the heady spring of 1902, the astute Eglinton had discerned in Yeats's and Griffith's literary-political project an anomaly disguised by shared enthusiasm. 'It remains to be seen', he concluded, 'whether this confusion of two essentially different things, idealism and patriotism, has bestowed upon Irish national literature the germs of new developments or has involved it in a mesh of error.'[153] The rise of petty-bourgeois patriotism, Eglinton's argument suggested, boded ill for the 'literary ideals in Ireland' aired in 1898. Class sensibilities would inevitably reassert themselves. And as the year drew to a close, the mesh knit by common cause was starting to unravel. If Yeats looked to a German philosopher and Griffith to a Hungarian nationalist, their search for European credentials guaranteed little more in the way of shared objectives. For the moment, Nietzsche and Kossuth were accommodated in the autumn issues of the *United Irishman*, but it would not last. Disappointed as he would be with Yeats, Griffith's interest in Hungary indicated a mind that responded more acutely to the potential of political strategy than to the long cultural games his ally had in mind. Yeats, for his part, was nurturing new possibilities. Buoyed up by the collateral of Annie Horniman's promises and Lady Gregory's matronage, his new aristocratic mien looked to different battles, through which

[150] Foster, *W. B. Yeats*, i. 584 nn. 68, 69.   [151] Yeats, *VP*, 1161.
[152] *United Irishman*, 1 Nov. 1902.
[153] 'The De-Davisization of Irish Literature', *United Irishman*, 31 May 1902.

he could assert his sense of authority and independence. The fragile unity, founded in the class-based interpretations of nationalism the heat of the Boer War had fused, had started to separate; and would soon widen with the forced-in wedge of a short play by J. M. Synge.

3

The Union of Sceptics, 1903–1906

In October 1903, in the wake of Synge's first publicly received play, *In the Shadow of the Glen*, Yeats made an appeal for a cultural critique which could, in recognizing the place and value of modern theatre, demonstrate the integrity of its own radicalism:

I would see, in every branch of our National propaganda, young men who would have the sincerity and the precision of those Russian revolutionists that Kropotkin and Stepniak tell of . . . who would not make a mob drunk with a passion they could not share, and who would above all seek for fine things for their own sake, and for precise knowledge for its own sake, and not for its momentary use.[1]

The appeal is notable for a number of reasons. It indicates the state of flux regarding Yeats's sense of political identity, fighting hard to 'hammer into unity' the influence of Morris and Nietzsche.[2] It shows, ironically, that ever-present element of polemical craft in his journalism, making 'momentary use' of exotic rebellion to help label as parochial the censorious attack Arthur Griffith was ready to mount. But Yeats's critique also reveals something more substantial, of which his own turbulent sense of self was a part. In appealing for the adoption of the 'precision of those Russian revolutionists', it manifested the kind of unstable alliance sought out by those who were at once hostile to the British regime and sceptical of the conservative nationalism challenging it. The troubled relationship in Ireland between the emerging theatre movement and advanced-nationalist groups would be portrayed by the latter as evidence of a reluctance to engage in 'the struggle'; but this analysis could equally be rebutted by indicating that the struggle was wider than such critics supposed, and that by exhibiting a reactionary response to new modes and themes in dramatic art it was they who were demonstrating reluctance.

[1] 'The Theatre the Pulpit and the Press', *United Irishman*, 17 Oct. 1903. In the eds.' introd. to *The Collected Letters of W. B. Yeats*, iii. *1901–1904* (Oxford, 1994), pp. xlviii–xlix, John Kelly and Ronald Schuchard have also remarked on this preoccupation with 'precision'.

[2] See Yeats to John Quinn, 6 Feb. [1903], in *Collected Letters*, iii. 312–13. Quinn similarly professed himself to be 'a Morris socialist'. Mary Lou Kohfeldt, *Lady Gregory: The Woman behind the Irish Renaissance* (London, 1985), 156.

As Yeats observed, such reluctance was rooted in the political identity of the groups concerned—an identity close to and influenced by bourgeois nationalist parties in Europe, whose aggressive reaction to the advances made on the Scandinavian or Parisian stage he often referred to. Yeats had remarked disingenuously that he had not the same friends as Ibsen. Yet his evocation of Narodniki caught precisely the common ground of heroic individualism, spiritual radicalism, and mental tenacity that had endeared Ibsen to the cadres of the left and the littérateurs of the 1880s and 1890s. It also recognized a bridge between his father's contacts in London (which had included Stepniak and Kropotkin),[3] his Fenian patron John O'Leary, and his more recent fascinations: from the vanguard to the avant-garde. In 1902, Cathleen ni Houlihan and Paul Ruttledge had already personified theatrical explorations in the Anarchistic 'propaganda of the deed'; by the end of 1903 Synge had begun advancing his case for the gallous story. It was not surprising, then, that Yeats should chose to evoke the author of *Paroles d'un Revolté* in that playwright's defence.[4] If the emerging theatre was to find allies in its pursuit of a form alive to a changing Ireland in a modern Europe, the more 'precise' critiques of those conditions evident in the developing ideologies of rebellion might suggest an opportunity for mutual aid.

That impulse arrived with a process of marginalization. The 'mesh of error' to which Eglinton had presciently referred was already becoming ever more apparent. Differences of 'idealism' became less clouded as pro-Boer patriotism died down, and as the class layering of nationalist identity separated out. Of particular importance was the rise of interest in the Irish Ireland movement and the *Leader*, which brought to bear a socially conservative agenda along with a model of the Catholic Gael. Despite D. P. Moran's avowedly even-handed abuse, this set up a sectarian opposition part of whose dynamic was to mask elements of conflict inside 'Catholic Ireland' by pointing out the real enemy. As J. J. O'Toole, one of the *Leader*'s main contributors, put it: 'If I say that an economically self-contained Ireland should be Celto-Catholic, I say it with no prejudice . . . but with a strong feeling that these Anglo-Protestants have . . . never ceased to be "the English in Ireland".'[5] Moran himself admitted that his

---

[3] William M. Murphy, *Prodigal Father: The Life of John Butler Yeats 1839–1922* (New York, 1978), 167, 188. R. F. Foster, *W. B. Yeats: A Life*, i. *The Apprentice Mage, 1865–1914* (Oxford, 1997), 268.

[4] Kropotkin's seminal pamphlet was published in Paris in 1885. For further elaboration of the influence of anarchism on nascent modernism see David Weir, *Anarchy and Culture: The Aesthetic Politics of Modernism* (Amherst, 1997).

[5] Under his pseudonym, 'Imaal'. *Leader*, 15 Nov. 1902.

argument was fundamentally polemic, glossing over complexity in favour of effect, and even tried a 'cruel to be kind' logic in justification: 'Our conviction is that if there is any potential Nationalism in Irish Protestants as a body that its growth will be stimulated by the fact that Irish Protestants, as a body, are painted up as anti-Irish Sourfaces.'[6]

Although Arthur Griffith kept such Protestant bashing at arm's length, it was a potent message and one his own political sums had to take into account. His faith in Yeats's powers might be maintained so long as his power base among the lower middle class remained unthreatened. Synge's arrival forced the issue, and the division over whether this emphasis could form the guidelines for the political content of the theatre was the central discussion of the following years. But Yeats's attachment to Synge itself evidenced the kind of makeshift alliance that the poet gestured toward when supporting *In the Shadow of the Glen*, a process of redefinition that was already firmly under way.

The year preceding Synge's debut had been fractious. Muttered challenges included those over Lady Gregory's first solo effort, *Twenty-Five*, whose protagonist, returning from America, purposefully loses a fortune playing cards with his ex-sweetheart's husband—too much of a fortune, it was argued by those anxious to deter emigration. Then in November 1902, Yeats had been displeased by the decision of two of the group's finest actors, Dudley Digges (soon to become secretary of *United Irishman* Publications Ltd.)[7] and Maire Quinn, to ignore his strictures and travel to Belfast to perform *Cathleen ni Houlihan* and *The Racing Lug* with the fledgling ULT. Further signs of dispute came the following month, when James Cousins offered his new play, *Sold*—'a comedy of real life in two acts'—to the company and published it in the *United Irishman*, under a heading which incidentally marked their recent change of name: 'Rights of production reserved by the Irish National Theatre Society' [INTS].[8] Yeats had been reading himself blind with the new collection of Nietzsche when it arrived, and, in the spirit of his influence, was inclined to exercise authority. Reckoning the play 'vulgar rubbish',[9] Yeats informed Gregory that 'Cousins is evidently hopeless & the sooner I have him as an enemy the better'.[10]

[6] Ibid., 3 Jan. 1903.

[7] William O'Brien Papers, NLI MS 13966.

[8] *United Irishman*, 27 Dec. 1902. It had been published a few days early in time for Christmas.

[9] Yeats to W. G. Fay, 26 Dec. 1902, in *Collected Letters*, iii. 284.

[10] Yeats to Lady Gregory, 26 Dec. 1902, ibid.

The interest of the newly retitled INTS in *Sold* had been indicated by a company vote in favour of production: but this was a product of desperation rather than wholehearted approval. William Fay was anxious about having enough Irish material to fill an evening—replying defensively to Yeats's questioning that his only critical criterion in judging the play had been length. Maud Gonne also agreed that it was 'full of bad jokes'.[11] (It was: Cousins deployed wordplay as low as 'murder fowl' in an attempt to leaven his stodgy tale of legal high jinks.) Eviction may have formed the play's premiss, but it was hardly the stuff of propaganda, and despite being championed by Russell was shelved with little further resistance.

At this point young Padraic Colum, son of a Longford workhouse master then working in Dublin as a railway clerk, contributed his first play. *The Saxon Shillin'* provided a clearer focus for burgeoning disputes—although here too oppositions remained less than crystal. Having appeared in the *United Irishman* in mid-November, Colum's Cumann na nGaedheal-prizewinning play was the dramatic equivalent of the Inghinidhe na hEireann's anti-recruiting campaign. The finale, in which a soldier is shot defending his family against eviction by the regiment he serves, gave a simple lesson on the implications of the betrayal of homeland/homestead. In this case it was William Fay who called on Yeats's support in pressurizing Colum to alter the ending in favour of something more complex—Yeats originally had given the play his blessing, contrasting it to *Sold* and rating it 'nothing against our dignity'.[12] *The Saxon Shillin'*, however, offered a bone of contention to a reading committee comprised of Griffith and Gonne as well as Yeats, Gregory, Russell, Ryan, and Colum himself.

Those among the nationalists who had supposed a constant stream of *Cathleen ni Houlihan*s were inevitably anxious about the direction of the company. Once the issue became one of whether the new company was towing the Cumann na nGaedheal line, artistic integrity presented itself as the alternative criterion. The schism widened as personal rifts appeared to underline political divisions. If keeping the Fays sweet was probably cause enough for Yeats to oppose *The Saxon Shillin'*, the seismic effect of Maud Gonne's marriage to John MacBride—an aftershock of pro-Boer enthusiasms—shattered a key point of contact. Padraic Colum may have been correct in asserting that his play was the issue upon which

[11] *The Gonne–Yeats Letters 1893–1938: Always Your Friend*, ed. Anna MacBride White and A. Norman Jeffares (London, 1992), 161.

[12] Yeats to Lady Gregory, 13 Jan. [1903], in *Collected Letters*, iii. 302.

'the link between the theatre and Cumann na nGaedheal was broken',[13] but personal chemistries catalysed the reaction. Yeats found out about the imminent matrimony in early February; the split over *The Saxon Shillin'* took place in a meeting on the 15th; on the 21st the ceremony took place.

Yeats's distressed pleading with Gonne indicates how swiftly he had superimposed Nietzschean codes onto the social configurations of Irish nationalism.

If you carry out your purpose you will fall into a lower order & do great injury to the religion of [pure] free souls . . . It was our work to teach a few strong aristo-cratic [*indecipherable*] spirits that to believe the soul was immortal & that one pros-pered hereafter *if one laid upon oneself* an heroic discipline in living & to send them to uplight the nation.[14]

The marriage seemed to manifest for Yeats a demeaning lower middle-class demagoguery that was guided by practical and political rather than artistic schemes of rejuvenation. To Yeats Maud Gonne's acceptance of the Catholic faith mirrored that opportunism which was allowing Irish Ireland to stress conservative and exclusive social models. And which, he added, had historically exerted a quietening effect on Irish republicanism. In order to challenge this direction, Yeats needed to make the change from figurehead to formative influence.

Yeats's assertion of his role as a leading light rather than just a Fay nominee was further emphasized by the triptych of one-act plays he produced that year; two of which, *On Baile's Strand* and *The King's Threshold*, Yeats took care to dedicate to each of the brothers. The plays themselves were testament to the swift changes Yeats was undergoing. The first, *The Hourglass*, was a peace offering to conventional Christian sensibilities and made common cause with the Church against the 'spear-man and catapult' of rationalism, 'Rhetoric and Dialectic'.[15] A 'wise man', given until the sands of the hourglass run out to redeem himself by finding a true believer, realizes his teaching has been too effective in erad-icating the faith he now needs to evade eternal torment. Failing even to cajole the play's idiot savant into such a declaration, his final submission to the will of God lifts him to a state of grace, while handily, the physical manifestation of his soul's departure in the form of a white butterfly gives the proof of the frantic spiritual argument to his sceptical followers. But the play found critics equally disinclined to take any lessons in piety from

---

[13] *The Road round Ireland* (New York, 1926), 278.   [14] *Collected Letters*, iii. 316.
[15] Yeats, *VP*, 594.

Yeats, at whom, as Arthur Clery put it, 'as a writer of morality plays . . . one feels inclined to look a little askance'.[16]

The charm of this early prose version of *The Hourglass* came partly from its triumph of naïvety. A neat choice from Lady Wilde's *Ancient Legends of Ireland*, Yeats's telling also carried something of her son's fairy-tale simplicity—a tone which finds confirmation as the patronizing sage finally relents and accepts the fool's view of man's vanity. If critics remained unconvinced, it was because the play seemed less conversion than conceit: far from renouncing 'Rhetoric and Dialectic' they remained Yeats's most valued tools. It was hard not to hear in the deathbed revelation 'we perish into reality'[17] one more ironic reiteration of symbolism's ascendancy over the simply mimetic.

On Baile's Strand confirmed suspicions. In a sense, it was a dramatic version of Yeats's pleas begging Maud Gonne to think again—an elaboration on what was for the poet a public rejection of a much-publicized love. Started before the split, the play evolved through revision to absorb those letters' disappointment and defeat, and in Cuchulain's love for the absent Aoife—'That hair my hands were drowned in!'[18]—the impact of loss. Inevitably, the political dimensions of those entreaties found their form too. The tragedy was wrought less out of the flaws in Cuchulain's heroism than from the constraints of conventional authority upon it, Cuchulain's allegiance to Conchubar eventually providing the High King with the mystical purchase that drives the hero, unknowingly, to murder his own son in single combat. The play travels a Sophoclean path through interrogation to tragic revelation, but despite the obvious symbolism of Cuchulain's doomed battle with the waves, the crisis in the play is forced not by unravelling fate but the subjection of individual, heroic will to political expediency. Set against the caste distinctions of nobles and beggarmen, it was not hard to discern in this Yeats's confidence in his new-found social status, his Nietzschian resentment of Griffith's criticism and Gonne's 'defection', combining to generate the tension that makes *On Baile's Strand* so tangible.[19]

Significantly however, Yeats's affiliations remained. His plays had drawn their subject from Irish legend, confounding Gonne's objection

---

[16] *Leader*, 28 Mar. 1903.   [17] *VP*, 636.
[18] Ibid. 513. The exclamation is present only in the late 1903 and 1904 versions. In the play's much revised (and much improved) form, largely finalized by 1906, Aoife's absence figures much larger, if less desperately.
[19] See also Otto Bohlmann, *Yeats and Nietzsche: An Exploration of Major Nietzschean Echoes in the Writings of William Butler Yeats* (London, 1982), 145–9.

that 'Neiche [*sic*] is not Celtic'[20] with their polemical use. Cuchulain's imperious independence, no less than Seanchan's stubborn resolve to 'Lie down upon the threshold till the King | restore to us the ancient right of the poets',[21] suggested a struggle within the ambit of nationalism rather than in antagonism to it.[22] When hostility to the visit in May 1903 of the new King Edward VII bound disputants together long enough for the National Council to form, it could still boast as its signatories Yeats, Edward Martyn, and the MacBrides.

This attempt at a representative body that could challenge the IPP was the first flowering of Griffith's rumination on Hungarian history and a forerunner of Sinn Féin. The popularity of the King's visit gave the gathering a measure of its own ambition. But the National Council helped broaden the base of the *United Irishman* to include links with bourgeois interests in the Dublin Corporation and the growing influence of the new nationalism checked whatever inclination there might have been on the part of consitutionalists 'to goad the people into concilia-tion'[23] after the 1903 Land Act. In this context, and despite the family ties between the Land Conference convenor Shawe-Taylor and Lady Gregory, there was no going back to pre-Boer alliances. Even when the estranged elements of the INTS divided over the rehearsal of Synge's play, with the 'propagandists' forming the rival Cumann na nGaedheal Theatre Company, differences remained more factional then fundamen-tal. The INTS might become isolated, but it could not be driven into the arms of the Establishment: it was too heavily tarred and stuck with the feathers of the white cockade for that.

Given the acute reorientation of Yeats it is tempting to see the follow-ing October's conflict over *In the Shadow of the Glen* in terms of a rather orthodox modernist distrust of democracy and cultural dilution, or even as symptomatic of the trimming of the theatre curtain to suit the Horniman cloth. Certainly the advent of a firm offer to fund an Art Theatre from Horniman, coinciding as it did with the debate, did noth-ing to dent confidence. Nevertheless it should be borne in mind that creative and critical personnel in the movement differed widely. Yeats's

---

[20] *Gonne–Yeats Letters*, ed. MacBride White and Jeffares, 169.

[21] Yeats, *VP*, 291. Reviewing *The King's Threshold* (performed on the same bill as *In the Shadow of the Glen*), Griffith wryly indicated his understanding of the obvious allegory: 'We hold it a pity that King Guaire did not hang Seanchan. Had he done so, Art would have been for all time his debtor.' *United Irishman*, 17 Oct. 1903.

[22] For Yeats's 'sinuous interweaving of loyalty and betrayal in the nationalist setting', see Edward W. Said, *Culture and Imperialism* (London, 1993), 280.

[23] D. P. Moran's typically pugnacious phrase. *Leader*, 15 July 1905.

April lecture 'Reform of the Theatre' certainly demonstrated once again an artistic assurance and detachment of Nietzschian proportions. But the argument took its force from a new-found alliance with a writer whose first works had been read in March and whose reception Yeats already knew would be problematic.

> We have to write or find plays that will make the theatre a place of intellectual excitement, a place where the mind goes to be liberated . . . If we do this we must learn that beauty and truth are always justified of themselves . . . They judge and are above judgement . . . I have seen plays of Irish country life by a new writer in which the persons speak out of the most powerful passions and yet never lose the country speech.[24]

As ever, Yeats had an eye to his own opaque drama as well as the advent of Synge—which, he hoped, could give stimulation where Synge administered shock. But lone attempts to rattle 'the beehives' of bourgeois sentiment like *The King's Threshold*'s assertion of bardic rights were too esoteric to outrage. Over the issue of Synge's play he could reinforce the self-justification of art as his guiding principle and make that principle palpable—worthy even—by fighting a battle over an excellent play not his own. Yeats's authoritarianism gained credence when he saw it allied (or unified, like Nietzsche and Morris) to a progressive cause portrayed as immoral from the popular press and the pulpit. The Ibsenite model was alive and well.

In the Shadow of the Glen had its first exposure on the stage of the Molesworth Hall in October 1903. Joseph Holloway commented ominously in his diary: 'Who knows what the reception of Synge's peasant play In the Glen with its French ideas placed in Irish atmosphere will be? All I know is that it is terribly unIrish in its sentiments.'[25] For Synge the repeated use of European culture to help define Irish arguments offered a more complex set of comparisons. Whereas other cultural commentators had found in French Catholicism a foil to British materialism, Synge sought in cosmopolitan modernity signs of liberation that might supersede both—as in his view, it had preceded them. 'The women of this island', he wrote of Aranmore, 'are before conventionality, and share some of the liberal features that are thought peculiar to the women of Paris and New York.'[26] His view of Ireland's westerners, as of those

---

[24] *United Irishman*, 4 Apr. 1903.
[25] Quoted in Robert Hogan and James Kilroy, *A History of Modern Irish Drama*, ii. *Laying the Foundations, 1902–1904* (Dublin, 1976), 70.
[26] *The Aran Islands* (Oxford, 1979), 121.

who opted out of Ireland's conventional society—tinkers, tramps, and lawbreakers[27]—invested with them that vitality Ireland would need to resist, not just imperial power, but other systems of control: religious, patriarchal, and capitalist. This romanticism owed much to his rejection of a strict Protestant upbringing and his ambiguous status as an Anglo-Irish gentleman of independent (if small) means with socialist sympathies.[28] It was also qualified, as his ever-darkening study *The Aran Islands* indicates, and as his reports on the progress of the Congested Districts Board confirm (Synge's conclusion, in 1905, stressed the importance of the Gaelic League and an urgent need for Home Rule to restore 'national life').[29] His recognition of the brutalities of peasant life checked sentimentality, offering a violent realism in dialectical tension with the idealized qualities and idealizing capacities of his characters. With Synge, vitality finds form in comic irreverence, but remains tragic in its association with deprivation—a position that placed him at once to the left of Yeats and those lauding the virtue of the small Catholic farmer.

Dublin's rumour mill was already grinding such grist by the week of Synge's debut. Despite this, the *United Irishman*, holding fire until the response of the public could be gauged, merely noted the details of *In the Shadow of the Glen*'s plot as described by John Butler Yeats.[30] Yeats the younger meanwhile delivered his pre-emptive strike 'What is a National Theatre?', not for the last time pulling rank as the author of *Cathleen ni Houlihan* to justify drama that did not have an 'obviously political intention'.[31] But the *Shadow* was in its own way as overt a statement as Yeats's *Cathleen*, implicating the sexual mores of Irish society—and particularly bourgeois adherence to them—in the crushing of a Celtic pagan spirit; an act that perpetuated Ireland's subjugation. Like *Cathleen ni Houlihan*, Synge's play was an aisling. Nora (the echo from Ibsen hardly coincidental)[32] symbolized Ireland, locked in loveless marriage with Dan (the Unionist establishment, constructively feigning death), being courted by

[27] Synge, 'In Wicklow, West Kerry and Connemara', in *Collected Works*, ii. *Prose*, ed. Alan Price (London, 1966).

[28] For a comprehensive treatment of the Protestant evangelism of Synge's formative milieu, see W. J. McCormack, *Fool of the Family: A Life of J. M. Synge* (London, 2000), 3–103, 431–6.

[29] 'Possible Remedies', the last in the series for the *Manchester Guardian*, pub. 10 June–26 July 1905. 'In Connemara', in Synge, *Collected Works*, ii. 340–3.

[30] *United Irishman*, 10 Oct. 1903.

[31] Ibid.

[32] Elizabeth Coxhead, *J. M. Synge and Lady Gregory* (London, 1962), 14. See also Christopher Murray, *Twentieth Century Irish Drama: Mirror up to Nation* (Manchester, 1997), 69–74.

bourgeois nationalism in the form of Michael Dara, but only gaining harsh freedom with a poetic tramp to whom liberty and poverty are synonymous.

The play brought swift condemnation from the *Irish Daily Independent*, followed by a vehement *United Irishman*, whose pages then opened a debate that testified to the divisions in the now polarized INTS. Arthur Griffith quickly identified the implications of Synge's play for Irish identity as conceived in terms of traditional family relationships and gender roles: 'Mr. Synge—or else his play has no meaning—places Norah Burke [*sic*] before us as a type—"a personification of the average"—and Norah Burke is a Lie.'[33]

Into the fray lepped (on the pro-side) the Yeatses, while on the anti-, Gonne MacBride joined Griffith. Yeats *père* noted the understandable sensitivity of those who apprehended Synge's theatre merely as a newer form of the stage calumnies the national theatre was supposed to displace. Ireland, once criminalized, had become instinctively defensive, resigning a native 'faculty for iconoclasm' in favour of the English platitude.

While Ireland stood in the dock the fierce-tempered part of the nation which moulded Swift's mind remained apart . . . But Ireland is no longer in the dock . . . Let her therefore put her house in order in accordance with her own judgement and conscience; let her begin the work of self-examination and self-accusation.[34]

For once father and son were in accord. W. B., having fought for the play with allusion to the Russian spirit of revolt, lit off the idea of a tradition of iconoclasm an incendiary article attacking the pillars of Irish Ireland. 'The Irish National Theatre and Three Sorts of Ignorance' attacked the Gaelic propagandist, conservative priest ('forgetful of the great traditions of his Church'), and opportunist politician. Such insouciance confidently intimated that such targets were all customary game in the voguish pastime of *épater les bourgeois*. The difference, Yeats marked, was that the standard-bearers of revolt were being corralled into conservatism: 'Extreme politics', he wrote, 'were once the politics of intellectual freedom.'[35]

Griffith climbed down considerably between 17 October and the following week, when he recanted any slur on Yeats's good name; but his riposte to Yeats the elder on the 31st made clear that he could only construe the *Shadow* as an insult, calculated or no. His objection, shared

---

[33] *United Irishman*, 17 Oct. 1903.
[34] J. B. Yeats, 'Ireland Out of the Dock', ibid. Another disputant at odds with the INTS was the critic James Connolly (sometimes mistaken for his more famous namesake, who had left Ireland for the United States earlier that year).   [35] Ibid., 24 Oct. 1903.

by many, was revealing. The national cause had been slighted not by an attack on patriotism, but upon a patriarchy that considered female subordinacy as an essential element of Ireland's claim to national distinction. Any suggestion to the contrary came from an implicitly anti-Catholic position incompatible with nationalism and obviously under alien influence:

> It remained for a member of the Society who spends most of his time away from Ireland, and under the operation of foreign influences, to represent, in good faith no doubt, adultery as a feature of Irish life, and to exhibit his utter ignorance of the Irish character by treating woman's frailty as a subject for laughter.[36]

Griffith and Synge differed less on the need for nationalism than they did on its nature; a difference amplified by Griffith's emphasis on the issue of whether or not the play was representative.[37] The *Shadow* could only have resonance in a society that had as a rule a restrictive, seldom transgressed marital order. Synge was not in the business of creating drama that reflected society: he had taken a folk tale in which the hoodwinked wife is punished for transgression, and in reversing the woman's role, had made an emancipatory fable.[38] His stylized realism and lyrical dialogue were employed to invest with romantic gravity those characters whose dramatic role it was to revitalize society. The play was thus not only a challenge to the status quo, but to the potency of those who apparently opposed it. Griffith's insistence that, despite Ireland's loveless marriages, 'in no country are women so faithful to the marriage bond'[39] implicated women's 'virtue' in a social fabric shot through with submission, political and domestic. Sensing Synge's gist, one contributor to the ensuing row linked 'sexual immorality' with 'the virility that builds up nations'.[40]

Such a comment naturally referred to a masculine virility rather than the sexual contract struck at a moment of domestic crisis by Nora and the tramp; but the point was sharp. Gender relations were a volatile element

---

[36] Ibid., 31 Oct. 1903.

[37] Griffith's discussion of the play's 'foreignness' was also somewhat disingenuous, since Synge had given a fulsome account of how the Irish and European folk tales showed common threads in 'A Story from Inishman', in the required-reading journal, *New Ireland Review* (10/3 (Nov. 1898), 153–6) and had offered to publish the story in the *United Irishman*. Griffith declined.

[38] Éilís Ní Dhuibhne-Almqvist, emphasizing the quality of Synge's folkloric skills, has suggested that the power of the play's adaption came from this twist, through which the playwright managed 'to reverse completely the anti-feminist timbre of the original tale'. 'Synge's Use of Popular Material in *The Shadow of the Glen*', *Béaloideas*, 58 (1990), 160.

[39] *United Irishman*, 31 Oct. 1903.   [40] 'Z', ibid., 21 Nov. 1903.

in nationalist identity politics. Suffragist organizations had existed in Ireland since the mid-1870s, but operated with a self-effacing gentility that left them remote from the turmoil of recent controversy.[41] On the other hand Celtic revival helped generate a militant women's organization, the Inghinidhe, individually and as a group an example for independent action, but whose political aims did not include adding any social goals to the ultimate prize of national independence.[42] The expected role of most women in the context of the revival was best expressed by a verse submission to the *United Irishman* that told the happy story of a Gaelic League Ireland in which the heroine had

> Set up a G.L. home in a G.L. farm,
> Was protected by a G.L. lover with a G.L. arm;
> Now a proud G.L. mother and G.L. wife,
> She believes in G.L. training and G.L. life;
> And this G.L. woman of a G.L. nation
> Find true happiness in her noble G.L. station.[43]

Alice Milligan and Maud Gonne MacBride may not have found such passivity edifying, but they, like Griffith, were aware that it was a position that had to be considered when taking sides on cultural issues. In particular, 'propaganda'—its purpose being to draw those who adhered to such social verities into support for the advanced nationalist position—would have to flatter to receive. This would necessitate the subordination of other elements of rebellion that involved class, sex, or generation, which might alienate potential converts. The Celtic Twilight might have successfully blurred such lines of division in nebulousness, but harbingers of social rupture like Synge would never do. Yeats's new *Samhain* principle of 'no propaganda but that of good art',[44] appeared like a depoliticized policy of *l'art pour l'art*, but instead operated in an inverse relationship to the Griffithite position. Hostile to notions of received opinion, the theatre offered space to voices silenced by its quite specific

[41] Cliona Murphy, *The Women's Movement and Irish Society in the Early Twentieth Century* (Hemel Hempstead, 1989), 16–18. The Irish Women's Suffrage Society (based in Belfast) was founded in 1873; the Dublin-based Irish Women's Suffrage and Local Government Association in 1876.

[42] For the anomalous situation of cultural nationalism regarding women's rights, as it pertains to the theatre movement, see Joseph Valente, 'The Myth of Sovereignty: Gender in the Literature of Irish Nationalism', *ELH* 61/1 (Spring 1994). He ascribes such contradictions to 'the slipknot effect of colonial hypermasculinity', 206.

[43] *United Irishman*, 28 Oct. 1905.

[44] *Samhain*, 3 (Sept. 1903), 4.

set of political ambitions. Rather than producing an increasingly rarified art, it became too rough for sensibilities more accustomed to gentle sentimentality.

The point was one made poignantly and with some irony by Gonne MacBride, who had converted to Catholicism through patriotic rather than religious conviction, and who, married despite her perception of the institution as an 'abomination',[45] would be separated from her new husband within the year. The theatre, she suggested, should sacrifice itself (as she had) on the altar of the nation's demands. Her plea for Celticism caricatured it more effectively than Moran ever had: 'In Ireland [the INTS] must draw its vitality from that hidden spring from which the seven fountains of Gaelic inspiration flow, where the red nuts of knowledge are ever falling.'[46]

This sweet vision found its realist equivalent with *In a Real Wicklow Glen*, a scenario devised to illustrate what Griffith insisted was 'the fact that all of us know—that Irishwomen are the most virtuous women in the world'.[47] The preferred version showed a noble Norah spurning a drunken suitor ('How dare you insult me, John Kavanagh. Ye know I am a married woman.').[48] Yeats, while exhibiting prejudices of his own, could hardly miss with his retort that such depictions of Irish men and women were mere daubs from 'the foreground of a young lady's watercolour'.[49]

Griffith's reaction to *In the Shadow of the Glen* was clearly personal— but it should be noted he had allowed the Queen's Royal Theatre production of *A Doll's House* a favourable notice earlier that year. Mindful of new links with the Dublin Corporation, his delayed judgement suggests a testing of the political water before he allowed his prejudices to be confirmed by the populist voice of the *Irish Daily Independent*. The European feminist rebellion might be tolerated as long as it did not disturb middle Ireland's expectations. In time Emmeline Pankhurst's Women's Social and Political Union, formed in Manchester in 1903, would bring it closer to home through inspiring Hanna Sheehy and Margaret Cousins to establish the Irish Women's Franchise League (IWFL), and with it a distinctly militant strain of Irish feminism.[50]

[45] Foster, *W. B. Yeats*, i. 284.   [46] *United Irishman*, 24 Oct. 1903.
[47] Ibid.
[48] Ibid. The scenario is also published in Hogan and Kilroy, *Modern Irish Drama*, ii. 148–52.   [49] *United Irishman*, 24 Oct. 1903.
[50] Rosemary Cullen Owens, *Smashing Times: A History of the Irish Women's Suffrage Movement 1889–1922* (Dublin, 1984), 60.

For the moment, the issue seemed in the mind of the nationalist right to be bound up with nefarious foreign influence, forces which might be construed as invasion or liberation. If the *Shadow* was Synge's *Cathleen ni Houlihan*, the landing of the French in his play consisted neither of the symbolist experiment nor nationalist tradition but of the Parisian liberality which might offer allegiance to Ireland's spirits of rebellion. Combined with that, the influence of French realists had done much to develop the very sense of social scope in Synge's plays against which his critics reacted, a scope permeated with left-wing ideas and, significantly, a pro-Dreyfusard attitude. Synge's decision to leave L'Association Irlandaise after a few months in 1897, when he wrote to Maud Gonne,[51] spoke of his discomfort with a militarism very much equated with the anti-Semitic mood of the time. If Moore had been compared with the 'filthy Zola', Synge's years in Paris made his praise of Anatole France particularly resonant, and displayed a clear indication of his own connection between the Dreyfus issue, socially progressive thinking, and a sense of humour with which he evidently identified:

Those who heard him speak in public at the time of the Affaire Dreyfus, and who remember the grave power of his words, will not be likely to find him—as some critics have found—a shallow sophist without sincerity or depth . . . No-one, it is possible, will consider . . . humorous optimism, even when completed, as Anatole France completes it, by socialistic ideals, as a high form of practical philosophy, but some may ask where at the present time we can find a better one . . . In his best work, while remaining true to the distinctive tradition of French writing—the tradition which had given us Frère Jean, Tartuffe, and Pangloss—he has contrived to express with curious exactness the irony and fatalistic gaiety which now form the essential mood of the French people.[52]

Such currencies of thought were also evident across Dublin's literary networks. The suggestion of a common platform for literary 'exactness' and the campaign for women's rights was already manifest in James Joyce and Francis Skeffington's double pamphlet of 1901, when the young Ibsenite's attack on the ILT came back to back with Skeffington's case for sexual equality in higher education, 'A Forgotten Aspect of the University Question'.[53] Their friendship is one example of the strands

---

[51] *The Collected Letters of J. M. Synge*, ed. Ann Saddlemyer, i. *1871–1907* (Oxford, 1983), 47.

[52] 'Three French Writers', in *Collected Works*, ii. 396. The other writers were Loti and Huysmans. Dated 1903, the article was later submitted to *Dana* but turned down by Eglinton. His reference was possibly to France's oration at the funeral of Zola, 5 Oct. 1902.

[53] Richard Ellmann, *James Joyce* (rev. edn., Oxford, 1982), 88–9.

that went to form left-literati combinations, in this case between nascent modernism, liberal Catholicism, and feminism. Their attempt to found a newspaper, the *Goblin*, failed,[54] but Skeffington (soon to take his wife's name and become Sheehy-Skeffington)[55] went on to co-edit the *Nationist* with Tom Kettle a couple of years later, before moving on to work on the *National Democrat* with Fred Ryan. Ryan, whose position as secretary of the INTS put him at the centre of theatre controversies, already knew Joyce, and it may have been on the basis of that relationship that Joyce flirted with the ISRP in that same year of 1903.[56] Though the limitations of even such fringe aspects of nationalism proved too constricting for Joyce, the affiliation between the two was more telling than suggested by his poem 'The Holy Office', a copy of which he forwarded to Ryan, among others. Both Ryan and Joyce sought to investigate those elements of nationalism with a tendency to racial exclusivity and parochialism; more particularly concentrating on the question of anti-Semitism, at that time once again becoming a topical issue.

Griffith was only too aware of the same axis opposed by the *United Irishman* in 1899. His report that Yeats's 'non-political' stance 'savours to us of the consideration of the feelings of the servants of the Englishman' was redolent of earlier conspiracy theories when the servants of the Englishman were the Jew, the Freemason, and the unreasonable Protestant. Certainly the visceral reaction to the *Shadow* suggested that Griffith might be taking on F. H. O'Donnell's mantle as a literary critic whose opinions were fed by ominously exclusive cultural and racial theories. When the emphasis shifted back to more explicit anti-Semitism, Griffith found that Fred Ryan remained a constant antagonist.

The opportunity for Griffith and Moran to air their anti-Semitic consensus came with the 'Limerick Pogrom'. The Jewish population of Ireland, as the only significant ethnic immigrant group, was experiencing increasing hostility from a nationalist movement already concerned about demographic trends. As one correspondent argued in the *Leader*: 'Ireland is at present being drained of its Gaelic population by emigration, and Jewish colonists are trooping in to fill up the places of the emigrants, and to turn Ireland into a filthy ghetto.'[57]

---

[54] Ibid. 140–1.

[55] Francis J. C. Skeffington married Hanna M. Sheehy, 27 June 1903. Leah Levenson, *With Wooden Sword: A Portrait of Francis Sheehy-Skeffington, Militant Pacifist* (Boston, 1983), 40.

[56] Peter Costello, *James Joyce: The Years of Growth, 1882–1915* (New York, 1993), 215. Unfortunately Connolly had already decamped to America and the two never met.

[57] *Leader*, 5 Sept. 1903. According to census figures, the Jewish population had increased

Jews, according to received wisdom, were so inculcated with the spirit of materialism that epitomized the Empire that their 'introduction' into Ireland was seen as final evidence of the British undermining of Irish identity. It was an image fixed on a Jewish pedlar stereotype with 'an oily, cross-eyed, subtle smile of self-apology and insinuating humility'[58] and backed by the conviction that 'the major part of the capitalists of the world are Jews'.[59] One contribution to a Gaelic League procession, demonstrating against the International Exhibition on in Dublin at the time, illustrated the logic:

The most striking tableau of Sunday's procession was that which represented a National versus an International Exhibition. The Internationalists were represented by a Jew pedlar with shoddy and gew-gaws whom Erin disdainfully turned away, turning to the Irishman who exhibited the sterling products of his country.[60]

When Michael Davitt, Standish O'Grady, and Fred Ryan had brought public attention to Fr. Creagh's denunciation of the Limerick Jews in January 1904, both the *United Irishman* and the *Leader* stepped forward to endorse the priest's exhortations for his flock to boycott and intimidate Jewish settlers. Griffith argued the policy should be extended:

To Father Creagh and the people of Limerick . . . we say well done. It is high time that the people in other cities of Ireland emulated the example of Limerick and freed themselves from the octopus grip of the Jewish usurers, who are swarming into this country to prey upon its people . . . all are threatened by these cunning and immoral people.[61]

The Hierarchy remained silent, as did Dublin Castle; and while Griffith's exhortations failed to provoke more widespread persecution, Limerick's Redemptorist congregation succeeded in its objective of driving out many of their Jewish neighbours.[62]

Davitt had long been a defender of Jewish rights, despite being guilty of anti-Semitism himself in his book *The Boer Fight for Freedom* and even in the process of denouncing the Russian pogroms in his powerful (and

---

from 472 to 3,769 from 1881 to 1901, of which 283 and 2,048 respectively were Dubliners. The Irish population had fallen from 5,174,836 to 4,458,775 over the same period. Louis Hyman, *The Jews of Ireland* (Shannon, 1972), 160.

[58] 'Cui Bono' (William Bulfin), *United Irishman*, 1 Oct. 1904.

[59] Griffith, ibid., 28 May 1904.

[60] Ibid., 19 Mar. 1904.   [61] Ibid., 30 Apr. 1904.

[62] For a more detailed account, see Dermot Keogh, *Jews in Twentieth-Century Ireland: Refugees, Anti-Semitism and the Holocaust* (Cork, 1998), 26–53.

aptly titled) exposé *Within the Pale*.[63] O'Grady, too, was capable of succumbing to rumours that Jews were seizing land from debtor peasants.[64] Indeed, their blemished records indicate how close anti-Semitism was to the natural parlance of Ireland, as of Europe generally, at the turn of the century. Yet when appealed to by the beleaguered community they had protested—partly because their sympathy was reinforced by a common wariness of clerical influence. It was hardly surprising that the division of support for Creagh's boycott largely fell along sectarian lines, with Protestants continuing to give Jewish shops custom; but scepticism of clerical moral leadership claimed a wider ambit. The local Church of Ireland bishop rallied to the cause, but he was not alone: one old Fenian fended off a threatening crowd until the RIC relieved his defence of a Jewish shop.[65] Beyond that, Limerick demonstrated once again that, however insular Irish Ireland, all sides of the cultural and political debate fed off international currents of thought. The Redemptorist Order of Limerick had originally been comprised of Europeans nursing revenge for the expulsion of their sect from France (thus directly influencing the locally born Creagh), and were here persecuting people expelled from Lithuania. And so, despite a gesture from Davitt indicating the opposite, the experience of oppression gave no guarantee of tolerance.

Griffith asserted his European credentials by pointing to the commonplace practice of persecution on the Continent: if Ireland were to take its place in the sun, the argument implied, it would need to recognize that such long-established customs of the civilized nations would be ignored at peril. Moran, if less extravagant in his sphere of reference, worked with similar assumptions. As in Europe, the Jew was particularly useful as an image of unscrupulous capital that could provide distraction from campaigns to establish and protect indigenous industrial concerns. So long as the revivalist movement's push-me-pull-you attitude to material self-sufficiency and spiritual integrity complicated the response to

---

[63] *Within the Pale: The True Story of Anti-Semitic Persecutions in Russia* (London, 1903). For his anti-Semitism, see p. ix, a statement belying the book's tone of dismay, esp. in his account of the Kinishov massacres, described as 'revolting deeds of medieval savagery', 107.
[64] *All Ireland Review*, 8 June 1901. O'Grady went on to report that 'we might fare worse, far worse than falling under the domination of that sagacious, far-seeing, noble and world considering race'. His afterthought may have been prompted by the recollection that his benefactor, Lady Desart, was, in Hubert Butler's words, 'a plump and plain little Jewess with high intelligence'. 'The Deserted Sun Palace', in *The Sub-Prefect should have held his Tongue, and Other Essays*, ed. R. F. Foster (London, 1990), 39–40.
[65] Keogh, *Jews in Twentieth-Century Ireland*, 31.

modernizing forces, the characterization of both Jew and Saxon as natural servants of Mammon presented a useful antidote to the paradox.

Given the bourgeois political implications of this, it was not surprising that of all the defenders of the Jewish community, it was Fred Ryan who could provide the most effective and sustained counter-attack.[66] His socialist perspective gave the necessary 'precision' required to place the issue in both European and class-related contexts.

Anti-Semitism . . . is the refuse of the Continental reactionary parties. It may seem good tactics on the part of corrupt militarists and capitalists to set the mob at the heels of the rich Jews. But the cause of liberty has nothing to gain by being associated with such tricks, and the very personnel of the parties who resort to them ought to warn us of their objects. Let us fight for liberty as liberty and put down capitalist greed as capitalist greed, but let us resolutely shut our eyes to questions of race and creed, which are only raised by reactionaries to create disorders in the camp of progress.[67]

If the camp of progress still had a tent in it marked INTS, it was partly because the split occasioned by the *Shadow* echoed across the advanced-nationalist spectrum. Ryan, for one, was not likely to be tempted away by the seceders. Critiques emanating from the left found more common cause with the object of Griffith's ire, and with its material. In December 1903, Colum offered up his second play, *Broken Soil*.[68] Its subject, a disruptive old fiddle-player stretching the restraint of his daughter's domesticity, gave the first indication of its author's gift for the topical. Its success confirmed the staying power of the INTS—like Colum's hero, irrepressible, if troubling. When, late the following February, Synge's tragedy *Riders to the Sea* first shocked the audience to silence,[69] and even hostile critics into appalled respect, the company was

[66] This campaign has latterly been echoed by left-wing revisionists, whose long overdue celebration of Ryan's role—esp. regarding Griffith's anti-Semitism—has led to further controversy (note e.g. the *Irish Times*, Aug.–Oct. 1984 and Aug.–Sept. 1992). See Manus O'Riordan, chief architect of the Ryan revival: 'Sinn Féin and the Jews', *Irish Communist*, 171–8 (Mar.–Nov. 1980); *The Rise and Fall of Irish Anti-Semitism*, co-authored with Pat Feeley and Jim Kenny; his two edited collections of Ryan, *Articles by Frederick Ryan* (Dublin, 1984) and *Socialism, Democracy and the Church* (Dublin, 1984). More recently, Terry Eagleton has taken up the cudgels: 'The Ryan Line', *Crazy John and the Bishop, and Other Essays on Irish Culture* (Cork, 1998), 249–72.

[67] *United Irishman*, 28 May 1904.

[68] The play was later revised into *The Fiddler's House*. Colum, *The Land and The Fiddler's House* (Dublin, 1909).

[69] 'The audience was so deeply moved by the tragic gloom of the terrible scene on which the curtains close in, that it could not applaud.' Diary entry, Friday 26 Feb. 1904. Holloway, *Joseph Holloway's Abbey Theatre: A Selection from his Unpublished Journal Impressions of a Dublin Playgoer*, ed. Robert Hogan and Michael J. O'Neill (Carbondale, Ill., 1967), 35.

consolidated rather than disturbed by calls for more 'sunshine' from the *United Irishman*.[70]

Broken Soil and *Riders to the Sea* indicated a darker radical edge to the new theatrical enterprise, complementing Yeats's hardening Celticism, but drawing on a contrasting political impulse. Yet a drama that determined to harness the despair, or the bitterness and frustration, of the homestead soon sat uneasily housed in the bijou arena of the Abbey Theatre. Yeats had spent Annie Horniman's money on a space that made followers of the INTS, attending the opening on 27 December 1904, blink in wonder. Yet, following the instructions of Horniman, the cheapest seats were set at an exclusive shilling. Well might Moran complain (reporting darkly how John Redmond's head had obscured his line of sight) that 'this *un*-commercial theatre bangs its doors on the despised sixpenny public'.[71] Nationalists likewise looked with distrust at the financial arrangements and wondered who owned the national theatre. And yet, as Moran's attitude indicates, the insulation from the commercial imperatives followed by the Irish entertainments industry still piqued expectation. If the question remained whether a theatre thus housed could remain sensitive to such tensions, it would only be answered in terms of the plays put on there.

Such issues were germane in Ireland at this time, when the Land Act had complicated the questions of identity and ownership: no longer just a case of nationalist tenant rights versus alien rack-renting absentee, but peasant proprietorship versus nationalization, pasture versus tillage, and farmer versus labourer.[72] The seasonal crises the national theatre suffered reflected consternation on the part of nationalists as to the impact of ownership on the struggle for independence. The land question had been, like the Boer War, an issue identified as belonging to the political bipolarity of Nation versus Empire. The implication of nationalist landowners in land purchase deals, in the extension of grazing rights and the devolution crisis, generated concern that the momentum achieved by cultural nationalism might be weakened by the materialist sop, and that the subsidy of *embourgeoisement* by the British would co-opt a new class of farm-owners.

[70] *United Irishman*, 5 March 1904.

[71] *Leader*, 7 Jan. 1905. Lady Gregory reassured doubters in private that the charge was only a temporary concession to Horniman's snobbery (as indeed it proved). 'I was always against a 1/- pit, but it was decided to let Miss Horniman have her way for about a year or so. I think we shall very soon be able to change it for a 6d one.' Letter to Colum, 9 Jan. 1906. Berg.

[72] Paul Bew, *Conflict and Conciliation in Ireland, 1890–1910: Parnellites and Radical Agrarians* (Oxford, 1987).

Padraic Colum's new play *The Land* took on such issues. Colum had declared that 'A poet . . . is the organ of self-consciousness in the social organism.' In consequence he viewed realism as an essential means of exploring the conditions of life in Ireland and making them more knowable, more understood. To preach to an audience converted in other times was to live in the past, and so inevitably fail both politically and artistically by refusing to speak of broad experience. 'Until we have absorbed normal national life we can say no patriotic thing in a new, in an intimate way. And we have offered the people less than our best, we have done work other than that which has come to our hand, and perhaps we have been false to our hour.'[73]

Intensely aware of the gap being opened between old and new generations by the accelerating pace of economic change, Colum's topical realism was expressed in an attempt to fix Ireland's 'hour' dramatically. *The Land* reported that Wyndham's Act was too little too late to restrain the young figures of Ellen Douras and Matt Cosgar from emigration, and was actually reinforcing the rigidity of the society that had helped generate their disaffection in the first place. What seemed miraculous for the older generation—possession—was scarcely enough for the new. A combination of Greek chorus, chant-like repetition, and layering of speech[74] emphasized the awe of ownership enveloping the couple's fathers, Martin and Murtagh:

MURTAGH COSGAR. Lands ploughed and spread. And all our own; all our own.
MARTIN DOURAS. All our own, ay. But we made a hard fight for them.
MURTAGH COSGAR. Ay.
MARTIN DOURAS. Them that come after us, will never see them as we're seeing them now.
MURTAGH COSGAR. Them that come after us . . .[75]

The *United Irishman*, in a favourable review, interpreted the strident figure of Ellen Douras as negligent of her responsibilities.[76] But the drama stressed that social stagnation was neglecting those who found (as did the fiddle-player in *Broken Soil*) the status quo suffocating. Ellen, like Synge's central figures of rebellion, is a character whose energy is essential to harness if mere landownership is to become ownership of 'The

---

[73] *Nationist*, 19 Oct. 1905.
[74] For reference to Colum's 'flat' midland dialogue, see Zack Bowen, *Padraic Colum: A Biographical-Critical Introduction* (Carbondale, Ill., 1970).
[75] *The Land* (Dublin, 1905), 17–18.
[76] *United Irishman*, 24 June 1905.

Land' of Ireland.[77] The absence of the means by which this might be accomplished—through economic and cultural alternatives to emigration—is an assertion of a realism that, while refusing to offer solutions, eloquently presented Ireland's problems. Well might the champions of realistic pessimism note with relief that the play 'contradicts all the expectations which such a title would have raised years ago . . . no evictions scenes, no sheriffs, land agents, redcoats'.[78] The play was alive to the complications which Unionist 'kindness', if it had not proved fatal to Home Rule, had certainly introduced.

When Ellen derides Matt—'Go back, go back. Make it up with your father. Your father will be glad of a labourer'[79]—she derides the subservience implicit in his intended return, noting in passing the shift in material relations as the land changed hands. Colum's play pointed out that as long as nationalists demanded uncritical views of the small farm, the unconvinced Ellens of Ireland would be difficult to persuade, and perhaps that group included Yeats, Synge, and himself. The message was all the more potent when viewed together with the available alternative. The Abbey's rivals the Cumann na nGaedhael Theatre Co., had merged into the Keating Branch-based National Players Society. Following less than successful attempts to produce a new *Cathleen ni Houlihan* by Maud Gonne and Maurice Joy,[80] Seumas MacManus[81] turned his back on the INTS to come up with the National Players' stock propagandist play, *The Hard-Hearted Man*.[82]

'Ireland', declared MacManus, 'is one of the nations wherein idealism has ever found harbourage . . . seeking shelter from the blighting frost of practicality.'[83] Consequently the critical expansion offered by realist

---

[77] Colum's play also drew attention to the crisis of a traditional political metaphor for self-government. See Philip Bull, *Land, Politics and Nationalism: A Study of the Irish Land Question* (Dublin, 1996), 94–5.

[78] *Leader*, 17 June 1905. The comment was probably also an ironic reflection on *The Saxon Shillin'*. [79] *The Land* (1905), 36.

[80] With 'Dawn' and 'The Message', *United Irishman*, 29 Oct. 1904 and 7 Jan. 1905 respectively. Gonne's 'Dawn' has been republished in Robert Hogan and James Kilroy (eds.), *Lost Plays of the Irish Renaissance*, i. *The Abbey Theatre* (Newark, Del., 1970), 73–84.

[81] Seumas MacManus, a prolific writer from Donegal, was one of the directors of 'Sinn Féin' Publishing and Printing Company. Despite his anti-emigration message, MacManus ironically spent more and more time supporting the League from the USA and in 1908 took an academic post at Notre Dame University. Philip O'Leary, *Prose Literature of the Gaelic Revival, 1881–1921: Ideology and Innovation* (University Park, Pa., 1995), 348–9.

[82] MacManus had already had his play *The Townland of Tamney* performed by the INTS in Jan. 1904.

[83] *United Irishman*, 15 Apr. 1905. The play was first put on in July 1904. It was widely performed afterward and hailed as the model nationalist drama. The *United Irishman* used its familiar gauge, remarking that 'it impressed the audience as no other play since

commentary was eschewed in favour of the conservative idealism of *In a Real Wicklow Glen*. Tackling much the same themes as Colum's, his play offered fulfilment in self-sacrifice rather than self-discovery, but to a vision in which the first duty of this generation is obedience to the last. His equivalent of Ellen Douras is William Breshlin, a young man whose desire to emigrate is depicted as neglect of his worn-out father. The 'hard-hearted man' of the piece is Maurice Ruddy, the neighbour who upbraids the errant youth for West Britonism, but retains enough faith in his underlying qualities to pay for his return from the United States (where he has proved a failure) and take him on as an agricultural labourer. At the close, Breshlin gratefully resumes his submissive role in the family and mode of production: 'Father you can give me . . . a fortune that's worthy of you and a fortune that will keep us both . . . I want you to give me—your blessing and a spade.'[84] Breshlin the errant emigrant could be a symbol for any of the prodigal sons or daughters of Ireland— the renegade artist, the socialist, the stifled feminist, the Unionist with a heart of gold—who had but to repent to be let back into bourgeois nationalism's frost-spared Eden. And start digging.

The dynamics of land and questions of possession go some way to explicate the split in the Abbey of Christmas 1905, when the INTS turned professional. *The Land* and *The Hard-Hearted Man* indicated a widening gap between left and the right as far as theatrical representation was concerned, whereas the ongoing processes of concentration of power at the Abbey opened a similar divide. This reflected, though different in so many other ways, ground shared by Yeats and Griffith.

During the period 1904–5, the *United Irishman* had outmanoeuvred its old enemy, the *Leader*. For all the ferocity and occasional brilliance of Moran's paper, which made plenty of capital out of mocking the Hungarian policy, it held a static position that could be outflanked by a faster-moving adversary. The recapitulation of Moran's tenets in book form, *The Philosophy of Irish Ireland*, was offset by Griffith's more pragmatic intelligence. Hence the swift change from the alien-sounding Hungarian Policy to the familiar cry 'Sinn Féin', which at once stole the

"Kathleen ni Houlihan" '. *ACS* admiring the occasional use of Irish in the play, called it 'the beginning of serious Irish Drama', 4 Oct. 1905. Synge, less appreciative, linked MacManus back to Sinn Féin and French anti-Semitism: 'God help us indeed if we are to fall into the hands of S MacManus or anyone like him . . . I would not be surprised if Sinn Féin had momentary success in Dublin—as the so-called Nationalism had in Paris at the time of the Dreyfus affair—but it will never touch the country.' Letter to John Quinn, 5 Sept. 1907, in *Collected Letters of J. M. Synge*, ed. Ann Saddlemyer, ii (Oxford, 1984), 46.

[84] Seumas MacManus, *The Hard-Hearted Man* (Dublin, 1905), 44.

clothes from and wrong-footed the opposition. Well might Moran complain that he had used the phrase in 1901 and the Sinn Féin Policy was nothing but the 'old Irish Ireland policy of the *Leader*'.[85] That could not stem the tide—at least for the moment—moving in Griffith's favour, and Moran looked on helpless as his rival took the name for his paper, changing the *United Irishman* to *Sinn Féin* in 1906. Even the John Kelly furnishing warehouse, whose advertising declared 'No Connection with Jews', changed its name to Sinn Féin Ltd.[86]

Griffith had continued to embellish his philosophy, so close in spirit to the ethos of the hard-hearted Maurice Ruddy. A central dynamic of the nascent Sinn Féin ideology was an anti-colonial element that led to a degree of identification with other movements in the British Empire, but did not extend to a critique of imperialism qua imperialism. Griffith's political and economic plan was to follow Hungary's and Germany's respective examples—one providing enough independence from Britain to enable the enjoyment of the material fruits yielded by the other. That this might involve something akin to Magyarization or Iron Chancellery did not concern. *The Resurrection of Hungary* and its partner *The Sinn Féin Policy*[87] were partly swift responses to the changing European situation: entente with Britain, the humbling of the army after the Dreyfus affair, and the separation of Church and State all altered the perception of France as Ireland's natural ally. In the autumn of 1905 the disillusion was voiced in a suggestion that Irish ambitions were best served in promotion of a German-American alliance.

I cannot recall that a single French paper has even alluded to the sentiments which the famous Entente Cordiale was received in Ireland—we exist so little in French estimation . . . It seems patent that Irishmen should do all in their power to promote friendship between the United States and Germany.[88]

Griffith's fascination with List and German militarism offer parallels to Yeats's infatuation with the cult of Nietzsche and his consideration for the wishes of Horniman. If Griffith's angry rejection of Synge made the 1903 split inevitable, Yeats's imperiousness following his sojourn in

---

[85] *Leader*, 11 Mar. 1905.

[86] Ibid., 22 July 1905. John Kelly boasted that 'our advertisement has, in our twelve months trading, closed four alien furniture stores in Dublin'. He went on to become a right-wing Sinn Féin boardman. *Irish Independent*, 22 Sept. 1913.

[87] *The Resurrection of Hungary* was first published in 1904; *The Sinn Féin Policy* in 1905. The latter pamphlet came from the text of Griffith's speech to the First Annual Meeting of the National Council, 28 Nov. 1905. Later editions, fittingly, saw them published together.

[88] *United Irishman*, 28 Oct. 1905.

America was an equally important factor in the division precipitated by the introduction of the cash nexus at the end of 1905. The influence of the theatre's patron, well catalogued,[89] might be seen as a Mephistopheles tempting Yeats's aristocratic pretensions with prestige; and certainly Griffith portrayed it thus. But Griffith's brand of corporatism, 'The Unity of Material Interests that Produces National Strength',[90] was no less possessed by the devil of class interest, however chauvinistically couched. Ideology aside, Griffith too had his patrons, and relations with well-heeled presidents of the National Council and Sinn Féin, respectively Edward Martyn and John Sweetman (the latter subsidizing the publication of *The Resurrection of Hungary*)[91] were necessary to Griffith's cause, despite his personal asceticism. In truth, Yeats and Griffith shared a similar trajectory, away from earnest Fenian rhetoric at the century's turn, toward an oddly similar emphasis on Georgian Ireland: Griffith, with the return to the 'King, Lords and Commons' of Grattan's 1782 constitution and penchant for dual monarchy; Yeats with his still-evolving Ascendancy fixation.

Equally, the shared chauvinism of both leaders remained, and their interpretations of Irish culture were iconoclastic, liberating, and rebellious—to a degree. Eglinton tried hard to articulate a relevant point in his *Dana* essay 'A Way of Understanding Nietzsche':

We have to bear in mind . . . an apparent inconsistency in the writings of Nietzsche, who, while praising power whenever he sees it exercised in history purely for the love of it, is clearly always on the side of those who confront the might of the world with the might of the idea, and for whom some limitation of the circumstance or character has been a 'school of genius'.[92]

Griffith and Yeats evolved their positions through opposition, and each saw the other as being implicated in what they opposed. In Griffith's (and Moran's) eyes, Yeats's use of British patronage to concentrate power into the hands of a Protestant directorate implicated the Abbey in familiar systems of colonization. If one thing validated Yeats's arrogation of control, however, it was his defence of dramatic experimentation in the face of those equally familiar bourgeois and religious systems of repression expressed by Moran and Griffith. Though ironically, each party was

---

[89] Thoroughly explored by Adrian Frazier, *Behind the Scenes: Yeats, Horniman and the Struggle for the Abbey Theatre* (Berkeley and Los Angeles, 1990).

[90] *The Sinn Féin Policy* (Dublin, 1905).

[91] Sweetman was an ex-MP and large Meath landowner, and soon to be chairman of the General Council of Co. Councils. Brian Maye, *Arthur Griffith* (Dublin, 1997), 97.

[92] *Dana*, 6 (Oct. 1904).

compromised by the very forces it assumed had corrupted the other, their 'school of genius' could still be said to confront some section of the 'might of the world'.

For those who could point to any number of alternative methods of finding a way forward for nationalist ideology, who wondered about such ideas maturing beyond opposition (or observed the dangers of anti-Semitism), such schools were confining. And in pursuit of alternatives, a union of sceptics often operated to counterbalance their voices in the nationalist forum. The review *Dana* was just such an alliance.[93] John Eglinton, whose cosmopolitanism Yeats had found so useful to offset his revivalism five years earlier, was a natural editorial ally for Fred Ryan, whose position in the INTS and experience writing for the *Worker's Republic* and the *United Irishman* gave him an overview of the current struggle. In its pages room was found for a diverse set: O'Grady, Joyce, Stephen Gwynn, George Moore, Colum, Russell, and St John Gogarty all contributed. But essentially it was a double-act interrogation. Eglinton, the good cop, made elegant forays into the possibility of a new paganism, criticized Nietzsche, or invoked the intellects in Ireland to freethink wherever possible, declaring that 'The great modern lesson that we have learned is that we must live creatively.'[94] Ryan, bad cop, continued to voice Connolly's distrust of distraction from bread and butter issues. Besides savaging Griffith's anti-Semitism and launching critiques of imperialism, he issued a hard-hitting series of articles on Catholic Irish Ireland for its neglect of pressing social ills and its right-wing pedigree, in particular the Catholic Truth Society—all signs, as he called it, of 'intellectual suicide'.[95]

Another target was the language movement. 'Is the Gaelic League a Progressive Force?' he asked in November 1904, provoking a fresh row in the *United Irishman* and *An Claidheamh Soluis*.[96] Such a debate served to indicate the extent to which the *Leader* had been isolated. Post-millennial wariness of pure cultural revivalism began to improve the stock of political nationalism. Ryan's probing forced Griffith to admit that the Sinn Féin movement only regarded Irish as the 'right arm' of the struggle, and

93 Terry Eagleton, 'The Ryan Line', in *Crazy John and the Bishop*, 257–8.

94 'Sincerity', *Dana*, 7 (Nov. 1904). 'Our idealists have begun to cry out for anarchy.'

95 Ibid. 5 (Sept. 1904). Ryan was at pains to link religion with right-wing ideology and nationalist preclusion of internal schism: 'Whenever anyone calls for a cessation of the political warfare and a "union of all classes" we know at once he is a reactionary, well meaning or otherwise . . . to refuse to face the intellectual battle, confident of the final victory of the right, is the attitude of the theological champions today.'

96 Ibid. 7 (Nov. 1904).

not, as the League would have it, the very soul.[97] The mechanics of propaganda still militated against the use of Irish, just as it militated against giving the national theatre free rein. Despite this (and the fact that Seumas MacManus had had a rather bitter exchange in *An Claidheamh Soluis* over their description of his writing as Anglo-Irish)[98] *An Claidheamh Soluis* froze out the *Leader* while referring to the *United Irishman* as its 'confrere'.[99] Such was enough to provoke allegations of a Leinster conspiracy from Moran, a charge reiterated through the editor's accusations of intimidation by Dublin's radical contingent during the Gaelic League rallies of 1904 and 1905. 'If the Coisde Gnotha did not expressly denounce the outrage, every thinking man would conclude that it condoned it, and the non-political Gaelic League would be regarded as an annexe of the Tin Pike and King Lords and Commons of Ireland Party.'[100]

Given the careful positioning of cultural-nationalist groups, *Dana*'s capacity for mischief made it ideal for the purposes of those who fell outside categories. Yeats, writing to George Russell in support of his defence of Plunkett's *Ireland in the New Century* (which had been badly mauled), had suggested another article. He added, 'I wish that "Dana" would say every month "such & such a paper has called Mr so & so such & such"—and do this exhaustively. I had a plan once for a thermometer of abuse.'[101] With unconventionality as its guiding principle, *Dana* was still the first port of call for any such defence, and this was both its quality and its failing. Synge had been impatient with its progress (and probably piqued by Eglinton's rejection of his piece on Anatole France), but finally considered it 'too good to get a paying circulation in Ireland'.[102] Its demise after only eleven issues left something of a gap on the margins of the nationalist spectrum.

It was succeeded, in September 1905, by the *Nationist*, a liberal Catholic 'Weekly Review of Irish Thought and Affairs', edited by Tom Kettle and Francis Sheehy-Skeffington and peopled by UCD graduates.

---

[97] *United Irishman*, 28 Jan. 1905.

[98] MacManus had suggested, 'I consider that you can have an Irish literature as easily as you can have Irish linen or Irish soap, irrespective of the language ingredient.' *ACS*, 10 Jan. 1903. By Aug. 1905 he had learned the error of his ways and had *The Hard-Hearted Man* translated by Tomás O Concheaniana. *ACS*, 12 Aug. 1905.

[99] *Leader*, 11 Mar. 1905.   [100] Ibid., 25 Mar. 1905.

[101] Yeats to George Russell, early Oct. 1904, in *Collected Letters*, iii. 658–9.

[102] According to Cherrie Matheson's memoir, 'John Synge as I Knew Him', quoted by McCormack, *Fool of the Family*, 183. He had earlier judged Eglinton an instance of 'pedantic degeneration'. *Collected Letters of J. M. Synge*, i. 88.

In its own way, the paper was a response to the hardening of Catholic opinion by seeking out the middle ground in a similar way to its Meath-based contemporary the *Irish Peasant*, whose new editor W. P. Ryan had just taken over from 'Pat' Kenny. The *Nationist* also had its European touchstones, guided by Kettle's Continental leanings:[103] the first two issues featuring articles praising the levelling Catholicism of Le Sillon, with Maurice Joy posing as Ireland's Marc Sagnier as if in response to Ryan's Jean Jaurès.[104] The house journal of the Young Ireland Branch of the UIL, the *Nationist* supported the IPP but toyed with constitutional separatism, and like other papers of the cultural-nationalist revival, it felt the constraints of mainstream political language while attempting to define its position: ' "Nationalist" was inadequate; it had been narrowed and cheapened down to almost blank nothing. We cast about for a fresher word; none offered, and we were compelled to invent one.'[105] Though its defamiliarizing life was shorter and less daring than *Dana*'s,[106] the *Nationist* provided a rallying point for liberal critics of ' "frankly Catholic" and "soi-disant Catholic" journals'[107] and defended the Abbey's overtly propagandist writers, Lady Gregory, William Boyle, and the darling of the paper, Patrick Colum.

Reacting against the less catholic Catholic assertions of cultural exclusivity as well as protesting against the Protestant configurations of the Abbey, the *Nationist* took up the middle ground that opened up as Sinn Féin/the National Players and the Abbey were forced further apart. Yeats had moved swiftly to turn the INTS into a joint-stock company that concentrated power with the writer-directors, rendering other INTS members mere employees. This removal of 'omov'[108] and the subsequent share deal inevitably resulted in an alienation compounded by Yeats's belligerence.[109] 'Mr Yeats may be going towards what he wants', complained Colum to William Fay, 'But he is not going towards what I

---

[103] Senia Paseta, *Before the Revolution: Nationalism, Social Change and Ireland's Catholic Élite 1879–1992* (Cork, 1999), 133.

[104] *Nationist*, 21 and 28 Sept. 1905. See also Ryan and Joy's clash in the *National Democrat*, Feb. 1907, in which Joy accused Ryan of being a 'stalwart' of the 'rationalist press'.

[105] *Nationist*, 21 Sept. 1905.

[106] The weekly journal ran from 21 Sept. 1905 until 29 Mar. 1906.

[107] *Nationist*, 2 Nov. 1905. The phrase was used in criticism of the *Catholic Young Man*.

[108] 'We refused and must still refuse "one man one vote" (an English radical cry)'. Lady Gregory to Colum, quoted in Hogan and Kilroy, *Modern Irish Drama*, ii. 61.

[109] Frazier, *Behind the Scenes*, 108–48.

want. My ideal is a people's theatre, and I'd rather write for the Gallery of the Queens than for a few people in the stalls.'[110]

The movement fractured again. Significantly, however, the splinter group did not attach to any existing amateur troupe, but attempted a new direction. The members of the Committee of the Theatre of Ireland illustrated a lineage of ideology and personnel which connected it to the recently defunct *Nationist*: Tom Kettle (chair), Maurice Joy, Padriac Colum (secretary).[111] To their number were added Gaelic Leaguers interested in the possibility of more language plays, Stephen Gwynn and Patrick Pearse; up-and-coming nationalist Constance Markievicz; disgruntled ex-Abbey players Thomas Koehler, the Walkers, and, angling for a publishing contract for new plays, George Roberts. Playwrights J. S. Starkey and James Cousins came on board, while George Russell gave moral support (himself having resigned) and Edward Martyn accepted his habitual role as president of the new organization.[112]

The Theatre of Ireland (Cluithcheoiri na hEireann) was not without its opponents, however. Critics could note that the change from INTS to NTS Ltd. had been voted for by the seceders themselves.[113] They could also acknowledge that the new order came from a playwright rather than a Protestant coup—Colum had after all been sought as a director and had resigned as much out of injured pride as political scruple.[114] And as all theatre people knew, there were bruised egos involved all along the way.

This missed the real reason for the break. Democratic instincts that were keenly sensitive to issues of ownership quickly resented the hierarchies imposed by professional status: it was no accident that *The Land* and the Abbey parted company at this stage. The Horniman dispensation allowed Yeats to play the landlord at the Abbey, as though it were the last house of the Ascendancy and the field of theatre his own imperishable estate. In fact it put the directors more in the category of tenant farmers, mindful of the (usually bad) mood of their benefactor, biding time while

---

[110] Colum to W. G. Fay, 9 Jan. 1906. Berg.

[111] Colum was elected secretary at the first meeting of the Provisional Committee, 18 May 1906; Kettle was elected at the third meeting (6 June) after Gwynn had held the post provisionally. Theatre of Ireland Minutes, NLI MS 7388.

[112] Ibid.

[113] The main vote was carried 14 votes to 1 (with no record of the objector); subsequent amendments by smaller margins. INTS Minutes, 22 Sept. 1905, NLI MS 7268.

[114] Colum (and all Dublin) got wind of Horniman's remark that he 'knew which side his bread was buttered on'. Colum's letter to Lady Gregory, 8 Jan. 1906, reveals that he voted for the share issue, although he chided himself for opportunism. Gregory's reply, 9 Jan. 1906, rejoined him by reminding him of the apathy evident in his non-attendance of some of the crucial meetings. Berg.

their own purchase scheme materialized. Indeed, the early failure of the Abbey to perform the play commissioned from Shaw, *John Bull's Other Ireland*, takes on another hue if one considers its satire too close to the bone for Yeats. In that play, considering the drawbacks of having Englishman Broadbent as the local Irish MP, Barney Doran declares 'Divil a matther if he has plenty o money. He'll do for us right enough',[115] and there is more than a little of this sentiment in the machinations of 1904 and 1905.

There was another echo, however. Francis Sheehy-Skeffington accused the breakaway group of acting 'through pique' while Fred Ryan, who had often acted as a go-between,[116] criticized any regressive return to 'backyard halls'.[117] Here was a leftist impatience with those unable to see the practical strengths of the Abbey, and its impetus. Shaw's play plotted similar divisions. The audience were denied his redrawing of political boundaries to accommodate the effects of capitalization: but also the subtler point made in the friction between the indulgence and rejection of Irish idealism, between the dreamer Peter Keegan and doer Larry Doyle. 'Every dream is a prophecy'[118] says the former priest Keegan, but is locked in the neurosis of deferment.[119] Doyle, the 'civil engineer', prefers to build, but with an indiscriminate resignation to the forces of 'progress'. It is their synthesis, the struggle to give substance to the fantasy, which redeemed Yeats's ambition in the form of a well-appointed theatre equipped to become a national forum.

Yeats did not always live up to the caricature used by his critics. All this contrasted with his adroit handling of the Gaelic League, which he continued to placate, carefully apologizing for being a writer in Ireland's last generation of English-users. Leaguers were impressed by what Pearse called this 'self denying ordinance',[120] particularly when the Abbey stage was made available to the Keating Branch for their performance of F. Dineen's remarkable play tackling souperism, *Creideamh*

---

[115] *The Complete Plays of Bernard Shaw* (London, 1934), 433.

[116] *Collected Letters of J. M. Synge*, ed. Saddlemyer, i. 141 n.

[117] Accusations made at an NLS discussion, 10 Dec. 1906. Holloway, *Holloway's Abbey Theatre*, 78.

[118] Ibid. 452.

[119] Eagleton's analysis of 'premature utopianism', which projects 'beyond the compromised political structures of the present . . . persuading us to desire uselessly rather than feasibly', has resonance here. Terry Eagleton, *Nationalism: Irony and Commitment* (Derry, 1988), 6.

[120] 'Mr Yeats and his Failure', *ACS*, 5 Mar. 1904. Quoted by O'Leary, *Prose Literature of the Gaelic Revival*, 335.

agus Gorta (Faith and Famine), in October 1905.[121] *An Claidheamh Soluis* reported on Yeats's speech 'On Literature' at University College, Dublin:

Except for the strange infatuation which makes him see a great dramatist in Mr Synge, Mr. Yeats's views on the position and purpose of his Theatre are entirely sane. 'It might be that this country in ten, twenty, or fifty years, would speak nothing but Irish, and there would be no space in it for them . . . still, they, dramatists, could only obey the words of the poet who said "Let us be merry before we die" ' . . . We recognize in the Irish National Theatre, so long as it is true to its best instincts, not a danger to, but an ally of, the language movement.[122]

This happily accomplished, and mindful of age-old maxims on the merits of publicity, Yeats prepared the way for *The Well of the Saints* by keeping Griffith in mind of Synge's crimes. The editor rightly described as 'logrolling'[123] Yeats's unnecessarily tenacious revision of the *Shadow* debate in the 1905 *Samhain* and thereafter in the *United Irishman*, but it served to confirm the prejudice that the Abbey was actively anti-nationalist, which was hardly an accurate assessment.

The directorate had its own union of sceptics, kept in place by necessity. Criticism of Yeats usually came in two parts—his use of English money and his use of Synge—both as examples of foreign influence. Yet the two were principally connected by the hostility of Sinn Féin to both. Synge, different from Yeats in demeanour as in ideology,[124] was attached to the Abbey principally because it was the one place in Ireland he could be played. In this matter he was clearly dependent on Yeats. The alacrity

---

[121] Dineen's play was set in North Kerry, 1847. There was an English text available to the audience, but original and translation are lost. Joseph Holloway, however, recorded it as an affecting drama in five episodes in which a poverty-stricken mother will not convert in order to receive relief. 'The last episode of all, the death of Mrs O'Sullivan's little ones of starvation—closes the drama, and created a deep impression. The staging of this scene was well done, and the vision of angels cast from a lantern on the back cloth the while, voices laden with a message of hope sang "off" as the mother distractedly watched her children's lives ebb away heightened the effect of the sad picture.' Holloway also records that Dineen refused to take the calls for 'Author' because he wanted no further connection with the theatre's reputation for 'irreligion'. Joseph Holloway Papers, NLI MS 1803 (2), 28 Oct. and 5 Nov. 1905.

[122] *ACS*, 22 Apr. 1905.

[123] *United Irishman*, 4 Feb. 1905.

[124] Synge's cordiality comes across strongly in many reminiscences (in contrast to Yeats): see e.g. Maire Nic Shiubhlaigh and Edward Kenny's account, *The Splendid Years* (Dublin, 1955); or William Fay and Catherine Carswell, who described him as being 'a joy to work with . . . a keen sense of humour and plenty of patience'. *The Fays of the Abbey Theatre: An Autobiographical Record* (London, 1935), 138–9.

with which Synge's work found its way into the Continental repertoire indicates how far he was part of a wider bohemian fringe, something Yeats had aspired to but only accomplished in London's paler manifestations.[125] In early 1906 he was busy trying to tempt the Deutches Theater, Berlin into directing *The Tinker's Wedding*—a play Yeats and Gregory had blanched at producing—with the appetizing promise of something 'too immoral for Dublin'.[126] Other instances of his frustration include his complaints that Yeats and Lady Gregory were excluding him from the tour programmes, and his growing resentment at Horniman (felt by all to some degree). If Dublin seemed too intemperate there was always the danger of Synge going east like Joyce before him and O'Casey after: but if anything, the harness of controversy seemed to bind him even tighter to his audience.

If, of the directorial triumvirate that emerged after Colum's departure with the Theatre of Ireland in 1906, Yeats was on the right, and Synge on the left, then Lady Gregory had emerged as the nationalist voice of the Abbey. And by sheer dint of the volume of her work she was a defining voice. Not only by giving substance to Yeats's lip-service to the League in her close working relationship with Douglas Hyde, but with her cunning dual output: Cloone cartoon shorts on one hand, subverting the authority of press gossip, and main-feature nationalist plays on the other, that either of the breakaway groups would have been happy to call their own.

In plays such as *Spreading the News* and *Hyacinth Halvey*,[127] set in the gossipy village of Cloone, the ideological basis to the dramas of rebellion and defiance evident in Synge and Yeats is displaced by a theatre of misapprehension. A character such as Barney Fallon, accused of murder through snowballing rumour with no more substance to it than his attempt to return a pitchfork to its owner, is a villain by accident. Similarly, in *Hyacinth Halvey*, the funniest of Gregory's short comedies, the hero's every deed demonstrates how the fates conspire to justify the glowing but spurious references from which he is attempting to disassociate himself. Misinterpretation forms the basis on which reputations stand and fall—almost as if these short satires were attempting to deconstruct criticism by questioning the dependability of language as a mode of communication. 'Some at least of these accusations', she remarked regarding a variety of attacks on the Abbey, 'must be founded on evidence

[125] R. F. Foster, *W. B. Yeats*; also Ronald Schuchard, 'W. B. Yeats and the London Theatre Societies, 1901–1904', *Review of English Studies*, 29/116 (1978).
[126] *Collected Letters of J. M. Synge*, i. 147.
[127] Lady Gregory, *Seven Short Plays* (Dublin, 1909).

as airy as that given in the case of the murder of Jack Smith [in *Spreading the News*].'[128]

Her tenuous plots added to the effect. In the Chinese whispers of Dublin politics Lady Gregory is just one more indistinct voice indicating her own obtuseness by ignoring the incredible credulity of her characters. The implication was that if the figures in the nationalist forum would only overcome their use of assumption then suddenly differences would evaporate. Unlikely perhaps, but Gregory supplemented the popularity earned for the Abbey by her short comedies with less subtle claims on nationalist audiences.

Her three longer plays of this period, *Kincora*, *The White Cockade*, and *The Canavans*, were confusing for those who took Yeats's posturing to heart. The former two plays are almost demonstrations to Alice Milligan that she could do it better, and indeed Milligan responded with praise and a demand that the press recognize not only Gregory's talent but her objectives also. 'I must say that nothing I have read in recent years seems so wholesome and so good for national propaganda as some of her writing, notably *The White Cockade*.'[129]

This was a statement made at the end of 1906, a year after the split between the Abbey and what had become the Theatre of Ireland. At each point her plays mitigated criticism. *Kincora* was produced soon after *The Well of the Saints*, qualifying the predictable criticism for Synge's play with a unanimously positive press response.[130] 'I really think Kincora a beautiful play,' wrote Patrick Pearse approvingly to Gregory, 'and (though Mr. Yeats dislikes the word) an excellent piece of *propagandism*.'[131]

The White Cockade, which but for the stringent Abbey copyright might otherwise have been destined for the Queen's Theatre, came out in December of the same year, just as the company was becoming more 'Limited' in scope. Although these plays are clearly nationalist— Sarsfield's speech declaring every champion of Ireland as 'a lover of a

[128] *The Arrow*, 1 (20 Oct. 1906).

[129] *Sinn Féin*, 31 Dec. 1906.

[130] Arthur Clery called it 'a pleasant and wholesome change . . . the vigorous product of a healthy mind'. *Leader*, 1 Apr. 1905; O'Grady 'a fine historical drama', *All Ireland Review*, 8 Apr. 1905; Griffith quite reasonably complained that it was too 'Fayish', *United Irishman*, 1 Apr. 1905.

[131] Pearse to Gregory, 29 May 1905. 'I have been trying in An Cleadheamh Soluis to promote a closer friendship between the Gaelic League and the Irish National Theatre and Anglo-Irish writers generally', Pearse continued. 'After all we are all allies. Plays like Mr. Synge's however, discourage me.' *The Letters of P. H. Pearse*, ed. Seamus Ó Buachalla (Gerrards Cross, 1980), 94.

beautiful sweetheart'[132] being a case in point—they are as oriented to a landed-class claim to nationality as Yeats's, the earlier plays of Martyn, or indeed the melodramas that dramatized the 'union of hearts' in the 1880s. *Kincora*, like much Celticist theatre, concentrated on the regal lineaments of Irish culture, the haughty Queen and decorous heroes, while *The White Cockade*, though castigating James II, had as its Cathleen ni Houlihan a dispossessed Catholic marquess. The ex-Countess Cathleen, perhaps, come to rattle her chains at the audience as a reminder that privilege was not of itself un-Irish.[133]

Lady Gregory occupied areas common to Yeats and his opponents, pointing out to both parties the overlap in their objectives rather than the estranged margins. Her own work was part of a process of persuasion that continually underplayed the differences the polemicists chose to heighten, remaining a point of contact between the Abbey and the wider ambit of the revival. She provided links between the Castle establishment, Yeats's aristocratic nationalism, Celticists, the League, and bourgeois one-nation inclusion; partly through her work, and partly though a sympathetic ear. True to her maxim 'To influence people, appeal to whatever is best in their nature',[134] Gregory constantly condescended to complaints about (and from) Yeats and Synge with soothing indulgence. In private, she could be possessed of acerbic disdain; but whereas her co-directors had a talent for controversy, she mollified with equal flair.

Part of the reason that Lady Gregory's assignations did not fall on entirely stony ground lay in her principle of reminding the public of the Abbey's continuing and growing status as a national institution, and in this campaign for understanding she had a boost from an unexpected source. The concurrent political evolution of the ULT would be one more factor adding force to the claim that the Abbey was an agent of cultural nationalism, vindicating the movement through evidence of regional theatrical dissemination.

As a bonus, it was clear that Gregory's ameliorating attitudes had added purchase here. While the power of the Church brushed with the various cultural-nationalist movements, over such questions as secular

---

[132] Gregory, *The White Cockade*, in *Collected Plays*, ed. Ann Saddlemyer (*The Coole Edition of the Works of Lady Gregory*, ed. T. R. Henn and Colin Smythe; Gerrards Cross, 1970), ii. 242.

[133] Gregory's friendship with Lecky would have put her in touch with the Davisite thesis that the 1689 Parliament was 'proof of the tolerance and pluralism of the Jacobite cause'. See R. F. Foster, *Modern Ireland, 1600–1972* (London, 1988), 144, n. 3.

[134] *Diaries*, 260.

education and the issue of compulsory Irish, the political situation in Ulster took on greater importance. Ethnic majority was a source of validation unavailable to nationalists in Belfast, though the founders of the ULT came in a direct line of descent from the caucus showcased in *Shan Van Vocht* and the subsequent popularity Ulster writers had enjoyed on the Dublin scene. The early themes of their plays clearly echoed those of their Dublin counterparts—including the apparent use of *The Enemy of the People*, in Lewis Purcell's *The Reformers* and *The Enthusiast*, and the study of the artist alienated by stifling peasant Puritanism, as in Rutherford Mayne's *The Turn of the Road* (which bore a striking resemblance to Colum's *Broken Soil*);[135] even the treatment given, again by Purcell, to the attractions of Celtic vigour over passive Christianity in his disappointingly wholesome play *The Pagan*.[136]

Following Hobson and Purcell's trip to Dublin in 1902, the nascent company had borrowed plays and players from their southern cousins, but nevertheless sought to strike out and generate material to suit local conditions. The early discussion over the nature of the ULT's remit in their magazine *Uladh* demonstrated that the luxury of militancy would be passed over in favour of the necessities of viability. With less room to manoeuvre, ideological differences were cautiously expressed, and questions of emphasis took on loaded significance. J. W. Good, *Uladh*'s editor, took the line that argued that confidence in regional difference lay at the heart of national strength.

We aim . . . at building a citadel in Ulster for Irish thought and art achievements such as exists in Dublin . . . we shall have our way, though the differences will always be within the generous circle of one nationality, just as one idiom may be, or the different character of the country and the coast, North, South, East or West, may be, and still be Ireland.[137]

Like the language movement, the theatre's best chance was to steer clear of politics: 'Without fear of compromising their political opinions, nationalist and unionist are preparing to co-operate in many things, and not least in literature for the honour of Eire.'[138]

On the other hand, it was argued, if the theatre was also to be 'national' then it should not emphasize its sense of regional difference. As one contributor put it: 'If we accept the broad fact that Ireland, of which Ulster is a part, is a nation, we must recognize that provincial differences

---

[135] Rutherford Mayne, *The Drone and Other Plays* (Dublin, 1914).
[136] *The Pagan* (Dublin, 1907)   [137] *Uladh*, 1/2 (Feb. 1905), 2.
[138] Ibid. 1/1 (Nov. 1904), 17.

will be quantitative rather than qualitative.'[139] These degrees of difference were represented by the familiar stylistic camps: the quasi-historical
Celticism of Hobson's *Brian of Banba*, with its welter of thees and thous
and the strident call 'Who will come to death?' vied with the Ibsenism of
Purcell.

In time Purcell's diligence and superior craft saw his wry realism win
the day. *The Enthusiast* in particular had resonance among those who were
trying to nurture the shoots of green recovery generated by cross-sectarian land and labour issues.[140] T. W. Russell had led a tenant-farmer revolt
against his Unionist masters in Ulster prior to the Land Act of 1903, and
his influence was still being closely watched.[141] The quixotic idealism of
The Enthusiast's protagonist, James McKinstry, attempting to sway
Ultonian farmers toward the cooperative movement, had a satirical
pessimism clear to those who saw it in the early summer of 1905. Russell's
power had waned, but the hopes and misgivings that surrounded the
Sloan-Crawford leadership of the Independent Orange Order and their
Magheramorne Manifesto meant its message remained fresh.
McKinstry's Plunkettesque appeal for a common practical solution to
'this damned division of the people'[142] prefigured Lindsay Crawford's
call for 'a patriotic party with a sound constructive policy' by just two
months. Purcell's play pondered the dangers facing cultural and political
innovation. At the close, McKinstry's enthusiasm falls prey to its own
naïvety, as the meeting he has called merely provides a new battleground
for well-worn conflicts, leaving the hero nursing a sense of futility.

The practical problem of how to nurture such tentative moves and still
treat national issues while remaining in business (the ULT had no subsidizing benefactor) gave rise to a pragmatism which allowed the company
to tackle topical subjects without falling prey to sectarian animosities.
This position could command a more varied constituency as an audience
and thus provide an alternative to McKinstry, with a less brittle enthusiasm and more subtlety. In this the ULT were not alone: on one hand,
Canon J. O. Hannay (George Birmingham), whose novel *The Seething Pot*

[139] 'Connla', ibid. 1/2 (Feb. 1905), 13.
[140] Hagal Mengel, *Sam Thompson and Modern Drama in Ulster* (Frankfurt on Main,
1986), 44–6, argues that the more romantic elements represented propaganda, and these
were 'squeezed out' by 'realistic social satire'. It seems more likely that the social satire
provided a more effective form of propaganda given Northern politics. Hence that fact that
of all the plays the London Dungannon chose to perform it was *The Enthusiast*.
[141] Bew, *Conflict and Conciliation*, 87–107.
[142] Lewis Purcell, *The Enthusiast*, *Uladh*, 3 (May 1905), first performed by the ULT on 3
May 1905.

had similar themes, could be found writing that spring urging T. W. Rolleston to act as a facilitator to get Griffith in contact with Crawford.[143] In a more republican direction, it was necessary to look no further than Patrick McCartan, who wrote to Joseph McGarrity (of Clan na Gael), optimistic about possibilities but realistic about cultural methods:

There was a meeting of the Independent Orangemen last night & they have taken a long stride in the right direction . . . in my opinion with the Gaelic League, like semi-literary, semi-political & patriotic (not perhaps all you or I would like) Dungannon Clubs & the Independent Orange movement the task to join Orange and Green will not after a short time be very difficult.[144]

The close correlation between the emergence of the Dungannon Clubs' new strand of republicanism and the even-handed cultural objectives of the ULT was not merely a matter of overlapping personnel. The realities of Northern politics similarly dictated that republicanism (particularly republicanism rooted in a Protestant tradition), for being more extreme politically, would have to be less exclusive than the constitutional nationalists in Joseph Devlin's Ancient Order of Hibernians (AOH). Unlike the *United Irishman*, which while giving lip-service to a Protestant nationalism had to keep on the right side of Catholic morality, the Clubs had to pursue a line which as well as being more radical was less culturally and more politically oriented.

No doubt Hobson's choice was influenced by his Quaker heritage, but as a consequence the theatre's role in serving the cultural wing of the nationalist cause could be freer and more nuanced. No surprise then, to see Hobson surfacing in the *Nationist*, arguing in November 1905 that 'The New Ulster, Catholic and Protestant . . . are men of new blood, begot of a blending of the races . . . There must be a blending of the ideal and the practical—a high aim.'[145] This goal could only be achieved once there was 'no sectarianism or sectarian systems of education, Catholic or Protestant'. The following January, Colum, spotted by one of the editors as having condemned *The Enthusiast* as 'immoral', was accused of being a 'Propagandist Despot'.[146] The playwright hastily admitted his error: 'I

[143] Andrew Gailey, *Ireland and the Death of Kindness: The Experience of Constructive Unionism 1890–1905* (Cork, 1987), 307–8.

[144] Letter dated 25 Nov. 1905. Joseph McGarrity Papers, NLI MS 17457. McCartan was one of those trained in the Dungannon Clubs who later came to dominate the Supreme Council of the IRB. The letter was written in approval of Bulmer Hobson's article in the *Nationist* (which he was also sending to the *Gaelic American*) referred to below.

[145] 'The New Ulster', *Nationist*, 30 Nov. 1905.

[146] 'The Propagandist Despot', ibid., 4 Jan. 1906.

judged "The Enthusiast" from a wrong standpoint. It is a piece of social satire, and the weariness of the idealist is satirized as much as the prejudice of his neighbours.'[147]

Distance from Dublin helped the Ulster company to minimize the differences that had twice split the NTS, and which probably appeared small beer compared to that between Orange and Green. As well they might. The Abbey plays of 1906 could hardly have been closer to the nationalist model, quickly blunting attacks that followed the split. By the end of the year Yeats could declare that the defensive remit of the new Abbey journal was proving redundant: 'We started the Arrow very largely that we might reply to hostile criticism . . . but we have no new enemies of late, and have played to large and growing audiences.'[148]

The Abbey accomplished this because Lady Gregory continued to produce plays that could be criticized only on an artistic level, while the gap left by Colum's departure was quickly filled by William Boyle. After a popular start with *The Building Fund*,[149] Boyle picked up on the ambiguity and fracture that surrounded the fears of *embourgeoisement* and its potential for compromising nationalism and presented them in his play *The Eloquent Dempsey*. It was a feat that appeared to earn Boyle Synge's jealousy, who had felt himself too noble a nationalist to record the 'horrible and awful . . . groggy-patriot-publican-general-shop-man who is married to the priest's half-sister'.[150]

Boyle restated the case in terms of a publican-councillor playing to the nationalist gallery and the royal box simultaneously, and finally coming unstuck. It was a play which warned of the perils of political Bunburyism;[151] a charge which looked back to questions of co-option implicated in the Local Government Act, the welcome offered to royal visits, and the devolution crisis, and which took on added significance given the Liberals' simultaneous general election breakthrough.[152] Jerry Dempsey,

[147] Ibid., 11 Jan. 1906.   [148] *The Arrow*, 2 (24 Nov. 1906).

[149] *The Building Fund* (Dublin, 1905).

[150] Synge to MacKenna, 13 July 1905. *Collected Letters*, i. 116–17. See also his letter to Yeats, 21 Aug. 1905, ibid. 125–6.

[151] Boyle's character Dr Bunbury was evidently a nod to Wilde, and in Boyle's hometown was a particular favourite. Synge to Lady Gregory, Ma. 1906. Ann Saddlemyer (ed.), *Theatre Business: The Correspondence of the First Abbey Theatre Directors: W. B. Yeats, Lady Gregory and J. M. Synge* (Gerrards Cross, 1982), 121.

[152] *The Eloquent Dempsey* had its debut at the Abbey Theatre on 20 Jan. 1906. Nationalist patrons would have discovered in that morning's papers the accumulating total for the Liberal landslide sidelined for the moment by Joseph Devlin's sixteen-vote victory in West Belfast. *Freeman's Journal*, 20 Jan. 1906.

caught having signed a welcome *and* a condemnation of the Chief
Secretary's visit, is opposed by both parties and forced out of office. In
the end, however, he declines the wages of betrayal in a funny and well-
constructed inversion of Ibsen's ever-popular template, becoming in the
process a friend of the people rather than their enemy. It was a neat ideological point, expressing confidence that democracy could control the
silver-tongued rather than destroy them. 'One word more!' is Dempsey's
motto, but finally he is convinced that the debased currency of nationalist oratory needs to return to the gold standard of action.[153]

If *The Eloquent Dempsey* cast questioning glances at the cake-and-eat-it
politics of constitutional nationalism, Boyle's third play, *The Mineral
Workers*, seems at face value a dramatic interpretation of Griffith's ideas of
political economy. There was still enough room, however, for a few digs at
Sinn Féin's expense while updating Martyn's earlier *Heather Field* discussion of constructive Unionism. Martyn's romance of the land forgotten,
Boyle's Sir Thomas Maguire (with the help of his remigrant engineer
Stephen O'Reilly) plans to excavate the equivalent of Ireland's cherry
orchards with a Lopakhin-like lack of sentiment. The problem revolves
around one stubborn landowner who refuses to join the landowning
consortium, and the various unscrupulous methods employed while they
try to convince him to do so. Kitty Mulroy, a farmer's daughter, is at one
point pressurized to marry the old man—perhaps a reference to Griffith's
prostitution of Nora Burke in the *Shadow* to the ideal of Irish woman-
hood. Yet Boyle always errs on the side of sympathy for the men who are,
after all, trying to get the best out of Ireland, even if as Kitty says, 'they'd
dig the groves of Paradise to bring that gold about them!'[154] And here, no
doubt, as Stephen Gwynn observed, was the reason that Boyle succeeded
where Synge failed—like Dempsey he made sure he played to the gallery.
Unfortunately, just a few months later, this same faith in the crowd would
lead him to a popular error of judgement.

The other directors did little to dispel the genial atmosphere that
prevailed during the close of the year. Yeats's experiments in modernizing the mythological repertoire in *Deirdre* and *The Shadowy Waters* met
with the customary equivocation that his verse quality compensated for a
lack of dramatic tension. Lady Gregory offered up one dreadful experiment in historical slapstick, *The Canavans*,[155] and more tellingly, an incisive one-act tragedy, *The Gaol Gate*.

---

[153] *The Eloquent Dempsey* (Dublin, 1911).

[154] *The Mineral Workers* (Dublin, 1910), 31.

[155] If W. G. Fay actually did (as reports suggest) succeed in making the audience laugh at

Outside the prison, Mary Cahel and her daughter-in-law Mary Cushin, mother and wife of Denis Cahel, wait, mourning their shame: for the word is he has turned informer. The gatekeeper, however, finally informs them that Denis Cahel had kept his council and ensured his execution, and they make for home, triumphant with the news of his heroism. Once again, Gregory used misapprehension as a weapon, unbalancing critics with a tragedy in which the bitterness of triumph is as much a reproach as the dangers of gossip. There was no doubting the visceral nationalism the playwright employed, daring the Abbey's attackers to misconstrue its message and the theatre's agenda. But the audience was impressed. With a sixpenny pit replacing the shilling minimum (not to mention the addition of a 'cheap new tea room')[156] the debut performances of *The Gaol Gate* and *The Mineral Workers* on 20 October 1906 were given to a crowded theatre. Joseph Holloway's diary heralded 'the era of success'.[157]

Meantime, the National Players struggled and drifted, and despite some success with old Alice Milligan and new Seumas MacManus pieces, *The Hard-Hearted Man* remained their most potent play. The Theatre of Ireland, too, was in abeyance. After a valiant stab at the first act of Ibsen's *Brand*, the group had to come to terms with the fact that Colum had wandered off and James Cousins had dried up, and fell back on reprising *The Racing Lug*. With the Gaelic League placated, a suspicious quiet hanging over the offices of *Sinn Féin*, and the *Leader* in abatement, it was unnaturally quiet. Unsurprising, perhaps, that a restive Yeats found himself alienating his co-directors with a plan for the cosmopolitanization of the theatre (in a late reprise of the debate in 1898).[158] The urgency that had surrounded the cultural-nationalist movement, subsiding in the face of the Liberals' control of power and a general tailing-off of millennial excitement, seemed to indicate there was going to be a conserving of energy for the long-haul politics that beckoned.

Yet the lull was at least in part due to the fact that Synge had had no new play performed for almost two years. With *The Playboy of the Western World* in rehearsal, the controversy-hungry poet need not have worried that Boyle's contented image of cultural excavation, or Gregory's pacifications,

---

(or with) the Elizabeth I impression scene, that would be testament enough to his comic genius. Lady Gregory, *The Canavans*, in *Collected Plays*, ii.

[156] *Leader*, 27 Oct. 1906.

[157] *Holloway's Abbey Theatre*, Sat. 20 Oct., 72.

[158] Yeats's call for verse speakers and foreign masterpieces found more subborn resistance in Synge and Gregory. Saddlemyer, *Theatre Business*, 175–202.

would continue unchallenged. Mary Cahel, at the end of her closing speech at the gaol's gate, cries with pride: 'The child he left in the house that is shook, it is great will be his boast in his father! All Ireland will have a welcome from him, and all the people in Boston.'[159] But Synge had imagined a different boast, and a different reception.

[159] *The Gaol Gate*, in *Collected Plays*, ii. 10.

4

The Room of Mirrors: The Debut of The Playboy of the Western World

The morning following the first performance of his new play, J. M. Synge wrote to Molly Allgood: 'It is better to have the row we had last night, than to have your play fizzling out in half-hearted applause. Now we'll be talked about. We're an event in the history of the Irish stage.'[1] *The Playboy of the Western World*, in accordance with its author's evaluation, remains as a text permanently situated in the context of its first performance, dominated by its status as gauge of the national mood in Ireland, January 1907. But Synge's words of encouragement for his actress-fiancée display a confidence born of intent. The *Playboy* was and remains intimately engaged with the response it first engendered because it was designed to do so. The Abbey staged a play; but Synge had created an *event*.

Synge was more direct than most about the purpose of his drama. Recalled W. G. Fay: 'He said to me bitterly one night, "the next play I write I will make sure I annoy them." And he did. As soon as I cast eyes over the script of *The Playboy of the Western World* I knew we were in for serious trouble.'[2] Lady Gregory and Yeats also had serious misgivings, but despite their success in trimming some offensive material away during rehearsal, Synge guarded his script 'like a tiger with its cub'.[3]

It is the play's reception that says most about the subtlety of the way in which Synge orchestrated the famous response. Lady Gregory's telegram to Yeats declaring all well ('Play great success')[4] after the first act passed without demur, indicated more than her combined nervousness and over-optimism—it showed an acute underestimation of the play. Given that contemporary criticism concentrated on Christy Mahon's

[1] *The Collected Letters of J. M. Synge,* ed. Ann Saddlemyer, i. *1871–1907* (Oxford, 1983), 285.

[2] E. H. Mikhail (ed.), *J. M. Synge: Interviews and Recollections* (London, 1977), 48.

[3] Lady Gregory to W. B. Yeats, 12 Jan. 1907, in Ann Saddlemyer (ed.), *Theatre Business: The Correspondence of the First Abbey Theatre Directors: W. B. Yeats, Lady Gregory and J. M. Synge* (Gerrards Cross, 1982), 205.

[4] *Our Irish Theatre* (London, 1913), 67.

The Room of Mirrors

parricidal proclivities, it also introduced an intriguing anomaly. It was in the first act that the young stranger, finding himself in the Flaherty shebeen, had revealed he was guilty of murdering his father. So why the cordial reception?

Part of the reason was the way in which that secret is extracted from Christy. This takes the form of a catechism that runs through the gamut of crimes both political and domestic in a process of elimination.

PHILLY. Maybe the land was grabbed from him, and he did what any decent man would do.

MICHAEL [*to Christy, mysteriously*]. Was it bailiffs?

CHRISTY. The divil a one.

MICHAEL. Agents?

CHRISTY. The divil a one.

MICHAEL. Landlords?

CHRISTY [*peevishly*]. Ah, not at all, I'm saying. You'd see the like of them stories on any little paper of a Munster town.[5]

The interrogation alludes to poverty as a result of 'broken harvest and the ended wars', thereby socially contextualizing theft, and ends with a hopeful suggestion that the young Mahon might be guilty of treason after 'fighting bloody wars for Kruger and the freedom of the Boers'.[6] Synge delicately asserted that the expectations of his Mayo community naturally reflected their closest concerns. Offering a catalogue of possible crimes, the examples chosen by Christy's inquisitors are—aside from the perennials rape, fraud, and bigamy—acts of resistance criminalized by the state. By doing so they acknowledged the political concerns of those in the theatre audience anxious for a play with an overtly nationalist message, for whom such issues would be foremost in their minds.

Synge's Mayo peasants' attitude to law saturated in class and colonial conflict is so hostile as to render illegality in general as laudable. Even Christy's frightened confession, 'I killed my poor father',[7] meets with acclamation rather than condemnation. He is swiftly taken on by Michael Flaherty as pot-boy for Pegeen's protection, on the rationale that 'the

---

[5] Synge, *Collected Works*, ed. Alan Price (London, 1966) iv. 69, 71.

[6] Ibid. 71. The Boer War reference was possibly inspired by Arthur Lynch, a Paris acquaintance of Synge's, who had returned from the war having won the Galway parliamentary seat in absentia. He was arrested and convicted for high treason (the last man condemned to be hanged, drawn, and quartered), but had his sentence commuted to life, and was finally released after serving only four months. W. J. McCormack, *Fool of the Family: A Life of J. M. Synge* (London 2000), 309; Donal P. McCracken, *The Irish Pro-Boers, 1877–1902* (Johannesburg, 1989), 107.

[7] Synge, *Collected Works*, vi. 73.

khaki cut-throats' will be kept at bay and 'the peelers is fearing him'.[8] Adroitly squeezing out the comic irony implicit in this inversion, Synge maintained an atmosphere sensitive to nationalists at the same time as highlighting that element of the absurd which carefully signposted the performance as artifice. 'Now, by the grace of God, herself will be safe this night, with a man killed his father holding danger from the door.'[9]

Considering that the sheepish piety of Shawn Keogh opened the act and it closed with the sexual jealousy of Pegeen and the Widow Quinn, eyebrows must have been raised. Add to this the suspicion in which Synge was already held by the nationalist contingent, and it is the ability of the playwright to contain his audience that impresses. After Act 1, Synge, like Mahon, had taken in his audience, and been taken in by them. Lady Gregory's telegram fitted well the protagonist's happy exit line, 'I'm thinking this night wasn't I a foolish fellow not to kill my father in the years gone by.'[10]

The audience would have been alert to the allegorical possibilities of the situation Synge was in the process of engineering. The notion that the killing of the father might be taken as a symbol of national rebellion was not without precedent. Arthur Griffith had used the same image in 1899 while criticizing John Eglinton for suggesting that modern Ireland was an offspring of the Union: ' "John Eglinton" is no true genealogist, and if the child cannot breathe and live in peace whilst the old man lives, does it not seem to be her part to knock the old man on the head?'[11]

Similarly, given exposure to the frequent symbolic use of the 'bard' as an instrument of social upheaval in Yeats, Colum, and Hyde as well as in Synge, Pegeen's crucial pointer, 'I've heard all times it's the poets are your like, fine fiery fellows with great rages',[12] would have piqued audience anticipation. One critic ('H.S.D.') afterward pondered the possibility of an obscure Moranite reading, with Christy as a kind of *über*-West Briton who woos, with ever-improving *rameis*, the soft-headed locals into admiring his attack on the fatherland. He remained unconvinced: 'Perhaps it is an allegory, and the parricide represents some kind of nation-killer, whom Irishmen and Irishwomen hasten to lionize. If it is an allegory it is too obscure for me. I cannot stalk this alligator on the banks of the Liffey.'[13]

The critic was closer to bagging an exotic quarry than he imagined;

---

[8] Ibid. 75.   [9] Ibid. 77.   [10] Ibid. 93.

[11] *United Irishman*, 10 June 1899, countering an essay by John Eglinton, 'On Regenerate and Unregenerate Patriotism', in the Dublin *Daily Express*.

[12] Synge, *Collected Works*, iv. 81.

[13] 'H.S.D.', *Evening Mail*, 27 Jan. 1907. Quoted in James Kilroy, *The Playboy Riots* (Dublin, 1971), 13.

but that he had been tempted to embark on this particular paperchase was hardly surprising. Synge left plenty of clues. At the start of Act II, Christy recounts to an inquisitive female audience the story of his crime, with added embellishment and exaggeration. To a crowd with a heightened political and cultural consciousness, whose criticism of drama often included the importance of 'holding the mirror up to nature', it was a scene that commanded attention. 'Didn't I know rightly I was handsome,' remarks Christy to his reflection, 'though it was the divil's own mirror we had beyond, would twist the squint across an angels brow, and I'll be growing fine from this day.' Then, disturbed in his act of reappraisal, Christy is mocked for his poorly hidden inversion: 'Well, I never seen that to this day, a man with a looking-glass held to his back.'[14] Such hints that genre and form were facing change were also reflected in the dialogue. The following retelling of his tale, recast as a melodrama complete with clichéd confrontation in tableau (' "God have mercy on your soul," says he, lifting a scythe; "or on your own," says I raising the loy.'), elicits a knowing recognition of fiction and the forms fiction takes. 'That's a grand story', interjects Susan. 'He tells it lovely', agrees Honor.[15]

At this point in time the audience at the Abbey endorsed the judgement of these two young women, responding generously to the burlesque calibre of Synge's, as of Christy's, tale. Metadramatic[16] and autobiographical elements of the *Playboy* have already received considerable critical attention, as has the Fanonesque quality of Christy's progress to independence.[17] But the combination of these elements with Synge's experimentations in audience manipulation forces the reader to reconsider the implications of the play. The *Playboy* becomes a critique of the theatre and the playwright (or playboy) and his relationship to the community, both personal and social in nature; and in extending his drama beyond the stage to the auditorium, Synge reaches into the realms of the truly avant-garde.[18]

---

[14] Synge, *Collected Works*, iv. 95. Declan Kiberd, *Inventing Ireland* (London, 1995), 176–7.   [15] Ibid. 103.

[16] Mary C. King, *The Drama of J. M. Synge* (London, 1985).

[17] See Declan Kiberd's reading of the *Playboy* as a tale of post-colonial liberation, 'J. M. Synge—Remembering the Future', which construes the play's finale as upbeat synthesis. *Inventing Ireland*, 166–88. For an equally illuminating focus on the irreconcilable elements of Synge's oeuvre, see Seamus Deane, 'Synge and Heroism', in *Celtic Revivals: Essays in Modern Irish Literature, 1880–1980* (London, 1985), 51–62; and *Strange Country: Modernity and Nationhood in Irish Writing since 1790* (Oxford, 1997), 143. The two approaches generate a fruitful dialectic.

[18] For a conceptual framework of the avant-garde as a critique of art's complicity in a culture of acquiescence, see Peter Bürger, *Theory of the Avant-Garde* (Manchester, 1984).

In his autobiographical writing, Synge concentrated on the spiritual and intellectual violence of his rebellion against the axioms of his strict Protestant upbringing. As if trying to personify a proto-modernist crisis of identity, he first found his earlier beliefs overturned by Darwin.[19] So involved was his religious and political identity in 'unreasoning loyalty',[20] his revelation implied a class and cultural consciousness which demanded a change of national allegiances. 'Soon after I relinquished the kingdom of God I began to take real interest in the kingdom of Ireland.'[21]

Constantly aware of his mother's bitter disapproval, his search for redemption informed his study of Irish and his apprenticeship in Celtic studies with De Jubainville, who became a personal friend.[22] Dabbling in Parisian bohemianism, Synge could bathe in the streams of international socialist thought, finding affinity in Marx and Morris, and in the modern currencies of French writing.[23] As a result, radical elements in cosmopolitan culture acted as a conduit through which the young writer could pass into an active role in Irish cultural nationalism. If it was Yeats that pointed the way to the Aran Islands in 1896, he was acting as a catalyst to, rather than the originator of, a change in Synge's personal chemistry. As Daniel Corkery later put it: 'It was Synge's European learning enabled him to look at Irish life without the prejudices of the Ascendency class coming in the way . . . Europe cleared his eyes of the fogs of prejudice, not entirely of course.'[24]

That 'not entirely' was a caveat of some significance, since Synge found class-consciousness came bound with an alienation and an anger. The notion that Synge's European exploits would do anything but confirm his Anglo-Irish penchant for defamation did not occur to many of his critics at the time. Synge, for his part, was frustrated by petty-bourgeois nationalism, annoyed at the League's policy of standardizing Irish, and impatient with the conservatism of the Catholic Church. If he had rebelled against and rejected the reactionary elements of his world using the weapons of modern thought, why could not other Irish nationalists overturn their conventionality? Sometimes that irritation could still

---

[19] McCormack records two reactions to Darwin, one at 15, the second a more mature and more profound reaction in his mid-twenties. *Fool of the Family*, 41–3.

[20] Synge, 'Autobiography', in *Collected Works*, ii. 10, 13.   [21] Ibid. 13.

[22] McCormack, *Fool of the Family*, 240.

[23] David H. Greene and Edward M. Stephens, *J. M. Synge 1871–1909* (rev. edn. New York, 1989), 52–77. Also Kiberd, *Inventing Ireland*, 175.

[24] *Synge and Anglo-Irish Literature* (Cork, 1931), 38.

sound close to old prejudice: at his most 'volcanic',[25] Synge looked
forward to a figure who would succeed where he had failed. Underscoring
the significance of his own familial rebellion, he wrote in response to the
Gaelic League's part in the popular umbrage taken at his play, a wild
letter 'Can we go back into our Mother's Womb?' (which remained unsent
and unpublished):

> I believe in Ireland. I believe the nation that has made a place in history by seven
> centuries of manhood . . . will not be brought to complete insanity in these last days
> by what is senile and slobbering in the doctrine of the Gaelic League . . . they dare
> not be Europeans for fear the huckster across the street might call them English.
>
> This delirium will not last always . . . some young man . . . will sweep over the
> backside of the world to the uttermost limbo this credo of mouthing gibberish . . .
> will teach Ireland again that she is part of Europe.[26]

Emulation of that avatar in the *Playboy* hinted at an allegory of liberation through generational revolt, a theme that had been troubling the
Abbey peasant for some time. H.S.D.'s notion of a 'nation-killer' might
also be a 'nation-builder', through precisely the convergence of influence
that critic found objectionable. Paradoxically, the play was judged 'absurd
and un-Irish', the product of decadent 'literary flaneurs of Paris' and yet
through this medium spoke 'the living breathing Irish peasant'.[27] Synge's
play left in the background the external forces of colonial oppression to
focus on the internal fissures that disturbed the notion of Irish Ireland
unity. The generational friction characterized by Christy's revolt was
reinforced by a domestic division of labour—'toiling moiling, digging,
dodging from the dawn till dusk'[28]—specifically relating to the impact of
emigration and indigenous ownership of the land. A new generation of
European revolutionary ideas were cousins of the native communism of
the Western Isles; conversely the structures of capital and possession
condoned in bourgeois nationalism were closely related to the imperialism that fostered them.[29] Social conservatism was part of a culture of
acquiescence Synge wanted Ireland to revolt against, just as he had.

---

[25] An epithet used by Synge's close friend Stephen MacKenna to describe the otherwise
mild-mannered playwright's extremes of temper. His portrayal of Synge as 'a most rabid
politician' provides a useful counterpoint to Yeats's depoliticizing portraits. His remarks
were made following an NLS discussion led by Maurice Bourgeois, 'J. M. Synge's Life in
France and his Relations to French Literature', reported in the *Freeman's Journal*, 23 Jan.
1912.   [26] Synge, *Collected Works*, ii. 399.
[27] Kilroy, *Playboy Riots*, 13.   [28] Synge, *Collected Works*, iv. 83.
[29] See e.g. the Marxist flavour of Synge's comments on Aranmore: 'It is likely that much
of the intelligence and charm of these people is due to the absence of any division of labour,
and to the correspondingly wide development of each individual.' *The Aran Islands* (Oxford,
1979), 106.

Besides the class conflict, another source of energy available to such change was the overcoming of low morale through lower morality; liberation through sexual and romantic attraction from an enervating passivity overtly connected with Catholicism—a dynamic applicable to women as to men. Christy's love for Pegeen, and hers for him, is thus the flip side of their energetic independence of mind, and freedom from the tyranny of expectation.

Christy gains the attention and acceptance of the village, learns the tricks of narrative and flattery, negotiates the Scylla of Shawn Keogh's material bribery and the Charybdis of Widow Quinn's sexual pragmatism. Halfway through the play he seems on course to win Pegeen, having struck a common chord of isolation as much as of action (notably, in the scene following Pegeen's brusque reaction to his female admirers, when they use the word 'lonesome' nine times in a brief exchange).[30] But Christy's easy passage is interrupted by the appearance of his notably alive father. In allegorical terms, the playwright's melodramatic crowd-pleaser receives an unwelcome dose of realism.

Padraic Colum's account of that first night attributed the mood-swing after the successful opening act to this manifestation of the elder Mahon, which disturbed the suspension of criticism brought on by the comic genre. 'That scene was too representational. There stood a man with a horribly-bloodied bandage upon his head, making a figure that took the whole thing out of the atmosphere of high comedy.'[31]

Maire Nic Shiublaigh, who considered the play an act of retaliation amplified by direction, agreed. After the first act's 'laughter at the right places', tension began to build in the second half. The comic tone was augmented by a darker mood, 'played seriously, almost sombrely, as though each character had been studied and its nastiness made apparent'.[32] Arthur Griffith, who weighed in against the play with customary gusto, made one of his central charges the use of outrageous language in this same scene; that it resulted from his mishearing the phrase 'dirty stuttering lout'[33] does not divert the impression that the sudden advent of Old Mahon produced a swift change in aspect.

The appearance of the father has two important elements. In the first place, it places limits on the effectiveness of personal revolt. The blow

[30] Synge, *Collected Works*, iv. 109–11.
[31] *The Road round Ireland* (New York, 1926), 211–12.
[32] *The Splendid Years* (Dublin, 1955), 81–2. A point well made by Nicholas Grene, *Synge: A Critical Study of the Plays* (London, 1975), 144.
[33] *Sinn Féin*, 2 Feb. 1907.

from the loy has not produced a surgical severance from the past: on the contrary, history is stalking our protagonists (Christy and Synge) to future confrontation. Secondly, it darkens the lines of allegory to become indistinct from the sombre itinerant realism. Synge is giving his attack on complacent idealization of the peasant new figurative definition; the elder Mahon is no longer an abstract. The brutal metaphors that underpin so much of the dialogue are here given dramatic presence and begin to hit home, 'as if', in Sheehy-Skeffington's words, 'the author had set himself to find out exactly how much his audience could stand'.[34]

At the beginning of Act III Christy's father enters, and sits with dramatic inevitability at the back of the shebeen. He embodies an incursion of the actual into Christy's parallel universe of heroic deeds and poetic romance. 'On the stage,' wrote Synge in the introduction to his play, 'one must have reality, and one must have joy, and that is why the intellectual modern drama has failed, and people have grown sick of the false joy of the musical comedy, that has been given them in place of the rich joy found only in what is superb and wild in reality.'[35]

Peasant speech, Synge argued, combined Mallarmé and Huysmans with Ibsen and Zola, 'as fully flavoured as a nut or apple'—and sometimes rather stronger: 'the wildest sayings in this play are tame indeed compared with the fancies that one may hear in any little hillside cabin in Geesala'.[36] Having given this defensive forewarning, the denouement prepared to combine the combustible elements into the fully-fledged representation of this heightened reality. Prior to this explosive moment, Synge kept the tension high, with Christy's success in the sports tempered into dramatic irony by his father's slow recognition. Through the celebrated love scene, in which Christy's poetic diction reaches its ripest flavour, impending discovery gives that added quality of beseeching to the lovers' hopeful intimacy. Happiness is tantalizing, as Synge enjoins the audience both with memories of his dramatic horsemanship (*Riders to the Sea*) and poetic lepping.

It is not the return of Christy's father who breaks the spell, however, but the return of Pegeen's. Darkly hinting at the mind-forged manacles Synge is about to rattle, Michael James Flaherty enters, singing, 'The jailor and

---

[34] *Irish Times*, 28 Jan. 1907. 'The hostile demonstration, manifestly spontaneous and sincere, was thoroughly justified', concluded Sheehy-Skeffington, though he added that the public should judge for themselves.

[35] Synge, *Collected Works*, iv. 53–4.

[36] Ibid.

the turnkey | They quickly ran us down'.[37] He then proceeds to defy the audience to contemplate tolerance of the lovers' potential marriage. His provocative description of the wake, 'six men, stretched out retching speechless on the holy stones',[38] marks the beginning of the play's finale, in which violent retaliation against the reality of violence on stage is extended to the auditorium. Michael '[*loudly, with horror*]' reminds the onlookers of the crime which they have so far condoned by their silence. 'You'd be making him a son to me an he wet an crusted with his father's blood?'[39]

The deposed fiancé Shawn dare not defend the honour of the community with an energy rooted in the same soil which produced Christy's, despite repeated prompting from the sidelines. Likewise Synge urges his audience to put off the timidity taught them by the constraints of commerce and religion. 'Take the loy is on your western side',[40] instructs Michael ambiguously. Shawn having fled in terror, Pegeen's father relents, apparently with enough of the West awake in him to want to see the isle peopled with 'little gallant swearers'.[41]

Offering briefly this drift toward romance, the play is again brought back to reality by the return of Old Mahon, and the swift disillusion and condemnation he brings with him. The indomitable symbol of the playwright's past returns to claim as his own the child of his time and tradition. Synge/Christy retaliates with confidence in the weapons of genius and unconventionality, promising to repeat the act of independence in a further flouting of natural law.

CHRISTY. If I am an idiot, I'm after hearing my voice this day saying words would raise the topknot on a poet in a merchant's town. I've won you racing and your lepping and . . .
MAHON. Shut your gullet and come on with me.
CHRISTY. I'm going but I'll stretch you first.[42]

Confident that his act will restore him to the confidence of the community, Christy is oblivious to the inevitably outraged response. He writhes like Proteus, changing form (donning drag as Widow Quinn instructs), but unable to escape the grip of the paradox of unconventional performance. The onlookers, desperate to leave the pattern of their lives undisturbed, can do nothing other than implicate themselves in the same 'treachery of law'[43] against which at the outset they had conspired to

---

37 Ibid. 151.   38 Ibid.   39 Ibid. 153.
40 Ibid. 157.   41 Ibid.   42 Ibid. 165.
43 Ibid. 173.

harbour Christy. 'If we took pity on you, the Lord God would maybe bring us ruin from the law to-day, so you'd best come easy.'[44]

The *Freeman's Journal* gave a report of the first night which still burned with indignation at 'this unmitigated protracted libel . . . this squalid offensive production'. This protraction, and the evident concentration of opposition to the play as the intensity of the final scene drew to its climax, is clear in its account:

He [Christy] pursues his father, apparently again beats him, and is followed in by the peasants, who proceed to tie him with a rope. The audience had stood this revolting story thus far. Now angry groans, growls, hisses, and noise broke out while the pinioning of Mahon went on. It was not possible—thank goodness—to follow the dialogue for a time. Mahon springs forward and bites the leg of one of his captors—his rival Shawn. The girls and others rush in with the father, now in his shirt sleeves and brandishing a weapon. A brutal riotous scene takes place. The groans, hisses and counter cheers of the audience drowned the words[45]

'A brutal riotous scene takes place.' The critic seems impervious to the wider dramatic irony of this phrase, which falls with such appropriate ambiguity between on- and off-stage activity. The 'great gap between a gallous story and a dirty deed'[46] had been revealed, as the transformation from auditor to eyewitness generates revenge—but is instantly closed again by the play in performance, when the gallous story *is* the dirty deed, creating its parallel audience reaction.

The *Freeman*'s report establishes the significance of the language not as an isolated instrument of provocation, but as the medium of unbearable action.[47] Lady Gregory's celebrated second telegram ('Audience broke up in disorder at the word shift')[48] created then and since a Cloonesque distraction from a more complex defensive outrage. The sexual limpidity of Christy's metaphor was no doubt of itself a violence to the image of peasant piety, and could only function as such in the context of a series of perceived calumnies built around the celebration of parricide. Yet the protestations only really took hold when the villagers take hold of the playboy with a hostility appropriate to this crime. The audience brutally reject Synge as author while their anger, bought to boil through calculated provocation, is given vent at the precise moment in the play that conservatism insists on betrayal, by society, of the artist. The Abbey became a room of mirrors; the audience part of the drama, ironically shouting down the action that they themselves perform.

44 Synge, *Collected Works*, iv. 169.
45 *Freeman's Journal*, 27 Jan. 1907.
46 Synge, *Collected Works*, iv. 169.
47 Grene, *Synge*, 145.
48 *Our Irish Theatre*, 67.

The seed of redemption in this process of self-abrogation is contained in the matching aura of failure that pervades the play's closing moments. The hard-headed Old Mahon returns once again, this time to be conclusively commanded by his transformed son. As he leaves, Christy addresses the assembly: 'Ten thousand blessings on all that's here, for you've turned me into a likely gaffer in the end of all, the way I'll go romancing through a romping lifetime from this hour to the dawning of the Judgement Day. [*He goes out.*]'[49]

Thus Synge snaps his fingers in the face of the audience, just as he did in front of his interviewer the following week, not caring 'a rap'.[50] But the final note is Pegeen's cry, 'I've lost him surely',[51] and in any version of the *Playboy* played with its darker side to the fore,[52] it is this note that carries the dominant theme. In this despondency can be heard the vertigo of alienation, the 'lonesome' condition of detached privilege experienced by Synge in his second visit to the Aran Islands; where community is that 'place and dignity from which we are shut for ever'.[53] Following the selfless dedication of the love scene Christy puts a comic mask and a brave face on tragic estrangement. Pegeen's cry is all the keener, put in the mouth of Molly Allgood, the Catholic actress to whom Synge wrote love letters with an attitude at once adoring and patronizing.[54] (Contrast this with Yeats, who in *Cathleen ni Houlihan* had with such confidence seen Maud Gonne in the role of Ireland personified.) Unlike the more optimistic *In the Shadow of the Glen*, this time the hero fails to get the girl. Neither does Christy's reunification with his father symbolize any profound sense of progress. He is not destined for a life of permanent revolution spurning bourgeois creature comforts,[55] but a simple reversal

---

[49] Synge, *Collected Works*, iv. 173.

[50] *Dublin Evening Mail*, 29 Jan. 1907. Quoted in Mikhail (ed.), *Synge: Interviews and Recollections*, 37–41.

[51] Synge, *Collected Works*, iv. 173.

[52] Subsequent productions of the *Playboy* were not only radically edited, but tended to be played with the emphasis on comedy. As W. J. McCormack has noted: 'Until the Lantern Theatre productions by Liam Miller in the 1960s, the harsh irony . . . seems to have been sedulously avoided.' McCormack, *From Burke to Beckett: Ascendancy, Tradition and Betrayal in Literary History* (Cork, 1994), 239–40.

[53] Synge, *Aran Islands*, 145.

[54] See *The Collected Letters of J. M. Synge*, ed. Ann Saddlemyer, i–ii (Oxford, 1983–4).

[55] As is suggested by Kiberd, *Inventing Ireland*, 175, 184. G. J. Watson's point that Synge experimented with a version which resulted in Christy's 'reversion to his father's cowed slave' is relevant here—Synge's portrayal of reaction toyed with utter failure before deciding on hollow success. *Irish Identity and the Literary Revival: Synge, Yeats, Joyce and O'Casey* (Washington, 1984), 80. Cf. also Synge, *Collected Works*, iv. 172, 173–4, for Saddlemyer's selection of alternative endings.

of the familial labour relations which first drove him to violence. His isolation, as he forces his 'heathen slave'[56] before him, renders him socially redundant as an agent of change.

Shawn Keogh and Pegeen burn Christy with the 'lighted sod', a symbol of an intense and exclusive collective identity rooted in the soil.[57] Their action and repeated threat to 'scorch' his leg echoes his refusal to beg for acceptance: 'what did I want crawling forward to scorch my understanding at her flaming brow?'[58] Synge has been scorched by his failure to relinquish in entirety that element of his Anglo-Irishness Corkery insisted on, to find acceptance in the community he serves. Yet though it is his condescension which marks him as defamatory, it is the revolutionary potential of his unconventionality which has caused his rejection. The fault, as well as the loss, is mutual.[59]

In the midst of manifesting his greatness as a playwright, Synge confesses failure by forcing divorce from his audience: an avant-gardist recognition of the paradox of artistic complicity. A sense of political impotence can force the artist either into ever greater arrogance until trapped in dead-end individualism, or into seeking refuge in a non-threatening institution of art.[60] In forcing the point to departure, however, the collaborative nature of the ensuing 'riot' suggests a common space which revitalizes form as a revolutionary agent. Exhausting genre toward conclusion, the first *Playboy* was not completed in comedy, melodrama, allegory, or tragedy but in the realms of the carnivalesque, baiting the audience into an ironic contribution.[61] The carnival of reaction generated on both sides of the proscenium partition blurred that boundary, as the

---

[56] Synge, *Collected Works*, iv. 169

[57] This was a politically familiar symbol: in the Land War protestors carried burning sods.

[58] Synge, *Collected Works*, iv. 169.

[59] Deane, *Celtic Revivals*, 53. Terry Eagleton's phrase 'Oedipal children of Ascendancy' works with obvious appositeness in relation to this dialectic. *Heathcliff and the Great Hunger: Studies in Irish Culture* (London, 1995), 235–40.

[60] Bürger, *Theory of the Avant Garde*, 26–7, and Terry Eagleton's use of Bürger in evaluating the Revival's revolutionary potential in his chapter 'The Archaic Avant-Garde', in *Heathcliff and the Great Hunger*, 273–319.

[61] For application of Mikhail Bakhtin's notion of carnivalesque to the play, see George Brotherton, 'A Carnival Christy and a Playboy for All Ages', in Daniel J. Casey (ed.), *Critical Essays on John Millington Synge* (New York, 1994), 126–36; and Nicholas Grene, *The Politics of Irish Drama: Plays in Context from Boucicault to Friel* (Cambridge, 1999), 107–8. Synge's carnival was not dramatic, but theatrical, however, and considered in this tradition, Synge's legacy is as significant for Artaud's Theatre of Cruelty—see Christopher Innes, *Avant-Garde Theatre 1892–1992* (London, 1993)—as for the more obvious (and self-aware) heir of his poetic peasant drama, Lorca.

principal players became Christy and the Abbey crowd, or their equivalents Synge and the shebeen locals, as the drama expanded into the theatre.

In the immediate aftermath, this obscure optimism was inevitably lost in the very oppositions it relied upon for effect. The spontaneity of 26 January soon became organized protest, as Fred Ryan later recalled:

Afterwards . . . it was very difficult to get a fair judgement. The first-night demonstration had set up prejudices and currents of feeling. Men, hearing that the peasant, as it was said, was maligned in the play, came to hiss; others, in order to protect, as they thought, the challenged freedom of the theatre, came to support. Others, again, hearing the peasant was maligned, came to applaud the malingers.[62]

The reports in the *Irish Independent* and *Freeman's Journal* during the following week, that cries of 'Sinn Féin' and 'Sinn Féin Amhain' could be heard from the protesters, imply that a proto-Sinn Féin combination of National Council and Cumann na nGaedheal support constituted the forty or so hardcore anti-play occupants 'forming a body on the right-hand side of the pit'.[63] *Sinn Féin* had certainly had its long opposition to the Abbey confirmed; Griffith declared blankly: 'Mr. Synge's play as a play is one of the worst constructed we have witnessed. As a presentation on the public stage it is a vile and inhuman story told in the foulest language we have ever had to listen to from a public platform.'[64]

Old enmities were resumed. Yeats had returned in time for the second performance and quickly took up the arguments he had used over *In the Shadow of the Glen*. As then, Synge, feeling ill, quietly took a back seat and left Yeats to mastermind the controversy. By the end of the week he had placed a suitably poetic ad in the papers claiming the nationalist moral high ground.

> He who strikes at
> Freedom of Judgement
> Strikes at
> The Soul of the Nation[65]

But this had already been undermined by Yeats's inability to resist his own sense of superiority. The protestors, he remarked, had 'no books in their houses'.[66] Observers in turn pictured him forth as a malevolent

[62] *Eye Witness*, 1 Feb. 1912.   [63] *Evening Herald*, 31 Jan. 1907.
[64] *Sinn Féin*, 2 Feb. 1907.   [65] Ibid.
[66] *Evening Telegraph*, 29 Jan. 1907.

creature, 'perched, like Poe's raven, upon a privileged staircase at the side of the stage'.[67] The impression of the Abbey as cultural battlefield was reinforced when W. G. Fay invited in the police on the second (Monday) night, and the following day when Lady Gregory drafted in Trinity undergraduates. Segregated by price (they sat in 3s. stalls, the nationalists in the 6d. pit), the antagonism became vocal combat, as the students competed with 'A Nation Once Again' by drunkenly intoning 'God Save the King'.

Playing out the dangers implicit in the *Playboy*'s end, Art and Audience had apparently dug in along the familiar lines of Irish cultural conflict.[68] The directors' marshalling of the forces of law and disorder became as great a focus of objection as the play itself. The following two evenings saw the worst disturbance, as Synge's delicate balance gave way to a reversal of roles. 'A scene of tumult ensued. The players in the orchestra sought safety for themselves and their instruments, and the characters on the stage crowded to the footlights to see the fun. The comedy on the stage was therefore stopped, and the comedy across the footlights was hilarious.'[69]

Escalating anger, though carried by organized protest, proved popular and infectious. Those arrested included stirred-up neutrals like Colum's father as well as agitators like Piaras Béaslaí. In court the next day, Yeats was again the visible face of the Abbey, as he gave evidence against Béaslaí (though not the elder Colum, who the directors did their best to protect),[70] who wanted to force the issue 'to the utmost extremity' for added political impact. 'They would then have the spectacle of a man brought to the police court for making a protest against an outrage on Irish nationality.'[71]

The severity of the legal response was not even, however. When Mr Wall KC replaced Mr Mahoney as court judge the next day, he showed less indulgence to the prosecutor Mr Tobias and Inspector Flynn. Reducing the standard fine to 10s. (Colum's father had been fined 40s.), Wall argued that the question of blame for the disturbance was far from clear-cut:

[67] *Irish Independent*, 31 Jan. 1907.

[68] David Cairns and Shaun Richards, 'Reading a Riot: The "Reading Formation" of Synge's Abbey Audience', *Literature and History*, 13/2 (Autumn 1987), 219–37.

[69] *Irish Independent*, 30 Jan. 1907.

[70] Colum was particularly grateful to Robert Gregory, whose 'prompt assistance' had saved his father from a night in the cells. Letter to Lady Gregory, 1 Feb. 1907. Berg.

[71] *Evening Herald*, 30 Jan. 1907.

It might be well to consider on the part of the Crown whether those who persisted in bringing forward theatrical procedure of such a character as to excite popular odium and opposition, and which could not be tolerated at all events in Ireland, where practically there were two worlds, one wishing to be at the throat of the other, and one wishing to avoid what the other wished to obtrude—whether those who were responsible for that should not themselves be brought forward.[72]

Wall's suggestion hinted at a renewed debate on the issue of an Irish censor, available to establish a legal framework for accommodating conflicting Irish sensibilities. But the suggestion, which was supported by the unionist press as much as nationalist, bespoke a broad consensus rather than factional interest. Here was the moral majority, rising up to subsume warring factions in confident conservative opinion; making ready to draw the sting of Synge's drama by keeping the 'two worlds' separate where he had forced them one into the other. Yet in doing so they also illustrated the playwright's point that such assertions were not merely of Ireland, but the international language of pious denial. If D. J. O'Donoghue argued that the public had to act as its own censor in the absence of an independent authority,[73] Alice Milligan attempted to prove a similar suggestion by pointing out that 'even the most brazen playgoers . . . require expurgated editions of Shakespeare'.[74]

A *Freeman's Journal* editorial brought the issue back to its political context, arguing that caricaturing and criminalizing the Irish were old methods of justifying repression.

Grossness of the language is, of course, an offence to be condemned. But the calumny on the Irish people, of which the play is an embodiment, deserves still more condemnation. Let us remember this calumny runs on old and familiar lines. It has ever been the custom of traducers of the Irish people to charge them with sympathy with all sorts of crime. Over and over again the same lie has been made the justification for coercion.[75]

It was an argument which, naturally, implied constitutionalist acceptance of the law as it stood. As such it rather begged the question whether such coercion might in turn be considered as likely to criminalize justifiable acts of resistance. The expectant questioning in the opening scenes of the *Playboy* was here revisited, with that impatient anticipation of criminal resistance performed by 'any decent man'. 'New' nationalists might read the *Freeman* and ponder it in terms of their frequent criticisms of self-satisfied MPs taking on the values of the parliament they

---

[72] Ibid., 31 Jan. 1907.   [73] *Freeman's Journal*, 4 Feb. 1907.
[74] Ibid.   [75] Ibid., 29 Jan. 1907.

were supposed to resist. The issue of for whose benefit Ireland's image was being idealized remained germane. If, as J. B. Yeats had suggested in 1903, Ireland was to climb out of the dock, the first step would not be defence but the refusal to recognize the court; to shift the paradigm as Synge had done. In time, physical-force nationalists would become sensitive to such implications. More immediately, the irony insisted that Yeats once again stray onto his opponents' turf, to stand indicted by the standards established by the play. Publicly contemptuous of calls for censorship, he defended the Abbey's actions on the basis that Synge's 'very new and harsh' vision was in the process of gaining quick acceptance,[76] but glossed over the quick bowdlerization he and Lady Gregory had performed in order to make the play more palatable. Just as recourse to an alien system of law had been a measure of acquiescence in the *Playboy*, the decision to rely on police protection struck another note off the play's resonance. Yeats chose to ignore the implications of having the DMP secure the peace (for which he was happy to take the credit), an elision easily exposed by Moran, who mordantly found 'Head-Constable Yeats a little reckless in the use of his "loy" '.[77]

Moran remained even-handed in his abuse, however, commenting that mainstream papers at the forefront of shoneenism could hardly cast aspersions: ' "Stone the 'Playboy' and let 'Kitty Grey' go free" is evidently the motto of the "Freeman"!'[78] Ever anxious to needle Griffith, he also conceded that (if unwise) the 'Abbey Theatre people' had indicated a certain 'pluck' in fighting the matter out.[79] As this indicated, opinions were not as simply demarcated as first appeared. Some commentators condemned both parties. Padriac Colum stated what many held to be self evident, that 'Police protection is the last thing with which an Irish theatre should wish to be associated', but also contended that 'the opposition . . . only prevented sane criticism'.[80] One Mary Costello wrote to the *Irish Independent*, appealing for a self-regulating discipline to restore order. 'We are becoming violently serious and self-centred', she warned. 'If this new development is not checked by a strong patriotic hand— which must be from among the powerful Gaelic movement—it will soon spread . . . turning patriotism into hysteria.'[81] Although this was wishful

[76] *Irish Independent*, 1 Feb. 1907.   [77] *Leader*, 30 Mar. 1907.

[78] Ibid., 9 Feb. 1907.   [79] Ibid., 30 Mar. 1907.

[80] Ibid., 31 Jan. 1907. Privately Colum wrote to Gregory offering to speak with Yeats 'on the freedom of the theatre . . . if it would be of any advantage' during the debate scheduled for the end of the week. He failed to do so, and one can only speculate that discretion proved the better part. Letter to Lady Gregory, 1 Feb. 1907. Berg.

[81] *Irish Independent*, 2 Feb. 1907.

thinking, it was echoed by an article (in Irish) in *An Claidheamh Soluis* which suggested that Yeats should have treated the disturbances 'as an internal dispute among Irish Irelanders, to be settled by them alone'.[82] Patrick Pearse had, in his editorial, advocated a boycott rather than a prevention of the production: the *Playboy* was 'not a play to be howled down by a little mob. It was a play to be left severely alone by all those who did not care to listen to it.'[83] Not always Pearse's supporters, the Keating Branch of the League found itself in sympathy with this line, the majority finding Yeats's appeal to liberal sensibilities more attractive than his method of reinforcing them.[84] The observation that the whole event, as far as Irish speakers were concerned, was outside the domain of the League, would have been persuasive. As Pearse put it, 'both [sides] are of Anglo-Ireland; wherein the true Gael, "who sees life steadily and sees it whole" may find a certain satisfaction'.[85]

This position in the League lends further weight to the evidence that it was a Griffithite group which provided most of the organized disruption, an impression compounded by voices closer to the Sinn Féin position who also took issue with their methods. In particular, criticism came from Bulmer Hobson's Belfast-based journal, the *Republic*, which presented the Dungannon Clubs' emerging line in its short life from December 1906 to March 1907. Bulmer Hobson would have been careful in setting out a stall distinct from the position held by Cumann na nGeadheal, as the Dungannon Clubs manoeuvred toward the alliance of April 1907. But the position also indicated that there was no simple correlation between nationalist conviction and the anti-play policy; and that in view of differences over the conservative goal of a return to 1782, Hobson may also have concluded that Griffith's opposition to the *Playboy* was further evidence of a lack of vision. The close connection between the Clubs and the ULT, combined with a more specifically political nationalism, fashioned a greater tolerance for the Abbey's misdemeanours.

Whatever may be the demerits of Mr. J. M. Synge's comedy, 'The Playboy,' we may confess we are not greatly enamoured of the new fashion in criticism that last week turned the Abbey into a bear garden . . . If the Ulster Literary Theatre satirized Orangemen, Nationalists would be up in arms should the lodges wreck a performance; but apparently Mr. Synge's burlesque of Irish peasant life can only be refuted by a strenuous application of a strong hand . . . the Abbey is purely the

---

[82] Noted and trans. by Declan Kiberd, *Synge and the Irish Language* (London, 1979), 235. Kiberd's speculation that Leaguers rather than 'Nationalists' were responsible for the protest (247) seems at odds with the evidence he presents of the Gaelic League's position.
[83] Ibid. 250.   [84] Ibid. 253.   [85] *ACS*, 9 Feb. 1907.

toy of a coterie. It has a perfect right to make experiments in its own fashion with national material drawn from Irish life, to claim a fair hearing for them . . . We who believe in Sinn Féin demand liberty of speech and liberty of thought, not merely for ourselves, but for every man and every party in Ireland.[86]

Such liberality was partly borne out of the drastic sense of cultural conflict that was evident every day in Ulster, beside which the Playboy 'riots' were minor indeed. Synge's artful display of boundary disruption spoke volumes to those operating cultural programmes in the pre-partitioned North. If Dublin divisions, such as they were, could offer no platform for dissidents whose views were no great distance from the central tenets of nationalism, what hope had the ULT, battling in the chasm between the Ancient Hibernian and Orange Orders?

If such a disparity of views indicated that a defence of the theatre without recourse to police action might have been possible, Yeats was taking no chances, realpolitik was the order of the day. With over fifty representatives of the DMP outnumbering the core protestors by Wednesday night, and stiff fines being imposed by day, the organized attempt to stop the play was forced into retreat. In an effort to avoid arrest, Thursday's fifth-night performance was disturbed only by synchronized coughing and sneezing fits.[87]

For those who like to puncture the self-importance of the central protagonists, such phenomena provided endless opportunities to lampoon 'the comedy across the footlights'. Not only the tragic elements of Synge's play found their echoes in the auditorium. Festive encounters played a descant to the disharmonies of the brooding central theme— sometimes literally, as the odd bugle call was heard above competing anthems, and drunken students attempted to amuse the crowd by murdering old tunes on the theatre piano. Yeats's patronizing manner was no exception; his regular bulletins to the press, had, the *Evening Herald* declared, also their 'comical side':

These read like notices posted outside the residence of some great man down with fever or the fashionable appendicitis. 'The audience was a little better tonight; they were less fevered, and rested a little between the acts.' Or, 'Visible improvement in the condition of the audience this evening. They were quite coherent, and recognised many fine passages in the "Playboy". On leaving they were able to stand and swallow a little nourishment.'[88]

[86] *Republic*, 7 Feb. 1907.
[87] 'Was It Influenza?', *Irish Independent*, 1 Feb. 1907.
[88] *Evening Herald*, 1 Feb. 1907.

'It is only the catastrophes of life that give substance and power to the tragedy and humour which are the two poles of art', wrote Synge.[89] The open debate arranged for the evening of Monday 4 February was the final act in a definitive controversy. Inevitably it operated, like the previous week's events, between those Syngian poles, with the serious discussion barely containing a general unruliness that was in constant danger of 'developing into hilarious farce'.[90]

Yeats, continuing the theme of fracture between artist and audience so forcefully generated in the play, made a speech of lip–curling disdain. Apparently anxious to provoke no less a furore than Synge (still conspicuous by his absence), Yeats's polemic seemed intent on twisting his attitude into the very caricature his critics had painted. Recounting a story of a priest in Liverpool who had apologized to an audience which had shown disapproval, he vaunted the directors' pedigree: 'They had not such pliant bones, and did not learn in the house that bred them a so suppliant knee.'[91] His defence of the *Playboy*, made later in the proceedings, drew further comparisons. The plot, he suggested, operated around the attractive vitality of the playboy as opposed to Shawn Keogh's alternative, 'docile to Father Reilly', exemplifying the degenerate deference evident in both the Liverpool priest and the Abbey audience. The obvious parallels bespoke the tendency of later events to echo the play's central themes: but Yeats, inevitably, had articulated only one side of the play's dialectic of estrangement.

Given his invocation of the Ascendancy, Yeats's description of the police as 'the means which every community possessed to limit the activities of small minorities who set their interests against those of the community' was ironic indeed. His warning against the 'tyranny of clubs and leagues' lost force through its wilful perversion of existing power relations and distinct echo of Unionist rhetoric.[92] It was hardly consistent with his own appeals to the audience of the basis of his nationalist credentials, including involvement in the Wolf Tone Commemoration and his authorship of *Cathleen ni Houlihan*. As Sheehy-Skeffington argued, the opportunity for firmer defensive ground had been lost by the failure to 'enlist the support of the public rather than the support of the garrison'.[93]

[89] Note (i) from notebook, 1908, in *Collected Works*, ii. 350.

[90] Dublin *Daily Express*, 5 Feb. 1907.

[91] *Freeman's Journal* report, 'Parricide and Public: Discussion and the Abbey Theatre', 5 Feb. 1907.

[92] The similarity of Yeats's terms to the *Irish Times* editorial (29 Jan.) condemning 'the organized tyranny of clap-trap patriots' may not have gone unnoticed.

[93] *Freeman's Journal* report, 'Parricide and Public', 5 Feb. 1907.

Against a backdrop of general approbation, seven speakers attacked the play and the Abbey both. The critic W. J. Lawrence proved the most articulate, wisely insisting on the first night as a true measure of the play's outrageousness. Yet his speech, perhaps with a complacency born of consensus, shied away from tackling the issues in any depth. Denouncing the play with a conservative eye to the decencies of the stage, he, like his fellow indicters, fell back on audience sincerity as a measure of conclusive criticism.

But the minority had their voices too, given room by the pro-*Playboy*, ex-*Irish Peasant* editor and chair for the day, 'Pat' Kenny.[94] Forceful defences of the *Playboy* were made. One insisted that as author of *Riders to the Sea*, Synge deserved the benefit of the doubt. J. B. Yeats continued to demonstrate support for the besieged playwright, despite attempts to shout him down, delivering a mischievous speech casting Ireland as a land of 'plaster saints' and Christy as a positive role model. Daniel Sheehan, a medical student and 'a peasant who knew peasants', echoed those sentiments with an interpretation that shocked several of the audience into leaving: 'The point of view [he suggested] was not the murder at all (hisses), but when the artist appears in Ireland who was not afraid of life (laughter) and his nature (boos), the women of Ireland would receive him (cries of 'Shame' and great disorder).'[95]

Such occasional and incisive readings indicated the wide space that could be taken up between the pit censors and Yeatsian politicking. These were the elements whose response to the play best correlated to the playwright's, finding frustration in the mutual conservatism of the apparently opposing poles. Sheehy-Skeffington, in calling down a plague on both houses, spoke for those alienated by both sides. He and Fred Ryan, in their effort to maintain the momentum won by *Dana* and the *Nationist*, launched their new monthly the *National Democrat* that February. The editorial of their second edition found it 'intolerable that a band of persons should invade a theatre, not to judge the play or to pass judgement, but to . . . prevent others hearing the piece'. But the ambiguous behaviour of Yeats was equally unprepossessing. 'To crown the whole absurdity, Mr. Yeats admitted the hissing was justified by excising, after the first night, some of the passages that were hissed, though this did not prevent his declaiming about the iniquity of "bowing the knee" to clamour.'[96]

[94] Kenny had made a forthright defence in his review of the first night, declaring 'I cannot but admire the moral courage of the man who has shot his dreadful searchlight into our cherished accumulation of social skeletons.' *Irish Times*, 30 Jan. 1907.

[95] *Freeman's Journal* report, 'Parricide and Public', 5 Feb. 1907.

[96] *National Democrat*, 1/2 (Mar. 1907).

This stance recalled Ryan's criticism of Yeats's recourse to clerical approval over *The Countess Cathleen*: his rationalism demanded consistency. Even when they shared the negative opinion of the play, the left-leaning littérateurs were also alert to the danger of indulging nationalist clubs whose politics had to be viewed with a critical eye. Ryan again called attention to Griffith's foreign policies, at that time applauding the 'courage and wisdom' of the Kaiser and the militarists of 'Der Flottenverein' for their attacks on German socialists.[97] 'Every jingoism, it seems, is noble but the jingoism of England', observed Ryan dourly, condemning Griffith's position 'as reactionary as the similar attempt some years ago to link [the Irish cause] with French chauvinism and Monarchism'.[98] As if to underline the internationalist point, Ryan was soon to depart to Cairo for a two-year stint co-editing *The Eygptian Standard* for the nationalist leader Mustafa Kamil.[99]

The *National Democrat* strove to make its readership aware of the perils of submerging different interests in a conservative nationalist vision. The opening editorial had expressed its concern that 'There are, it is to be feared, too many in the Nationalist ranks today who regard the attainment of Irish autonomy either as an end in itself, or, if a means to an end, to the establishment of a conservative regime, supporting and supported by ecclesiastical and capitalist hierarchies.'[100] To guard against such dangers, it was essential to 'cultivate in the people a consciousness of the social needs and remedies'. This required both 'a clear recognition of [the] international solidarity of democracy' and 'an imperative need in Ireland for freedom of speech and opinion'.[101]

If the editors could not quite make the leap from their radicalism to that implicit in the *Playboy*, their contributors could. 'Conventionality' came under attack, most noticeably from ex-Abbey seceders.[102] Thomas Koehler found the on- and off-stage counterpoint, arguing that Synge and Christy displayed parallel examples of liberation essential to a nation with ambitions to independence. The argument bore a striking resemblance to Synge's unsent letter to the Gaelic League.

---

[97] *Sinn Féin*, 2 Feb. 1907.

[98] *National Democrat*, 1/3 (Apr. 1907).

[99] Terry Eagleton, *Crazy John and the Bishop and Other Essays on Irish Culture* (Cork, 1998), 254.

[100] *National Democrat*, 1/1 (Feb. 1907).   [101] Ibid.

[102] See also A. Lloyd, 'Patriotism and Drama', ibid. 1/2 (Mar. 1907). For the appropriate freight of the term 'conventionality' in the context of theatre as a 'convention', see the discussion in the introd. by Raymond Williams, in his *Drama from Ibsen to Brecht* (London, 1958).

Such a modern Firebrand [Synge] . . . suddenly cast into the midst of conventional circles in Dublin was bound to cause an explosion . . . We pride ourselves that our country in its struggle for national individuality is in the full tide of the movement that has been making itself felt everywhere in Europe during the past century. And yet the little incident of Mr. Synge's play goes on to show that the lightest impact of an idea, not only current, but rampant in modern Europe, sets our minds in such a commotion that we scarcely know what we are doing . . . behind the by-play and the frivolity, behind the cynicism and the whimsicalities, there lies a very definite principle, and something that is of supreme importance to a people claiming their rights as a nation. It is this, that no laws or conventions can restrain the natural or fundamental instincts of humanity.[103]

Just as the play found in the combined act of provocation and self-criticism a defiant radicalism which challenged the pessimism inherent in its manifestation of alienation, so such readings elevated the element of rebellion in the *Playboy* into its central message. The publisher of the play, George Roberts, writing in the *Shanachie*, gave this paradox an Arnoldian gloss; 'a continued retreat from the actual', he suggested, 'is at the basis of [the Gael's] nature, at once his strength and his weakness, and often the mainspring of his action'.[104] He had, perhaps, observed in the play, in Synge, and in the audience, a more general impulse to find in the rejection of this world a preferable one. Time would tell whether it might be possible for the more progressive elements in nationalism, in facing the violent implications of realism, to recoil into the future rather than the past. For the moment (January 1907) the *Playboy* was situated in its status as an occasional piece, defined by the complex dynamics of a performance of audience as well as actors, in turn defining those dynamics in time. As Roberts said: 'It is because Mr. Synge has discovered and revealed this so supremely that his plays are as typical and as representative of Irish life as it is possible for drama to be.'[105]

---

[103] 'T.G.K.', 'The Island of Sinners', *National Democrat*, 3 (Apr. 1907). Koehler, a solicitor and theosophist, and key to the Theatre of Ireland's break with the INTS, was, like Roberts, part of George Russell's circle, which makes this defence of Synge all the more remarkable.

[104] 'A National Dramatist', *Shanachie*, 2/3 (Mar. 1907), 58.

[105] Ibid.

5

'The Loy in Irish Politics',[1]
1907–1909

The sensitivity to social and political nuance displayed in the *Playboy* lived long in the mind of nationalist Ireland. Despite the bitter criticism Synge's play received, topical activity in cultural-nationalist circles continued to suggest almost uncanny parallels. One such was offered by a natural heir to those organs of the left-literati alliances that had sprung up in the preceding years. The *Irish Peasant* staggered from its Kilkenny home after a bruising encounter with the Church, in which Cardinal Logue had threatened censure and the paper's proprietors backed down.[2] A week after the *Playboy* riots it took refuge in the more varied political atmosphere of the metropolis, where W. P. Ryan, now owner as well as editor, re-established it as the *Peasant and Irish Ireland*. His first editorial mused on the role newspapers might perform in encouraging social rejuvenation:

Can they play an exalted part in modern life, or in that Irish life which to us is the most interesting part of humanity? Can they really stir the faith and enthusiasm of men and women? In the rush and burden of the day can they be made an artistic expression of truth, of human drama, of national mind and feeling and fortune?[3]

The *Peasant*, like the *United Irishman* before it, continued to consider the need to 'stir the faith' and 'the artistic expression of truth' to be part of a single ambition closely allied with the realization of national identity. Yet Ryan's tone, which highlighted the demands modernity would make on the fourth estate, betrays the thoughtful approach that would in time draw the editor into conflict with 'Official' Sinn Féin as well as the Catholic Hierarchy. His social conscience and anticlerical inclinations, particularly in the sphere of education, put the *Peasant* in the tradition of

---

[1] *Irish Nation and Peasant*, 17 Sept. 1910.
[2] Virginia E. Glandon, *Arthur Griffith and the Advanced Nationalist Press 1900–1922* (New York, 1985), 21–2.
[3] 'The Press and the Nation', *Peasant and Irish Ireland*, 9 Feb. 1907.

'rationalist' press championed by his namesake in *Dana* and the *National Democrat*, and the 'modernist' Catholicism supported in the *Nationist*.

Ryan's predecessor on the *Irish Peasant*, 'Pat' Kenny, had found in the *Playboy* elements of his own criticisms of Irish Ireland philosophy, which he published later that year in *The Sorrows of Ireland*. This tract, rather in the tradition of Plunkett's *Ireland in the New Century*, angered national-ists[4] by arguing that the Irish ought to reform the British Empire from the inside into 'an association of nationalities for the common good'.[5] At the same time, amongst Kenny's celebrations of industrial and agricultural Sinn Féinism and criticisms of political nationalisms, are passages which display insight into the mood of the time. In particular, that of genera-tional frustration finding new political direction:

Thirty years of resolute ruin and organised inanity . . . these are obvious enough even for peasants; and now their sons, at least in the towns, are beginning a new rebellion, against their own tyrannies, which have always been the basis of other tyrannies. A new leaven sets up its ferment in the old mass . . . The leagues live shorter lives, and 'split' into more numerous sub-divisions. We have added phil-ology, folk-lore and economics to the new causes of cleavage . . . As yet it is 'chaos,' but most promising chaos. We are a sociological chrysalis.[6]

In the short term, those familiar with the machinations of nationalist groups might have taken Kenny's observations as evidence that he was losing touch. Far from threatened by 'numerous sub-divisions', the formation of the Sinn Féin League seemed to indicate a growing consen-sus. In April the merging of Cumann na Gaedheal and the Dungannon Clubs stole the march on the National Council, but only until September, when all three joined under the Sinn Féin banner and Griffith's policy.[7] But the IRB-backed clubs still maintained independent views on matters theatrical; and these reflected deep political differences with some subtlety. The final issue of the *Republic* remarked on the first perfor-mance by the ULT in Dublin, held in the Abbey Theatre that Easter. Applauding the move, Hobson emphasized that such points of cultural contact between North and South were still significant means of provid-ing political momentum. 'The gulf that had divided Ulster from the other provinces is due more to the lack of knowledge than to essential

---

[4] Francis Cruise O'Brien, e.g., accused him of moving from nationalist anticlericalism to 'the anti-clerical buffoon of "Saturday Review" Toryism'. *Leader*, 18 Jan. 1908.

[5] *The Sorrows of Ireland* (London, 1907), 71.

[6] Ibid. 67.

[7] Richard P. Davis, *Arthur Griffith and Non-Violent Sinn Féin* (Dublin, 1974), 24–35. Despite their differences, the three organizations had overlapping memberships.

differences of outlook or temperament, and the theatre in striving to bridge that gulf is engaging in a work of vital importance to the Irish nation.'[8]

Whatever their differences, the ULT was performing *The Pagan* and *The Turn of the Road* at the Abbey, and performing a nationalist service.[9] Just as the *Republic* had chimed in with its message of tolerance at the time of the *Playboy*, so the timely appearance of the Northern troupe stressed the fact that hostility to the NTS did not correlate precisely to degrees of nationalism. The Dungannon Clubs, though overtly republican, had a consistently more liberal approach to the arts as a matter of practical necessity, and thus a less aggressive attitude to the organization offering their dramatic sibling a Southern audience.

Hobson's motives in seeking out the *Peasant*, rather than *Sinn Féin*, when he folded the *Republic* showed a similar dynamic. Anxious that the republican ethos of the Clubs should not be swallowed up by the pending amalgamation he realized that if a platform was to be held (or captured) by radical separatism it would have to be outside Griffith's domain. As he wrote to Joe McGarrity, his close political associate in Clan na Gael: 'I have arranged to amalgamate with the Peasant, our name being put on the front page along with theirs. This will give us the Peasant as an organ, & our writers will work for it, & if in a years time we want to start again, we can have the name.'[10]

Theatrical and political alliances owned as much to expediency as to ideology. The republican clubs found themselves allied on the left of nationalism because of practical concerns as much as any positive common commitment: because as a marginal element of a marginal element they had, whatever their ambitions, to 'work for' a paper critical of Griffith's conservative separatism. Similarly, though the ULT went to the Abbey for its performances, Fred and Jack Morrow, the ULT's ex-stage manager and designer, went to work for the Theatre of Ireland when they moved to Dublin.[11]

[8] *Republic*, 28 Mar. 1907.

[9] The ULT performances were organized by Ulsterman and co-founder of Maunsel & Co., George Roberts (as already noted, pro-*Playboy*) with a mind to publishing the plays. According to Rutherford Mayne, Lewis Purcell managed to book the lucrative Easter week because of an oversight on the NTS's part. Rutherford Mayne, 'The Ulster Literary Theatre', *Dublin Magazine*, NS, 31 (1955), 19.

[10] Hobson to McGarrity, 22 Mar. 1907. The name of the *Peasant* (and other organizations and publications in this correspondence) is in transparent code. The first line reads 'I have arranged to amalgamate with the xpgvgwe'. Joseph McGarrity Papers, NLI MS 17612.

[11] Maire Nic Shuibhlaigh, *The Splendid Years* (Dublin, 1955), 89.

A parallel in North–South relations between the ULT/Theatre of Ireland and the *Republic/Peasant* evolved, which worked in similar ways in relation to the Abbey and Sinn Féin. In both cases groups of lesser mass united to offset the orbital pull of the dominant organization. In the case of the Clubs and the *Peasant*, however, one of the properties they used to keep Griffith's influence at bay was a more open cultural mind— and this would continue to have positive implications for the Abbey. The liberal dimension of the *Republic*, partly evolved through their own theatrical experiment, was an element which recommended it to the ambitions for cultural uplift Ryan had in mind.

A couple of years ago some of those keen and earnest spirits gave us a taste of their quality in *Uladh*, a periodical of real distinction and ability . . . Towards the end of last year several of the same eager band gallantly started a weekly organ of national and literary thought, the *Republic*. They are now deep in the engrossing work of the Sinn Féin League, and the labour of a weekly paper is too much . . . It has been decided that the *Republic* will be incorporated into our paper. Thus our readers will gain further national and literary thought and more Ulster news generally.[12]

The *Peasant* thus broadened its base both geographically and ideologically. If as much a process of coalescence as an attempt to offset Griffith, this nevertheless introduced a radical critical combination that competed with his ideological influence. The implications for Irish Ireland attitudes to the theatre were positive, as the broad church of the *Peasant*, if still critical, was at least less condemning than Griffith's disappointed hostility.

The feeling was, to all intents and purposes, mutual. The Abbey directorship's long-standing policy of saying one thing regarding political drama and acting another remained. The ULT was made welcome. The visit allowed the host a little reflected glory, made a quiet case for the benefits to the nationalist community accrued from the Abbey's existence, and at least partially detached it as an institution from the 'house style'. Certainly, those who might attend ULT or Theatre of Ireland productions could still stay away from the NTS's—and be provided with new comparisons by which the Abbey's sink into decadence could be measured. 'There are no theories here,' commented Griffith approvingly of the northern troupe, 'no feeling of the ultra-modern literary school.'[13]

But there was little evidence of 'ultra-modernity' in the NTS's new season either. Principles of 'art for art' could not be followed indiscrim-

---

[12] *Peasant*, 18 May 1907.   [13] *Sinn Féin*, 6 Apr. 1907.

inately while the Sinn Féin boycott had decimated attendance.[14] The directors employed the same strategy against the 'rule of silence'[15] that had brought them through previous crises—playing as many pieces palatable to nationalist taste as possible, which in the absence of Boyle meant digging into Lady Gregory's back catalogue. March 1907 saw the revivals of the *White Cockade*, *The Gaol Gate*, and *Hyacinth Halvey*, along with Yeats's most Catholic-friendly creation *The Hour Glass* and the ubiquitous *Cathleen ni Houlihan*. In terms of nationalist content, the (well-attended)[16] Theatre of Ireland productions of *The Fiddler's House* (Colum's revamped *Broken Soil*) and Milligan's *Last Feast of the Fianna* were less political and a tad stale. In addition to the Abbey opus came new fare from Gregory's stall, *The Rising of the Moon* and *The Jackdaw*, the former of which had already been published and was long anticipated.[17] Continuing the examination of the favourite themes of, respectively, conciliation and misunderstanding, these plays were a timely response to Alice Milligan's open letter in the Dublin press that had called on Lady Gregory 'to exercise due control and not permit the managing directors' advertising tendencies to spoil the high standard of art which up till almost recently has been unmarred'.[18]

Given the events of January and February, Gregory might well have congratulated herself on her continuing reputation as the honest partner in the Abbey triumvirate, building ever more spindly bridges across the divide between artist and society. Her gift for placatory diplomacy was still deployed in minimizing damage and reconciling opposites for the greater good. She had cajoled Yeats back into the fold, maintained her working relationship with Hyde,[19] and written of the directors' responsibility as

[14] Takings figures (dated 21 June 1907) show the post-*Playboy* fallout quite starkly. With a full house of 562 people notionally yielding £32+, week-long runs reliably generated takings of around £50 at the end of 1906. After '*Playboy* week' generated an unprecedented £158. 10s. 1d., this revenue almost halved, bringing in only £24. 19s. 10d. for the last week in Feb., and little more than £30 in early Apr. The drop was even more marked for the two-show performances put on every Saturday between Jan. and May: before the *Playboy*, these averaged £35; in Mar. £17 (despite a fairly successful *Rising of the Sun* debut); by the Apr. barely £10. Frank Fay Papers, NLI MS 10952 (1) (ii).

[15] As Lady Gregory described it to John Quinn, letter 17, Aug. 1907. Berg.

[16] Robert Hogan and James Kilroy *A History of Modern Irish Drama*, iii. *The Years of Synge, 1905–1909* (Dublin, 1978), 185.

[17] *The Rising of the Moon* had been first published in *The Gael* (New York, Nov. 1903); it carries the enthusiasm and conviction of the earlier period, and sat particularly well with the older established elements of the Abbey's nationalist repertoire, of which it quickly became a part. [18] *Sinn Féin*, 2 Mar. 1907.

[19] As if to emphasize the point 3 Apr. 1907 saw the first production of their joint play, *The Poorhouse*, which had first been published in *Samhain* in 1903.

censors. Meanwhile, she continued to effect a practical mediation between Yeats's call for European masterpieces and Synge's commitment to distinctly Irish drama, by producing her Kiltartan-flavoured adaptations of Sudermann and Molière.[20]

The Rising of the Moon was an earlier play, but had a fresh message. Gregory's police sergeant and his Fenian quarry found enough common ground to suspend the dictates of social function and explore deeper roots of a shared culture with inherent nationalist sympathies. Who could doubt those sympathies were shared by those producing a play which depicted a green pimpernel? And even if the directors had drafted in the DMP to quell opposition, might not any one of these men have been happy to join in a chorus of the popular song, given the chance? At the close of the play, the sergeant who had begun talking of duty ends by covering for the escapee. The police uniform might indicate respect for the rule of law, but did not necessarily impel craven obedience to *all* forms of political authority.[21]

To complement this tack, *The Jackdaw* reached further into that world of demented misapprehension visited in *Spreading the News* and *Hyacinth Halvey*, this time precipitated by Nestor Cooney who chooses to donate ten pounds to his struggling cousin by 'buying' a token jackdaw. The absurd ferocity with which the villagers pursue their new-found resource results eventually in the wrongful indictment of the benefactor on a murder charge. A warning against the perils of mass hysteria, *The Jackdaw* had a darker mood than Gregory's earlier comedies, coloured as it was by Synge's combination of depiction and provocation. Gregory's advice to Irish Ireland was to avoid spurious scapegoating and observe her own cool detachment. 'What about the other classes?', she complained in the *Arrow*. She and her friends had admired 'the spiritual beauty' of F. Patrick Dineen's play about souperism, *Faith and Famine*, 'though we believe its picture of Protestant bigotry to be not only a caricature but an impossibility'.[22] The example chosen was telling—F. Dineen, president of the Keating Branch of the Gaelic League, was an old guard advocate

---

[20] Molière's *The Doctor in Spite of Himself*, first produced Apr. 1906; *The Rogueries of Scapin*, Apr. 1908; and *The Miser*, Jan. 1909; Sudermann's *Teja*, Mar. 1908.

[21] The difference between civil and political law was not always so easy to draw, a point which would find surprisingly topical reinforcement when the RIC faced a mutiny over the Belfast strike that year. Later again, Dublin Castle (in Mar. 1912) vindicated Gregory's nationalism by declining to lend the uniforms they customarily offered for theatrical use, on the grounds that ' "*The Rising of the Moon* was derogatory to His Majesty's forces" '. Quoted by Lady Gregory, *Our Irish Theatre* (London, 1913), 60.

[22] *The Arrow*, 1 June 1907.

of Church control over education,[23] and a seasoned opponent of progressive ambitions to make the new university a secular institution. There was a suggestion there that Catholic intellectuals should take care not to be misunderstood as a homogeneous bunch, sharing one set of views and values; if Lady Gregory could take the effort to discern the complexities cultural issues involved, maybe they could reciprocate.

Inevitably, the Anglo-Irishness of the Abbey directorate militated against her protestations—and the overriding implications of social status inevitably belittled differences in the politics of each director's drama. Lady Gregory's uneasiness can be traced to her proselytizing family (a skeleton exposed by George Moore in *Vale*, 1914); taint by association threatened to negate her personal contribution to the revival.[24] The anxiety was piqued now that a similar dynamic seemed apparent in the literary sphere. Lady Gregory's resentment at being tarred with the same brush as Synge and Yeats was understandable, given the decision of the Gort District Council, who refused to accept her charitable donations for local workhouse children.[25] Though she might take solace in the charges of hypocrisy made against the 'self-sacrificing nobility' of the Council from within the republican camp,[26] the deeper implications of their decision provoked her most soul-searching play, *Dervorgilla*. Gregory's sense of having committed an act of betrayal in allowing an English stage-manager (Ben Iden Payne) into the Irish National Theatre had, she said, provided her initial inspiration,[27] but the mix of injury and culpability suggested a tale of unassuageable class guilt.

The intense one-act piece (set in 1193) portrayed Dervorgilla in forgotten old age, reflecting on her legendary crime: with her long-dead husband Diarmuid, she had invited the 'Gall' into Ireland. Now a charitable dispenser of largesse, including the prizes for the children's sports, Dervorgilla first has her conscience raked by a travelling poet, and then her servant Flann (as he attempts to quieten the troublesome bard) is murdered by English soldiers. In the aftermath her secret is revealed and her gifts spurned. One did not have to look far to see the element of self-scrutiny. Services rendered to national theatre as a popular dramatist—

---

[23] For Dineen's exploits, see W. P. Ryan, *The Pope's Green Island* (London, 1912), esp. ch. 10, 'The Fear of Liberal Catholicism', 122–35.

[24] Adrian Frazier, *George Moore 1852–1933* (New Haven, 2000), 390–1.

[25] In a neat connection between the troubles in Gort and her choice of genre, Gregory described the situation to Quinn as being 'like all Irish life, a comedy to those who think, a tragedy to those who feel'. Letter, 17 Aug. 1907. Berg.

[26] 'F.A.' in the *Republic*, 14 Feb. 1907.   [27] *Our Irish Theatre*, 58.

'Look at all the weight of gold the Abbey got from her and the golden vessels upon the high altar'[28]—were rooted in a vain attempt to atone, through acts of cultural compensation, for the original sin of national betrayal.

This was not a simple message of contrition. The tying together of solemnly rejected material charity (in the play) and artistic contribution (of the play) pleaded for the separation of class, cultural, and nationalist agendas. Through the language of remorse Gregory made a claim to common ground. The critique of the Ascendancy offered by Sinn Féin had little in the way of ideological condemnation of privilege or patronage, and nor had this: the purchase of redemption in *Dervorgilla* fails for no other reason than the protagonist's inescapable place in national political history. This was a play petitioning for the right to be bourgeois-nationalist despite the traditions of aristocratic unionism, but with a foreboding of rebuttal on the basis of the 'two civilizations' model of cultural politics. The anxiety that this punishment might be just—and perhaps that her adoption of nationalism had accepted it was just— nevertheless shadows Gregory's appeal. The fear is given form in the Dervorgillian nightmare, as described by this Eve of the Anglo-Irish: 'I dreamt last night that the people knew me, that they knew my story and my sin.'[29]

In the spring of 1907, such thinking seemed ominously appropriate, but by the time of the play's opening night in October less rather than more so. The cultural rejection reinforced by traditional generational rebellion and delivered by what Dervorgilla calls 'the swift, unflinching, terrible judgement of the young'[30] was proving more complex than Moran's crude polarities. Sheehy-Skeffington's 'Dialogues of the Day' were sensitive enough to pick up on more complex realignments once the heightened disputes of the winter had subsided:

'I like your candour,' said the Bookman. 'It makes me sometimes wonder why women want to take part in the farce called politics.'

'To give it some seriousness,' replied the Mere Woman, 'and to defend their interests against idiots like the Oughterard District Councillors, who resolute [*sic*] about the disgraceful state of affairs produced by having "females" as the only teachers in a certain Western parish.'

'Wasn't that the body,' asked the Bookman, 'which condemned The Playboy of the Western World, without either seeing or reading it?'

---

[28] Gregory, *The Collected Plays*, ed. Ann Saddlemyer (New York, 1970), ii. 96.
[29] Ibid. 99.   [30] Ibid. 110.

'Some of these Rural District Councillors,' said the Engineer, 'are badly in need of a fresh democratic element.'[31]

The sense of common cause between engineer, bookman, and 'mere woman' (in antagonism with the Sinn Féin Curate and the Nationalist Barrister as well as the Unionist Baronet) recognized that the northern republicans were not the only nascent militant interest that might disrupt the Irish Ireland happy-family view of advanced nationalism. The 'fresh democratic element' would find form as well as expression in 1908, as the emergence of the IWFL and the Irish Transport and General Workers' Union (ITGWU) questioned the assumptions of conservative nationalist ideology.

That challenge was mounted from the pages of the *Peasant*. The paper's series 'Irish Work and Workers', which had begun life as reportage on the progress of native industry, began to record the discomfort of split loyalty. One anguished Sinn Féiner felt torn between his responsibility to his workmates whose membership of the Amalgamated Society of Railway Servants had improved his conditions, and the clear anti-union message that Griffith had long been espousing. 'On one side my mates consider me a scab, a blackleg; on the other, I'm simply doing my duty as a citizen of the Irish nation. What am I to do?'[32]

The social agony aunts of the *Peasant* would have an important new factor to consider while pondering the response to this entreaty. Christy Mahon, troublesome newcomer incarnate, had found another parallel in James Larkin, who on the eve of the *Playboy*'s first night had stumbled off the Liverpool boat and into the cultural-nationalist shebeen, as the new Irish organizer of the National Union of Dock Labourers. Swiftly taking stock of the reduced circumstances of the unskilled in Belfast, Larkin had by the summer of 1907 marshalled the Dockers and Carters into generating a strike of unprecedented dimensions.[33]

The prospect of Catholic and Protestant labourers combining in an industrial dispute revived possibilities of cross-sectarian working-class unity; but it was a unity which could only be maintained if the drive of Larkin could be matched by leaders in Britain. Once the police mutiny of

---

[31] *National Democrat*, May 1907. The 'Dialogues' had first appeared in the *Nationist* in late 1905. Sheehy-Skeffington then briefly printed them in pamphlet form, before turning to the newspaper pages of the *National Democrat*, the *Peasant and Nation*, and occasionally *Sinn Féin*. Levenson, *With Wooden Sword*, 48–50.

[32] *Peasant*, 18 May 1907.

[33] John Gray, *City in Revolt: James Larkin and the Belfast Dock Strike of 1907* (Belfast, 1985).

late July–August implicated national authority in the dispute, the strikers found that, despite support offered by Lindsay Crawford in the *Ulster Guardian*, and the more grudging encouragement of Tom Sloan and the Independent Orange Order, Larkin could never keep his leader Tom Sexton on side.[34] Without such an agreement or the backing of the TUC, the Belfast dockers could never gain enough consensus within their own organization to take on the RIC, the Shipping Federation, and the British Army. The Ulster working class emerged from the dispute more painfully divided along sectarian lines than ever.[35]

That Larkin should be sent South in defeat, 'out of harm's way',[36] was indicative of the widely held belief that Belfast was bound to be a unique incident in Irish trade-union militancy, just as that city's industrial capacity was unique in Ireland. As long as the class war was limited to Belfast, the advanced nationalist press in Dublin found little need to comment. But there were those who sensed the importance of the northern strike. Sheehy-Skeffington's 'Engineer' had complained that August:

I should have thought . . . that that strike in Belfast was our own business—the business of all Ireland. I should have thought parliamentarians and Sinn Féiners would be vying with each other to show sympathy with the strikers. Yet no prominent man of either party has done so, and the exploitation of the affair has been left to the English labour leaders and the Independent Orangemen.[37]

With the English labour leaders and the Independent Orange Order at the last proving ineffective, the failure of Sinn Féin to support the strike looked all the more like wilful neglect. But if one lesson had been learned by Larkin it was that the conditions which forced down the wages of the unskilled in Belfast—a surplus of cheap labour—were true throughout Ireland.[38] Both the wage differential with British workers and the added militancy which could be harnessed in a country used to land war and

---

[34] The Dungannon Clubs, studiously silent on the strike issue until the police mutiny appraised them of the revolutionary potential of the labour dispute, issued a statement on 2 Aug. 1907: 'The RIC are finding out at last that they are all sons of Ireland before they are the sons of the English government and that, if they strike, it will not be the heads of their brother Irishmen they'll hit.' Quoted in Gray, *City in Revolt*, 131.

[35] Henry Patterson, *Class Conflict and Sectarianism: The Protestant Working Class and the Belfast Labour Movement 1868–1920* (Belfast, 1980).

[36] Larkin's status, as C. Desmond Greaves put it, was 'reduced to that of a wandering trouble shooter'. *The Irish Transport and General Worker's Union: The Formative Years 1909–1923* (Dublin, 1982), 81.

[37] In the last edn. of the *National Democrat*, Aug. 1907.

[38] Despite modest progress, by 1914 unskilled workers in Ireland could still expect to earn wages 25% lower than their British counterparts. Cormac Ó Gráda, *Ireland: A New Economic History 1780–1939* (Oxford, 1994), 238–9.

nationalist organization, lent power to the argument for an Irish labour movement no longer dependent on a less feisty head office based somewhere in England. Out of the Belfast strike came the ITGWU and out of that came a serious headache for Sinn Féin, who would soon no longer be able to dismiss the labour movement as simply another aspect of Anglicization.

And out of the process generally came the *Peasant*'s new mood of enquiry and criticism to trouble the nationalist verities of the IPP and what, with the National Council's consent, had become the fully amalgamated Sinn Féin League. Concomitant with the rise of working-class activity came a changed perception of social ills for which existing nationalist ideology provided little preparation. It was an uncomfortable experience that not surprisingly brought to mind the drama of Synge. One piece of reportage on a visit to 'dirty Dublin' recorded the new reality:

Another matter which disappointed us was the large number of intoxicated women to be met . . . Some vile expressions . . . are introduced into every sentence by a large number. Walking the streets many a word grates on the ear, and let us pray that J. M. Synge may never lay a future plot and dialogue in this city.[39]

Of course Synge had calumnied the West, not laid bare the slums, but that he might take theatre to such extremes was a disturbing notion. And that sense of disturbance was ambiguous—if the journalists at the *Peasant* were still following the course of spiritual uplift recommended by W. P. Ryan at the start of 1907, why were they pre-empting Synge by taking their copy from such insalubrious material? While continuing fractures in nationalist and class interests were exacerbated by generational rifts, the sheer confusion was enough to qualify cultural condemnation. As W. P. Ryan reflected later over the differences of opinion generated by the novels of George Birmingham:

Older Catholic clerics and a Board of Guardians were wroth with him; young priests and Catholic press-men defended him. They did not agree with all the criticism, but they knew that Irish life was a rather complex and comprehensive thing, which very few knew as a whole, and the more delineation of it, the more criticism of it we had, the better.[40]

[39] *Peasant*, 4 May 1907. It is perhaps an idle conjecture that Griffith, to whom housing improvements were the limit of social policy, might have been provoked to such a position by the mere thought.

[40] *The Pope's Green Island*, 43. Birmingham (the Revd J. O. Hannay) came under fire for his series of novels satirizing Irish society, *The Seething Pot* (1905), *Hyacinth* (1906), and *Benedict Kavagagh* (1907). Ryan nevertheless criticized him for being of the 'peace-making Protestant' type (42), who fudged their attacks on the clergy for fear of being labelled anti-Catholic.

It was not so surprising then, to see this ideological leeway reflected in the Abbey's output. The autumn of 1907 saw the first evidence of the withering post-Syngian dramas that would dominate in the next few years. George Fitzmaurice's *The Country Dressmaker*, a tale of interminable wranglings amongst materialist matchmakers and their plans for farmer's daughter Julia Shea, depicted love's young dream 'as the ox going to the slaughter'.[41] The play offered itself as retaliation, heralding the arrival of young blades eager to blunt their realism on any number of sacred kine.

But the bloodletting would have to wait a little while. Though attempting to recast *Cathleen ni Houlihan* as an attack on 'an ignorant, undisciplined bourgeoisie',[42] Yeats was adopting Gregory's more mollifying attitude. No better instance of this could be found than her emasculation of *Where There is Nothing*, which re-emerged as *The Unicorn from the Stars* (or, as *Sinn Féin* dubbed it, *Where There is Less*).[43] The revolutionary nihilism of the original was toned down to reveal a less incendiary philosophy.[44] 'My business is not reformation but revelation', Martin Hearne explains to his flame-blackened followers. 'I was mistaken when I set out to destroy Church and Law. The battle we have to fight is fought out in our mind.'[45] Gregory tempered Paul Ruttledge's anarchistic edge with respectable nationalist devices: his successor Hearne was made an artisan, rather than an aristocrat; the materialist service he leaves is in the pay of the crown; his visionary status defended, if misunderstood, by Father John; he is killed not by a lynch mob, but by the police—and then unintentionally. Gregory had made a play at once more nationalist and less revolutionary—a transformation at which a tiring Yeats declared his 'delight'[46]—a play which betokened the gap opening up between the co-

---

[41] Fitzmaurice, *Five Plays* (Dublin, 1914), 56. Yeats, who thought the play 'much worse' than the *Playboy*, was mystified by a positive reception due partly to a change of mood and partly to the continued absence of more vociferous opponents. Letter to John Quinn, Oct. 1907, *The Letters of W. B. Yeats*, ed. Allen Wade (London, 1954), 495.

[42] Yeats's recasting of the play came in a speech to the NLS, 10 Feb., 1908. Dublin *Evening Mail*, 19 Feb. 1908.

[43] 'Evan', *Sinn Féin*, 30 Nov. 1907.

[44] See Katherine Worth's introd. to the Irish Dramatic Texts edn. of the two plays (Washington, 1987). A detailed history of this collaboration, as of other Yeats-Gregory plays, has been produced by James L. Pethica, 'Dialogue of Self and Service: Lady Gregory's Emergence as an Irish Writer and Partnership with W. B. Yeats', D.Phil. thesis (Oxford, 1987), 206–39.

[45] Yeats, *VP*, 704–5.

[46] The comment was given in the introd. to *The Unicorn from the Stars and Other Plays* (New York, 1908). *VP*, 712.

authors and those keen to pick up the creative baton from the now ailing Synge.

This was further evident in the following spring, when *The Piper* threatened a repeat of the previous year's unrest. The play itself was a case study in the cruel-to-be-kind school of nationalist drama, this time in the guise of historical realism. The action revolved around a fractious group of soldiers retreating in the wake of defeat at the hands of the British. In a state of collective denial, the only one who will accept the truth—that they are 'bet'—is Black Mike, who declares so repeatedly to no avail. Declining his leadership, slowed by their captive and refusing to recognize the peril of their position, they are overhauled and massacred.

Amplifying the dogged declarations of his central character, Norreys Connell (Conal O'Riordan) posited his side of the 'Unended Argument',[47] that in order to progress, Ireland and the audience must resist self-flattery—and consequently should resist the temptation to attack the play's rude honesty. Yeats's (successful) gambit of defending the play by invoking Emmet and Parnell,[48] appealing to the romance of the noble and deserted leader, cleverly embellished this theme with its clear parallels for his own imperious defence of theatrical liberty against the imprecations of the mob. But impressed as O'Riordan was by Yeats's reading, his thoughts were less with the poet's Nietzschian aristocracy of action than with the foot soldier of Fenian rebellion whose lot it was the artist's duty to deglamorize. This did not mean a denigration of patriotic sacrifice— just that it should neither be promoted as *dulce et decorum* nor dismissed as the ugly face of nationalism. O'Riordan wrote:

My friend Yeats sees in black Mike the figure of Parnell . . . But black Mike is not only Parnell. He is many men braver and less fortunate; his bones do not lie in any trim necropolis: they crumbled in rain and wind on the hillsides or in quicklime in the prisonyard. Black Mike is the type of noble fools, who for their country suffered ignoble deaths . . . is the rebel who, placing liberty above the Ten Commandments, is denied by the respectable; but not by me.[49]

Whereas hitherto Yeats had depended on a certain structure of support for his well-publicized disdain for popular nationalism, by early 1908 several props were looking less secure. Relations with Horniman were poor, Synge was ailing, the Fays had left. Sailing closer to the position of

---

[47] The play's full title was *The Piper: An Unended Argument*. Conal O'Riordan, *Shakespeare's End (and other Irish Plays)* (London, 1912).

[48] *Freeman's Journal*, 17 Feb. 1908; Hogan and Kilroy, *Modern Irish Drama*, iii. 215–17.

[49] *Shakespeare's End*, 11–12. This passage comes from the introd., which takes the form of an open letter to Joseph Conrad, to whom the vol. is dedicated.

his closest ally Lady Gregory was the obvious course. And so, even if Yeats chose his models from the nationalist pantheon carefully, *The Piper* affair revealed the signs of continued popular pressure on his public position, being the first fracture in the Abbey's 'apolitical' façade. That he interpreted the play as less radical than judged by its author not only suggested he was critically engaged in cutting the 'burning sod' from political possibility as he had done from the *Playboy*. It made plain in theatrical terms a similar process that was taking place in cultural nationalism—the expansion in confidence of middle-class ideology at the expense of dispirited marginal movements. As a disappointed and disillusioned Frank Fay observed, 'The Dublin people are beginning to fight Yeats with his own weapons. He calls "bourgeois" and they retort "bourgeois yourself".'[50]

It was not altogether surprising that Yeats found a new ally in the *Leader* at this time—Moran had always been a champion of what he considered open-eyed pessimism. William Dawson applauded *The Piper* as 'a plea for fight versus talk, and for the recognition of unpleasant truth rather than indulgence in glorious make belief'.[51] The warmth of this review was no exception. He had already wavered in his observation of the boycott to see *The Country Dressmaker*, declaring that 'Time dulls the sense of injury',[52] while Daniel Corkery gave a glowing appreciation of the Abbey in a series on the 'Institutions of Dublin':

To get the quintessence of the Abbey, you must go to a matinee; there is nothing like it to be had in any city in the world outside Dublin: but this Dublin does not seem to know. There might be thirty present on some occasions, or twenty, or less—but what you felt about the authors, the actors, the orchestra, about everything was: how very kind of them![53]

Such sentiments were not out of place in the *Leader*; D. P. Moran's acerbic flair was fading. The one-time champion of the GAA would soon write without irony that 'football is football, and Rugby, Gaelic,

[50] Frank Fay Papers, NLI MS 10952 (2) (i), letter to W. J. Lawrence, 27 Feb. 1908.

[51] *Leader*, 22 Feb. 1908. Yeats's reputation had also improved as the result of his behaviour at a dinner for Lady Aberdeen: accused of pandering to the Castle, Yeats defended his appearance as an accident which through 'courtesy' he could not escape. Reports then filtered through that he had embarrassed the company by calling for a Catholic university in an after-dinner speech. Moran was most contrite. Ibid., 23 and 30 Nov., and 7 Dec. 1907.

[52] Ibid., 12 Oct. 1907. 'If his [Fitzmaurice's] characters were sordid and unromantic,' he commented, 'they were at any rate human.'

[53] Ibid., 5 Oct. 1907. The account was the result of Corkery's first visit to the Dublin theatre in Aug. 1907. Patrick Maume, *'Life that is Exile': Daniel Corkery and the Search for Irish Ireland* (Belfast, 1993), 20.

Association strike us, outsiders, as merely the same thing governed by arbitrary rules—the thing football is common to all'.[54] Moran was certainly not exhibiting the behaviour of an editor growing in confidence as the Catholic star rose in its zenith; perhaps because the two elements closest to his heart, the Church and the Gaelic League, were increasingly in conflict as education became a focus for projected cultural ambitions. Though the battle for essential Irish in the National University would help the growth of the League,[55] Moran considered that such struggle was alienating precisely that section of society that would be necessary for victory. Early in 1907 he had chosen to urge on the Munster Feis in their bid to woo the big bourgeois into the fold with an air of fatigue, and even regret:

Irish Irelanders have carried about as many positions as possible by crude assault during the last few years . . . we may claim that we led the assaults; but the assaults have been continued long after their utility had ceased . . . Businessmen have to be taken tactfully . . . and the lack of tact is, we fear, one of the chief reasons, if not the principal reason, why the League has not made the progress that might reasonably have been expected in recent years.[56]

This disconcerting occupation of the middle ground seemed to be reciprocated by the staging of W. F. Casey's gentle satires on the urban middle class, *The Man Who Missed the Tide* and *The Suburban Groove*, which appeared among the national theatre's debuts in 1908, and which were welcomed by 'A Bourgeois at the Abbey' as Dawson unashamedly confessed himself to be.[57] Yeats approached on a more symbolic level; *The Golden Helmet* reintroduced the implacable Cuchulain as a self-effacing diplomat striving for equanimity among his friends-if-rivals, offering his head that 'the quarrels of Ireland shall end'.[58] The respect earned from the mischievous spirit (of the nation) gives his hero the prize—but the air of capitulation spoke volumes about Yeats's weariness with the constant confrontations of theatre politics. The mood deepened when Yeats gave notice in *Samhain* that when the Horniman subsidy ended the directors planned 'to hand [the theatre] over to some management that will work it as a business, while keeping its artistic aim'.[59]

---

[54] *Leader*, 20 Feb. 1909.

[55] Shane O'Neill, 'The Politics of Culture in Ireland 1899–1910', D.Phil. thesis (Oxford, 1982).

[56] 'The Gaelic League and the Commercial Classes', *Leader*, 16 Mar. 1907. See also 'The New Idea of the Munster Feis', ibid., 4 May 1907.

[57] Ibid., 22 Feb. 1908. Dawson also confessed he did not know exactly what that meant.

[58] Yeats, *VP*, 251.   [59] *Samhain*, Nov. 1908, 2.

This fatigue was not limited to Moran and Yeats. Confronted by the uphill struggle against Liberal dominance in the post-1906 parliament, and uninspired by the intermediate battles over devolution, the National University, 'essential Irish' as requisite for matriculation to that University, and the latest Land Bill, many of those who had led the field *c*.1899–1900 were beginning to lose ground. Griffith still had confidence in his own staying power, and castigated the Abbey for 'giving it up'[60]— but he too was being closed down.

In particular, the Sinn Féin Policy's broad appeal was beginning to undermine Sinn Féin's political stability. IPP MP C. J. Dolan's switch of allegiance from mainstream nationalism, and the subsequent North Leitrim election, offered hope that frustration would generate a split in the IPP. The defection, however, remained an isolated incident that indicated a power to influence rather than convert. The IPP comfortably retained the seat,[61] and new departures provoked by the pressure of Sinn Féin remained within the auspices of the UIL and IPP, including the AOH—Devlin's shock troops of Catholic consensus—and the left-leaning 'ginger' group of the Young Ireland Branch of the UIL.[62] The latter included Francis Cruise O'Brien, a writer whose regular column in the *Leader* had contributed to that paper's change of direction;[63] along with Sheehy-Skeffington and Tom Kettle continuing the constitutionalist-separatist argument first floated in the *Nationist*. While having sympathies with the Sinn Féin League such groups still considered the longer Westminster route better signposted than Griffith's short cuts to Home Rule.

Still, North Leitrim had provided a tantalizing glimpse of what might be possible. The new party was posed a classic choice between a strong vanguard and a popular base that would provide a better platform on

[60] 'Inanities at the Abbey', *Sinn Féin*, 10 Oct. 1908.

[61] Michael Laffan, *The Resurrection of Ireland: The Sinn Féin Party 1916–1923* (Cambridge, 1999), 29. The IPP secured 72.8% of the vote, but Griffith viewed the contest as an important step in raising the Sinn Féin profile. Nevertheless, a large proportion of the UIL concurred with one of Dolan's most vociferous opponents, and editor of the *Sligo Champion*, McHugh, in regarding Sinn Féin as 'a handful of Dublin cranks'. Ciarán O Duibhuir, *Sinn Féin: The First Election 1908* (Manorhamilton, 1993), 20.

[62] Patrick Maume, *The Long Gestation: Irish National Life 1891–1918* (Dublin, 1999), 63–5.

[63] The tendency to characterize the *Leader* purely on the basis of its more notorious (and usually earlier) excesses serves the model of exponential Catholic militancy but ignores the change of tenor. See e.g. Conor Cruise O'Brien's unnecessary consternation over his father's 'puzzling' contributions in *Ancestral Voices: Religion and Nationalism in Ireland* (Dublin, 1994), 50–2.

which to compete with the IPP. Already enemies were happy to question Sinn Féin's revolutionary credentials. The *Leader*, though easing off on West Britons, continued to pour ridicule on the 'Sham Fenians', aka the 'King, Lords and Commons Party', or (pointing to their previous 'feather bed "revolutionist" President') the 'Martynites'.[64] Attempting to drive a wedge between the radicals and the conservatives in the Sinn Féin alliance, Moran called on the leaders to demonstrate their contempt for British rule by withholding taxes. The new Sinn Féin president John Sweetman's response was not likely to inspire anything but disdain from neo-IRBers or further giggling from Moran and his chums. 'I pay direct Income Tax on my residences. If I were to refuse to pay it, my furniture would be seized for the amount, and I would not be imprisoned, but even if I were imprisoned, how would that help Ireland? I never recommended anyone to get himself imprisoned.'[65]

What Sweetman wanted through defence of his property, the de facto leader Griffith was hinting at through design. His sounding-out of a united front with Nationalists over Irish finances, exploiting popular antagonism to the 'People's Budget', betokened his desire to emphasize common economic ground with mainstream conservatives.[66] *Sinn Féin* had already changed in emphasis from cultural issues to economics, and adopted a less discursive style that signified tight editorial control. While it campaigned aggressively on issues such as essential Irish and the Council Bill, the plays and poems which had festooned the *United Irishman* were largely missing, replaced by long series such as that on List's 'National System of Political Economy'. As in the paper, so in the party, as P. S. O'Hegarty complained to fellow young-blood Terence MacSwiney:

A.G. is not the A.G. of the U.I. Far from it. He has let his mind run to . . . materialistic bread and butter points like Patent acts, and so on, and day by day he disregards more and more of the larger issue . . . I go to every convention and fight like a wildcat on essential points . . . Then someone gets up and asks 'What does Mr Griffith think?' He simply says a few words and they follow him blindly.[67]

---

[64] *Leader*, 14 Dec. and 17 Aug. 1907.

[65] Ibid., 10 Aug. 1907. Moran also drew attention to Sweetman and Martyn's cattle-driven estates, noting that the latter rented land to Lady Gregory's brother, Mr Persse. He recommended she write a play on the issue, 'The Cattle Drive of Tulira', ibid., 21 Dec. 1907.

[66] The keen-eyed Cruise O'Brien spotted what he called 'The Overtures of Sinn Féin' and asked 'Does this resolution indicate a new pacific on the part of Sinn Féin Organisation?' Ibid., 21 Nov. 1908.

[67] P. S. O'Hegarty to T. MacSwiney, 9 Aug. 1907. O'Hegarty was attempting to persuade MacSwiney, who had left the Sinn Féin League, to rejoin and help change it from inside. Terence MacSwiney Papers, UCD P48b/378.

The disgruntled vanguard, denied space in Sinn Féin policy and paper, found their outlet in the *Peasant*. But the *Peasant* was far from hostage to the republicans—responding with more purpose to the urgency of calls to address social grievances and working-class concerns. Throughout the autumn of 1908, while the Abbey was recouping its audience, the recrudescence of labour as a political force, heralded by the Larkin-lead carters' strike in Dublin, provoked a long debate on the relevance of socialism to Irish Ireland. Sinn Féiners like P. S. O'Hegarty might argue that 'class war would play England's game',[68] but were influenced enough by opponents like 'Eoin' and Connolly to concede the need to tackle social ills.[69] Larkin's accusations of the hefty share-ownerships held by Redmond and Sweetman in the Grand Canal Company were comprehensively reported. One bright contributor, reviving the dormant issue of European parallels, observed from the examples of Poland and Germany that nationalists and socialists could form alliances in opposition, but seldom in power.[70] By the close of the year W. P. Ryan, who had once joined Griffith on the industrial committee of the Gaelic League, took the argument to Sinn Féin, and reprinted his hostile lecture 'Has Sinn Féin a Serious Social Policy?' in his last issue of 1908. Labelling them as a reactionary group disguising bourgeois interests under the 'exceedingly pathetic' guise of class conciliation, Ryan suggested they go in the opposite direction from Moran and Griffith to find allies in the lower rather than the upper classes.

There is a serious drawback in the pioneering of Sinn Féin. The pioneers . . . belong mostly to the middle classes, and have a frigidly conservative notion about what they call the rights of property and their own place in what they call the social order—but which some of us consider to be both anti-social and anti-Christian.[71]

The 'frigidly conservative' ethos of the advanced-nationalist right was facing severe disruption from a source rooted in class conflict, a force of a larger ideological nature than that which separated nationalist methodologies. Here was the other side of that modernism coin which feared the greasiness of bourgeois-democratic tills; seeing in popular politics the opportunity to redefine and erase the hypocrisies of establishment moral-

---

[68] *Peasant*, 7 Nov. 1908.

[69] See 'Eoin', 'Sinn Féin and Socialism', ibid., 31 Oct. 1908 and James Connolly 'The Two Sides of Sinn Féin', ibid., 23 Jan. 1909, which stressed compatibility on the national question while attacking Sinn Féin's economic teaching.

[70] Ibid., 14 Nov. 1908.

[71] Ibid., 26 Dec. 1908.

ity rather than complicity in them. As James Connolly would put it in a heady inversion of the Yeatsian view: 'All hail . . . to the mob, the incarnation of progress!'[72]

The trend had the power to impress at least one old advocate of Ascendancy revivalism, in Standish O'Grady. No doubt inspired by his patron, the Kilkenny Owenite Otway Cuffe,[73] O'Grady advocated in his series 'Life and Liberty: Letters to a Dublin Clerk' a radical scheme of agrarian communes which would respiritualize downtrodden scribes and wrest power from profiteering farmers.[74] But if the occasional defender of the landed class might extend his anti-urban proclivities toward sympathy with the city scriveners, in a general mood of *embourgeoisement*, the *Peasant* found few friends among Sinn Féin allies or Ascendancy opponents for its new stance.

Flushed by the success of the revival of *Deirdre* in November, Yeats sensed a new mood abroad in the pit. 'Here and there,' he wrote to his father, 'I already meet a young man who represents something which I recognize as new, and which is not of my time—he is very often a sort of Catholic by the by.'[75] This 'sort of' Catholicism, democratic or modernist Catholicism, was (as Yeats indicated) an aspect of that generational rebellion which contested paternalism in all elements of social interaction and with which the themes of the *Playboy* continued to resonate. The laity would be brought on to a more equal footing with the Fathers, and within the confines of the Roman Catholic Church some young priests found themselves contesting the authority of the Hierarchy, particularly over the role of the Church and Irish language in education.[76]

---

[72] 'Labour, Nationality and Religion: Being a Discussion of the Lenten Discourses against Socialism delivered by Father Kane, S.J. in Gardiner Street Church, Dublin 1910', in *Collected Works*, ii (Dublin, 1988), 410.

[73] For the background to O'Grady's U-turn, his relationship with Cuffe and his sister-in-law Lady Desart, see W. P. Ryan, *Pope's Green Island*, 257–66, 270; and Hubert Butler's essay 'The Deserted Sun-Palace', in *The Sub-Prefect Should Have Held His Tongue, and Other Essays*, ed. R. F. Foster (London, 1990), 35–50.

[74] O'Grady's articles, which appeared in the *Peasant* Nov. 1908–30 Jan. 1909, also earned him the respect of James Connolly, who considered him an unwitting fellow disciple of Fintan Lalor: 'In our day another great Irishman, Standish O'Grady, perhaps the greatest litterateur in Ireland, has . . . urged the formation of co-operative communities in Ireland as an escape therefrom. It is curiously significant how little Irishmen know of the intellectual achievements of their race, that O'Grady is apparently conscious of the work of his great forerunner in that field of endeavour.' Connolly, *Labour in Irish History*, in *Collected Works*, i. 113.

[75] W. B. Yeats to J. B. Yeats, 27 Dec. 1908, in, *Letters*, ed. Wade, 513.

[76] On the antagonism between 'Fathers' and sons over education, see David W. Miller, *Church, State and Nation in Ireland 1898–1921* (Dublin, 1973), 222–6, 242. Miller, however,

The question remained whether the Abbey had resigned its place as part of a critical movement. Not, it seemed, so long as it remained targeted by conservatives. Connolly, viewing events from the United States, diplomatically construed the anti-bourgeois instincts of 'art for art's sake' and liberal religious departures as equally welcome signs. 'My hand goes out to W. B. Yeats', he declared:

The decadence of capitalist society is evident in every field in which human thought expresses itself; it is seen . . . in the shakings and adjustments of religious doctrines to suit the new conditions, as is illustrated in the Christian Socialism of Protestantism and the Modernism of Catholicism, it is evidenced in literature, art, and the drama and in each and every case in which such manifestation comes within the ken of a socialist it is his duty to recognise the good work that may be in it without abandoning his own view.[77]

Various strands of rebellion—republican, socialist, liberal Catholic, communitarian, feminist—existed in antagonism to established and mainstream notions of acceptability. In the *Peasant* the criticism of the theatre was sometimes that it failed rather than excelled in this function. P. S. O'Hegarty, atheist, republican, and bibliographer[78] suggested Yeats had reneged on his duty by choosing not to revive the *Playboy* in 1908.[79] But on the whole he was inclined to agree with Connolly, contending that

neglects to consider the international dimension to this issue. When O'Hickey's dismissal from Maynooth over his threatening pamphlet *An Irish University or Else*—led him to Rome seeking reparation, his eventual failure must be seen in the context of the support of elevated Gaelic Leaguers (like W. P. Ryan and William Gibson) for the liberal Catholic movement in France and the Pope's encyclical against modernism in 1907.

[77] 'Intellectuals and Socialism', *Harp*, 6 (June 1908). In the *Harp* (the official organ of the Irish Socialist Federation in America) Connolly found more space for artistic matters than in his earlier journalistic incarnations: praising *The Countess Cathleen* and *The Laying of the Foundations*, as well as reprimanding J. B. Yeats for eulogizing the Irish for the benefit of an American audience (*Harp*, 3, (Mar. 1908)).

[78] For P. S. O'Hegarty's role as mainstay of the London Dungannon Club, see Richard P. Davis, *Arthur Griffith and Non-Violent Sinn Féin* (Dublin, 1974), 28; for his bibliographic skills, Wayne K. Chapman and James Helyar, 'P. S. O'Hegarty and the Yeats Collection at the University of Kansas', *Yeats Annual*, 10 (1993), 221–38.

[79] *Peasant*, 31 Oct. 1908. See also the criticism of Yeats in his own terms on 17 Oct., in an anonymous letter addressed to the attention of the poet: 'You hate the bourgeois, yet to all appearances you bow to their opinion . . . Artists form an aristocracy to themselves, and consequently the principle of noblesse oblige should prevent an artist holding any parley with popular opinions, or bow to popular standards . . . this will not be so difficult if he just bear in mind the dicta of Ibsen that "the majority is always wrong." ' Yeats naturally took such criticism in good part, and strove to cultivate connections with O'Hegarty (unaware, of course, that his son would eventually marry O'Hegarty's daughter), promising him in Dec. 1908 to lecture to London Sinn Féin groups. R. F. Foster, *W. B. Yeats: A Life*, i. *The Apprentice Mage, 1865–1914* (Oxford, 1997), 399.

'The work of the National Theatre Society is on the whole national and on the whole good', and aggressively condemning the conservatism of those who had ostracized the Abbey and divided the theatre movement:

> Many years ago it used to be a dream, a vision to work towards a theatre in Ireland where Irish plays would be produced regularly by Irish actors. Towards it, with mighty faith, the early workers worked. When it came, when the vision became a reality—it was elbowed out into the outer darkness because it would not fit its genius into grooves, because it reserved the right to perform plays freely, and refused to bind itself to conventional themes and conventional treatment. The conventionals have had their way, they have done their best to alienate and drive out of the country genius which would not conform; they have hindered the National Theatre Society . . . they have hindered the dramatic movement.[80]

Seen in this light, one can recognize a close relationship between two of the important new Abbey plays that autumn season, *When the Dawn is Come* and *The Clancy Name*. O'Hegarty's defence emphasized the perils of an orthodoxy blind to alternatives because it cast out men of vision who were prepared to criticize or object; in his complaint can be discerned a link between frustration at Griffith and softening attitudes to the Abbey. The author of the first, Thomas MacDonagh, had appeared in Dublin in the summer of 1908 to help open St Enda's, the bilingual school set up by Pearse. His play, *When the Dawn is Come*, took the vision-versus-convention dynamic and dramatized it into a revolutionary context, portraying an Irish war council on the eve of the final battle. The 'man of vision', leader and poet Turlough MacKieran, is an imperious figure who (in a scene oddly prescient in its anticipation of the Treaty debate) argues for the pure republic against the Griffithite compromise. Though touted as 'The first Sinn Féin drama',[81] this play was arguing young intellectual affinity for the Dungannon Clubs and the IRB. 'In brief, the basis of the treaty offered to us is this—full freedom in our land, with our own laws and governance, under the foreign crown, with a joint council of their state and ours.'[82]

Turlough's advice—'If they want peace, let them give all'—is fore-shortened however, as the discovery of his unilateral subterfuge against the enemy is mistaken for treachery. He is tried by his erstwhile comrades on the council, some of who are anxious with disbelief, others for whom

---

[80] 'National Drama—The Situation', *Peasant*, 3 Oct. 1908.

[81] E. W. Parks and A. W. Parks, *Thomas MacDonagh: The Man, the Patriot, the Writer* (Athens, Oh., 1967), 102.

[82] Thomas MacDonagh, *When the Dawn is Come: A Tragedy in Three Acts* (Dublin, 1908), 21.

his apparent guilt is confirmation of long-held suspicions. Fortunately, however, Turlough has kept the faith of the army, and leading in the field, he dies redeemed in arms and the deliverer of his nation.

In practical ways the production indicated that the Abbey might be there to facilitate rather than stifle national sentiment. MacDonagh had been helped by Synge's editorial pen,[83] and clearly owed much to Gregory in terms of construction. Their ministrations could not redeem the ponderous solidity of MacDonagh's dialogue, but made playable a lesson valuable for the theatre's popularity. This drama not only projected MacDonagh's ambitions, it held up the lone artist-nationalist protagonist as a misconstrued genius whose stratagems were too long and complex to be safely challenged by short-sighted politicians or generals. Though Yeats was reportedly less than enthusiastic about the finished product,[84] *When the Dawn is Come*'s political kudos and neo-Seanchan advocacy of the poet's role showed an obvious sympathy with his position.

The pitfalls and hypocrisies of 'the conventionals' pointed out by republicans tied in with the realist impulse to satirize the world of 'pathetic illusion' exposed by W. P. Ryan in the *Peasant*. Lennox Robinson's *The Clancy Name* was a direct attack on cultural conservatives' obsession with keeping up appearances. The murderer John Clancy, killed while heroically saving a child from a runaway cart, is surveyed 'with a terrible quiet satisfaction'[85] by his mother who is saved thereby from the public disgrace of his confession. Her attitude to the maintenance of the 'Clancy Name'—or the fictive construct of the typical peasant that disallowed aberration—mirrored criticism of the *Playboy*, as it would that of Robinson's own work. 'I'm not going to let you disgace me and the Clancy name, John. Think of your father's three brothers, all priests; think of your aunt married to a gentleman in Dublin; think of me, a poor widow woman, who's always been respected and looked up to by the neighbours.'[86]

The *Freeman's Journal* obligingly provided the text parallel to Sarah Clancy's plea:

Has it come to this, that acceptance to the ranks of writers at the Abbey Theatre

[83] Johann A. Norstedt, *Thomas MacDonagh: A Critical Biography* (Charlottesville, Va., 1980), 55.

[84] According to a rumour heard by Joseph Holloway, Yeats was reluctant to allow the play to go on, and had to be prevailed upon to do so. Hogan and Kilroy, *Modern Irish Drama*, iii. 229.

[85] *Two Plays: Harvest; The Clancy Name* (Dublin, 1911), 77.

[86] Ibid. 76.

is subject to the writer black-guarding his countrymen and countrywomen, setting
up to the public a shocking and libellous picture of their methods and character-
istics? . . . one can see no just reason why a representative member of the distin-
guished family whose name has been so flagrantly and gratuitously mentioned . . .
should not apply at once for an injunction to stop the further perpetration of a
libel on the good house of Clancy.[87]

Robinson offered a melodramatic depiction of youthful iconoclasm,
not innocent but eager for the clean air of controversial honesty; and his
ambitions were not lost on the doyens of the Abbey, who took him on at
the age of 23.[88] Yet the sense of appetite for the more distasteful aspects
of Irish life showed by the new wave of realists and so resented by the
Freeman's Journal was not entirely to Yeats's taste either: he considered
the result too naturalistic. What Robinson's work possessed was a sense of
bitterness akin to the topical radicalism of the *Peasant*, which had its roots
in the neglected social 'dirt' beneath Ireland's romantic self-image.
MacDonagh coupled it with the still present but less confident republican element, tentatively setting the day of reckoning 'Fifty years hence'.
United in admiration of Synge,[89] their appearance at an Abbey that was
taking strength from intra-nationalist frictions emphasized how marginalized elements could coalesce under the auspices of an established institution.

The very institutionalization of the Abbey, like Sinn Féin's semi-
popularity, was nevertheless fraught with its own tensions. Grudging
respect was due and given, at least partly because, like the new University,
the Abbey was something tangible at a time of scant accomplishments.
But the danger of losing forward momentum and being lost in the mainstream affected leaders of the dramatic movement no less than it
did nationalists. To those outside the Dublin scene, like Corkery or
O'Hegarty, occasional snapshots of the Abbey gave a more accelerated,
clearer picture of its development than those who had to suffer prolonged
overexposure to its stock repertoire. These last certainly included the
directors themselves, who were relying on young blood to keep from slip-
ping into the good books of the *Freeman's Journal*. It also included those

---

[87] *Freeman's Journal*, 'The Abbey Theatre', 9 Oct. 1908.

[88] Lennox Robinson, *Curtain Up: An Autobiography* (London, 1942), 23.

[89] See MacDonagh's unstinting praise in his obituary piece on Synge in *T. P.'s Weekly*, 9
Apr. 1909, also in Hogan and Kilroy, *Modern Irish Drama*, iii. 267–8, and his later defence
in *Literature in Ireland: Studies in Irish and Anglo-Irish* (Dublin, 1916), 16, 48. Robinson's
sense of inadequacy as Synge's replacement—they never met—pervades his history
Ireland's Abbey Theatre. That said, Robinson claimed his first inspiration as being *Cathleen
ni Houlihan* and *The Rising of the Moon*. *Curtain Up*, 17.

who had dropped out of the NTS fearing co-option and the pull of Horniman's strings, and who were continuing the battle to produce alternative and implicitly more noble and nationalist fare.

O'Hegarty had argued that his reappraisal of the NTS might allow for a reunification of the theatre movement. The Theatre of Ireland had performed at the Abbey since late 1907, and had particularly impressed the *Peasant* school of criticism with their discovery of the dramatic talents of Seumas O'Kelly. Unlike Seumas MacManus, the earlier propagandist champion of the National Players, O'Kelly was intent on mixing social messages with social criticism in his plays. *Matchmakers*, which provided a sympathetic contrast to Fitzmaurice's *Dressmaker*, had pleased the *Peasant* critic with a blend that seemed after W. P. Ryan's heart, 'free from the obscurations of sex problems and "typical" peasants singed with the heat of maudlin sentimentality'.[90] Despite this the Theatre of Ireland remained a poor cousin, not merely lacking the funds available to its professional counterparts, but by all accounts lacking direction and artistic coherence also. It remained true that while acting talent was available from ex-Abbeyites, the Theatre of Ireland failed to entice the Fays or get Boyle to join it, while Colum, technically its biggest playwrighting name, remained uninspired.[91] The paucity of material was underlined by performances of a by-now stale catalogue, including plays like Martyn's *Maeve*, Russell's *Deirdre*, and Milligan's *Last Feast of the Fianna*; while the artistic incestuousness of the peasant play became all too evident when one year Colum's *The Fiddler's House* was followed the next by Rutherford Mayne's *The Turn of the Road*, with an uncomfortably similar plot. Both plays, appropriately enough, dealt with domestic oppression of creative spirits; inoffensive Abbey fare of the pre-*Playboy* type. Like the rest of the Theatre of Ireland's material, it was scarcely as nationalist as *The Rising of the Moon*, *When the Dawn is Come*, or indeed *The Piper*. Nevertheless, as the National Players declined from 'disgrace'[92] into anonymity, the Theatre of Ireland gained in stature as the foremost champion of 'genuine vital life-giving National Theatre'[93]—a reputation jealously guarded by *Sinn Féin*.

[90] *Peasant*, Dec. 1907.

[91] Colum managed only two plays for the Theatre of Ireland: *The Fiddler's House*, a reworking of *Broken Soil*, and *The Miracle of the Corn*, an insubstantial one-act miracle play.

[92] Joseph Holloway described the National Players' 1907 Samhain productions as 'a disgrace to the theatre' on the basis of their execution rather than subject matter—the reverse of his appraisal of Synge. Hogan and Kilroy, *Modern Irish Drama*, iii. 188.

[93] *Sinn Féin*, 7 Dec. 1907. In the same report 'Garach' described the Abbey as 'a plague house whose pestilential disease-laden atmosphere must be avoided at all costs by those who cherish a lingering regard for their health'.

Frank Fay, en route to the United States in the spring of 1908 and hearing a report of Synge's latest bout of illness, wrote to W. J. Lawrence that 'I hope he exaggerates; because if anything were to happen to him, it would give the whole movement into the hands of the two selfish children that would then be cocks of the walk.'[94] Yet despite Synge's failing health and the air of ingratiation given off by the Abbey, what Fay acidly characterized as the 'Gregorization'[95] of the theatre was being offset by new contributors. The year 1908 had showed a new spirit abroad, one that could be communed with at the Abbey, via either the NTS, or, occasionally, the Theatre of Ireland. This mood was pervasive enough to be independent of the notional positions propounded by the leading lights, but not to overcome nominal differences. Although O'Hegarty might point out that these were more apparent than real, for Horniman in particular, appearances counted. The ferocity of her opinions seemed to grow in an inverse proportion to her power over Yeats, but her ire occasionally found a target that played well with his predilections. So it was with the Abbey's guests. In the end, it was nothing more substantial than an advertising error that gave her the opportunity to attempt an exorcism of new nationalism. With a calculated overreaction, Horniman jumped on a mistaken press billing of the Theatre of Ireland as 'The Abbey Theatre Company' as an abuse of profession reputation and forbade her enemies in the other group the use of the theatre.[96]

The Theatre of Ireland, galvanized by rejection, came up with an effective counterpunch in their April 1909 production of Seumas O'Kelly's finest play, *The Shuiler's Child*. The playwright's capacity for social comment threw a wide net over topical issues: the trawl included bureaucracy, the poor law, single parenthood, pauperism, depression, and homelessness. (The poor law in particular had come in for considerable scrutiny—Griffith for instance vote-catching on the promise of outdoor relief which would 'spare able-bodied men and women . . . the humiliation of being obliged to enter the workhouse'.)[97] At the same time, they were issues that concerned social policy rather than pure nationalism.

[94] Frank Fay Papers, NLI MS 10952 (2) (i), 24 May 1908.

[95] Ibid., (2) (ii), letter to W. J. Lawerence dated 1912. In this letter, as in many others, Frank Fay puts the blame for their resignation on the departure of Boyle and his plays, whose popularity he believed gave an important counter-balance to Yeats and Gregory.

[96] The accident stemmed from ULT–Theatre of Ireland interaction. Mayne's *The Turn of the Road* came from the ULT repertoire (made available through the Morrow brothers' connection) and it was Mayne's boss from the (English) William Mollison Company who naïvely assumed that the Dublin theatre movement was unified.

[97] *Sinn Féin*, 22 Feb. 1908.

The forces of the state as represented by an officious Anglo-Irish matron—played by Constance Markievicz—contrived to extend a connection between elemental personal rebellion and national defiance.

Rebelliousness was something nationalists were anxious to harness, and as usual, the image of the family carried notions of typicality and with it the customary national representation. The struggle on this particular battlefield was fought over the custody of a child, between the natural mother and shuiler (a 'walker' who sings for sustenance) Moll Woods, and the adoptive parent Nannie O'Hea; between a demystified agent of the unconventional, creative and itinerant, and a bulwark of the Irish homestead. This was potentially a chalk-circle test of maternity claims on the Irish future between bohemian revolutionary and right-thinking conservative. O'Kelly's play suggests that these forces could be complementary rather than conflicting and that this understanding was necessary to prevent a destructive split. The violence and intelligence required to outwit the forces of the state are Moll's—the fruit of that 'wild' sacrifice, the freedom of her offspring, is entrusted to the care of Nannie and her stable family-based environment.[98]

The Shuiler's Child was in a practical sense an advocate of the forces it was attempting to describe; that the central roles were exclusively womens' made it a rarity indeed—only Gregory's *Gaol Gate* could be offered in comparison. At the same time, a deep-seated conservatism kept O'Kelly's discussion centred in the 'natural' female domain. Militant feminism was an agent of rebellion of which advanced nationalists were simultaneously suspicious and envious. The Inghinidhe na hÉireann, who had launched their paper *Bean na hÉireann* in 1908 to cater for nationalist women, disregarded suffragism, arguing that the desired republic would surely enfranchise women when the time came.[99] Nevertheless the suffragists' passion for direct action was occasion for respect: Arthur Griffith, quoting Christabel Pankhurst, was suitably chastened by the use to which she had put the example of Irish politics.

'Let women suffragists be warned by the experience of the Irish Party, and resolve that until Government action is forthcoming, they will, in spite of sympathetic utterances whether made by political leaders or by the rank and file, continue to wage war upon a Government which denies them constitutional liberty.'

A few years' courageous fighting outside 'the House' has transformed

---

[98] *The Shuiler's Child* (Dublin, 1909).

[99] Virginia E. Glandon, *Arthur Griffith and the Advanced Nationalist Press 1900–1922* (New York, 1985), 128.

women's suffrage from an academic question into a great political issue. Twenty-one years of 'fighting on the floor of the House' has killed home rule and left Irish Parliamentarianism to be pointed out by English ladies as the acme of political imbecility.[100]

The comparison was suddenly more immediate with the advent of the IWFL, founded by Margaret Cousins and Hanna Sheehy-Skeffington in 1908 as a response to Pankhurst's lead, thus providing a distinctly militant feminist alternative for nationalist women.[101] D. P. Moran, Arthur Clery, and Thomas MacDonagh all agreed in the pages of the *Leader* that the IWFL—who had just held a meeting at the Abbey—were right in principle even though, by putting that scruple 'before nationality', they bore the mark of West Britonism.[102] Cruise O'Brien suggested that the suffragists would not command support because 'the free Ireland of tomorrow will be sane enough to give Irish women their proper status in a civilized polity ... will have no fear that woman will become less womanly because she is treated as a rational being, and as a compound of a child's doll and a patent cooking apparatus'.[103] However, while he and his brother-in-law, fellow Young Irelander Francis Sheehy-Skeffington, might chafe at the UIL conference, mainstream conservative Catholic opinion was inclined to keep women 'mere'. The more radical Irish nationalist movement remained torn between recognition of a modern woman whose capacity to champion the cause had many examples, and a model close to that condemned by Cruise O'Brien. Like socialism, it was an issue that kept the notion of cultural nationalism in flux, as it reminded practitioners of the novelty of certain social dynamics. The daughter of Houlihan, in both realistic and symbolic senses, was turning out to be a character of some complexity.[104]

This very complexity exposed the assurance with which responsibility for the incorrupt root of Irish culture had been foisted on the peasant. Minority movements had to ponder on the forces that concentrated their

---

[100] *Sinn Féin*, 5 Sept. 1908.

[101] As Cliona Murphy has noted, the IWFL was also at pains to resist the Pankhursts' tendency to treat it as merely a branch of the WSPU; a similar problem to that Larkin faced with the British trade-union movement. *The Women's Movement and Irish Society*, 77.

[102] *Leader*, 13 Mar. 1909.

[103] Ibid., 18 Jan. 1908.

[104] Critical discussion of women's representation in revival drama remains limited to the central canon, or to more obvious aisling and myth-based symbolism. See Elin Ap Hywel, 'Elise and the Great Queens of Ireland: "Femininity" as constructed by Sinn Féin and the Abbey Theatre, 1901–1907', in Toni O'Brien Johnson and David Cairns (eds.), *Gender in Irish Writing* (Milton Keynes, 1991), 23–39, and David Cairns and Shaun Richards, *Writing Ireland: Colonialism, Nationalism and Culture* (Manchester, 1988).

power in the towns. Lennox Robinson's *The Cross Roads* (put on in the same month as O'Kelly's play) portrayed the youthful, vivacious advocate of new agricultural methods, Ellen McCarthy, returning to the land eager enough to put up with an arranged marriage in order that she might organize a model farm, an example to all. To this end she sacrifices her love for a fellow Dublin radical, Brian Conor. Seven years on, Ellen has become a prisoner of ambition, cursed for her unnatural rejection; and Brian, who arrives intent on writing a book cataloguing her achievement, finds that while the region has prospered she and her husband are destitute and defeated. In a denouement commenting retrospectively on *In the Shadow of the Glen*, *The Land*, and *A Doll's House*, Conor agrees to fabricate 'a grand optimistic book' that might keep a 'girl that was going to the States . . . at home'.[105] Ellen on the other hand is left locked in by a pub-bound brute of a jealous husband who promises to thrash her upon his return. The final scene indicted peasant-culture romantics and propagandists with an obvious Ibsenite inversion: '[*Goes out. Ellen remains sitting at the table staring in front of her with sad, hopeless eyes. The key turns in the lock with a sound of dreadful finality.*]'[106]

New thematic strains in modern politics, serving to complicate the direction of Irish nationalism, could be dealt with either head on with earnest symbolism, or with the irony preferred at the Abbey. In different ways, *The Shuiler's Child* and *The Cross Roads* reflected changing attitudes to the issues for which the theatre had originally been attacked. In 1903 *In the Shadow of the Glen* had run into trouble because of its subversion of the feminine ideal—six years on Robinson was manipulating the audience into willing the wife toward independence; and in doing so posing the question whether Irish Ireland idealism was in danger of being locked into a conservative peasant cultural vision. On tour that year, the programme sought to make the point unmissable by partnering it with Synge's earlier controversial play.[107]

Robinson's retrospective commentary—'Maybe we loved [Ireland] more deeply, but just because we loved her so deeply her faults were clear to us'[108]—suggests that as well as the frustration young writers felt with the limits of chauvinist idealism, their mood was also borne of cultural confidence. His native Cork had its deep divisions, but they existed most violently within a solidly Nationalist camp, in which power-brokers

---

[105] *The Cross Roads* (Dublin, 1910), 48.   [106] Ibid. 53.
[107] *Leader*, 8 May 1909.
[108] *Ireland's Abbey Theatre: A History, 1899–1951* (London, 1951), 84.

fought out an intense faction fight. William O'Brien, the IPP dissident, whose newly founded All For Ireland League waged a bruising row with the UIL, had a formidable power base there. Cork inevitably had its unionist and nationalist divide, but its chief battle was a rivalry rather than an opposition.[109] This atmosphere both benefited and bedevilled native talent. Cultural nationalist initiatives, such as the League or the radical clubs affiliated to Sinn Féin, found themselves further marginalized by an absorbing conflict.[110] That writers emerging out of that margin were more hostile than most to Nationalist rhetoric was perhaps not so surprising: but it was perhaps also true that a Cork so solidly nationalist and yet so bitterly divided encouraged as well as invited criticism. The desire to explore fresh social issues and to contribute to reassessment became bound up with that confidence needed to produce the sceptical dramaturgy Robinson and other local writers preferred. And as other 'Cork realists' would find, bringing such wares to Dublin also brought their criticisms into the heart of the debates generated by pressing issues of class and gender.

In part Synge's legacy was his stimulation of these dramatic essays. The influence of his more experimental departures was less evident. Of the Abbey's new crop of authors, only George Fitzmaurice felt inclined to test dramatic convention in terms of language and symbolism, with his obscure elaboration on the obsessions of art object and utility, *The Pie-Dish*.[111] Fitzmaurice's isolation in Dublin demonstrated the immediacy of the political and social debates, demanding as they did dramatists' undivided attention. In Ulster, however, different conditions pertained and a different emphasis evolved. The ULT's task as a nationalist theatre was somewhat more precarious, involving as it did the possibility of an audience reaction more hazardous than mere anti-*Playboy* heckling. That danger made for a greater degree of invention. If realism was employed for uncontroversial, comic satires on the Ultonian work ethic like *The Drone* (Rutherford Mayne's popular portrayal of a preternaturally lazy farmer remained a staple),[112] it was too obvious an idiom for political material. When, at the close of 1907 Lewis Purcell and Gerald MacNamara (Harry Morrow) produced a play that dealt with the battle

[109] Peter Hart, *The I.R.A. and its Enemies: Violence and Community in Cork, 1916–1923* (Oxford, 1998), 42–4.

[110] See Liam de Roiste's memoirs, serialized in the *Evening Echo* from 19 Aug. 54.

[111] Fitzmaurice, *Five Plays*.

[112] Mayne, *Selected Plays*, ed. John Killen (Belfast, 1997).

of the Boyne and the siege of Derry, necessity dictated a different tack. As Mayne later reflected: 'To anyone who knows the city well, it might easily have had the same result as throwing a lit match into a barrel of gun-powder.'[113]

Suzanne and the Sovereigns was 'An Extravaganza' that sweetened its satiric medicine with the indiscriminate humour of a (sustained, three-act) burlesque—which for added measure took advantage of the festive cheer of the Christmas season. Kings William and James, rendered equally ridiculous, fight their war not around claims for the throne or religious grievance, but in love-struck pursuit of the heroine. The general silliness made for, as the local review put it, 'one huge gargantuan gigantic giggle from beginning to end'.[114] But this pantomime horse of a play had its Trojan aspects too: smuggling into the view of its audience the absurdities of sectarianism. The constant lampooning of the monarchs and relentless disrespect for tradition had a flavour of that Protestant separatist ethos out of which the theatre group had sprung, and which found it as easy to question ultra-Catholic mores as Loyalist mythology. And at the close of the play, the moral is that Ireland's ills are only exacerbated by outsiders, who in the end and only after much havoc, see the place as a bane rather than a boon. William and James, having both lost in love, find friendship, but with one remaining bone of contention:

KING JAMES [*Taking William's hand*]. Till death, brothers.
KING WILLIAM. And to prove my sincerity I am willing to forego part of the fruits of my victory. I will allow you to keep Ireland.
KING JAMES [*Anxiously*]. But—but—.
KING WILLIAM. Nay, do not thank me. You shall be King of Ireland, while I am to reign in England.
KING JAMES. No, no, no. I will not hear of it. I could not think of depriving you of Ireland.
KING WILLIAM. Brother, I insist.
KING JAMES. I must refuse———really I—I don't want it.[115]

However wry the acknowledgement of this disdain for things Irish, the joke suggested the feeling be mutual. The peoples of the North, in a like-minded spirit of camaraderie, should likewise admit their absurd attach-

---

[113] 'Ulster Literary Theatre', 18.
[114] *Nomad's Weekly and Belfast Critic*, quoted by Kathleen Danaher Parks, 'Gerald MacNamara: Ulster Playwright', D.Phil. thesis (Delaware, 1984), 37.
[115] Gerald MacNamara and Lewis Purcell, *Suzanne and the Sovereigns*, in Kathleen Danaher (ed.), *The Plays of Gerald MacNamara*, a special edn. of *Journal of Irish Literature*, 17/2–3 (May–Sept. 1988), 52–3.

ment to these ciphers of foreign authority and similarly reject them. In a sense, that the audience laughed took them some way down this path, as their consent to accept the licence of humour became an act of complicity in the relegation of their differences.

The play did not merely find its form through avoiding confrontation, although it did, in actor David Kennedy's words, 'skate over the thin ice of political and sectarian animosities'.[116] The patently fabricated historical figures in *Suzanne and the Sovereigns* fed off regularly touring stock-melodramatic histories like O'Grady's and Whitbread's, and as they did so commented knowingly on a sentimental and overblown image of the past. The ULT's objectives required a propaganda that tried to belittle history to make it easier to handle, pocketable, superable. Happily resigning the real as the necessary condition of modern theatre, the ULT—and Gerald MacNamara in particular—kept admirably aware of another range of possibilities.

MacNamara's response to Synge was to ponder his unrealities. If *Suzanne* flirted with a less sinister version of the carnival, *The Mist That Does Be On The Bog* (subtitle: *A fog in one act*) toyed with metadrama, satirizing the side of Synge that claimed authenticity. A light-hearted proto-Pirandellian tour, *The Mist* was set in a Connemara cottage rented by a group of Ulster actors obsessively honing their method. Assuming local guise, they welcome a wandering tramp, who after engaging them in a conversation of high Syngese turns out to be a playwright from Dublin also seeking out 'local colour'.[117] The wandering playwright, Clarence St John, having fallen for an actress, Cissy Dodd, mistakes the owners of the house for her still role-playing parents. After a farcical conversation he pleads:

CLARENCE [*To Bridget*]. For heaven's sake, tell me—are you real?
BRIDGET [*Angry*]. Real is it? Am I real? Micheal Quinn, do you hear me insulted in my own house?[118]

When the ULT performed *The Mist* at the Abbey in November 1909, the conceit was complete. If the actors' inability to cope with the range of accents marred MacNamara's dialogue,[119] it served up the fog even thicker. An actor from Belfast playing a Dublin playwright pretending to be a tramp, asking an actor playing a Connemara farmer's wife—now

[116] 'The Ulster Region and the Theatre', *Lagan*, 1/2 (1946), 53.
[117] Danaher (ed.), *Plays of MacNamara*, 62.
[118] Ibid. 68.
[119] As 'Jacques' complained in the *Irish Independent*, 27 Nov. 1909.

doubting that the actor's character is an actor only imitating a Connemara farmer's wife—if she is 'real' posed a precociously modern question. Using the Synge-song as its satirical starting point, *The Mist* briefly pointed up realism's post-*Playboy* shift away from stylized language and self-aware dramaturgy towards the apparent, perhaps naïve, transparency of social commentary. Along with *Suzanne*, *The Mist* gave notice that the limitations of realism in terms of political possibilities in the North could also translate into recognition of its limitations as a form. But the process operated the other way round, too; the ULT's muted politics also deprived them of a seriousness that might lead such ruminations to fuller expression. Conceptual elegance was often lost in sketchy wittiness and a lack of ambition that bespoke a complex joke rather than a profound exploration.

Just as the Abbey continued to patronize the ULT and Yeats praised them for their 'serious artistic work'[120] the adventures of the northern troupe were broadly held within the ambit of the alliances arranged around left nationalism. MacNamara was not a republican, but his Protestant nationalism chimed easily with the tradition out of which the ULT had sprung, and as a Morrow, he had seen two of his brothers link up with the Theatre of Ireland. Republicans naturally maintained their support for the ULT: not just founder members like Hobson, writing for the (now *Irish Nation and*) *Peasant*, and J. W. Good, another IRBer editing the *Northern Whig*; but other left-leaning literary Ulstermen like the London Dungannon Club stalwart (and editor of the Gaelic League monthly *Inis Fail*), Robert Lynd.[121] In 1907 republican defence of the *Playboy* had brought the ULT closer to the Abbey, and the *Peasant*'s position confirmed that allegiance. By 1910 the continued use of the Abbey's stage confirmed both that theatre and the ULT as component parts in the array of options that had begun to challenge nationalist norms.

Yeats had caught a fleeting glimpse of the spirit of 'alternative nationalism', but such delicate shading was bleached out by the death of Synge and grave illness of Lady Gregory, events which for him stained the entire nationalist community with shared guilt.[122] Two years of flux were cut

[120] *Samhain* (Nov. 1908), 5.

[121] Robert Lynd, *Irish and English Portraits and Impressions* (London, 1908). Lynd and Good had both been members of the Belfast Socialist Society, a Connolly-influenced group set up by Alice Milligan's brother Ernest in 1898. See John W. Boyle, *The Irish Labour Movement in the Nineteenth Century* (Washington, 1988), 204.

[122] Yeats, 'Estrangement: Extracts from a Diary Kept in 1909', *Autobiographies* (London, 1955), 482.

away, and Yeats felt himself back in the winter of 1907 facing the howling mob; and always at their head, defining their actions, the philistine arche-type incarnate. 'I wrote a note a couple of days ago', he intimated to Gregory, 'in which I compared Griffith and his like to the Eunuchs in Rickett's picture watching Don Juan riding through Hell.'[123] If Yeats despaired of taming the protean popular hostility he characterized as the Abbey's inevitable lot, he would hardly have considered an anti-censor-ship issue a likely bridle.[124] Yet if anything was to reaffirm the complex-ity of the Abbey's relationship with a nationalist audience, it was the production, in August 1909, of G. B. Shaw's *The Shewing-Up of Blanco Posnet*.

This play had been banned on the grounds of blasphemy by the Lord Chamberlain, under whose auspices the British censor operated, but whose authority did not extend to Ireland. Responsibility for perfor-mances there rested with the issuing—or retraction—of the patents under which each theatre operated, bestowed by the Lord Lieutenant. While Lord Aberdeen had to give due attention to the decision made in England, he was under no obligation to enforce it in his jurisdiction. Once it became clear Dublin Castle would try to prevail upon the directors to withdraw the play, Gregory and Yeats were aware of the opportunity to reverse the polarities which had made political kudos and artistic licence mutually repellent properties.[125]

Lady Gregory, fully convalesced, orchestrated operations with an audacious verve (which won the lasting affection of Shaw), fuelled by confidence in the strength of their case. 'I wish they would forbid it, we have such a strong hand,' she wrote to Shaw, 'the publicity might bring us

---

[123] Yeats to Lady Gregory, 8 Mar. 1909. *Letters*, ed. Wade, 525. The image was, of course, to reappear in 'On Those that Hated "The Playboy of the Western World", 1907'. *Collected Works of W. B. Yeats*, i. *The Poems*, ed. Richard J. Finneran (rev. edn., London, 1991), iii.

[124] Yeats's poem 'At the Abbey Theatre' enquires of Douglas Hyde 'Is there a bridle for this Proteus | That turns and changes us like his draughty seas?' *The Green Helmet and Other Poems* (1910), in *Collected Works*, i. 96. For Hyde's adroit response advocating his use of a shared tradition ('Therefore we step together'), see Foster, *W. B. Yeats*, i. 455.

[125] The play was forwarded to the Under-Secretary for Ireland on 9 Aug. 1909 after two submissions for the 'License for Representation' by English theatres, His Majesty's Theatre (by Beerbhom Tree) and the Manchester Gaiety (by Iden Payne), had met with refusal. It is worth noting the extra fillip that the Abbey had managed to produce a play which Horniman's other place and other manager could not as a result of *English* judgement. *Blanco Posnet* was finally given a licence after St John Ervine pleaded its case for the Repertory Theatre Liverpool and given its British debut on 10 Apr. 1916. BL, Lord Chamberlain's Correspondence, MS 1916/91.

capital to start again.'[126] The Abbey's victory was arrived at by playing off nationalist and liberal sensibilities, but in the end this was possible because the play stretched neither particularly far. Throughout the negotiations between Gregory, Yeats, and the Under-Secretary Sir James Dougherty, what impresses most is the inviting embarrassment of the officials (newly appointed Liberal Home Rulers)[127] and the glee with which Lady Gregory fixed their squirming consciences with the pin of the Abbey's intransigence.[128] Such exchanges brought out some dialogue as classically Shavian as anything in the play itself, including Dougherty's assertion of Lord Aberdeen's good will: 'He is a supporter of the drama. He was one of Sir Henry Irving's pall bearers.'[129] Constructive Unionism was being deconstructed yet again, as external authority and internal freedom came into conflict. But discomfort at Dublin Castle indicated two things: that official opinion was not behind the censor except to the extent demanded by duty, and that more overt support could be found for the Abbey's position amongst liberally minded members of the Castle set without professional responsibilities. To these could be added the attention of international intelligentsia, relaying to a wider audience a response that would reflect on the Empire itself.[130] The Viceroy's threat lacked conviction, and once Shaw had begun canvassing such support to vote with their feet, to fill the circle and gallery as well as the pit, it was revealed as a tempting bluff.

Everything hinged on the tenuous nature of the censor's objections. *Blanco Posnet* was a play set in the American West, depicting the finding of religion, and the rehabilitation of the protagonist following revelation and self-sacrifice. The manner rather than the message led to the censor's refusal to let two scenes past. In the first Blanco complains of the Almighty's crafty omnipotence, declaring 'He's a sly one. He's a mean

---

[126] Lady Gregory to Shaw, 15 Aug. 1909. D. H. Lawrence and Nicholas Grene, *Shaw, Lady Gregory and the Abbey: A Correspondence and Record* (Gerrards, Cross, 1993), 24.

[127] McBride, *Greening of Dublin Castle*, 124–58.

[128] For an admirable dissection of this interaction, see Lucy McDiarmid, 'Augusta Gregory, Bernard Shaw, and the Shewing-Up of Dublin Castle', *PMLA* 109/1 (Jan. 1994), 25–44.

[129] Laurence and Grene, *Shaw, Lady Gregory and the Abbey*, 17.

[130] 'Jacques' described the scene in the *Irish Independent*: 'From London and the provinces they came. Berlin, Munich and Vienna were represented, so was America. Men near me made desks of their knees. They wrote and wrote.' Hogan and Kilroy, *Modern Irish Drama*, iii. 297. Among the visitors was James Joyce, reviewing for the Italian press. Joseph Holloway, *Joseph Holloway's Abbey Theatre: A Selection from his Unpublished Journal Impressions of a Dublin Playgoer*, ed. Robert Hogan and M. J. O'Neill (Carbondale, Ill., 1967), 129.

one.'[131] Yet he only does so as part of a rediscovery of his better self, having given up on a stolen horse to help a dying child, in the knowledge he returns to severe justice. In the second contested scene the desperate hero points the moral finger at Feemey, declaring 'I accuse the fair Euphemia of immoral relations with every man in this town.'[132] Yet this phrase too is acted in an ironic context, merely serving to highlight the double standards of the crowd: their moral superiority is thrown into relief by the prostitute's (and Blanco's) susceptibility to compassion. Censoriousness similarly stood indicted. The censor had, it appeared, taken the part of Blanco's hypocritical brother Elder Daniels, who demands he 'Speak more respectful, Blanco—more reverent'.[133] Shaw, like the God he was held to have blasphemed, was 'a sly one' out to catch the censor in the moral conundrum presented by his refusal to use the 'fair' euphemism, and had succeeded. The ironic sanctity of his message allowed approval from the public if not from public office, and thus served to bring the censor's role into question more effectively than if it had outraged popular sensibilities.

Blanco Posnet allowed the directors to campaign against censorship on a nationalist ticket because its relative innocuousness minimized the likelihood of a backlash. At the same time, the timidity with which nationalist papers approached the defiance of English law brought to the fore the lurking connection between radicalism and unconventionality. Gregory and Yeats had come out with a declaration of independence worthy to be read on the steps of the Abbey:

One thing, however, is plain enough, an issue that swallows up all else, and makes the merit of Mr Shaw's play a secondary thing. If our patent is in danger, it is because the decisions of the English censor are being brought into Ireland, and because the Lord Lieutenant is about to revive on what we consider to be a frivolous pretext, a right not exercised for 150 years, to forbid, at the Lord Chamberlain's pleasure any play produced in any Dublin theatre, all these theatres holding their patents from him.

We are not concerned with the question of the English censorship, now being fought out in London, but we are very certain that the conditions of the two countries are very different, and that we must not, by accepting the English Censor's ruling, give away anything of the liberty of the Irish theatre of the future.[134]

---

[131] Shaw, *Complete Plays of Bernard Shaw* (London, 1934), 593.
[132] Ibid. 597.   [133] Ibid. 593.
[134] Hogan and Kilroy, *Modern Irish Drama*, iii. 290.

Griffith's response in *Sinn Féin* was to urge caution and non-confrontation in a manner reminiscent of John Sweetman's fear for his furniture. 'The directors of the Abbey Theatre . . . by their blundering, have opened a road for the revival of the exercise of this disused power.'[135] Playgoers, though, should quietly dismiss provocation from typically degenerate Abbey fare for the benefit of the wider dramatic movement. Likewise Moran: 'Mr. Yeats's incontinent scramble for notoriety . . . had forced Ireland into the controversy, and now, having done the damage, he wants to pose as the leader of Irish democratic freedom, and apparently had got the soft, the very soft, side of some Irish Irelanders.'[136]

Moran was accurate at least in the latter part of his assessment, to the extent that even Griffith changed his mind in the wake of the play's success. Blanco Posnet's query seemed most apt: 'Why should He go . . . soft on a rotten thing like me? Why did I go soft myself? Why did the Sheriff go soft? Why did Feemy go soft?'[137] Griffith for one had pressing considerations. *Posnet* had arrived the same week as the launch of the *Sinn Féin* daily newspaper, the first edition of which hit the streets on 23 August 1909. The launch of his party's new flagship could hardly benefit from unnecessary fault-finding. It served both long-lasting enemies to make a common platform. Gregory sent out emissaries to *An Claidheamh Soluis* and *Sinn Féin* to seek support; Yeats gave an interview published in the *Sinn Féin* daily on the day of the play's debut. Consequently, amid unanimous self-congratulatory puzzlement at the censor's idiocy, *Blanco Posnet* was declared 'moral, reverent and worthy'.[138] A week later, in a review of Lady Gregory's *Seven Short Plays*, it was made clear that despite the past, the door was open for reconciliation. 'With a finer sense of nationalist trust and prudence, and a more general courtesy towards brother artists, the Abbey would inevitably become the premier theatre in Dublin, and be assured of the support it will shortly need when attempts are being made to curtail the liberty of the Irish dramatic movement.'[139]

The *Posnet* episode became an uncanny inversion of the *Playboy* fracas. The gradual reacceptance of the Abbey by those alienated in the earlier battle was largely confirmed by the least 'racy of the soil' production yet staged there. Its success depended on flattering the audience that

135 'The Castle and the Theatre', *Sinn Féin*, 21 Aug. 1909.
136 *Leader*, 21 Aug. 1909.
137 Shaw, *Complete Plays*, 602.
138 *Sinn Féin* (Daily), 26 Aug. 1909.
139 Ibid., 1 Sept. 1909.

their discerning sophistication would recognize that it was as inoffensive as its subtitle suggested—'a sermon in crude melodrama'.[140] *Posnet*'s plot had a criminal entering the bosom of a community after failing to save an infant, whereas Christy had alienated one by trying to murder his father. The generosity of Shaw's community, locating in the redemption of Blanco its own potential for redemption, contrasts with the hostility of Synge's, who damn themselves in damning Christy. Shaw had made a great case for prodigals and given the Abbey, like his ostracized harlot Feemey, a heart of gold in the process.

Posnet deposited the mantle of protectors of the arts on a community wary of the privilege but willing to be honoured. W. P. Ryan again made the point in the *Irish Nation and Peasant* that the progress at Abbey Street contrasted with inertia elsewhere in public life, placing the theatre alongside the language movement:

We are on the whole a poor and unproductive people nowadays. In art, literature, drama, music—apart from Gaelic League and Abbey achievements—we originate nothing ... The Abbey conductors are standing for an important principle, dramatic and national, and it is earnestly to be hoped that Irish opinion will be strongly and unmistakably on their side.[141]

Consensus behind the Abbey over *Blanco Posnet* should not be misconstrued, however. The calm at the eye of the whirlwind—the play itself—allowed Gregory to realize a cross-class unity of support for the theatre which could pave the way for relieving Horniman of her ownership. Establishing the Abbey as an Irish National Institution-in-waiting required a play that could satisfy national pride on the issue of censorship without impinging on a national sense of propriety. The very unlikelihood of finding such a piece of drama emphasizes the fragility of Lady Gregory's and Bernard Shaw's accomplishment.

That the *Irish Nation and Peasant* could by now be expected to back the NTS, was not surprising given their convergent paths in the post-*Playboy* period. Its constituent elements of liberals, socialists, and republicans epitomized the 'young' nationalist contingent frustrated with what they considered the self-defeating naïvety of contemporary nationalism. In this they formed a natural sympathy with the strand of up-and-coming realists beginning to emerge at the Abbey. The Abbey directorate had been more anxious to ameliorate than offend, and Yeats's lofty posturing was tempered by the recognition that they had pursued a less exacting

---

[140] Shaw, *Complete Plays*, 589.   [141] *Irish Nation and Peasant*, 28 Aug. 1909.

agenda in defence of Art than the contemporary caricature suggested. Their success in attracting the loyalty of new brash authors at the same time as attempting to smooth the way to commercial independence allowed them both the gloss of bohemianism *and* the glow of popular theatre.

With the erosion of its reputation as the home of Ascendancy recidivism, even a drift into commercialism could make the Abbey appear repoliticized. And this contrasted with those, who, shifting from purist nationalist positions in the same direction, appeared *depoliticized*. Griffith, while launching the *Sinn Féin* daily, was making moves to make Sinn Féin more of a mainstream political force. That IRB faction which had originated with the Dungannon Clubs was finding it more and more difficult to rest on their shovels while he undermined the already compromised ideal of national independence. When Griffith's long-nurtured ambitions to foster an alliance with William O'Brien came out into the open in December 1909,[142] the republican activists who had provided so much of the party's coherence since the North Leitrim election of 1908 rebelled. Using the cutting edge of *Irish Nation and Peasant* reports, the young Turks dealt a series of savage blows that left the headquarters of the movement split, and its elders staggering on to what appeared by October 1910 to be 'the last stages of its inglorious existence'.[143] Well might W. P. Ryan muse under the headline 'The Loy in Irish Politics':

We begin to wonder if Mr. J. M. Synge was thinking of Irish politics when he revelled in the fantastic demoralisation of 'The Playboy of the Western World.' Our politics becomes more and more like that topsy-turvey drama . . . In fact, the 'da' destroying loy is becoming dangerously popular . . . rumour has it that even Sinn Féin parents expect a touch of the loy at the coming convention.[144]

While the Abbey directors continued to bar the door against their erstwhile fellows from the Theatre of Ireland, and continued to produce only English-speaking drama, they might also expect to receive flak and the occasional condemnation from all nationalist groupings. Yet Gregory and Yeats, despite anxieties over isolation, had found virtue in marginality, and had kept the vitality of their project alive through a continual supply of fresh blood: possible because despite competitors they remained the first port of call for aspiring talent. Griffith in contrast had responded to

[142] Richard P. Davis, *Arthur Griffith*, 60–4.
[143] *Irish Nation and Peasant*, 10 Sept. 1910.
[144] Ibid., 24 Sept. 1910.

the disappointment of the post-millenial slow-down by striving to accommodate the mainstream, and in doing so had led his party into the blur of faction long the domain of the IPP and the UIL. And as his stock declined, so that of the Abbey, and the cultural touchstone of Synge's plays, improved.

Two burgeoning elements in what Pat Kenny had called Ireland's 'sociological chrysalis' were finally beginning to split the husk of the Sinn Féin League. In addition to the physical-force republicans, the socialist movement was achieving greater definition as Connolly returned from America to join forces with W. P. Ryan, Fred Ryan, and Larkin in setting up the Socialist Party of Ireland in September 1909 and the *Harp* in the offices of the *Irish Nation and Peasant*, while poaching P. T. Daly from the Sinn Féin executive en route.[145]

In spite of local strife, the dramatists of Cork were also finding focus. Founding the Cork Dramatic Society (CDS) in the image of its Dublin and Belfast counterparts, Daniel Corkery heralded the *Playboy* as 'Synge's greatest play', stating that 'realism of literature is at least stirring up hope in human souls'.[146] It is hard not to see the continued social introspection occasioned by rising working-class consciousness as informing such an observation. But the dynamic of generational rebellion continued its interplay with class antagonism. Corkery went on to assert that 'people fall in love not with Christy Mahon, the murderer, but with Christy Mahon the romancer'. The romance of revolt had been revivified by the return of Tom Clarke (also in 1907) to an IRB already benefiting from the Dungannon Clubs. Corkery's first production at the CDS, *The Embers*, picked up on younger republicans' tendency to look back beyond the 'lost generation' of materially softened constitutional nationalists to the Fenian tradition. Old John O'Loughlin passes the tradition to a vilified Lawerence Kiely who in turn conveys 'the flame of nationality'[147] to a new generation.

Complementing this mood, Terence MacSwiney contributed work romantic in form as well as substance, with his atavistic verse play *The Last Warriors of Coole*.[148] Yet of these early plays of the CDS, the most

---

[145] C. Desmond Greaves, *The Life and Times of James Connolly* (London, 1961), 235–9.

[146] *Cork Free Press*, 28 Oct. 1910.

[147] *The Embers*, pub. in Robert Hogan and Richard Burnham (eds.), *Lost Plays of the Irish Renaissance*, iii. *The Cork Dramatic Society* (Newark, Del., 1984), 36. Corkery's play was based on the return of Jeremiah O'Donovan Rossa to Cork in 1905. Maume, *'Life that is Exile'*, 21.

[148] *The Last Warriors of Coole*, in Hogan and Burnham (eds.), *Lost Plays*, iii. No reference was intended, I feel sure, to the ageing veterans of the cultural battle holed up in Lady Gregory's demesne.

interesting is another of MacSwiney's, one which in the aftermath of a bitter ITGWU strike on the Cork quays, briefly attempted to address the gulf of interest between his fiercely spiritual Catholic nationalism and the urgent anger of the workers. *The Holocaust*, set in a Cork slum, replaced the relentless ocean of Synge's *Riders to the Sea* with the equally implacable misery of poverty. Polly Mahony is set to lose the last of her five children to TB; Father Cahill, trying to ameliorate her suffering, is caught between his own sense of anger at the complacent bourgeois Doctor and his duty to restrain the same violent impulse in the child's unemployed father. Although the ending is overwrought, with MacSwiney trowelling on tragedy by having the mother die too, the curate's crisis of conscience carries a convincing sense of ambivalence toward visceral socialism.

My God! My God! The misery of it all, the misery of it all, where will it end? where will it end? . . . Christ, justice for this suffering child! We have no divine patience: we will do wild things and leave the great thing undone. If we arraign them who make these horrors, they can crush us and we are futile. Justice would endure annihilation, but to be futile.[149]

From the same school of Cork realism came the work of Thomas C. Murray, and, though he took a more direct route to the Dublin stage, Lennox Robinson: playwrights attempting to 'out-Synge Synge'. This impulse, though reacting against popular manifestations of Catholic nationalism, would continue to resonate with issues of (and conflicts between) militant labour and republicanism.

Yeats, in measuring the accomplishment of the theatre in 1910 against the failure of Irish cultural ambitions, took rejection of Synge as the most telling symptom of nationalist narrowness of vision. Similar goals to those aired by W. P. Ryan back in 1907—'the nobleness of emotion associated with the scenery and events of their country'—were to be associated with the gifts of 'great poets'. 'Patriotic journalism', could offer only an exhausted, frustrated cipher: 'They are preoccupied with the nation's future, with heroes, poets, soldiers, painters, armies, fleets, but only as these things are understood by a child in a National School, while a secret feeling that what is so unreal needs continued defence makes them bitter and restless.'[150]

In this judgement Yeats was less than just to those who had evolved through a different trajectory. Liberals and socialists alike nervously

[149] Terence MacSwiney Papers, UCD 48b/296, 4.
[150] W. B. Yeats, 'J. M. Synge and the Ireland of his Time', in *Essays and Introductions* (London, 1961), 311–41.

beheld the conservative Catholicism of the AOH now flexing its muscle. At the 'Baton convention' of the UIL in 1909, strong-arm tactics had kept any dissent from the mainstream party line to a minimum; the 'Molly Maguirism' of the AOH's violent operations against trade unions proved brutally effective, and bitter battles offered by IPP factions like the O'Brienites in Cork were equally unedifying. Elsewhere, republicans marked the opportunism of Griffithite Sinn Féin, now uncomfortably close to this coercive centre. Yet Yeats's criterion for vision was accurate: and it was small wonder that a sizeable contingent from these elements might look back at the previous three years and reconsider the popular judgement of Synge's work. 'Its flavour', remarked republican young blood Ernest Blythe, 'is not so much of the nut or the apple as of the tomato—one must get use to it to appreciate it.'[151]

[151] *Irish Nation and Peasant*, 24 Aug. 1909. The 20-year-old Blythe ('Cairdre'), a Gaelic Leaguer and IRBer from Antrim, continued his review of the *Playboy* in Belfast by criticizing the directors for continuing with the bowdlerized version. 'Nobody now considers it a libel on the Irish race', he urged. 'That view was only dug up by rioters in justification of their conduct.' Blythe later became minister for finance in the first Free State government, and was responsible for providing the Abbey Theatre with a state subsidy in 1925. He became a director of the Abbey in 1938 and eventually (a notably conservative) managing director, 1941–67.

6

Ghosts *and Spectres: Theatres of War, 1910–1916*

Attempting to describe the role of Ireland in the Englishman's political psychology, Tom Kettle wrote in 1911 that it was 'the one *péché de jeunesse* of his nation that will not sleep in the grave of the past . . . This spectre haunts the conscience of England to incite her not to a deed of blood but to a deed of justice.'[1] Had he paid his text of *Hamlet* closer attention, the contagion of the categories of blood and justice might have given him greater pause. As it was, the return of the IPP with parliamentary leverage in 1910 gave MPs like himself the opportunity to urge that their patient preparation should finally prove effective, and that the genie of Irish nationalism could be coaxed back into the bottle of Home Rule. The problem was that the ghost of Irish past appeared in different guises to different people; and neither would it appear alone, but in company with the spectre of syndicalism and the ghoul of impending war.

Parnell's shade, like that of Hamlet's father, pervaded the scene; it was a presence that personified expectation. The sense of a historical echo with a twenty-year lag heightened the topicality of that already current notion of generational difference, prompting much retrospective analysis of Ireland's progress. Not all agreed with Kettle's prognosis. One contributor to the IRB's new 'organ of an uncompromising national ideal', *Irish Freedom*, concurred with an editorial contempt for Westminster, adding: 'The conduct of Irish politics since Parnell's death has afforded the world a classic instance of how not to do it. The history of the past twenty years is sad, if grimly amusing, reading for an Irish nationalist.'[2]

What 'Fearbolg' wished to stress, however, was not merely the inadequacy of the IPP but of the Irish Ireland generation that had challenged it, obsessed with an anaemic cultural nationalism to the detriment of political drive:

---

[1] *The Open Secret of Ireland* (London, 1912), 15–16.
[2] *Irish Freedom*, first issue of the neo-Fenian monthly, Nov. 1910.

The non-political theory of the Gaelic League was a disastrous mistake, disastrous for the Gaelic League and disastrous for national politics . . . [in the first place] it tended to create in the public mind the idea that the Gaelic movement was a mere academic thing, utterly unconnected with the realities and struggles of life, in the second place by drawing off so much of the youth and intellect and idealism of the country from the political movement it helped lower the tone of political life.[3]

This was fast becoming a typical position. Having the IPP essential to a Liberal majority brought on a feeling of *déjà vu* in the Irish polity and presented a familiar backdrop against which intervening accomplishments could be measured. On the face of it, the failure of cultural nationalism to produce a sustainable fever of Gaelic identity had reinforced rather than provided an alternative to the establishment. Confronting the overambitiousness of populist Leaguery, the Coiste Gnótha had fixed its hopes on educational institutionalization, intending to accomplish systematically what enthusiasm could not. League campaigns focused less on the increasingly ill-attended Oireachtas, where the manifestations of Irish linguistic endeavour could be beheld,[4] more on securing the National University, compulsory Irish, and teacher-training programmes. The emphasis therefore shifted toward the National Board and legislative redress, the domain of the IPP; away from revolutionary de-Anglicization toward a kind of Fabian gradualism.[5] The position of a still-cautious Pearse ('A Revolution Needed') was a case in point: 'There are many obstacles in the way of Irish progress, but there are few that with sound education we could not remove. The greatest obstacle that faces us now is the foreign and false system of education that holds sway in our schools.'[6] This vision carried the seeds of future cultural policy but suggested another generation might be required to harvest it. That this necessarily slow revolution might be a long time bearing fruit put the onus back on to more tangible ambitions, providing another impetus to the refusion of practical politics and cultural nationalism.

---

[3] 'Fearbolg', *Irish Freedom*, Jan. 1911.

[4] For self-searching concerns over 'lukewarm' public response, see *ACS*, 23 July 1910 and 15 July 1911. John Sweetman pointed out (*ACS*, 26 Sept. 1911), that the League had been a victim of its own zeal by printing all posters advertising the Oireachtas in Irish, incomprehensible to most Dubliners.

[5] Compulsory Irish, though popular within the IPP, was not uncontroversial, however: see Patrick Maume, *The Long Gestation: Irish National Life 1891–1918*, (Dublin, 1999), 98–100.

[6] *ACS*, 8 Apr. 1911.

Yeats, whose *Golden Helmet* had become *Green* to point up its allegorical significance, lectured the Ard Craobh in March 1910 on the limitations of the language revival. His argument subtly picked at the League's fraying confidence. The great artistic movement of the future, he had 'no doubt' would be in Irish. But, he contested, 'the beginning of success in literature was distrust in journalism', and he went on to question Hyde's first commandment: 'One of the things that Synge feared was that Ireland was going to be denationalized, that Ireland was going to be de-Irished by English commonplace literatures being translated in the Gaelic tongue and spread through Ireland.'[7] Yeats's flattery was thus typically strategic. He generously suggested the League's activities could command a profound influence on the cultural health of the nation; then snatched the prize back by asserting that Irish as well as English could be the tongue of crass materialism. In the League's assumption of its superiority might begin the origins of its own failure.[8]

An Claidheamh Soluis responded defensively, pointing out its interests went beyond 'The sale of Galway tweeds or Dripsey woollens'. Yet, significantly, the collective cap was reluctantly doffed in the recognition of Yeats's authority in literary matters. 'When Mr. Yeats speaks on the conditions under which literature is created and on the attitude that encourages its growth he has the wisdom of a sage, and Ireland owes him much for the example he has set in his devotion to literary ideals.'[9]

Although League stalwarts could still claim that the Theatre of Ireland and the Abbey were 'sacrificing lasting fame'[10] by excluding Irish-language plays from their repertoire, the gap in quality of the dramatic material was large enough for Yeats to patronize League efforts. The stage was open for Irish-language companies to use, if the NTS itself did not perform plays in Irish. And the gap was large enough too for the League to acknowledge. As was frequently stated, for Irish theatre to be good Gaelic League propaganda it had to be of high enough calibre to command attention; to achieve that, Yeatsian criteria of excellence were seen as necessary, including elimination of overstrenuous politicking and sensationalism. Language enthusiasts recognized the inevitable paradox, sometimes painfully. 'Everything is so perfect at the Abbey', mourned one critic, 'that the Gaelic League feels ashamed . . . Beautifully staged

---

[7] 'The Tragic Theatre', *Irish Times*, 9 Feb. 1910.

[8] As an example of the attitude Yeats was criticizing, see *ACS*, 29 Jan. 1910. 'The Irish language is the most effective weapon against the evils which inevitably follow from the possession of a knowledge of English.'

[9] *ACS*, 19 Mar. 1910.   [10] Ibid., 4 Mar. 1911.

and performed plays in English are a danger to our hopes for self-expression in Irish.'[11] Although the cry went up for original pieces, with a few exceptions the response continued to be a rehashing of Hyde or translation of Yeats's and Gregory's shorter plays.

The whole process exacerbated the sense of a synthetic movement, which brought the question of long-term success back into the equation. 'Irish drama will not come in a year or in a generation . . . The growth of the new drama must be from the soil', as one commentator put it.[12] When it did emerge, it would use the slipstream of the existing theatre, as was demonstrated when two bona-fide Irish-language theatre companies emerged in 1913. The first, Na Cluicheoirí, became instant Abbey regulars. Na hAisteoirí (set up by Piaras Béaslaí, who had turned to writing Irish drama after his part in the *Playboy* trials) successfully toured the country until forming the basis for Gearóid Ó Lochlainn's An Comhar Drámuidheachta, which provided Irish drama to Abbey audiences in the mid-1920s.[13] Theatre would have a rearguard rather than a vanguard role in the Irish language revolution, and thus came fairly low on the list of priorities. Other than the odd article and an annual fit of consternation following the Oireachtas, treatment of such matters remained a rare distraction from *An Claidheamh Soluis*'s campaign for educational reform.

From the fertile soil of a thoroughgoing Irish education might spring the brave regenerates who would redeem Ireland's honour. But that left a hole in the self-regard of the present generation, products of what Pearse called the 'Murder Machine' rather than Connolly's hoped-for 'Palaces of Education'.[14] It was a rationale exacerbated by the reflection that even the best intellects would be frustrated unless their skills could be employed in every aspect of national life, including government: and that meant a different kind of revolution, or acquiescence. Nationalists found it hard to escape the logic of theatre that drew its matter from a despised contemporary

---

[11] 'Na hAisteoirí', *ACS*, 19 Apr. 1913. Quoted by Philip O'Leary, *The Prose Literature of the Gaelic Revival, 1881–1921: Ideology and Innovation* (University Park, Pa., 1995), 321.

[12] *ACS*, 8 Jan. 1910. Following the poor Oireachtas of 1911, Padraic Colum developed this idea (*ACS*, 5 Aug. 1911), arguing that the League would be better advised to cease competition for a Dublin theatre base, and instead concentrate on a practical scheme to build a tradition of drama in the Gaedhealtacht. He suggested a marionette theatre as a potential method of creating 'centres of dramatic activity in places where Gaelic life is full'.

[13] O'Leary, *Prose Literature of the Gaelic Revival*, 302, 305–6.

[14] Pearse's pamphlet *The Murder Machine* (pub. Dec.1916), summarized his articles from *Irish Freedom* and the *Irish Review* 1913–14. Connolly's phrase appeared in *The Re-Conquest of Ireland* of 1915, which comprised reworked articles from the *Irish Worker* and *Forward*, 1912–13. Connolly, *Collected Works*, i (Dublin 1987), 254.

system with inevitably dysfunctional products. The new battery of Abbey plays continued to force their discomfort.

The Cork realists' particular skill was in taking the agricultural vocabulary of cultural commentators and dramatizing it, pushing to the fore the material issues that had already begun to corrupt the clean lines of Irish cultural forecasting. In Lennox Robinson's *Harvest*, the schoolmaster William Lordan is a sower of seeds whose germination results in a veritable sheaf of vice. The promising children of the Hannigan family, forced up against the 'straight lines drawn between the classes',[15] are distorted by either frustration or ambition. The most promising have become the most depraved. Mary, portrayed with especial enthusiasm, had been drawn by her lust for 'excitement and splendour and colour'[16] into prostitution; Patrick, the only one to succeed, has become a government minister who has disowned his filial and national identity. This 'snivelling coward who's changed his name and his religion for fear he'll be thought a dirty Irishman'[17] declines to help his farming family, which has been brought to bankruptcy by funding his and the others' studies.

Birthright's unfortunate representatives of the younger generation fail to accomplish even this much. In this, the first of T. C. Murray's plays to be performed at the Abbey, Hugh Morrissey appears to be the epitome of Irish wholesomeness, with the latest cultural equipment. Yet his self-indulgent pursuits alienate his materially minded father Bat who is more worried about the future of the farm. Hugh floats on, fatally unaware of the seething resentment generated by the unequal distribution of rewards both in their household and beyond it. Just as his younger sibling Shane declares, 'The sweat o' my body an' my life is in every inch o' the land, and 'tis little he cares with his hurling an' his fiddling, an' his versifying an' his confounded nonsense!'[18] so Bat Morrissey expresses disdain for the farmhands, who have the temerity to expect eggs for breakfast. Tradition and rebellion are presented in violent flux: the play drives forcefully to its fratricidal climax, the division of labour having become an insupportable weight, too heavy for family structures to bear. The madness of Tyrell's *Heather Field* schizophrenia is here revisited in Shane and Hugh's internecine strife, but complicated by the corruption and alienation possession has brought. *Birthright*, which opened to immediate popularity, reads like a retrospective prologue to the *Playboy*.

---

[15] *Two Plays: Harvest; The Clancy Name* (Dublin, 1911), 43.
[16] Ibid. 49.   [17] Ibid. 59.
[18] *Birthright* (Dublin, 1911), 14.

The realist impulse to sour an already turning perception of Irish life tackled a range of issues that once again widened the ambit of the Abbey. Though the Theatre of Ireland remained outside the hallowed walls, Padraic Colum had been readmitted, with a late and last return to form, *Thomas Muskerry*.[19] The laurels stolen by *The Shuiler's Child* could be won back by a new play critical of the workhouse system. This time care for the previous generation rather than the next is the gauge of human-ity—Muskerry's Learesque reversal of fortunes as workhouse master reveals the cruelty both of the system and the values propagated by it. The coup was complete when the Abbey produced *The Shuiler's Child* itself in November 1910, with a reacquired Maire Nic Shiublaigh to play the lead. R. J. Ray contributed to the barrage of reassessment with *The Casting Out of Martin Whelan*, though his political satire shared only the cadence of Shaw's subtle controversiality.

The combined impact of these plays secured the evil reputation of the Abbey Theatre among mainstream political nationalists: 'Thus, in practi-cally direct sequence,' complained the *National Student*, 'we have been given *The Cross Roads*, *Thomas Muskerry*, *Harvest*, *The Casting Out of Martin Whelan*, plays the power of which no one may deny; but also which remain eminently depressing. It remains to state that *Birthright* is temperamentally in close agreement with its predecessors.'[20] Or, as the *Evening Telegraph* remarked upon *Harvest*: 'a mere seething pot of vice, filth, meanness, dishonour, dishonesty and duplicity'.[21] Yet despite accu-mulating a reputation of hostility for and from nationalists, the Abbey emerged out of 1910 with its audience intact. This owed a good deal to the well-publicized wrangles over Horniman's ill-tempered withdrawal from Irish theatre. Not merely in the sense that it compensated for nationalists' disappointment over the public apology issued when the theatre failed to close during the official mourning for Edward VII. Then an apparently daring snub had turned out to be simply a mix-up over delayed telegrams between Robinson and Gregory.[22] Like the promising election of 1910, the loss of subsidy seemed like a victory for the waiting *demos*, forcing the directors out of over-comfortable detachment back into

---

[19] *Thomas Muskerry* (Dublin, 1910). The play was dedicated to 'T.M.K.'—Colum's close political and journalistic ally Tom Kettle.

[20] Robert Hogan, Richard Burnham, and Daniel D. Poteet, *A History of Modern Irish Drama*, iv. *The Rise of the Realists 1910–1915* (Dublin, 1979), 49.

[21] Ibid.

[22] For an account and analysis of the King's death debacle, see Adrian Frazier, *Behind the Scenes: Yeats, Horniman and the Struggle for the Abbey Theatre* (Berkeley and Los Angeles, 1990), 232–8.

close proximity with the body politic. Yeats and Gregory might embark on a campaign to woo the great and good into pledging enough funds to maintain the theatre's independence, apparently bringing the evolution back full circle to the ILT, but the beast had outgrown such provision. Part of the essential dynamic of the following years would be the continued expansion of the NTS Ltd: the development of a second company, prolonged tours both national and international, and a varied programme that had room even for those who had departed on less than friendly terms—including William Boyle. But this expansion was now hooked to the box office, and it was not always easy to discern whether it was the Abbey or its audience that was 'the element which absorbed'.

Nationalist opinion was as usual in more than one mind. Though the Abbey was often accused of pandering to the ruling elite, it was noticeable that, as one frequenter complained, 'neither the balcony nor the stalls are ever full, whereas the pit is usually crowded'.[23] The stubborn resistance of the well-heeled to the overtures of Yeats and Lady Gregory could now be interpreted as a dereliction of national duty, a symptom of West Britonism. Reporting on committees engaged in fundraising for the London-based Shakespeare Memorial Theatre, *Irish Freedom* remarked:

The majority of their Irish sympathisers ostentatiously cold-shoulder the Abbey, and make no effort to supply the few thousands required to establish it on a sound financial basis. To rub shoulders with the *élite* of English society is to help art; to give the Abbey the backing it needs might come perilously near financial treason.[24]

And vice versa. It was a measure of the Abbey's increased stature since *Blanco Posnet* that while it was as de rigueur as ever to criticize the decadence of its fare, it had become essential viewing. Anticipated premieres such as the posthumous performance of Synge's *Deirdre of the Sorrows* in January 1910 drew 'all literary Dublin'.[25] As an institution it was more confident of its national status than at any time in its history, 'even fashionable'[26] as Yeats remarked, apparently nonplussed that his elitism should have found such popularity.

---

[23] *Irish Nation and Peasant*, 5 Nov. 1910. The writer attributed the change in fortunes at the Abbey to the return of Colum and Boyle, 'the plucky action of the management' over *Posnet*, and 'later the withdrawal of the Horniman subsidy'.

[24] 'English and Irish National Theatre', *Irish Freedom*, Nov. 1910.

[25] Joseph Holloway, *Joseph Holloway's Abbey Theatre: A Selection from his Unpublished Journal Impressions of a Dublin Playgoer*, ed. Robert Hogan and Micheal J. O'Neill (Carbondale, Ill., 1967), 133.

[26] W. B. Yeats to his father, 24 Nov. 1910, *The Letters, of W. B. Yeats*, ed. Allen Wade (London, 1954), 555.

Yeats, however, was quick to realize that the writers who were starting to define the Abbey were developing quite a different relationship with the audience, and that those who viewed them as a natural product of his and Lady Gregory's directorship were mistaken. Just as Synge's work had been distinctly removed from Yeats's theatrical ideal, so his disciples evolved greater distance. 'These men are the historians of their times, in a way that we are not', said the poet with typical acumen.[27] The hyper-criticality of the realist school above all documented two elements of the Zeitgeist deeply at odds with the self-congratulatory mood of pre-Home Rule Bill Ireland: the socialist and the republican.

The role of the *Irish Nation and Peasant* as a sanctuary for both of these interests began to falter late in 1910, when the grind of inadequate funding and equipment finally convinced W. P. Ryan of his need to explore other avenues.[28] The array of talent available to the paper combined to form the Irish Nation Propaganda Committee, with an impressive roll-call including Francis Sheehy-Skeffington, Jim Larkin, James Connolly, Fred Ryan, William O'Brien, P. T. McGinley, Robert Lynd, and P. S. O'Hegarty. Their statement, pledging to continue the work of the *Irish Nation*, the 'advocacy of nationality and democracy in the highest and broadest sense in Ireland',[29] conveys both the significance and limitations of W. P. Ryan's paper. The various forces it harboured, once allies out of necessity, could no longer be happily contained in one organ. The republican element, focusing on the need to bolster an IRB alternative to *Sinn Féin*, set about printing *Irish Freedom*. The left faction, aware of the need to evolve a thoroughly working-class publication to promote the ITGWU and the Socialist Party of Ireland, fell to creating the *Irish Worker and People's Advocate*.

Throughout 1911, the progress of the ITGWU continued to gather momentum, moving like a thundercloud against the wind of bourgeois nationalism. Connolly, organizing in Belfast particularly, found himself

---

[27] *Cambridge Daily News*, 25 May 1910, quoted by Hogan, Burnham, and Poteet, *Modern Irish Drama*, iv. 72. Yeats took care to place Synge in the same category as himself and Lady Gregory, as 'individualistic'.

[28] Ryan had considered resigning in Feb. 1909, citing the 'crippling . . . difficulty' of the 'inadequacy of the working capital'. By Dec. 1910 the 'preposterously humble equipment' and lack of finance had led to a marked deterioration in the quality of the paper, and its last issue was produced 21 Dec. 1910. William O'Brien Papers, NLI MS 13966, and *Irish Nation*, 10 Dec. 1910.

[29] William O'Brien Papers, NLI MS 13966. The other members of the committee were: W. P. Ryan, P. J. O'Shea, Robert Coates, Nelly O'Brien, M. J. Fitzgerald, W. O'Brien Hishon, and J. F. Ennis.

under fierce attack from the AOH as well as predictable opposition from employers and the Orange Order. Yet still the ITGWU made progress, and such was the confidence during the dock-strike summer of 1911 that some commentators took Connolly's ability to poach Hibernian and Orange musicians to form the 'Non-Sectarian Labour Band' as an intimation of more profound unity.[30] The Ulster arena billed all the major contemporary themes: religion, unionism, nationalism, and socialism. A powerful trade union movement was a relatively new player in an old contest, and thus provided a clear link between generational and class rebellion. Such antagonisms made for good drama, and the Abbey 'historians' could compensate for lack of refinement with the force of contemporary relevance. St John Ervine's *Mixed Marriage* was crude but important. Making its debut in March 1911, it looked back to 1907 and forward to the coming hostilities. When Michael O'Hara convinced the Protestant patriarch John Rainey to speak for unity in the strike, he advocated the simple thing so hard to achieve: 'a chance t'kill bigotry and make the men o'Bilfast realize that onderneath the Cathlik an' the Prodesan there's the plain workin' man'.[31]

Critics found fault with Ervine's powers of construction, and with good reason—an act appears to be missing, leaving the concluding riot scene perfunctory and dissatisfying. But whatever the flaws of the fourth, the third act contained a fine episode defining the tragic fragility of the anti-sectarian class-based political project. John Rainey, having agreed to speak against religious bigotry in favour of the common cause, is full of his new role, 'a gran' work, t'make peace'.[32] His test is closer to home than he realizes, however, since his eldest Hugh has already declared to the sympathetic mother Mrs Rainey his intention to marry a Catholic girl, Nora Murray. Though intent on keeping their pledge secret until after the strike, the couple are overheard by John Rainey, who to the horror of his wife, his children, and O'Hara, reverts to type in anger: 'It is a Papish plot, the strack. How can A belave anythin' else whin A see it goin' on in me own house. Me son taken thrum me be a Papish wumman!'[33]

The tradition of Irish realism which worked so many national and political themes through the symbol of family and family unity, was

---

[30] C. Desmond Greaves, *The Life and Times of James Connolly* (London, 1961), 265. See also (e.g.) 'Ulster Won't Fight', *Irish Freedom*, Feb. 1911: 'The new generation has a shrewd suspicion that whatever form of Government is adopted it will still have to slave nine or ten hours a day for a living wage, and it won't make a penny difference in its pay whether a green flag or a Union Jack floats over Dublin castle.'

[31] *Mixed Marriage* (Dublin, 1911), 11.   [32] Ibid. 22.   [33] Ibid. 31.

crucially drawn upon by Ervine. Its message was more acceptable in Dublin for being an attack on Orange bigotry, but its title was well chosen, referring to a subject as relevant in Catholic as in Protestant households, and as pertinent to *Ne Temere* as it was to any dock strike. Michael O'Hara, frantic with concern for the repercussions of Rainey's decision, tries to persuade Hugh and Nora to sacrifice their love for the greater good. Mrs Rainey, rebutting this idea and the male tendency for confrontation ('A wish there wus Or'ngeweemen'[34]), tenaciously bring the politics of culture back to the domestic sphere: 'Can't ye see, they're doin' the very thing ye want Irelan' t' do . . . Him an' her, Mickie, are bigger than the wurl', if ye on'y knew it.'[35]

The inevitability of Rainey's betrayal has dramatic force because of the tension between his prejudice and the new-found attraction of an alternative politics. Rather than craft plot and character development, Ervine in turn took resonance from the politics of North-East Ireland since 1907, making the tragedy of *Mixed Marriage* the tragedy of Ulster. When first performed, his sobering essay seemed a timely lesson on the subject of tolerance and unity, undercut with the author's Fabian schooling.[36] But the concluding portrayal of Nora's futile death in a mêlée of sectarian violence was soon to be brutally confirmed by the shipyard persecution of Catholics and trade-unionists in 1912.[37]

Critics recognized in the new school a symptomatic crudity, but not all adopted the judgement of Ernest Boyd on art's most 'insidious enemy—popularity'.[38] G. Hamilton Gunning gave a more delicate evaluation of the Abbey's current form in the *Irish Review*. After criticizing the 'gunshot school of drama' for blending Synge and Yeats with melodrama, he went on:

However unsubtle and lacking in imagination the latest Abbey drama is, it is healthy . . . The special form of decline evidenced in the work of Murray, Robinson and Irvine [*sic*] is the most healthy and progressive form of decline from which any art can suffer . . . The audience in the Abbey is a fine virile audience, mostly composed of young, hard-working people who take their drama seriously

---

[34] Ibid. 35.   [35] Ibid. 32.

[36] Norman Vance, *Irish Literature: A Social History: Tradition, Identity and Difference* (Oxford, 1990), 176.

[37] Austen Morgan, *Labour and Partition: The Belfast Working Class 1905–1923* (London, 1991), 128–30. Morgan notes that as a result of the conflation of labour and sectarian disputes, in addition to Catholics many other 'suspect' workers were expelled from the shipyards, particularly trade-unionists and Protestant dissidents such as Independent Orangemen.

[38] 'The Abbey Theatre', *Irish Review*, 2/ 24 (Feb. 1913), 632.

as in Russia they take their politics and parliaments. Such an audience will develop with the development of the theatre.[39]

If the realists were intent on topicality at the expense of finesse their reward was an audience sensitive to political intimacy, with such drama no longer smuggled in under the blanket of aestheticism. This relationship could continue to exude 'health' partly because of the process whereby Abbey writers could continue to be seen as at one with the legions of Ireland's 'progressive' youth.

Edited by Bulmer Hobson, *Irish Freedom* nervously surveyed the vigour of the socialist movement, cautiously positioning itself behind the workers, a stance due as much to mutual enemies as mutual interest. The northern republican project had had hardly less difficulty with the 'Frankenstein monster' of Catholic militancy than with the terrors of Orangeism.[40] On the bitter rail dispute of 1911, a leading article eschewed old rivals: 'The surest way to rivet the chain of English dictation more tightly around the necks of Irish Railway workers is to preach the policy advocated by the "Independent" and "Sinn Féin" of unconditional and humiliating surrender.'[41] The republican mind, having cast out Griffith as an aberration, needed to look round for a new idea to help modernize the basic tenets of advanced nationalist ideology. Characterizing the Griffithite experiment as a bid for bourgeois support helped redefine an old-style Fenian philosophy tempered with a more precise anti-imperialism and a tinge of social progressivism.

The temporary suspension of the Sinn Féin movement is often cited as a throw back, but it is nothing of the kind . . . the principles of the Sinn Féin Policy are as sound today as they ever were. The movement is temporarily suspended because some of its leaders directed it into an '82 movement, thinking they could collar the middle classes and drop the separatists; but when the separatists were dropped there was no movement left.[42]

Asserting themselves as the true heirs to the discomfited generation of interred heroes, republicans still had to respond to either or both of two vibrant options: Catholic and proletarian identity. Though methodology remained far more germane to *Irish Freedom*, its editors still felt the need

---

[39] 'The Decline of the Abbey Theatre Drama', *Irish Review*, 1/13 (Feb. 1912).

[40] See *Irish Freedom*, Apr. 1911. 'This narrowing down of nationalism to the members of one creed is the most fatal thing that has taken place in Irish politics since the days of the Pope's Brass Band . . . Mr Devlin himself is beginning to find that this Frankenstein monster he has created will prove a menace instead of an aid.'

[41] Ibid., Oct. 1911.   [42] Ibid., Jan. 1912.

to define a projected social policy—what type of republic should Ireland be? Social visionaries were prompted to come forward: 'though the task is beyond us,' admitted the editorial of September 1911, 'there may rest a latent unsuspecting ability in some of our readers'.[43]

Most nationalists, mainstream or extreme, would have made their postcard answer clerical rather than communist. The strides made by the AOH were mirrored by new offensives by the Catholic Truth Society and Vigilance Committees, who were equally indisposed toward all elements of progressive Ireland: socialism, suffragism, and, of course, 'decadent' literature included. D. P. Moran, having moved the *Leader* into the unfamiliar waters of liberality, took note of the changing tone of Irish affairs. Revd R. Fullerton, a scourge of the left, contributed a series, 'Priestcraft and Patriotism', and his book *Socialism and the Workingman* (based on his denunciations of left-wing evils in the *New Ireland Review*) was recommended.[44] From early 1911 tentative support for the IWFL was withdrawn, and they began to be characterized as 'self-advertisers trying to imitate their English sisters'. By the summer of 1912 they had become 'the Virago Suffers and the Skeffy gang'.[45] Although Moran argued for checks on capitalism—his social panacea was the minimum wage[46]— these were, like the Catholic Truth Society itself, attempts to 'save thousands of Irish Catholic wage-earners from being led astray by the delusive dreams of infidel socialism'.[47] An essential part of Moran's resumption of normal service was a vigilant attitude to the latest crimes of the Abbey Theatre, applied with sharp sectarian spin. 'If Lady Gregory never tried to "save" Connacht Papists with bowls of soup and pieces of hairy bacon,' he wrote of the tour in the summer of 1911, 'she is in a way making up for it by hawking the "Playboy" in England.'[48]

The link between attacks on the marginal progressive and literary elements was identified quickly by Fred Ryan, who though in London editing Wilfred Scawen Blunt's anti-colonial paper *Eygpt*, nevertheless

---

[43] Ibid., Sept. 1911.

[44] *Leader.* 'Priestcraft and Patriotism' ran Nov. 1910–Jan. 1911, while *Socialism and the Workingman* was puffed 15 July 1911.

[45] *Leader*, 14 Jan. 1911, 3 Aug. 1912. Moran half-heartedly appealed against violent attacks made that week by Catholic militants on a suffragette demonstration, while continuing to heap abuse on them as 'not only unsexed but . . . denationalised'.

[46] An idea developed in response to Revd Fullerton's address at the Catholic Truth Society, 'Capitalists, Labourers and the Buying Classes', ibid., 19, 26 Oct., and 9 Nov. 1912.

[47] Ibid., 2 Nov. 1912.

[48] Ibid., 3 June 1911. Moran's allusion to proselytism pre-empted George Moore's disclosure of Persse family history by two years. But as Adrian Frazier has noted, the allegation had long been county gossip. Cf. *George Moore, 1852–1933* (New Haven, 2000), 391.

kept a practised eye on Irish politics. Reporting on the conference of the Catholic Truth Society, he noted an old enemy of the *Irish Peasant*, Cardinal Logue, in the chair.

A much deeper and more sinister motive actuates the real directors of the present crusade than the mere exclusion of reports of divorce cases and criminal happenings . . . The most Rev. Dr Clancy, Bishop of Elpin, addressed a letter to the Chairman of the local Vigilance Committee for the Suppression of Immoral Literature in Sligo . . . 'the Literature,' says Dr. Clancy, 'which is calculated to debase and vitiate the public mind is opposed not only to morality but also to dogma . . . the great danger of the future will not be a revolt against Faith so much as a revolt against the natural order of social and commercial life. In a word, the Christian war cry for the future should be "Le Socialisme, voilà l'ennemi." ' So that while Dr. Foley would suppress Rationalist literature Dr. Clancy would proscribe socialism. Perhaps another Bishop might put the Woman Suffrage movement under a ban.[49]

The strands Ryan had pulled together would become more tightly drawn by the political crises of 1913. For the time being, however, Ireland contemplated the possibility of Home Rule. The realist command of the Abbey's stylistic identity brought its own sense of generational change. Although old hands like Colum and Boyle made appearances, the sense of a new wave was palpable. The death of Synge was echoed by a partial withdrawal of Yeats from the business of theatre. Lady Gregory provided a forceful tour management, but her steady output of plays only charted creative decline. No longer finding her temporizing oeuvre satisfactory for a polarizing Ireland, she wrote one bitter play, *The Deliverer*, before lapsing into a series of saccharine acquiescence, *The Bogie Men*, *McDarragh's Wife*, and *Damer's Gold*.

Written in the summer of 1910, *The Deliverer* looked, with everyone else, back to 1890–1. Gregory had been stung out of Dervorgillian angst by frustration at class and sectarian hostility. Moses/Parnell—'the King's Nursling'—is rejected and stoned by the people he leads, before being fed to the King's cats in a scene that exuded disgust. Ill-bred ingratitude, the allegorical homily implied, was threatening a violent recurrence: and with the lesson came a taste of the author's usually shaded capacity for imperious disdain. Malachi (possibly Redmond), the one faithful Parnellite, warns 'Put the malice out of your heart or we are all destroyed'[50] in true

[49] 'The Latest Crusade', *Irish Review*, 1/12 (Jan. 1912).

[50] Gregory, *The Collected Plays*, ed. Ann Saddlemyer, (New York, 1970), ii. 274. The biblical pretensions of *The Deliverer* were so thin that the play was included in the second (1912) volume of *Irish Folk-History Plays*, along with *The Canavans* and *The White Cockade*.

Gregorian fashion, but the playwright herself had been overtaken by the bitterness which she warned would blight this generation, as it had the last. 'Wandering, wandering I see,' concludes Malachi, 'through a score and through two score years.'[51]

The logic had a specific as well as a general cultural application. Yeats had characterized his role in the radicalization of the theatre during the Boer War in similarly biblical terms, and *The Deliverer* can also be seen as a remonstration with audiences to remember his innovative leadership with less hostility. It was a pertinent point, given the introduction at this play's premiere of the Gordon Craig screens championed by Yeats. His tireless explanation to the press was that the new system of machinery, fresh from the Art Theatre in Moscow, allowed the use of light rather than paint, to suggest rather than convince, and meant 'the abolition of realism'.[52] The suggestion was rather that his aesthetic imput had in effect become a silent partner in new performance. Choosing that old stalwart *The Hour Glass* to share the scenic experiment merely underlined the fact that, endless revision aside, Yeats was intent on redeploying his creative energies.

The Deliverer was more of an aberration than a bid for the gap left by Yeats. The poet had high hopes for Lord Dunsany, whose *King Argimenes and the Unknown Warrior* was performed two weeks after Gregory's in January 1911. The play's similarities led Dunsany to suspect plagiarism;[53] but it was as likely a shared capacity to conjure the Zeitgeist. The plays' strengths, moreover, were quite different. Next to *The Deliverer*, *King Argimenes* has the quality of an essay, clever where Gregory is visceral. Though Yeats had mourned Dunsany's failure to find 'Slieve-na-mon nor Slieve Fua incredible and phantastic enough',[54] the play was a manifest allegory complete with vanquished King and soothsayers prophesying impeding calamity to spoilt courtiers. The King-made-slave Argimenes finds an 'old green sword'—symbol of unearthed culture and tradition restored, and despite Dunsany's exoticism, doubtless an accessory to Yeats's *Green Helmet*.

Nationalism resurrected, then, but with a palimpsest of complications. Once he has used the weapon to reclaim the throne, Argimenes gives thanks to the unknown warrior who first wielded it: 'Aye, though thou

[51] *Collected Plays*, ii. 277.   [52] *Evening Mail*, 9 Jan. 1911.
[53] R. F. Foster, *W. B. Yeats: A Life*, i. *The Apprentice Mage, 1865–1914* (Oxford, 1997), 435, 609 n. 10.
[54] W. B. Yeats, introd. to *Selections from the Writings of Lord Dunsany* (Dundrum, 1912), p. iv.

wert a robber that took men's lives unrighteously, yet shall rare spices smoulder in thy temple.'[55] Like the sword, this has a double edge to it. On one side, the 'unknown warrior' asserts a sense of mystery and unknowableness about history embedded in culture alone (legitimizing Dunsany's own sense of the fantastic). On the other, it suggests that the function of historical culture in a revolutionary period operates independently of an intimate and accurate knowledge of that mythic past. The essayist concludes that the product of the revolution will not be material redress—Argimenes's fellow slave Zarb is kept in his place when the King returns to power—but rather a sacralization of culture defined in its revolutionary role, a temple open equally to slaves and 'the noble and the mighty'.[56]

The canonization of Parnell had overarched intermediary interest in pagan lore as a cultural strategy for writers (particularly Ascendancy writers) anxious to neutralize clerical influence. Swords and sorcery from the mists of time lost relevance at a time when historical reference was becoming more myopic. Lord Dunsany's dramatization obliquely documented the decline of Irish mythology as a dramatic staple. The Babylonian air of Argimenes complemented the biblical tenor of *The Deliverer* and both plays sat well with the medieval mystery plays directed by Nugent Monck at the Abbey early in 1912, and those produced by Pearse at St Enda's. It was testament to the gathering confidence of realism that the other genres seemed employed to represent that rising force, whether by allegory or as a demonstration of histrionic ecumenicalism. Moses as Parnell, couched in regional dialect, pleaded nationalist lineage, Protestant inclusion, Catholic tradition, and artistic tolerance all at once.

Critics of the Abbey remained ready to rebuff such advances, but as it was, minders of the Gaelic psyche would take lessons from American, rather than Irish, Ireland. Bulmer Hobson's friend and correspondent Joe McGarrity rallied the Philadelphian Clan na Gael to protest where the AOH and civic authorities had failed, at the performance of the *Playboy* by the Abbey company in January 1912. It was an indication of the speed with which Synge had become a cultural symbol that the Clan's protest, in contrast to the Dublin upheavals, took careful preparation—the branch had set up a subcommittee in anticipation to discuss and recommend action. In addition to an orchestrated hiss, it fell to McGarrity to state the objections of his fellow theatregoers—'I protest against this play which is

55   Lord Dunsany, *Five Plays* (London, 1914), 65.
56   Ibid. 79.

a libel on Irish character and a gross misrepresentation of Irish peasant life.'[57]

The furore in the United States only highlighted the status Synge already enjoyed as a cultural touchstone. W. P. Ryan, reviewing the collected works, had praised the 'now fairly appreciated' *Playboy*, and wondered when a production of the *Tinker's Wedding* would be possible. 'The playing', he mused, 'would be a piquant test of Ireland's sense of humour, sanity, and sympathy.'[58] Thomas MacDonagh, responding to concerned friends in New York, gave a similarly elevated response: 'It is very hard for us here to feel any great interest in the new Playboy row. It is a little like going over the Parnellite split again, with Synge and Parnell dead too.'[59] Moran, in contrast, scathingly took such revisionism as evidence of the 'tame and weak "intellectuals" here' when compared to their more robust American counterparts.[60]

Two more of the tame and weak, Fred Ryan and Padraic Colum, engaged in a good-natured discussion which explored the question of Synge's legacy with a little more subtlety. Ryan strove carefully to separate the Yeatsian myth from the reality. Synge's work had been made a necessary antidote to the 'old dreamy and moon-gazing Abbey peasant', which nevertheless had established a counter-tradition that was guilty of excessive morbidity. While Synge's work had been 'written without malice', the new realists wrote 'to justify an attitude'.[61] Fred Ryan's rare independence—wrought between support for Irish and Egyptian nationalism, and given to wider notions of socialist anti-imperialism—nevertheless spotted opportunities for synthesis. Careful to praise the Abbey for its 'great and valuable work for Irish drama', he suggested *Mixed*

[57] Joseph McGarrity Papers, NLI MS 17501. Thomas O'Grady, a correspondent of McGarrity's from Sligo, asked earnestly for an extension of the protest. 'I hope that if you can do anything to put down Yeats and his plays in America you will also do it . . . when writing this I feel ashamed that we ever feathered such a vandalised ruffian in Sligo.' ibid., MS 17644.

[58] 'A Singer "O" the Green', *Daily Chronicle*, 4 Feb. 1911. T. R. Henn was not as alone as he thought in characterizing Synge's work as 'anti-clericalism . . . of the liberal-agnostic Continental tradition'. *The Plays and Poems of J. M. Synge*, ed. T. R. Henn (London, 1963), 43.

[59] Johann A. Norstedt, *Thomas MacDonagh: A Critical Biography* (Charlottesville, Va., 1980), 150. The letter, printed in its entirety (149–53) as part of app. A, 'The Hackett Correspondence', was addressed to Dominick and Jack Hackett, 5 Nov. 1911. MacDonagh goes on to make a robust defence of Synge (and Yeats), esp. his female characters, who were, he argued, 'finer than nuns'.

[60] A prescient comparison made in the *Leader*, 28 Oct. 1911.

[61] ' "The Playboy of the West" and the Abbey Peasant: A Curious Development and its Inner History', *Evening Telegraph*, 13 May 1911.

Marriage as a play apart from the norm, a useful model for writers seeking to avoid lurching between a 'super-mundane' notion of moral superiority and a Syngian vision of 'demented selfishness'.[62]

The thrust of Ryan's argument located in Ervine's art a direction for the violence of Synge's dramatic legacy; fixed (as his own critical powers had been fixed) on the rising questions of class conflict. Colum defended the instincts of his co-practitioners of new drama, but his position tested rather than dismissed his correspondent's case. Contemporary writers, he argued, had to respond to the world as they experienced it. By implication, if that meant the realism of the labour struggle, it would soon tell. He encapsulated his position with a remark that still catches the light: 'Says the Eastern proverb—"A man is more like his own time than his own father." The dramatist is the child of his time and his locality.'[63]

Mixed Marriage had placed such confidence under scrutiny—a play where the rebelliousness of youth, given form in fresh class awareness, was constantly under threat from habits of deference. Nevertheless Ervine's emphasis made it clear the play's thesis placed a special onus on those writers capable of elucidating this struggle. The playwright's role was to be more like his time and less like his father than most; in other words, to be part of a self-conscious vanguard. 'Young Dramatists', Ervine himself asserted, were the voice of the 'Young Irishmen'. 'Above all,' he wrote, 'they will mock the Old Irishmen. Ridicule is the weapon by which the self-satisfied may be destroyed and with ridicule the Young Irishmen will arm themselves against the Old Irishmen.'[64]

Self-satisfaction in 1912 was a sizeable target. Redmond's apparent Home Rule Bill triumph, delayed by the Lords, came under prolonged scrutiny and disillusion fermented. Ulster Unionism flared into open rebellion, betraying early confidence as overconfidence. As manufacturing interests began to look for an opportunity to curb the growing influence of the ITGWU, a labour crisis loomed. Militancy found favour. The failure of Tom Kettle to press for a women's suffrage amendment fractured the alliance that kept the 'Young Ireland' UIL radical,[65] while the sustained opposition of IPP MPs to suffragist Bills gave rise to the *Irish Citizen*. James Cousin's (later Francis Sheehy-Skeffington's) suffragist paper, unlike its republican opposite *Bean na hÉireann*, demanded

[62] 'The Irish Peasant: Is He a Moral Freak?', ibid., 3 June 1911.

[63] Ibid., 20 May 1911.

[64] *Sir Edward Carson and the Ulster Movement* (Dublin, 1915), 81–6.

[65] Maume, *Long Gestation*, 122. Sheehy-Skeffington's personal sense of betrayal was acute. *Irish Citizen*, 3 Aug. 1912.

women's voting rights get equal billing with the national question. And once again, the feminists gave other factions lessons in law—and window—breaking.[66]

Robinson, Murray, and Ervine if anything seemed more temperate in 1912, showing that if they were to be of their own time, they could redress a reputation for gratuitously critical realism. But if *Patriots*, *Maurice Harte*, and *The Magnanimous Lover* were less fierce than the respective authors' earlier plays, their better-tempered edge still bit. Robinson's *Patriots* pulled an audience by virtue of its title that left the theatre, according to one of the Abbey's biggest critics, 'deeply impressed'.[67] The ghost of Irish past exhumed by Robinson is James Nugent, a released prisoner of vague Fenian provenance who returns to gauge the efforts of a generation. Willie Sullivan, functioning as young idealist, hails his return 'like Christ coming to Earth again twenty years after his ascension'.[68]

First shown on 11 April, the same day as the Home Rule Bill was introduced to the House of Commons, the play dwelt on the far-from-banished tensions that attended it. Robinson had evidently been reading the advanced-nationalist press. Nugent's language is that of *Irish Freedom*, contemptuous of parliamentary bills and dismissive of cultural pretensions—'all right in moderation, but . . . apt to draw people's attention away from the main thing'.[69] A brief exposure to the local 'League' confirms his fears about an apathetic Ireland. The closing act of the play alludes carefully to the greater political sensitivity of uncommercial theatre which, like Nugent, is incapacitated by a materially distracted society. The old warrior builds his hopes on a triumphant public meeting, but in the end, the great comeback speech remains undelivered—because Nugent has his audience stolen by 'them moving pictures at the Town Hall'.[70] Instead it is he who is lectured by family and friends on a blinkered and destructive creed they assure him is happily passé. The spirit of '67 is, according to Peter O'Mahony, 'Not dead . . . but grown wise': 'Ireland is going to be very prosperous, very well-to-do one of these days, but she's never going to fight again. She's got courage still, but it's a

---

[66] *Irish Citizen*, 22 June 1912. Suffragist confidence extended to an appropriate appropriation of nationalist iconography. Reviewing *Cathleen ni Houlihan* early in 1913, Helen Hayes remarked: 'The struggle of women today, however repulsive its militant side may be to those who do not understand, to the seeing eye is like a young girl with the walk of a queen.' Ibid., 22 Feb. 1913.

[67] 'Jacques' (J. J. Rice) of the *Irish Independent*. Hogan, Burnham, and Poteet (eds.), *Modern Irish Drama*, iv. 196.

[68] *Patriots* (Dublin, 1912), 19.   [69] Ibid. 26.   [70] Ibid. 37.

different sort of courage. She's got to fight her own self now. I drilled secretly twenty years ago for Ireland, now I make bread for Ireland— that's progress.'[71]

Despite his words of compensation for the IPP and Irish Ireland, Robinson maintains a tone of disappointment and lost nobility that undermines and deconstructs this message. The old Fenian is not left isolated: as in Corkery's earlier *The Embers*, idealistic youth still resists the apparent consensus. While Nugent is finally broken by his wife's accusation that he is to blame for their crippled daughter Rose, young Willie remains besotted with her, just as he continues to loathe the 'money-making commercial life'[72] that has mocked her father's expectations.

Patriots had an elusive separatist flavour; both Nugent and O'Mahony's 'well-to-do' speech were cheered during performance. Perhaps, warmed by the title, the audience missed the suggested Irish Ireland–physical force opposition, both elements coexisting so happily in unreflective mythology. Robinson's inconclusive tone refrained from pushing his audience toward the possibility that they also might be a complacent community who needed to re-examine their relation to flesh-and-blood revolutionaries. Operating from a different perspective, Jim Larkin could make the point, in his own way. Quoting O'Mahony's speech for his readers, he remarked:

And then the audience rose as one man and cheered and clapped their hands and all was well. Good old shopkeepers.

But do the Abbey patrons think they are the earth? And because they, the smug parochials, may have comfortable jobs, nice homes to live in, and the males can afford chocolates for the hens, and the hens can get the opportunity to display their shoulder charms. Do they think they are Ireland?[73]

This made all the more sense following as it did the labour leader's celebration of the Home Rule Bill—on the grounds that it would disabuse naïve workers of bourgeois one-nation philosophy. 'Without economic freedom, political freedom is but a name and a delusion.'[74] Robinson had demonstrated that if the new realism bit, it was because the

---

[71] *Patriots*, 42.   [72] Ibid. 41.

[73] Editorial, 'The Abbey Patriots', *Irish Worker*, 13 Apr. 1912. Larkin displayed a familiarity with the company that establishes him as a frequent Abbeygoer: 'Donovan improves, and the great Sara still unsurpassable. Kerrigan seems able to undertake any and every part, a real artiste. Sinclair and O'Rorke—well, they are Sinclair and O'Rorke, and that's everything . . . Young Power should try and forget his pals in front, and that he is not understudying Robert Emmet.'

[74] 'Shall the Bill be a Final Settlement?', ibid.

writers were disappointed romantics, driven, not given, to satire. As with socialists, approval was contingent.

The Magnanimous Lover drew the *Irish Worker* into closer collusion, and widened the alliance to engage feminists. Ervine's reputation with the *Worker* was already secure as author of *Mixed Marriage*.[75] When his new piece threw the 'smug parochials' into outrage, correspondents were ready to take up the cudgels on his behalf. Ervine's central character, single parent Maggie Cather, robustly declines the returning leaf-turner Henry Hinde, who intends to make good his earlier betrayal. Hinde's new religious caring sensibility assumes the victory of consensus, but the social dynamic has left him behind. From *In the Shadow of the Glen* via *The Crossroads*, the new woman had learned to get along better without Mr Righteous. The *Irish Citizen* could only applaud, judging *The Magnanimous Lover* 'a very serious contribution to the literature of feminism in Ireland' and recommending readers 'miss no opportunity of seeing this play'.[76]

Critics baulked at the language, but as with the *Playboy*, trouble with words gave articulation to a deeper affront. Maggie Cather was one of a number of creations, including James Stephens's 1911 *Julia Elizabeth* and Francis Sheehy-Skeffington's 1914 *The Prodigal Daughter*, that responded to old presumptions with confident predictions. They were, like the suffragists harassed on Dublin's streets, simply too outspoken. Responding to new calls for a censor, Ervine turned on his attackers, inverting their accusations: 'The Dublin dramatic critics are the symbols of the decadence in Dublin: they are exhausted men, holding their fingers to their lips and whispering, "Oh hush! Oh, hush!" '[77] Articles in the *Irish Worker* agreed, Delia Larkin inveighing the readership to recapture Abbey seats from the 'rank snobbishness that is the rotten core of the middle class': 'This play was realism, was life as it is (unfortunately), therefore it was "Art" in the truest sense. I think we all know how it was received. Who was it, may I ask, who so unjustly criticised it? Who but some of the so called cultural folk, the lovers of "Art" .'[78]

The doyens of *Irish Freedom* had already found common ground with a view that was wary of the limitations of 'cultured folk' and middle-class disdain for abrasive drama. Responding to the American debacle, a

---

[75] *Irish Worker*, 19 Oct. 1912.   [76] *Irish Citizen*, 13 Sept. 1913.
[77] *Irish Times*, 22 Oct. 1912.
[78] 'D.L.', 'The Newer Drama', *Irish Worker*, 16 Nov. 1912. See also 'Mac', 'A Talk about the Newer Drama', ibid., 9 Nov. 1912: 'everyone knows that St. John Ervine can write and that the whole trouble about "The Magnanimous Lover" is that it is too true'.

triumvirate of Hobson, MacSwiney, and O'Hegarty had mounted a campaign to convince a doubting republican audience to reassess the benefits of new theatre. MacSwiney put a plague on both propagandist and art houses. Melodrama that 'makes our heroes ridiculous'[79] was as bad as coterie theatre just out 'to shock the bourgeois'.[80] O'Hegarty disagreed. Shocking the bourgeois was natural and necessary.

Writing is a bubbling forth of the revolution of the soul . . . practically all the Abbey plays—to specify the particular point at issue—are revolts. What is 'Harvest', unflattering though it is, ugly though you may call it, but a revolt against the waste of intellect called 'Education' in this country—the artist's passionate arraignment of it? What is 'Where There is Nothing' but a revolt against all conventions? . . . The plays are nearly all revolts against something or other, something which we may not like but which a lot of us are not prepared to face. The artist faces it; and eventually the people follow.[81]

What O'Hegarty, Hobson, and MacSwiney agreed upon was the need to secure some kind of ideological grounding (despite requests still undefined) for the republican movement. While Hobson intended to devote himself to a sociological survey of nationalism, MacSwiney's was to elucidate 'The Principles of Freedom'. O'Hegarty's cultural incursions were an element of the same project.[82] Picking up the thread of his *Irish Nation and Peasant* cameos, he fastened a connection between artistic courage and a political marginality ripening into favour. 'Eventually the people follow' would be an essential trope of revolutionary as of literary cadres in the modern revolutionary period. Romantic Fenianism was becoming infected with the reckless confidence of modernism; falling prey to the cosmopolitan shock of the new that had been seen as so dubious in Synge and so decadent in Yeats. It showed a new spirit abroad when Pearse could write to Kettle in May 1912 that 'many of the aspects of modern Europe were old features of ancient Ireland'.[83]

[79] MacSwiney (MacSuidhne), 'The Principles of Freedom IX: Literature and Freedom—The Propagandist Playwright', *Irish Freedom*, Feb. 1912.

[80] 'Literature and Freedom—Art for Art's Sake', ibid., Mar. 1912.

[81] 'Art and the Nation', ibid.

[82] O'Hegarty wrote to MacSwiney (25 Oct. 1910) relaying a request from Hobson for material for the first issue of *Irish Freedom*. Hobson then wrote to MacSwiney declaring him a man of like mind, and thereafter (25 Apr. 1911) emphasizing the importance of stressing 'the Ethics of Resistance to Civic Power' and telling him of his sociological project which he hoped to publish that autumn. 'You and I', he wrote (28 Apr. 1911) 'seem to be almost the only writers who see the necessity [of a moral outlook].' Terence MacSwiney Papers, UCD MSS. P48b/317–24, 380.

[83] *The Letters of P. H. Pearse*, ed. Séamus Ó Buachalla (Gerrards Cross, 1980), 268.

The range of socialist, feminist, and republican responses showed that despite gathering strength, the clericalist centre failed to extend its cultural agenda to all sections of nationalism. As the crisis deepened, mainstream presumptions, including populist denunciations of the Abbey, came under greater scrutiny. It was a process of qualification that mitigated sectarian criticism of the theatre: in the judging of plays there existed criteria other than religious conviction and social origin. Even the most conservative critics had to acknowledge that occasionally their influence could be discerned as new works took account of the strength of feeling.

T. C. Murray's new play *Maurice Harte* conveyed the grim claustrophobia of a young man forced against his inclination into the priesthood for familiar reasons: family solvency, pride, and the security of siblings' arranged marriages. In tragic consequence the eponymous Harte suffers a complete mental collapse. But Murray made the local priest a kind man, and ran the finished product by four priests for pre-performance benediction. In Murray's world, the suffocated generation was still tragic—but blame was more difficult to apportion. The writer considered it more important to capture something of 'the note of Irish Catholic life'.[84]

Maurice Harte was a crowd-pleaser, and a play which complicated condemnations of Abbey style with a more sympathetic interpretation of middle-Ireland aspirations: 'If the farm isn't too big sure 'tis nearly a freehold since we went to the land court?'[85] Murray referred back to the novelty of ownership Colum had first tapped in the *The Land*, mitigating criticisms of materialism with reminders of long denial. Still, misgivings lurked not far off. Murray's abrupt ending heightened the sense that Mrs Harte's caoine for the loss of uncomplicated Gaelic Catholicity ('A Mhuire! Mhuire! Mhuire!')[86] had been voiced too early, before a more intense and personal tragedy made manifest the gap left between Church and modern youth.

Maurice Harte as a character had something of his author's caution. His fate is that of a less callous Stephen Daedalus, sacrificing personal fulfilment at the altar of the altar. *Maurice Harte*'s fate as a play was not far removed, purposefully flying into the nets, as it were, 'of nationality, language, religion'.[87] Despite his attempt to distance his art from the

---

[84] T. C. Murray, letter to Joseph Holloway, 17 June 1912. *Joseph Holloway's Abbey Theatre*, 153–4.

[85] *Maurice Harte and A Stag at Bay* (London, 1934), 49.

[86] Ibid. 41. Irish for 'O Virgin!'

[87] James Joyce, *A Portrait of the Artist as a Young Man*, ed. Chester Anderson and R. Ellmann (London, 1964), 207.

aggression of his fellow realists, the emphasis spoke of what they had in common. Like Robinson and Ervine, Murray was content to pick the element of Ibsen from Synge and leave the rest, and with good reason. As O'Hegarty's position celebrating 'revolt' demonstrates, practical application of realism to the Irish farm was risqué enough for stiffening sensibilities. Pushing forward on all fronts as Synge had done seemed foolhardy.

George Fitzmaurice on the other hand, selected another set of influences. *The Magic Glasses* combined an oblique symbolism, an acceleration of Synge's stylized dialogue, and exaggerated figures like the healer Mr Quille ('A swarthy devil! Holy Father, the cut of him and he blowing out of his two yellow cheeks!');[88] all collapsed into one frenetic act. The fantasy life Jaymony Shanahan samples in 'the top loft' finally is the cause of his death, 'his jugular cut by the Magic Glasses'[89] through which he had viewed a bewitching world. Here in miniature was a reworking of the 'gallous story' and its dangerous interface with the real; but lacking the capacity to make that danger felt across the footlights. Irish audiences were puzzled rather than provoked, and Fitzmaurice's next play, *The Dandy Dolls*, remained unperformed until 1945.

Only the ULT remained to cater for the absurd, and well it might. Here too the reaction against Celticism was evident, as events in the North made any myth of pagan unity seem ever more untenable. The ULT, so adept at bringing theatrical pragmatics to bear on an increasingly unlikely cultural task, could no longer lighten the poisonous atmosphere of 1912, when the persecution of Catholic workers in July was followed by mass signing of the Solemn League and Covenant in September. Rutherford Mayne's *Red Turf*,[90] a tale of a land dispute forced to violent conclusion by haranguing insistence, had seemed apt at its premiere in December 1911. A year later Gerald MacNamara's *Thompson in Tir-na-n-og* documented the failure of the ULT to narrow the divide.[91]

Thompson in Tir-na-n-og dramatized the issues elided by later

---

[88] *The Plays of George Fitzmaurice: Dramatic Fantasies* (Dublin, 1967), 7.

[89] Ibid. 16.

[90] *The Drone and Other Plays* (Dublin, 1912), 115–29. It does not take much to build a Frielesque reading from such ominous statements as old man John Heffernan's suggestion of how the argument might be resolved: '[*with demure malice*] It's the map will do it surely. Isn't it by the maps all the great lords and ladies be holding of their estates, and be buying and selling of them.' Ibid. 121.

[91] The same theme is given more pedestrian treatment in William Paul's *Sweeping the Country*, produced by the ULT at the same time. Both plays were reproduced at the Abbey in Jan. 1913.

commentators in *An Claidheamh Soluis*, particularly the crucially ignored
connection between the virulent response to the Home Rule Bill and the
Ulster Volunteer movement. In doing so Gerald MacNamara also illustrated the gulf separating the world of romantic mythology from the realities of Belfast politics. Thompson, an Ulster Protestant from Scarva,
finds himself magically transported to the world of Irish heroes. At first
assuming the residents to be inmates in a lunatic asylum, problems of
communication are superficially resolved by a spell allowing everyone to
speak English. The visitor soon comes into conversation with fellow
Ulsterman Cuchulain of the Ford:

CUCHULAIN. Alone I have routed an army.
THOMPSON [*Patronisingly patting Cuchulain on the shoulder*]. Good man! Good
    man!
CUCHULAIN. As I swept into battle with my gold bronze chariot, whole nations
    have trembled to hear the Ulster war cry upon my lips.
THOMPSON [*very excited, slapping Cuchulain on the back*]. True blue! Ulster will
    fight and Ulster will be right. [*Assuming a military tone of voice*] Form fours!
    Left turn! Quick march!   [*Exit L.*][92]

The parlance of war and armaments had changed, but was still close
enough to allow contrary notions of independence to be uttered at
complete cross-purposes and remain disguised by new militarist enthusiasm. Cuchulain and Thompson's discussion presaged two seminal articles: Eoin MacNeill's 'The North Began' and Patrick Pearse's 'The
Coming Revolution'. MacNeill, against the faded backdrop of *An
Claidheamh Soluis*, famously held out the Ulster volunteers as a sign of
rebellion against British rule and an example to all Irishmen;[93] Pearse
declared outright that 'the Gaelic League, as the Gaelic League, is a spent
force'.[94] Like Cuchulain they could celebrate common use of force with
Thompson, but only so long as it was abstracted from the ends to which
it might be put. And as with Thompson, the incompatibility of reality
with the fantasy of consistency between Irish and Ulster Volunteerism
would finally out. MacNamara's Gods and Heroes first decide to put the
trespassing Orangeman on trial, and then, in a macabre finale, burn him
to death. The knockabout burlesque of the ULT was abruptly ended, in
grim and prescient bewilderment.

---

[92] *Thompson in Tir-na-n-og* (Dublin, n.d.). First produced at the Grand Opera House,
Belfast, 9 Dec. 1912.
[93] 'The North Began', *ACS*, 1 Nov. 1913.
[94] 'The Coming Revolution', *ACS*, 8 Nov. 1913.

THOMPSON. But what am I doing on you? What's wrong with me?

HIGH KING. That is beyond my ken . . . but sure we are that you can't remain in this peaceful land. You must stand or perish in the test. Take him away, and build a fire round the prisoner.[95]

The polarization of Irish politics that would characterize the next decade was neatly prefaced by the ULT's production. But the pantomime season saw another performance, in less grand surroundings but equally in tune with the tenor of the times. Set in a Dublin garret of 'abject poverty', Andrew Patrick Wilson's *Victims* put into the mouth of desperate Annie Nolan a dark reflection: 'the joys of life are only secured after fighting'.[96] When acted through by the Irish Workers' Dramatic Club at Liberty Hall on Boxing Day, the play intimated that conflict in 1913 would be at least tripolar; complications of class, gender, and generation would insist as much as issues of nationality.

The Christmas edition of the *Irish Worker* nevertheless had a positive air. James Connolly wrote stirring words of encouragement; W. P. Ryan contributed a short story (ironically titled 'On a Tram Car in Wonderland'). Standish O'Grady, who had been continuing his series 'To the Leaders of our Working People', wrote on a more familiar subject, 'Heroes and the Heroic', while St John Ervine wrote an approving review of James Stephens's *The Crock of Gold* in his piece 'After Home Rule'. His message, like his fellow contributors', was one that held out the redefinition of national culture as a prize for the dispossessed:

It is not to the landlords and the slumlords, rich men and sweaters, gombeen men and money-lenders, that you must entrust the re-creating of Ireland. Such craftsmen as these will spoil the work, for they will think solely of themselves. It is you, the poor men and the men without avarice in their hearts, who must make the Ireland of our dreams.[97]

A sense of youthful vigour inspired by newly acquired sense of power and purpose informed the Irish working-class movement. Not only a movement with legitimate grievances and a goal of social justice, but one with an ineffable sense of the modern. As Larkin put it—'A new nation is in birth, a newer type of man and woman is being formed amongst the working class; a new era opens out to us.'[98] It had the added attraction of compatible nationalism and internationalism, liberal artistic taste, non-

[95] MacNamara, *Thompson*, 31.

[96] *Victims and Poached* (Liberty Hall Plays no. 1, Dublin, n.d.), 13.

[97] *Irish Worker*, 20 Dec. 1912.

[98] 'The Passing Years', ibid., 24 May 1913 (being the paper's second birthday).

sectarianism, and a healthy distaste for Nationalist reassurance. Earlier advocates of the revival might have carried the torch for the peasant; a newer literati not merely observed the latent, repressed force of the urban working class, they empathized like to like. After much scoffing from cynics like Moran, a statement like Wilson's 'This is a commercial age. It is an age of industrial discontent and unrest',[99] encapsulated the divergence of elements in Irish society supposedly bound by mutual, national, ambition. No one was happier to oblige confirmation for such an observation than the man who was the antagonist of both the literati and the socialists—the president of the Dublin Chamber of Commerce, William Martin Murphy.

The magnate had seen the expansion of trade-union influence as Connolly pursued his piecemeal improvements in local disputes and Larkin managed new unions into amalgamation with the ITGWU. The transport and the newspaper industries, of closest concern, were becoming more and more affected by union organization. No area of Dublin life stood outside the workers' sphere of influence, a fact underlined by the arrival of William Johnson at the Trades Hall in March 1913. The general secretary of the National Association of Theatrical Employees had come to establish a branch dedicated to the eradication of the 'practical slavery' backstage of Irish theatres.[100]

Workers at the front were as important as workers behind. Count Markievicz's amateur Dublin Repertory Theatre (successor to the Independent Dramatic Company) chose well when they organized in August a production of Galsworthy's *Strife*, to be performed at the Gaiety. This tale of implacable capital and labour fighting to a standstill[101] was open to conflicting interpretations, but the *Irish Independent* and the *Irish Worker* agreed on one point. The play was dated. 'The next strike stage work', predicted the (Murphy-owned) *Independent*, 'will give us the true picture of the modern industrial strife—the strike monger rising from obscurity to the possession of a fat salary.'[102] Wilson, who was

---

[99] Ibid., 1 Feb. 1913. This remark drew from Sean O'Casey a forceful defence of Gaelic culture as an essential element of the Irish revolution, sparking a debate between the two which continued until 8 Mar. See C. Desmond Greaves, *Sean O'Casey, Politics and Art* (London, 1979), 59–60.

[100] *Irish Worker*, 22 Mar. 1913, 'Theatrical Workers Organise'. 'At night when the audience are enjoying themselves thoroughly . . . many men, whose wage is scarcely enough to keep body and soul together, have to work in a heated and unhealthy atmosphere.' Ibid., 5 Apr., 'The "Theatre" from "Behind" '.

[101] Galsworthy, *Five Plays* (London, 1984).

[102] *Irish Independent*, 12 Aug. 1913.

to provide this 'next strike stage work' positioned *Strife* as evidence of a pre-syndicalist need for compromise:

> That was the usual ending to sectional strikes a few years ago—compromise and dissatisfaction . . . The federal scheme of organisation was hardly thought of when Galsworthy wrote 'Strife' but nowadays it is making great headway . . . that fact makes 'Strife' a little out of date as a social document, but nothing can ever detract from its greatness as a play.[103]

A week later, the warning signs that Murphy was gearing up to test the resolve of the new movement were proved timely. The union was proscribed at the Dublin Tramway Company; a strike threatened in retaliation; Murphy and the Employers' Federation responded with a lockout.

The following six months concentrated the familiar elements of cultural antagonism focused through the lens of class war. The old left-literati combination, forged in isolation and marginality, took on a vigour lent by the conflict's seismic scale. Forces of the nationalist centre brought to bear all the anti-socialist elements available upon the strikers, mobilizing the AOH, anxious to display the reassuringly responsible attitude required in a statehood-in-waiting. As one contributor to the *Independent* put it: 'The present state of affairs gives the citizens of Dublin a splendid opportunity of showing to the world their fitness for future self Government . . . Larkinism must be destroyed if our trade and industries are to be continued on a firm basis.'[104]

Fought in the context of the nationalist search for social identity, it was inevitable that the strike should take on, by the very merit of its materialism, a cultural dimension. Murphy represented not merely the employers' interests, but the incarnation of bourgeois philistinism. As a disciple of Harmsworth, transformer of the London *Daily Mail*, he had brought mass production methods to the Irish newspaper industry, and as such was the chief importer of journalese;[105] he had spearheaded the Corporation's refusal to fund the housing of Hugh Lane's collection of modern art (a condition of its bestowal); and, making his credentials for *bête noire* satisfyingly complete, he had been one of the Parnellites' scourges in the wake of the Chief's disgrace.

---

[103] *Irish Worker*, 16 Aug. 1913.

[104] *Irish Independent*, 5 Sept. 1913.

[105] See Murphy's own account, *The Story of a Newspaper* (Dublin, 1909). With typical Nationalist Liberal rhetoric, Murphy promised the *Independent*'s reportage would help to 'bring about a better feeling amongst different classes, and promote a more cordial co-operation amongst those holding different political views of the common good of our country', 6.

Just as the Dublin Trades Council had resolved under Larkin's leadership to support Lutyens's design for Lane's collection, the literati closed ranks with the trade unions to fight the common enemy. Suffragists also took up the challenge: 'We believe', declared the *Irish Citizen*, 'it is the special function and destiny of the women's movement to stand between the movement of Labour and the movement of culture, and to link the two.'[106] The national issue had become not resistance to modernizing materialism, but its direction—the struggle to make it an agent of justice might be redemptive, perhaps even nationally defining. Now if Brehon Law was invoked, it was as a precedent for native feminism[107] or syndicalism.[108] George Russell, whose open curse 'To the Masters of Dublin' had withered all elements of the establishment,[109] took his cue from Connolly when he addressed the Albert Hall that winter:

I am a literary man, a lover of ideas, but I have found few people in my life who would sacrifice anything for a principle . . . Yet these men are the true heroes of Ireland today, they are the descendents of Oscar, Cuculain [*sic*], the heroes of our ancient stories. For all their tattered garments, I recognise in these obscure men a majesty of spirit. It is in the workers in the towns and in the men in the cabins in the country that the hope of Ireland lies.[110]

'The degraded slaves of slaves more degraded still'[111] offered with their act of rebellion a progressive nationalist option. Middle-class nationalism was presented as constructive Unionism's close cousin, intimate with and implicated in systems of imperial control. Infected with the implicit hypocrisy of the posited freedoms available to such programmes, the Catholic Church's condemnation of the strikers underscored political divisions grounded in class rather than ethnic ideology. More explicit hypocrisy became evident in the shocked forcible restraint of attempts made to evacuate some of the poorest children to sympathetic families in England. Going down to the North Dock to witness this 'famous insult to

[106] 'Art, Labour and Suffrage', *Irish Citizen*, 27 Sept. 1913.
[107] Ibid., 6 Sept. 1913.
[108] W. P. Ryan, *The Labour Revolt and Larkinism* (London, 1913), 5–6.
[109] George Russell, *Irish Times*, 7 Oct. 1913. Russell was encouraged by W. P. Ryan to produce a follow-up letter, but Russell declined on the grounds it would be 'counterproductive'. Letter to W. P. Ryan, W. P. Ryan Papers, UCD, LA11/A/30.
[110] Donal Nevin (ed.), *Trade Union Century* (Cork, 1994), 243. The other speakers at the meeting included G. B. Shaw, Sylvia Pankhurst, Connolly, and Delia Larkin. Using the customary yardstick of all traitorous pronouncements, Moran once again bound together elements of rebellion against the conservative notion of Irishness. 'The hairy fairy has done the "Playboy" trick on the platform of the Albert Hall, London.' *Leader*, 15 Nov. 1913.
[111] James Connolly, *Irish Worker*, 30 Aug. 1913.

Ireland', D. P. Moran noted approvingly the 'haranguing priests ... the type of Irish priest that must have pulled us through the Penal days'.[112]

But it is a measure of the moral certitude of writers siding with workers that their response should match clerical vituperation.[113] Reactions had the impression of release, given with an opportunity of implicating Catholic censorship in a condemnation of conservatism per se. James Stephens spat his denunciation:

They have been able to advertise themselves as the Saviour of Ireland's Children, through a piece of machine-made, theatrical sentimentality which would be laughable if it were not revolting ... Tell them that although Ireland has more priests and policemen than any other country in the world; it is still the worse in education and in art, and in the art of living; that in Ireland wages are low and living is high; that humanity is rotting under their care; that intellect is stagnant; that dirt is the rule instead of the exception; that men are housed like pigs, and are fed worse than pigs, and are educated not at all in our so-Christian land. We well learn that they are making us pay too high a price for the privilege of being called the Isle of Saints.[114]

Yeats too welcomed the opportunity to claim the moral high ground, taking care like Russell and Connolly to spice his grievance with the heavy irony of biblical inflection. His complaint carefully implicated militant mainstream nationalism in imperialist repression of 'civil liberties', naturally using cultural debasement as its chief instrument.

I charge the Dublin Nationalist newspapers with deliberately arousing religious passion to break up the organisation of the working man with appealing to mob law day after day and I charge the Unionist Press of Dublin and those who directed the police, with conniving at this conspiracy ... I want to know ... why the authorities ... have permitted the Ancient Order of Hibernians to besiege Dublin, taking possession of the railway stations like a foreign army.[115]

---

[112] *Leader*, 1 Nov. 1913.

[113] A prime example has been quoted by P. J. O'Farrell, *Ireland's English Question* (London, 1971), 269–70, and F. S. L. Lyons, *Culture and Anarchy, in Ireland, 1890–1939* (Oxford, 1979), 96, but is choice enough to stand repetition. From Michael J. Phelan SJ, 'A Gaelicised or a Socialised Ireland—Which?', *Catholic Bulletin*, 11 (Nov. 1913): 'Immoral literature' and 'lewd plays' were 'mere puffs from the foul breath of paganised society. The full sewerage from the cloaca maxima of Anglicization is now discharged upon us. The black devil of socialism, hoof and horns, is amongst us.'

[114] 'Come Off that Fence!' *Irish Worker*, 13 Dec. 1913.

[115] *Irish Worker*, 1 Nov. 1913. The letter had its origins in a speech at a peace meeting at the Mansion House on 27 Oct. Interrupted halfway through, Yeats reworked it and sent it to Larkin's paper. R. F. Foster, *W. B. Yeats*, i. 500.

Just as in the *Posnet* controversy, it pointed up helpfully the argument that it was the theatre's progressive element that had led it into trouble with the same social forces.[116] James Stephen's reference to 'machine-made theatrical sentimentality' drew a link between Yeats's agents of repression and commercial nationalist melodrama. At the Queen's Theatre in Brunswick Street, the latest exponent P. J. Bourke produced stirring tales set against the rising of 1798. Formula drama with larger-than-life heroes and heroines conversing in a dialogue of stock riposte and cliché, such plays as Bourke's *When Wexford Rose* provided cheap and cheerful entertainment. If good for morale, the plays remained, like their predecessors, close to the worn phrases of the Nationalist centre. The *Freeman's Journal* was still the Queen's ally; even in plays depicting revolution, the all-important love interest was wrought in the tight confines of social caste.

The threads tying drama to lockout were stronger in theatre which dealt with contemporary problems. The Markieviczes had pulled out of the Irish Repertory Theatre because their production of Birmingham's *Eleanor's Enterprise* at the Gaiety was considered too risky by the management. The comic plot of a well-intentioned upper-class Irish Irelander on a mission among the peasantry, only to find herself re-educated by the experience, was deemed too incendiary considering Constance Markievicz's active support for the unions and the republican scout movement Fianna Éireann. Perhaps sensing the influence of Mr Murphy, the Abbey pointedly entertained the couple before the Count's departure for Poland.[117]

Such actions might be seen as purely gestural, but given that the Abbey Theatre had come of age as a new theatrical institution, its stance would always go beyond the merely token. And there was more substance to solidarity than lip-service. Yeats was keen to push the production of Seamus O'Brien's play *Duty*, which he read mid-November. Ostensibly a light-hearted farce, the play featured three tippling members of the RIC arresting two citizens for the same offence—and for 'Singin' songs of a

---

[116] The connection was not all one way. Helena Molony, the proprietor of the *Worker's Republic* and an Abbey actress, had applied Jim Larkin's make-up prior to his theatrical appearance, in contravention of his bail, to address the massed ranks of strikers from the balcony of the Imperial Hotel. The disguise, chosen with some humour, was of an aged clergyman. W. J. Feeney, *Drama in Hardwicke Street: A History of the Irish Theatre Company* (London, 1984), 66.

[117] The symbolic nature of this gesture is all the more apparent considering Lady Gregory's intimation to Yeats that she would 'sup with [Markievicz] with a very long spoon'. Letter, 2 Nov. 1912, Berg.

nature likely to cause rebellion an' theatenin' to exterminate the whole
Royal Irish Constabulary'.[118] Yeats, connecting the politics of lock-in and
lockout, liked it because he thought it subversive: 'For at this moment it
is exceedingly topic[al] as the police are generally supposed to have been
drunk during the late riots . . . I would postpone the play about the critics if necessary to ensure this coming while the strike is on.'[119]

The Critics kept its slot, its neat satire on censoriousness (over a sordid
play that turns out to be *Hamlet*) being too tempting to pass up.[120]
Nevertheless *Duty* was on stage before Christmas, and along with it
Seumas O'Kelly's latest piece, *The Bribe*. This story of accomplished
youth frustrated by the vested interests of local capital and influence drew
together familiar themes of local government corruption, setting its
drama around the election of a medical officer to the Garrymore dispen-
sary district. The rising Dr Luke Diamond, the best man for the job, is
stymied by nepotism, perpetrated when the incumbent Dr Power
O'Connor[121] bribes the shopkeeper John Kirwan into selling his vote. As
a consequence, Diamond is at the play's close Australia-bound, while
O'Connor's incompetent son fails to save Mrs Kirwan and baby from
unnecessary death in childbirth.

O'Kelly, as was the tradition, borrowed heavily from Ibsen—particularly in the off-setting of Act II's public meeting against the back-room
politicking of Acts I and III. O'Kelly, however, invested his public enemy
with no ironic misrepresentation; and unlike *The Shuiler*, the enemies of
The Bribe are the agents of indigenous capital. The update of Land War
is Class War, in which Diamond, suing for favours, feels like 'the slave of
the last generation approaching the landlord on a gale day with his hat in
his hand and his heart in his mouth'.[122] Those watching Power O'Connor
did not have to go far to find a corresponding type. His central speech
criticizing 'half-baked socialists like Diamond' had more than a passing
similarity to *Irish Independent* editorials which throughout the latter half
of 1913 had continued to declare Larkinism 'the most insidious form of a
despicable cult'.[123]

[118] *Duty and Other Irish Comedies* (Boston, 1916), 35.

[119] W. B. Yeats to Lady Gregory, 15 Nov. 1913. Berg.

[120] St John Ervine, *The Critics, or a New Play at the Abbey Theatre* had its debut on 20
Nov. 1913.

[121] This was undoubtedly a pointed reference to the ex-Fenian and anti-Parnellite, John
O'Connor Power, used here as a cipher for self-interest.

[122] *The Bribe* (Dublin, 1914), 9.

[123] *Irish Independent*, 15 Sept. 1913.

We have got to kill the spirit that is plucking at the vitals of our public institutions by this immoral and deadly subdued rage that is continually seeking the overthrow of the established and even divine authority . . . *Every time my hand falls from this forth in this fight it will come down with the weight of gold.*[124]

Nor is it altogether impossible to discover in the play's counter-denunciations, the protestations of literary and labour voices alike:

The men that sell the interests of the poor will breed a generation that will sell its country . . . that humbug Morrisey has gone through thirty years of rotten transactions such as this with the piety and his patriotism for his magic passport . . . There he sits, twelve stone of moral corruption, beaming and cheerful, his lips ready to slobber about God's poor while he fingers in his greasy pocket the gold that bought him.[125]

The superimposition of two prevalent concerns, generational responsibility and material corruption, placed the lockout as a culturally defining moment, no less profound for the Employers' victory in early 1914. That *Sinn Féin* stood shoulder to shoulder with the bourgeois press, the Employers' Federation, and the Hierarchy—fulminating against 'the vile and destructive methods of demagogues posing as labour leaders'[126]—in an effort to protect Irish industry, suggested eloquently to alienated socialist and republican elements that its integration into the mainstream was now complete. They could look from Murphy to Griffith and from Griffith back to Murphy and see small distinction. Irish nationalism had established its sense of cultural difference in terms of material as well as political tradition or religion. The conditions of industrial Ireland which *Sinn Féin* was so assiduously out to protect, having become complicit in systems of oppression characterized as 'un-Irish', exposed anomalies in nationalism as a creed of liberation. The phantom of independence had become shadowed by the spectre of syndicalism, and the parlance of freedom reformulated in terms of class. However deeply buried labour interests might become, the troubling questions of Ireland's social philosophy remained unexorcized. Many a future examination of Ireland's soul would be ghost-written by the left.

---

[124] *Bribe*, 13. The emphasis is the original.

[125] Ibid. 25–6. St John Ervine, writing on the atmosphere of the time, used three examples of literary exposure of corruption in Ireland: Fred Ryan's journalism, Yeats's 'September 1913', and O'Kelly's play. *Sir Edward Carson*, 84, 108.

[126] Griffith ('Lasairfhíona'), *Sinn Féin*, 6 Sept. 1913. Quoted by Pádraig Yeates, *Lockout: Dublin 1913* (Dublin, 2000), 133. As Yeates points out (353–7), Griffith's hostility derived from a protectionist corporatism, clear from his article 'Sinn Fein and the Labour Question', *Sinn Fein*, 25 Oct. 1913: 'It is the right and function of the Nation to say to Labour . . . I am the Nation—your father and the father of Capital also, and in my house my children shall not oppress the other.' Ibid. 355.

The dynamics of this process is nowhere more eloquently presented than in *The Lord Mayor*, by the novelist (and bank manager) Edward McNulty, in which solicitor Gaffney saves Mr O'Brien from his creditors in order to help him become Lord Mayor on a Nationalist ticket, intending to use him as a puppet. Major Butterfield, a British agent, attempts to bribe O'Brien for this own ends, but his appeals are neutralized by O'Brien's daughter Moira, full of youthful republicanism. Finally the new Lord Mayor declares himself his own man, 'neither run by clique nor castle'.[127] The pivot of the drama, though, is the role played by the speech-writing Kelly, a lowly clerk whom Gaffney instructs.

GAFFNEY. Put all the top-gallery catches into it. You'll get them out of the newspapers, or political speeches, if you don't recollect. You know what I mean?
KELLY. Wave the Green Flag—Sunburst—Ireland will yet be free—I think I know, sir.[128]

For all its melodrama, Kelly's hack speech still possesses enough quality to rouse Moira, who declares it 'glorious . . . it makes my heart thump and thump'.[129] She is astounded, therefore, when her enthusiasm elicits his declaration of indifference to the national question. During cross-examination, the clerk reveals the true source of his inspiration.

MOIRA. If Ireland was free and a Republic you'd be better off.
KELLY. Not a bit of it. I'd be just the same. There would be a change of government officials, but that wouldn't change me.
MOIRA. Then how is it you can write all these beautiful sentiments about tyranny and freedom and all that?
KELLY. Because, when I use the word 'England,' I really mean 'Gaffney'. When I speak of 'Ireland', I mean myself. Just listen . . . [*reads*] 'Fellow citizens, England, the rich and prosperous England, grinds the face of Ireland. England is the greatest bully and tyrant that walks the earth. It is the unfortunate destiny of Ireland to be in the power and grip of that accursed despot.' And so on.[130]

Kelly is alienated from the nationalist struggle because of this class position; his ogre is too local to put aside immediate enmity in favour of common identity. Yet political culture ironically decrees his ire fires speeches with precisely that end. Class antagonism inadvertently stiffens nationalist resolve, as the energies of material struggle revivify otherwise stale national rhetoric. Under the sympathetic direction of A. P. Wilson,

---

[127] *The Lord Mayor* (Dublin, 1917), 50.　　[128] Ibid. 14.
[129] Ibid. 20.　　[130] Ibid.

these themes received appropriate emphasis and met with an appropriate audience response. According to Lady Gregory, 'one of the most applauded sentences in *Lord Mayor* was "where is the use of patriotism if we can't get our wages raised" '.[131]

O'Brien's moment of truth comes because his first temptation is proffered by old creditors. Experience provokes him to reject them out of revenge; but this act prepares him to dismiss from principle Major Butterworth. O'Brien evolves beyond the colonial pressures towards independence, and his concluding resolve is inspired by the marriage, actual and symbolic, of Moira and Kelly—the pure republican and the penniless scrivener.

As vehicles for investigating the complicity of stale forms of government and rhetoric in the dead weight of status quo, Diamond and Kelly could go so far. They represented well the 'pen slave',[132] but only by extrapolation the manual worker. It would be another year, during the Christmas of 1914, before *The Slough* by A. P. Wilson would bring the tenements to the Abbey stage for the first time. But, by then, it was as a bitter epitaph on the struggle ground down between the two stones of forced destitution and lack of solidarity from British trade-unionism; and even, with a glance at the wider picture, on the burial of the Socialist International under an avalanche of European nationalism.

Rumblings on the Continent and division of colonial spoils focused nationalist minds considerably, as had happened over the Boer War. After a period of relatively insular political consciousness, crises in North Africa from 1911 onwards relit arguments over Ireland's international position. Again, those very issues had affected nationalist positions. Griffith's *Sinn Féin*, consistent with its roots in the South African issue, stuck to its policy of using British involvement to index evil. While independence movements in India and Eygpt were generally applauded, revelations on Belgian atrocities in the Congo (whose discovery eventually led Roger Casement to Irish republicanism) were dismissed as attempts to 'blacken the character of a little Catholic nation'.[133] German ambitions to quell enemies within ('Atheists, Liberals and Socialists')[134] and without (England) were sympathetically recorded. *Irish Freedom*, however, had begun to combine its more thoroughgoing anti-imperialism with a zeal for devastation. O'Hegarty's reflections were typical:

---

[131] Gregory to Yeats, 16 Mar. 1914. Berg.
[132] A phrase used in the *Irish Worker* describing wage levels among clerical labourers, 21 June 1913.
[133] *Sinn Féin* (Daily), 4 Jan. 1910.   [134] Ibid., 10 Jan. 1910.

No peace hypocrite of them had the decency to suggest that the Congo natives had rights, and that the whole filthy European gang should be burned out of the country . . . Give us war, say we. War in our time, O Lord. Send the lightning of thy thunderbolts through the tyrant nations of Europe: let them rend and tear each other; to the end that the crucified nations shall have freedom and nobility at last; and that the earth may purge itself in good red blood.[135]

The combination of a more solid and consistent international ideology with such apocalyptic imagery betokened the warmer reception given by the intelligentsia of the separatist fringe to European modernism. The resistance of Irish nationalists to the *fin-de-siècle* seemed passé to republicans frustrated with that lost generation of liberal procrastination. For some a gamble on 'the new' seemed preferable. With it came, as in Pearse's educational project of St Enda's, a mixture of progressivism, social conscience, and militarism. The celebration of abstract violence at his school contrasted oddly with the reduction in real teacher–pupil hostility.

Pearse's Irish-language play *An Rí* (The King) made manifest this conjunction in terms of performance; a young innocent takes on the mantle of power, supplanting the soiled hands of a failed generation. The old King, who had 'made spoils and forays' and 'oppressed the poor',[136] has through corruption forfeited success. The child, intoning his commitment to Holy War, is similar to earlier depictions of the child-Christ such as *Isoagán*, but here innocence is a qualification for just slaughter. Language is still a weapon, the advantage of St Enda's in the slow revolution of culture, but a simpler revolt has emerged. Pearse, ready by 1913 to join the higher echelons of the IRB, suggested that the time had come for the Sword of Light to give way to a more contemporary weapon. Understanding incentive and reward as important educational inducements, he offered a rifle as a prize to his Irish class. Like his genuine insights into education, which came from his study of Continental advances, the notion that impending war was both a manifestation of civilization's decadence and an intimation of its latent nobility was intensely European.[137]

Pearse's graduation, from a cultural nationalist hostile to artistic experimentation to a physical-force critic of 'convention', brought one particular insight which affected his political methodology. O'Hegarty's

---

[135] *Irish Freedom*, written post-Agadir crisis, Sept. 1911, voices prophesying war.
[136] Pearse, *Collected Works*, 52.
[137] For an overview, see Modris Eksteins, *Rites of Spring: The Great War and the Birth of the Modern Age* (London, 1989).

phrase 'eventually the people follow' resonated in Pearse's series 'From a Hermitage' into a theory of revolution. His first model of vindicated victim was, of course, Christ—and second, Emmet—but he picked up on a theme that had been rehearsed since Yeats's 'Crucifixion of the Outcast', in recasting Synge in the same mould. 'When a man like Synge, a man in whose sad heart there glowed a true love of Ireland, one of two or three men who have made Ireland considerable in the eyes of the world, uses strange symbols which we do not understand, we cry out that he has blasphemed and proceed to crucify him.'[138]

In the ensuing months as the lockout appeared to be stealing national-ist momentum, Pearse defended the right to strike and organize without sanctioning socialism (he was, he said, 'nothing so new fangled').[139] However, his dark condemnations of those who represented a hypocriti-cal moral majority once again hit upon Synge as a source of—implicitly violent—revelation.

There are incongruities which disgust, or at any rate ought to disgust ... an employer who accepts the aid of foreign bayonets to enforce a lock-out of his workmen and accuses the workmen of national dereliction because they accept foreign alms for their starving wives and children, is such an incongruity; a public body in an enslaved country which passes a resolution congratulating a citizen upon selling himself to the enemies of that country ... an Irish Nationalist, unable to pull the trigger of a gun himself, who sneers at the drillings and rifle-practices of Orangemen, is such an incongruity. The Eastern and the Western Worlds are full of incongruities of this sort; each of them matter for a play by Synge.[140]

While Pearse was cogitating on the relationship between rebellion and avant-garde, the renewed interest in foreign influence was becoming more evident in the theatre. Yeats and Lady Gregory had maintained some contact with the outside world through occasional productions of Sudermann: the second company gave the Abbey room to experiment without sacrificing their commitment to indigenous talent. In May 1913 a fundraising production of *An Rí*[141] was imaginatively twinned with the Irish premiere of Rabindranath Tagore's tale of a young innocent's

[138] 'From a Hermitage', *Irish Freedom*, June 1913.
[139] Ibid., Oct. 1913.
[140] Ibid., Nov. 1913.
[141] Pearse's positive view of the literary elite certainly did not suffer from Yeats's decision to go ahead with this performance—coming from the director's office, Pearse is reputed to have remarked, 'Its true you know. Only a great artist can afford to be greatly generous.' Ruth Dudley Edwards, *Patrick Pearse: The Triumph of Failure* (London, 1977), 171.

triumph in death over the material (and colonial) world, coincidentally titled *The Post Office*.[142] Earlier in the year, Hauptmann's *Hannele* had been chosen with its topical balance of Christian idealism and social realism. Two productions of Strindberg were also aired, one of which, *There are Crimes and Crimes*, wittily documented the outré goings-on of a French theatre crowd tempted by Nietzschian amorality. With fame and infamy inverted according to shifting and contingent codes of behaviour, this was a play to invite scrutiny of the ephemeral quality of popular critical judgement. As Mary Colum commented on the productions: 'Strindburg deeply shocked his own generation . . . The work of a man of genius very commonly shocks people until his ideas become part of the general consciousness. A wild fight was once waged around that comparatively tame play, 'A Doll's House'. Far fiercer fights have been fought round Strindberg.'[143] Or, as Madame Catherine, *There are Crimes and Crimes*'s rather Lady Gregory-like figure, says: 'I have got beyond an opinion in this matter. Have you not seen angels turn into devils just as you turn your hand, and then become angels again?'[144]

The devil Ibsen having become an angel through gradual acceptance, political advance, and repeated exposure, the Strindberg productions no doubt whetted the appetite of those who found the Abbey, if topical, over-parochial. This was particularly true of two of Pearse's entourage, littérateurs and editors of the *Irish Review*, Thomas MacDonagh and Joseph Plunkett.[145] In 1912 MacDonagh, disillusioned after a poor production of his eccentric play *Metempsychosis* by the terminally faltering Theatre of Ireland, had made an abortive attempt at trying to set up a new company with Frank Fay. Plunkett also had tasted the sweets of applause after his exotic confection *The Dance of Osiris* had been performed in a series of benefits in the summer of 1913.[146] When in April they published an article in the *Review* by Edward Martyn calling for a new theatrical departure in Dublin, they recognized the opportunity to join forces.

[142] *The Post Office*, trans. Devabrata Mukerja (London, 1914).

[143] *Irish Review*, Apr. 1913.

[144] *There are Crimes and Crimes*, trans. Edwin Björkman (London, 1912), 52.

[145] MacDonagh and Plunkett had wrested control of the *Irish Review* from Padraic Colum when Plunkett bought out the journal in June 1913. Colum, who had edited the review for two years, expected the editorship to remain with him, and was greatly disappointed with the Plunkett–MacDonagh alliance which emerged. 'My only concern', he wrote to MacDonagh, 'was that the only free organ in Ireland should cease to exist. It is all nonsense to think that Plunkett can help the Review as I helped it. He is a delicate young man who may have to put the whole thing aside on a doctor's order.' Letter (draft), 20 June 1913. Berg.

[146] Feeney, *Drama in Hardwicke St*, 44–6. For *Metempsychosis*, see *Irish Review*, Jan. 1912.

Ostensibly, Martyn's article was old hat. Longing for the return of his *Heather Field* glory days, the ex-Sinn Féin president's 'Plea for the Revival of the Irish Literary Theatre' eschewed the Abbey. Martyn argued for an organization that would serve an intellectual elite, while the competition sacrificed quality in their attempt to be 'fashionable'. The theatre of ideas was about the select and for the elect. 'The peasant's primitive mind', he explained, 'is too crude for any sort of interesting complexity.'[147]

Unfortunately, Martyn could not quite justify his own press, nor see the irony in the failure of *The Dream Physician*,[148] a 'complex' satire on ex-ILT enemies provoked by George Moore's stinging reminiscence, *Hail and Farewell*.[149] Nevertheless, the Irish Theatre, as it became, served as an experimental space for the use of the republican literati, showing both their own work and that of obscure Continentals. In the course of the following year the Irish Theatre produced, as well as Irish-language plays, two of Chekhov's works, *The Swan Song* and *Uncle Vanya*, Villiers de L'Isle Adam's *The Revolt*, and such non-peasant works as Mac-Donagh's *Pagans* and Eimar O'Duffy's *The Phoenix on the Roof* and *The Walls of Athens*. Appropriately, the first performance of 1916 was Strindberg's *Easter*.

Pagans, first performed in April 1915, caught the fascination with things European. The previous year had seen the National Volunteers grow into a sizeable army, 75,000 strong at the time of the landing of guns at Howth in July 1914, 170,000 by the start of the war. John Redmond's unexpected pledge in September to use them not merely in defence of Ireland, but 'wherever the firing line extends'[150] had provoked the pending split with separatists, 11,000 of whom took the name Irish Volunteer and Eoin MacNeill for their leader. The breakaway conventions were held at the Abbey Theatre.[151] MacDonagh's new play was no rerun of *When the Dawn is Come*, however, but an effete drawing-room love triangle

[147] *Irish Review*, Apr. 1914.

[148] Esp. the lines put into the mouth of Martyn's caricature of Yeats, Otho: 'I know I ought to be very thankful for being given so magnificent an intellect.' Martyn, *The Dream Physician* (Dublin, 1914), 5.

[149] Moore brushed off the attack, but as Adrian Frazier notes, *George Moore*, 396–7, *Hail and Farewell* had made him fair game in Dublin, and Susan Mitchell's *George Moore* found its mark where Martyn failed.

[150] F. X. Martin, *The Irish Volunteers 1913–1915: Recollections and Documents* (Dublin, 1963), 148.

[151] Both Irish Volunteer conventions, 25 Oct. 1914 and 31 Oct. 1915, took place at the Abbey. *Irish Volunteer*, 31 Oct. 1914 and 6 Nov. 1915.

featuring a fled husband (John Fitzmaurice), his socialite wife Frances, and bohemian soulmate Helen Noble—*A Modern Play in Two Conversations*, as the subtitle admitted. *Pagans* flirted with feminism,[152] while drawing on Continental preoccupations. Well might the reader ask the author the same question asked of John: 'Where have you been lately—Norway?'[153]

In fact John Fitzmaurice has been contemplating—while standing in the Louvre gazing at the *Victory of Samothrace*—not adultery but the necessity of throwing himself into revolution. 'I know that the great opportunity is at hand . . . politics will be dropped here, and something better will take their place.'[154] MacDonagh was intimate with all the latest political developments, along with Pearse and Plunkett—like them a member of the Irish Volunteer Central Executive, and more importantly, of the IRB Military Council. What the play signified in its muted way was the victory of the unconventional: sexual liberality, cultural arrogance, and in its highest form, the marginal but self-convinced psyche of insurrection. Anglo-Irish literature justified itself through being another element of change, finding modern European alliances in its revolt against English influence. 'It enters literature at a period which seems to us who are of it as a period of disturbance, of change . . . Its mode is not that of the futurists or the writers of *vers libres*; but still, coming with the work of these, it stands as another element of disturbance, of revolution.'[155]

Europe, as well as supplying the focus and opportunity for revolt and the arms for its operation, was an essential source for its authority. As *Irish Freedom* claimed the month war was declared: 'Ireland is primarily an European Island, inhabited by an European people who are not English, and who for centuries appealed to Europe and the world to aid them in ceasing to be politically controlled by England.'[156]

Pagans airily posited the essential role of otherwise rootless intellectu-

---

[152] Flirting, perhaps, in a literal sense; *Pagans* can be seen as MacDonagh's troubled reflection on his unrequited love for Mary Maguire, the suffragist who had gone on to marry Padraic Colum. He was, however, according to the *Irish Citizen* (reviewing MacDonagh's *Thomas Campion*), 26 July 1913: 'one of the many poets and literary men who have publicly associated themselves with the women's movement'.

[153] *Pagans: A Modern Play in Two Conversations* (Dublin, 1920), 29. As Feeney has suggested, this is a clear reference to Ibsen. *Drama in Hardwicke St*, 84.

[154] *Pagans*, 38–40.

[155] MacDonagh, *Literature in Ireland: Studies in Irish and Anglo-Irish*, (Dublin, 1916), 7.

[156] 'Germany is not Ireland's Enemy', *Irish Freedom*, Sept. 1914. The article is an updated version of 'Ireland, Germany and the Next War', printed in the *Irish Review*, July 1913, by 'Shan Van Vocht'.

als in the business at hand, an Ireland at war. As such it needed to determinedly ignore the popular view that since the suspension of Home Rule, that business would take place in Flanders. For those in the IRB it required still more—to outface the consensus of fellow Irish Volunteers who, if they agreed the issue was national, also thought it would be raised on the back of public revulsion to British involvement, most probably against the imposition of conscription. IRB organizers as senior as Bulmer Hobson (still intent on popularizing republicanism) who wished to keep channels to the National Volunteers open found themselves tainted.[157] In this context cultural elites promised a logic with cachet. Maintenance of minority conviction was served by the performance of unpopular but critically acclaimed foreign drama. To a degree Chekhov provided MacDonagh and Plunkett with that solace Noh supplied to Yeats: inoculation from opinion.

If partly stimulated by a defensive psychology, the policy of the Irish Theatre was providing much-needed stimulation to Dublin drama. With the Abbey company often away touring America, England, and the Irish hinterland, and the second company often cutting its teeth on one-act plays, the variety and quality of new material began to suffer. After *The Lord Mayor*'s premiere in March 1914, pickings were scarce. The best material was provided by the vivid realist-melodrama of J. Bernard MacCarthy, whose *Kinship* included a convincing portrayal of hunger,[158] and R. A. Christie's *The Dark Hour*, a sort of comic version of James Cousins's early boat-crossing tragedy *The Racing Lug*. Abbey writers still appeared to be following the advice of Christie's character Wandering Danny, who on being asked for the newspaper replies, 'Let you be readin' th' good interestin' parts . . . Th' agricultural news or th' poetry column, an not th' shady history o' th' big people'.[159]

This was certainly the case with A. P. Wilson, who had been taken on as manager of the theatre after Lennox Robinson had resigned, a victim of the financial pressure brought by box-office dependency.[160] Although

[157] See Bulmer Hobson's own, still-angry account, *Ireland Yesterday and Tomorrow* (Tralee, 1968), 68–78.
[158] *Kinship* (Dublin, 1936). MacCarthy was another of the crop of dramatists to emerge from Cork, his first play *Wrecked* (Dublin, 1922) being produced by the CDS in Jan. 1913.
[159] *The Dark Hour* (Belfast, 1950), 12–13.
[160] Robinson resigned following poor attendance during the industrial unrest and a less than successful American tour. Wilson fell prey to similar problems when the war again depleted audiences, and after him St John Ervine proved perhaps the least capable in coping with the constant cash crisis, a problem exacerbated by his accelerating shift toward Unionism brought on by the war.

initially considered with some suspicion, Wilson earned his spurs producing *The Lord Mayor* and proved to be one of the ablest of the Abbey managers until his departure in May 1915,[161] when St John Ervine took over.[162]

The most remarkable product of Wilson's industry by far was *The Slough*, which he wrote, acted in, and directed. Exploring the possibilities of overcrowding a tight dramatic space, his curtain opened on the tenement-dwelling Hanlon family, confined and in conflict. The father Peter, out of wilful defiance and drunken belligerence, is refusing to pay his union dues, while his long-suffering wife finds solace in the stair-head banter of her neighbour Mrs Kelly. Two of their mature children have stifled ambitions—Jack the ubiquitous junior clerk and Peg a glamour-dazzled shopgirl—while the third Anne is a factory worker with an ominous cough. In and out of the constant mêlée of Hanlon life arrive the heralds of the larger manifestation of social faction; 'Jake Allen's General Union' is preparing for industrial action with a tactic as yet unfamiliar:

MRS KELLY [*to Mrs Hanlon*]. Edward says this strike will be different to everything that's gone before it. Its going to be fought in a new way, he says. I forget what was the word he used. Oh, aye, it began with Syn—yes, I mind that—Syn—Syn—something or other . . . Edward was just saying today before he went out to the Committee Meeting at the Union Hall that the Syn—whatever it was—army would very soon lead the toilers out of the slough of poverty.[163]

The committee meeting at the Union Hall forms the second act of *The Slough*, and at its centre is Jake Allen—unmistakably Larkin—energetically dispensing justice with little regard to formal procedure.[164] As the

---

[161] Wilson returned to Scotland, where he became instrumental in setting up the Scottish National Players and the Scottish National Theatre Society in 1921 and 1922 respectively. David Hutchinson, *The Modern Scottish Theatre* (Glasgow, 1977), 43–7.

[162] 'Extremely capable & works very hard,' reported Gregory approvingly to her co-director, 'I sometimes think he will turn us all out & remain in possession.' Letter to Yeats, 22 Feb. 1914. Berg. Her worries became rather less jocular when Wilson began to take the actors' side in pay disputes, or wrangling with Gregory about touring *Duty*. Ostensibly forced out because he had failed to rehearse *Deirdre of the Sorrows* for tour, Wilson's main crime was in stirring up the company. 'He is so useful in business that one wishes to forget these things, but we cannot do so', wrote Lady Gregory. Letter to Yeats, n.d. (May 1915). Berg.

[163] Wilson, *The Slough*, BL Add. MS 1914/35, fos. 15–16. This play, whose influence on O'Casey is so palpable, was previously thought lost. Fortunately Wilson submitted a copy to the Lord Chamberlain, seeking a licence for a production at the Liverpool Repertory (10 Dec. 1914).

[164] As Emmet Larkin has noted, James Larkin was 'seldom mindful of the impartiality of the chair'. *James Larkin: Irish Labour Leader 1876–1947* (London, 1989), 173.

strike vote reaches its climax, Hanlon, who has been debarred in his absence, compounds his fate by turning up late and drunk to popular disapprobation. Committee niggling no match for Allen's easy rapport with the rank and file, the brief glimpse into Liberty Hall is pure late summer 1913, burgeoning with confidence in new-found strength.

ALLEN. No man can say that the same strike is not needed. We must teach the masters once and for all that they cannot longer play the tom-fool with the labourers of this City, and every workmen's organisation is with us.
CHORUS OF MEMBERS. Hear! Hear!! Good Enough! and general acclamation.[165]

But this was not a play, like *The Bribe* or *The Lord Mayor*, for labour in ascendancy. *The Slough* closed like *Mixed Marriage* before it with the forces for social redress overwhelmed by lack of solidarity. Anne's death from consumption in a house pilloried for scabbing, is like Mary's end from a stray bullet, a tragedy symbolically confirming the broader pessimism of Wilson's bitter recriminations.

MRS KELLY. It seems to me that the whole strike has been a very troublesome business, and that it would have been better if it never had taken place.
EDWARD. Ah, now, don't say that, Mother. We must try every means in our power to lift the toilers from the slough of poverty.
TOM. Aye, and when we have tried every means in our power, when we have exerted every tissue, fibre and muscle in the lifting process, we'll still see the toilers wallowing, sinking, struggling, choking in that Slough![166]

'Next to a war', commented the *Irish Times*, 'it is probable that nothing holds so much that is tragic and dramatic as a strike.'[167] Nothing so much, it might be averred, as a failed one. An essential aspect of *The Slough*'s success was its timing. It was indeed performed next to a war, in which ground gained by socialists was swiftly being eaten up by issues of international conflict. Wilson himself had produced a recruiting play, *A Call to Arms*, at the Abbey only a month before. When *The Slough*'s battered personae left the stage for the last time their departure was an appropriate reflection of labour's depleted forces. Fred Ryan had died suddenly in London in 1913 and in October 1914 Larkin left for America, leaving James Connolly in charge of the Irish Citizen Army.[168] Denied

[165] Ibid. 43.
[166] Ibid. 58–9.
[167] 'The Irish Theatre', *Irish Times*, 2 Nov. 1914.
[168] Sean O'Casey, Wilson's obvious heir, had already left the Irish Citizen Army after failing to expel the Countess Markievicz for her 'bourgeois tendencies'. Gary O'Connor, *Sean O'Casey, A Life* (New York, 1988), 84.

through industrial defeat and the attractions of war his militant class, Connolly's undiminished taste for revolutionary action could only be made manifest through the remaining military vanguard. Though O'Casey's *The Plough and the Stars* would again give dramatic form to friction between socialist and nationalist objectives, the increasingly assertive redefinition of the British State at war was making choices starker. Connolly in late 1914 could still reflect on how during 1913 'the men and women of genius, the artistic and the literati, hastened to honour and serve those humble workers whom all had hitherto despised and scorned'.[169] In 1915 attention turned away again to issues and allegories of nationality.

Room for manoeuvre was considerably reduced. The advanced nationalist press came under severe restriction: *Irish Freedom*, the *Irish Worker*, and *Sinn Féin* were all proscribed.[170] New titles sought to compensate (*Irish Volunteer*, *Worker's Republic*, *Scissors and Paste* respectively) but editors had to take care with the increasingly sensitive Dublin Castle censors.[171] Theatres were similarly constrained. When *O'Flaherty V.C.*, Shaw's worldly recruiting play for Irish audiences had the kibosh put on it by the British military, he and Lady Gregory found their attempts to overcome objections *à lá Posnet* were met with short shrift.[172] As W. F. Bailey wrote to Yeats: 'There is no use threatening them—they are not in the mood for that.'[173] Nor were they in the mood for P. J. Bourke's melodramas of '98. When Bourke, opting for a change of scenery, chose to stage *For The Land She Loved* at the Abbey instead of the Queen's, the authorities blanched at stock speech given sudden force through context. The dastardly Colonel Johnston to United Irishman Robert Munro:

---

[169] *Irish Worker*, 18 Nov. 1914. Connolly was reviewing *Disturbed Dublin* by Arnold Wright, a history of the lockout commissioned by the Federated Dublin Employers. Nevin (ed.), *Trade Union Century*, 245.

[170] Censorship of the press was legislated for under the Defence of the Realms Act from 15 Aug. 1914, but was not applied vigorously to the Irish press until 2–3 Dec., when military authorities combined with the DMP to suppress these papers, plus *Eire* (Griffith's second try at a daily) and Cork's *Fianna Fail*. Virginia E. Glandon, *Arthur Griffith and the Advanced Nationalist Press, 1900–1922* (New York, 1985), 147–51.

[171] Advanced-nationalist press opinion began with open hostility to Irish soldiers fighting in France, but gradually changed (esp. after Gallipoli) to a stance of opposition plus pity. Benjamin Zvi Novick, 'Ireland's Revolutionary War?: Nationalist Propaganda, the Great War, and the Construction of Irish Identity', D.Phil. thesis (Oxford, 2000), 43–9.

[172] Augustine Birrell commented sympathetically: 'The military is not a good authority to which to submit a play. I don't think they would have passed *Henry V*.' Leon Ó Broin, *The Chief Secretary: Augustine Birrell in Ireland* (London, 1969), 152.

[173] D. H. Laurence and Nicholas Grene, *Shaw, Lady Gregory and the Abbey: A Correspondence and Record* (Gerrards Cross, 1993), 108.

I have to remind you that owing to the unsettled state of the country we find that you are the leader of a dangerous conspiracy, which is found to incite people of this country to a breach of the peace by an armed force . . . for the purpose of obtaining for the people of Ireland what they call their rights and Freedom—an act which is punishable by death.[174]

Ervine, chastised by Castle officials for allowing this 'piece of sedition', pleaded ignorance, but promised not to allow Bourke back onto the Abbey stage.[175] The stakes had risen. The Abbey was in a straitened financial situation—like all of the Dublin theatres suffering from shrivelled attendance. Bourke's use of the stage and Shaw's new play were intended as revenue boosters. At the same time, the Castle censors' remonstrations suggested that they thought of the Abbey, if a little wayward, essentially as part of the establishment. The complaint about Bourke was not so much against the play as against the Abbey's elevating imprimatur giving it cachet. A Queen's–Abbey combination was perhaps a little too reminiscent of *Cathleen ni Houlihan*; so long as melodrama remained confined to entertainment, it lacked potency.

The Castle's caution was based on a fear of drama as potentially incendiary, an understandable but misdirected anxiety. When Lennox Robinson staged his Emmet play *The Dreamers* earlier in the year, Yeats had recommended it on the grounds that it 'may well grow to be the most popular play we have . . . it is topical & should be put on at once'.[176] Its topicality was not uncomplicated, however, and as a result Yeats's hopes were not fulfilled. Robinson's theme had been to juxtapose the romance of Emmet with a grim historical realism treating his isolation in a corrupt Dublin. After a familiar love scene in the first act, the second act featured an experimental pastiche of bar-room discourse emerging out of 'half a minute of a babble of undistinguishable conversation' as the Dublin battalion fails to stir from its present pleasures. Emmet ends recasting his aspirations as naïvety: 'Sarah, tell me, was there anything in it but a boy's romantic dream? . . . when the rabble behind me began to loot and murder, oh Sarah, truth and justice seemed very far away.'[177]

Without that backdrop of growing working-class organization, agitation, and philosophy which gave the new realists their progressive air, Robinson reopened the gap between a modernist elite and any popular

[174] *For The Land She Loved*, in Cheryl Herr (ed.), *For the Land They Loved: Irish Political Melodramas 1890–1925* (Syracuse, 1991), 326.
[175] Seumus De Burca, *The Queen's Royal Theatre Dublin, 1829–1969* (Dublin, 1983), 4.
[176] Yeats to Lady Gregory, 6 Dec. 1914. Berg.
[177] *The Dreamers* (Dublin, 1915), 57.

movement that might travel with it. A contemporary link between the visionary and lagging audience appreciation was reinforced by his unconventional treatment. 'Robert Emmet's dream came down to him through—how many?—generations. He passed it on undimmed. It is being dreamed today, as vivid as ever and—they say—as impractical.'[178]

Terence MacSwiney had also written a play called *The Dreamers*—published in 1914 as *The Revolutionist*—which dwelt on similar concerns more overtly, and in a contemporary setting. It also marked the demise of the CDS, which dissolved with the establishment of a Cork branch of the Irish Volunteers in December 1913. Their theatre space, An Dun, became a drilling hall.[179] But MacSwiney was still attracted by the romance of theatrical idealism. Hugh O'Brien, debating at the Wolfe Tone Club, declares himself 'less of a democrat now than when we began the work':

> We acted in the belief the country would gradually be won over. I have come to feel it will not be so. The people will receive a shock and come over together.
> CONN. The time is too tame.
> HUGH. The time will always be—as dangerous as we make it.[180]

Even before the beginning of the war, MacSwiney had elevated the position of the IRB over that of the executive of the Irish Volunteers. The bulk of the Volunteers, under the leadership of MacNeill and Hobson, considered themselves realists, whose actions would faithfully reflect the national mood. For them, the time would be 'too tame' until either the Volunteers were attacked or conscription turned popular opinion in favour of revolutionary action—'success in the operation itself, not merely some future or political advantage' as MacNeill put it.[181] Sean MacDermott and Tom Clarke, the physical-force men at the core of the IRB, finally found strategic form following MacDonagh, Plunkett, and Pearse, who as 'dreamers' conceived of their role as catalysing, inspirational, and insurrectionary. And the appeal remained histrionic: nothing advanced Pearse's role in the Military Council like his graveside rhetoric in August 1915 eulogizing O'Donovan Rossa, declaring 'Life springs

[178] *Dreamers* preface [p. v].

[179] Patrick Maume, *Life that is Exile: Daniel Corkery and the Search for Irish Ireland* (Belfast, 1993), 37.

[180] MacSwiney Papers, *The Dreamers*, UCD P48b/297. *The Revolutionist* (Dublin, 1914) had its controversial debut at the Abbey on 24 Feb. 1921, within a year of its author's death while on hunger strike. 'We felt we were laying a wreath upon the grave', Lady Gregory told his widow Muriel. Quoted by Robert Welch, *The Abbey Theatre 1899–1999: Form and Pressure* (Oxford, 1999), 78.

[181] Eoin MacNeill, 'Memorandum I [Feb. 1916]', in F. X. Martin, 'Select Documents: Eoin MacNeill on the 1916 Rising', *Irish Historical Studies*, 12/47 (Mar. 1961), 234.

from death'. The fundamentally different approaches inspired corresponding tactics. The Irish Volunteers, making public assent an important criterion, were increasingly attracted by guerrilla action. The IRB, without public validation, were drawn not only by inclination but by audience mechanics into the symbolism of a theatrically open confrontation.

At the Irish Theatre in Hardwicke Street such differences could be discerned. In early 1915, prior to being drafted in by Hobson[182] to contribute guerrilla plans of campaign to the *Irish Volunteer* (as 'hedge fighting' theorist J. J. O'Connell's assistant),[183] Eimar O'Duffy's plays were performed. O'Duffy, commensurate with his more populist approach, later lampooned the Irish Theatre's penchant for 'Scandinavians and Russians' as a taste for 'not very interesting ideas and not very common emotions . . . uninteresting to the sane and logical mind of Ireland'.[184] Happy enough to have plays produced, the themes of this drama were nevertheless consistent with his position. *Phoenix on the Roof*, for instance, inverted the notion that visionary insight would be the preserve of an educated elite. He depicted any such elite as more likely to be typified by an *haut bourgeois* household such as his own (O'Duffy's father was a prominent dentist),[185] ineffectually debating the existence of the mythical and metaphorically Fenian bird that has alighted on their roof and set it ablaze. Terence Quigley, frantic to persuade his friends of their ignorance, points to the admiring crowd: 'The phoenix has the multitude on its side.'[186]

The Walls of Athens invested in the Mother Courage-like stall-minder Phryne the symbolic power of commerce to exploit war and public misery. The effective pragmatist Theramenes, by merit of his realism, wins out above the demagogue Cleophon, who has been driven to extremism by Phryne's blackmail. Though it was not easy to discern the 'comedy in allegory' in this plot (Phryne has been interpreted variously, as both Queen Victoria and the Shan Van Vocht[187]) the moral clearly recommended

---

[182] Dudley Edwards, *Patrick Pearse*, 241.

[183] Charles Townshend, *Political Violence in Ireland: Government and Resistance since 1848* (Oxford, 1983), 291.

[184] As part of O'Duffy's satirical rendering of what he called the 'Eclectic Theatre' in *Printer's Errors* (Dublin, 1922), 74.

[185] Robert Hogan, *Eimar O'Duffy* (Newark, Del., 1971), 14.

[186] W. J. Feeney (ed.), *Lost Plays of the Irish Renaissance*, ii. *Edward Martyn's Irish Theatre* (Newark, Del. 1980), 18. The text is as first published by the *Irish Review*, 20 Jan. 1923.

[187] As Queen Victoria in an unconvincing explanation by Feeney, *Drama in Hardwicke Street*, 89–90; as the aisling by a contemporary reviewer in *ACS*, 24 Apr. 1915.

realism and pragmatics over ideological zeal as less vulnerable to corruption and more sensible to suffering.

In the opposite corner from O'Duffy was the IRB's most effective propagandist. Pearse's *The Master* gave notice, through the suitable conduit of St Enda's schoolboy actors, of his emergence from the Hermitage to defy sovereign authority. In the play King Daire tempts pupils away from the Master Ciaran, in order to isolate and exterminate the teacher for preaching his newfangled Christian gospel. Phantoms of self-criticism appear in the form of Daire's interrogation—'What vile cause has not its heroes? Though you were to die here with joy and laughter you would not prove your cause to be a true one'[188]—but they are fleeting. Ciaran's obstinate faith finally prompts the Archangel Michael to appear in his defence, and even before this divine corroboration, Pearse's use of early Christianity as an example of vindicated minority has silenced any doubts.

In Pearse's final play *The Singer*, redemptive sacrifice as proselytizing force has entirely replaced the gradualism of education: this was not a play for schoolboys. Yet it was, significantly, for the performing artist. MacDara is a poet with the gift to animate and to provoke, and his songs are rumoured to contain 'irreligion and blasphemy against God'. His famous final speech declares for gesture:

DIARMUID. We thought it a foolish thing for fourscore to go into battle against four thousand, or maybe, thirty thousand.
MACDARA. And so it is a foolish thing. Do you want us to be wise? . . . the fifteen were too many. Old men, you did not do your work well enough. You should have kept back all but one. One man can free a people as one Man redeemed the world . . . I will stand up before the Gall as Christ hung naked before men on the tree![189]

The Messianic strain is self-evident. But *The Singer* also recalls Pearse's reflections on Synge: misunderstood, crucified, redeemed. Drama as cultural-political gesture, so expertly deployed by the dead master in the *Playboy*, was a reversible equation. A sufficiently gestural insurrection could amplify the tradition of heroic failure into national revelation. The theatre of war could resign metaphor, and in the Rising, be staged as production: part mystery play, part melodrama, part avant-garde provocation. Besides, as Pearse was at pains to point out in 'Peace and the Gael', human sacrifice may have been a cause of outrage in Ireland, but it was all the rage in modern Europe.[190]

---

[188] Pearse, *Collected Works*, 98.　　　[189] Ibid. 43–4.
[190] Dudley Edwards, *Patrick Pearse*, 245.

James Connolly responded to Pearse's glorifications of war by describing them as the ravings of a 'blithering idiot',[191] but the logic of the theatre of revolt was a convincing one. Pearse had set Lalor up among the demanding furies of the Irish past, and Connolly, whose impatience for revolution overcame his suspicion of the republicans' promotion of method over ideology, was pulled onside. His one and only theatrical work, produced at Liberty Hall on 26 March 1916, though called *Under Which Flag?*[192] offered nothing red in a clear choice of national colours. Connolly predictably showed a gift for humorous dialogue, and pointedly warned off any potential informers in the audience. But what is interesting about this play, set in '67, is that though it finished as an upbeat example of propaganda—

Gone! They are gone where countless thousands of the Irish race went before them, where it may be countless more will go after them. They are gone to fight for Ireland . . . the Irish Republican Brotherhood has sent out the call and all over Ireland in this March night the true sons of Erin are once more marching out to battle.[193]

—it was in fact suddenly thoroughly realist, with an almost ironic topicality: history itself was about to become propaganda.[194]

On Easter Bank Holiday Monday 1916 the IRB, joined by the Irish Citizen Army, mobilized their forces, occupying strategic buildings in Dublin city centre. Countermands issued by the circumvented Irish Volunteer leadership had limited their numbers to under 2,000, and localized the fight to Dublin. In front of the GPO, chosen as the insurrectionary headquarters, Pearse performed the inaugural act of the Irish revolution. Reading aloud the Proclamation of the Republic he declared: 'Ireland, through us, summons her children to her flag and strikes for her freedom.' A week of bitter fighting followed, the rebellion was comprehensively crushed, and its leaders executed.

The form of such dramatic political action owed no small debt to the

[191] *Worker's Republic,* 25 Dec. 1915.
[192] *Under Which Flag?,* NLI MS 13945. The play was rediscovered and read through, in its second ever performance, on 13 May 1969 to raise money for a Francis Sheehy-Skeffington Memorial.
[193] Ibid., fo. 31. The lines were spoken by Sean Connolly, the Abbey actor who was killed during the Rising. His portrayal of the blind '48 veteran Dan McMahon, according to the review by Sheehy-Skeffington, 'dominated the entire second act'. *Worker's Republic,* 8 Apr. 1916.
[194] A less intentional example of synchronicity came with the Irish Theatre's choice of Strindberg's *Easter* for production in early Mar. 1916. MacDonagh, not at that stage privy to the IRB's executive decision, was, like Martyn, nonplussed at Plunkett's instant resignation.

theatre's repeated use as a forum for cultural debate, antagonism, explication, and abuse. Writing *Ghosts*, the first in his series of final essays, Pearse had thanked Ibsen's shade for his 'inevitable' title.[195] For Pearse, as for many others, 'the nation is the family in large':[196] the dedication referenced the wisdom of a play for its insights into the family's secret guilt— but also conjured the vision of a man whose unpalatable truths had sweetened into favour. With this in mind, no doubt, he briefly accepted Parnell into his pantheon of heroes before concentrating on the four apostles of Tone, Davis, Lalor, and Mitchel. In hoping to join them he had keenly observed the force of display as well as the display of force. Ibsen and Synge, as much as any of his political icons, demonstrated the temporal nature of popular displeasure and the value of audience manipulation. It was a device which could find recognition in the least sympathetic, as it found the assent of Ireland's most diligent theatrical agent: 'for is it not the custom in Ireland as in tragedy for the victory to remain with the dead?'[197]

[195] 'Ghosts', in *Collected Works*, 221.
[196] 'The Sovereign People', ibid., 343.
[197] Lady Gregory, 'What was their Utopia?', a draft of an unpublished plea for the revolutionary manifesto, written 16 May 1916. Berg.

Conclusion
Mahon and the Echo

Man.

> .   .   .   .   .   .
>
> Did that play of mine send out
> Certain men the English shot?
> Did words of mine put too great strain
> On that woman's reeling brain?
> Could my spoken words have checked
> That whereby a house lay wrecked?
> And all seems evil until I
> Sleepless would lie down and die.
> *Echo.* Lie down and die.[1]

W. B. Yeats secured in his *Last Poems* a powerful claim on those willing to study the operations of Irish culture in the pre-revolutionary period. The insistent questioning of 'Man and the Echo'; the last review of his dramatic work in 'The Circus Animals' Desertion'; and that dark, left-open image of misconjured myth in 'The Statues'—'When Pearse summoned Cuchulain to his side, | What stalked through the Post Office?'—demand for their author a primary importance in the processes which led Ireland into violent rebellion. Such poems were the latest of Yeats's redrawings of pride and anxiety in his role as Ireland's mage-laureate and the 'onlie begetter' of the *Spiritus Mundi* of Irish insurrection.

Like all Yeats's revisions, these poems make apparent his need to control the attention of literary and historical enquiry and alter it in his image. They also, equally typically, and pre-emptively, mock that attempt.[2] In 'Man and the Echo' the 'Echo' serves to amplify the doubt in the persuasive rhetoric of the poet, but also takes the interrogation out of rhetoric into demi-dialogue. The poem thus becomes a suggestion of

[1] W. B. Yeats, 'Man and the Echo', in *The Collected Works of W. B. Yeats*, i. *The Poems*, ed. Richard J. Finneran (rev. edn. London, 1983), 345.

[2] Yeats's claims have been famously contradicted by Auden ('poetry makes nothing happen') and lampooned by Muldoon ('If Yeats had saved his pencil-lead | Would certain men have stayed in bed?'). But their judgement is more of a commentary on their own anxieties than a convincing judgement on the political influence of Yeats's literary practice or indeed of literary practice in general.

(pre-)Beckettian self-combat, as Yeats's literary conceit undermines his political arrogance. This tiny drama gives formal recognition to the thematic focus of the poems: when Yeats ponders his influence in Irish politics, the play, not the poem, is the thing that troubles his conscience. Trying to answer for us and for himself the riddle of his place in the maelstrom of the revival, his poetry is pulled out of place—back to the theatre and its effects.

Locating the theatre as the place of speech and echoes, however, inevitably challenges Yeats's notion of his singular importance. His suspicion that *Cathleen ni Houlihan* had been a cultural wrecking ball anticipates Raymond Williams's observation that of art forms, drama is 'the most social'[3]—and thus the most politically effective. But in claiming guilt he neglects the fact that his collaborator, Lady Gregory, had shared the authorship of that play, and much of the dynamism of the theatre movement of which it was a part. Small mention either, of the circumstances of performances, the role of Maud Gonne, the Inghinidhe, of Frank and William Fay, of the audience. Such elisions beg the question of what other dramas, and what other politics, were operating beneath the broadest overviews and assertions. If what Yeats's retrospection pulls from his poetry is dialogue, it is to the wider dialectics of cultural causation we must turn in assessing the role of drama in the politics of pre-Revolutionary Ireland.

This was not, as it has often been characterized, a period of inexorable tribalistic polarization. Prior to the contraction of political options that came with world war, revolution, and partition, Ireland's future was less rigidly cast. Just as Ernesto Laclau and Chantal Mouffe have sought to theorize radical possibility from the starting point of the 'variety and richness of Marxist discursivity in the era of the Second International'[4] it has been my contention that a similar wealth of possibility in nationalist ideology—including of course the socialist—was a contemporary feature of Irish cultural politics. Despite his fears and best intentions, Yeats must take his (still central) place in an array of voices and reverberations that multiply the complications of responsibility beyond the personal. That process, it must be said, is one that mirrors the shift away from the nationalist—or Whig—teleology that Yeats was relying upon for

---

[3] *The Long Revolution* (London, 1961), 246.
[4] *Hegemony and Socialist Strategy: Towards a Radical Democratic Politics* (London, 1985), 4.

his effect.[5] To reverse back through 1916 to the discourse anterior to that date is to decompress the national story line; in other words to open out the narrative into what Francis Sheehy-Skeffington had called the 'Dialogues of the Day'.

It is such an interruption to narrative that constitutes the parameters of this book. Ireland's theatre tradition did not start in 1890; and, as I have attempted to demonstrate, the search for an Irish national drama, like the wider revival, had less definite beginnings. But Parnell's fall produced a schism in which drama became part of the vocabulary of dispute. Naturally that role was to type, no less than precisely apposite. During the next quarter-century drama became the most potent of forms in an artistic renaissance that was crucial to Ireland's national ambitions; and this formal pre-eminence, so evident in the nationalist discourse of the time, was in part due to the performance of debates of which it was itself a manifestation.

Cultural nationalism did not replace Nationalist constitutionalist politics; it did offer a broader terrain for battles within nationalism to be fought upon. And this was specifically useful for Parnellites who in the early 1890s saw literary nationalism as offering much-needed cachet to the struggling minority interest—likewise the radical options available in physical-force and labour movements. The Chief's adultery invited such vituperation from social and moral conservatives that gender politics were also brought to the equation. Thus an alliance between the literati and emerging radical interests was established: which, despite fragmentations, digressions and personality clashes, remained remarkably durable. Within the broad camp of nationalism, such forces tended to coalesce in antagonism to the more conservative agenda, particularly as it was evident in bourgeois and petty-bourgeois chauvinism. Yet still, that broad camp remained to temper oppositions within what remained the broader opposition to the status quo.

Irish theatre in all its variety operated across this wide spectrum. But the ambition of self-consciously national drama was part of the reason that this cohesion held. Drawing on an anti-colonial ethos which considered British influence to be most palpable in the commercialization of culture, Irish drama was inevitably drawn to European forms which had already begun to kick against bourgeois convention and social conser-

---

[5] Homi K. Bhabha, (ed.) *Nation and Narration* (London, 1990); R. F. Foster, *The Story of Ireland: An Inaugural Lecture delivered before the University of Oxford on 1 December 1994* (Oxford, 1995).

vatism. Writers were drawn to both mythic and realist strands of this impulse, and in application to a distinctively Irish subject matter, added a new strand of resistance: an aspiration toward a dramatic autarky hinting at a political equivalent. The famous manifesto of the ILT, while not the first word on the subject, brought these objectives into focus.

National drama was thus a counter-hegemonic force: 'When all is said and done', admitted D. P. Moran in 1910, 'the Abbey represents the chief verb "to do".' In other words, as Adrian Frazier has argued citing Walter Benjamin's criterion of literary ethics, it 'put an approved apparatus' at the disposal of a multitude of consumers'.[6] But as Frazier also demonstrated, there were internal tensions and struggles. Anti-commercial imperatives gave playwrights essential space to explore their rather new subject, but also—and partly because of this—rendered their exponents prone to an elitism that understood the artist as a self-justifying category. That elitism had a tendency to draw on resources that brought its affiliations into question, based as they were in existing systems of privilege. In the case of the ILT, constructive Unionism offered an establishment seal of approval; and yet, when the wider colonial politics of the Boer War polarized opinion, nationalist predilections overrode the notionally 'apolitical' consensus upon which the cross-party support was based. Similarly, the patronized Abbey established at the centre of Irish culture a forum for debate, but was only possible at the cost of allowing benefactor Annie Horniman excessive control. The set-up valorized playwrights at the expense of other aspects of the theatre, and discarding the democratic instincts of the INTS, concentrated power into the hands of a directorship all the more obnoxious to nationalist opinion for being exclusively Protestant. It was little wonder that the theatre movement split, and sometimes left the Abbey looking isolated. Upon closer inspection, however, it is evident that the directorate was never the monolith critics suggested: while Synge operated on the left, and Yeats on the right, Lady Gregory's centrist, diplomatic attitude proved an indispensable attribute. As a result, the Abbey continued to produce drama that refused to conform to hostile caricature, whether from cultural-nationalist opponents or its neurotic sponsor. Autonomy at the Abbey made the production of an unexpected variety of plays possible and meant that by the time the subsidy was replaced by the box office, an audience alert to a drama given to conflict rather than reassurance had been assembled.

---

[6] *Leader*, 5 Nov. 1910; *Behind the Scenes: Yeats, Horniman and the Struggle for the Abbey Theatre* (Berkeley and Los Angeles, 1990), 136–7.

The importance of that conflict-driven—dramatic—sensibility was crucial to the success of the theatre movement in both aesthetic and political terms. Ireland in the early twentieth century was a nation in dispute. Unionism in the south, west, and east of Ireland was a distinctly minority opinion, but if nationalism was the popular persuasion, it was far from uniform. Those who began to push the cultural agenda as part of a more radical, separatist line from the 1890s were continually frustrated by the support that parliamentary party politics still commanded. The weekly newspapers and monthly journals that gave voice to new alternatives were far from in accord either; D. P. Moran's *Leader* and Arthur Griffith's *United Irishman/Sinn Féin* rarely concurred even on their rejection of the Abbey's latest work. Still, conservative nationalists tended to require that the Irish theatre present an agreed view, self-congratulatory and committed to the vision of an Ireland uncomplicated by internal frictions. From the point of view of a radical project, the pitfalls of this were swiftly evident. Nationalist ideology, no less than theatre practitioners, drew upon anti-colonial cultural instincts and European influences in equal measure. If the Boer War brought new vigour to advanced nationalism (and widened religious tolerance), the heightening of Catholic and ethnic essentialism rendered its advocates prone to European nationalism's anti-Semitic and anti-socialist mores. Arthur Griffith's politics called upon the Uitlander and the Anti-Dreyfusard as well as the republican tradition; his alert utilization of the political and economic strategies adopted in pursuit of Hungarian and German nationalist objectives similarly offered repressive as well as emancipatory potential.

Behind these schisms class divisions were inevitably in play. While conservative middle- and lower middle-class intellectuals expressed disdain for what they perceived as literary quasi-aristocratic posturing, they reserved their most trenchant abuse for precisely those theatrical subjects that reliably proved scandalous to bourgeois sentiment. Such episodes were characterized as typifying the tendency of Anglo-Irish writers to attack the Irish people. But they were more particularly driven by hostility to writers that attacked the Irish middle and lower middle classes.

Criticism of right-wing nationalism came from several quarters. On an issue like anti-Semitism, liberal and left could combine with a separatist anticlerical animus (though it is always possible to discover anti-Semites amongst these groups too). A similar 'union of sceptics' operated in the sphere of nationalist aesthetics, querying the hostility shown to the Abbey Theatre, while remaining critical of its leadership. An attack on Irish bourgeois assumptions could be understood as a damaging 'parting shot' from an elite that was being gradually divested of its power, thanks to land reform and the forward march of cultural-nationalist battalions. But it could also be construed as a challenge to the credentials of an ideological formation that while resistant to British imperialism happily confirmed the capitalist and patriarchal structures available to a European state-in-waiting.

Ireland imported modern art and ideology from both Britain and the Continent and with both came the fractures and oppositions that modernity made necessary (and possible). One such import was working-class activists. Equipped with skills developed in the industrially advanced, divided urban centres of Scotland and Northern England, Connolly and Larkin returned to the land of their fathers with the news that the sword of modernization was double-edged. Connolly's arrival in 1896 gave the gradual advance of the Dublin working class a new theoretical bite and provided his fledgling ISRP with an Internationalist perspective. Larkin's appearance in Belfast in 1907 brought trade-union militancy and soon the ITGWU. Both men were crucial to the formation of the Socialist Party of Ireland in 1910. As the working-class politics of Ireland's urban centres grew in confidence, so another challenge was made to the assumed ideals of what kind of society the new Ireland might be.

Similarly refocused was the rise in feminist thinking and action. Radical nationalist politics at the turn of the century was generally exclusive of women—and thus required the formation of alternative organizations for female involvement. The Inghinidhe na hÉireann was one such, with the useful side-product of providing actresses to the nascent theatre movement. More radical still were those no longer prepared to subsume a feminist analysis of Irish society to nationalist goals. Irish suffragists asked for more than enfranchisement:[7] at stake was a reassessment of the principles of identity confidently fixed by those pressing most for their country's independence. And, with the appearance of the IWFL, that reassessment became tactical rather than merely philosophical. As Hanna Sheehy-Skeffington put it in 1911, 'An outlawed section of the community never received its rights except by revolution or the threat of revolution.'[8] Militant feminism gave nationalists cause to reflect on the relative hesitancy of their own movement, and by the time of the *Irish Citizen*'s appearance in 1913, issues that had seemed peripheral were offering to come centre stage.

---

[7] Louise Ryan, 'Traditions and Double Standards: The Irish suffragists' Critique of Nationalism', *Women's History Review*, 4/4 (1995).   [8] *Leader*, 11 Feb. 1911.

The rapidity with which such issues opened up Irish politics in the first decade of the twentieth century repeatedly shifted the ground upon which criticism of the theatre could be made. Constituency and audience were in flux. Among radical nationalists, the increase in class and gender consciousness drew support away from the right and the aesthetic that went with it. Drama that got under the skin was celebrated as a disturbance, a necessary irruption in keeping with political change. Griffith's hostility, once a signature of advanced-nationalist conviction, became identified with the conservatism apparent in his wider politics. Part of the reason for this was the momentum of a conservative Catholic nationalism that was gaining force and claiming the centre ground. D. P. Moran, whose cultural broadsides had seemed so outré in 1900, was soon wooing bourgeois interests more gently; Arthur Griffith likewise found himself none too distant from the Nationalists he had once denounced. They had been overtaken by events.

Despite the dominance of the centre ground in Irish politics by the IPP before the war and by Sinn Féin afterward, class and gender issues were never so marginal as to prove irrelevant—that would be to misconstrue the nature of their marginality. Their power derived from the fact that the margin they occupied was that of the leading edge. It was a tenet of nineteenth-century nationalism that stifling Ireland's industrial capacity had been central to the Act of Union, and few at this stage demurred from an economic orthodoxy that assumed industrialization would therefore arrive all the more quickly with political autonomy.[9] Economic expansion North and South pre-1914[10] was accompanied by trade-union activism that echoed a European as much as any imperial pattern and suggested that despite Catholic corporatist teaching and the culture of the Gael, such divisions might prove unmanageable. Certainly, within a colonial paradigm, modernization could always be construed as a process that concealed within the concept of the 'new' a rationale that continually co-opted Ireland into accepting imperial systems. But modernity being an unstable not a stable condition, it also sustained conflicts along several lines of fracture, including, but not limited to, the notion of a resisting 'tradition'. The idea of the 'archaic avant-garde' posited by Terry Eagleton has neatly expressed the opportunity of that dialectic, so evident in the Celticist emphasis of the early dramatic revival.[11] But the impulse

---

[9] Cormac Ó Gráda, *Ireland: A New Economic History 1780–1939* (Oxford, 1994), 347.
[10] Ibid. 381.
[11] *Heathcliff and the Great Hunger: Studies in Irish Culture* (London, 1995), 281, 307.

toward the more temporally grounded idiom of realism was no less radical, picking up as it did on changing emphases within cultural nationalism. The sensitivity to class and gender represented other lines of fracture, and offered possibilities of resistance that extended through modernity, levelling Empire and encompassing Europe. The modern thus appeared not merely as the new but as the going-to-be-new, fuelling a destabilizing politics of anticipation that exercised the whole, not merely the periphery of Irish politics. Anticipation was what made the ideological skirmishes of the period so hard fought, the theatre so controversial, the lockout so bitter, and what led many initially to interpret the Easter Rising as more likely a Red than a Republican rebellion.[12]

It also gave the generational friction of the times its edge. Claim and counter-claim to the title 'Young Ireland' did of course hark back to the 1840s, to Thomas Davis and the *Nation*'s project of creating a new Ireland through 'national historical awareness'.[13] Such bids were equally Janus-headed, however: while young republicans, Gaelic Leaguers, left-leaning Nationalists, and literary provocateurs all claimed the validity of tradition, it was at least in part the tradition of upstaging a stale old-guard. They celebrated their generation as a freshly inspired and capable one. Youth therefore occupied another impatient marginal position fretting at the pace of change; old lags who once claimed its force, like Yeats (*vis-à-vis* James Joyce's militancy) or Griffith (*vis-à-vis* republican militancy) were apt to find themselves its targets in turn.

During the period 1890–1916, class, gender, and generation were all factors increasingly disturbing the nationalist mind. And this process had important repercussions for the theatre movement. In terms of finding the logic of an audience response, David Cairns and Shaun Richards have demonstrated the usefulness of taking Hans Robert Jauss's notion of an 'horizon of expectation' to gauge the moment literary (dramatic) forms break taboo. Any literary historian of the period must consider the first performance of *The Playboy of the Western World* as a crucial point in the revival, and it must be seen in the context of the conflicting interests and changing values of the audience. Synge's avant-gardist event wrought theatre from the very act of pushing aesthetic horizons. But it is also essential to view the synchronic moment (taking into account the

    [12] J. J. Lee, *Ireland 1912–1980* (Cambridge 1989), 30.
    [13] Joep Leerssen, *Remembrance and Imagination: Patterns in the Historical and Literary Representation of Ireland in the Nineteenth Century* (Cork, 1996), 147.

profoundly social nature of the aesthetic advance)[14] in the context of the diachronic processes that give that moment meaning. Nationalist response to the *Playboy* was complex and changing. Given the increasing influence of progressive nationalism that dramatic week was soon something to reflect back upon. For many radicals, Synge's depiction of violent youth lionized was, in hindsight, insight. Any audience attitude to an event must change as the horizon of expectation recedes; and so its approach to the coming 'event horizon' must also change in response to its own adaptability. In an increasingly self-consciously modernist moment, taste becomes less reception than prediction.

It is in this context that the success of realism in the Irish theatre must be considered, and reassessed. In a period when fair representation of the 'Irish' was a defining criterion for nationalist critics, portrayals of the Irish family in particular were disposed toward allegorical readings. They could not but become part of the debate over which and what Ireland was depicted, and in whose interests any censorship might be exercised. The working-class consciousness evident in the *Peasant* and later in the *Irish Worker* recognized in dramatic realism—particularly a new strain of urban realism—an opportunity for contesting the political 'realities' offered by bourgeois ideologues. Frederick Ryan, who so capably articulated socialist, anti-imperialist internationalism, was correct in observing that it was the *Playboy* that 'without malice' had evolved a new strain of harshly critical realism.[15] Yet through the growing capacity of that critical spirit to find an audience came also the reassessment of Synge's play: his provocation was marked out in the dramatic history of subsequent productions, demanding of nationalist converts a historicization of audience dynamics. And if such realism was a step back from the experimentation Synge offered, the tragic form it often took was no mere dampener reminding disputants of the impossibility of their task. Given the burgeoning confidence of working-class politics, such plays acted in straitened circumstances as a register of anger over existing injustice. The tradition of urban working-class drama which began with Fred Ryan; continued with Terence MacSwiney, St John Ervine, Andrew Patrick Wilson; and was to have a last late flowering in the work of Sean O'Casey,

---

[14] As noted by Cairns and Richards in terms of their adding a Gramscian spin to Jauss's theory. 'Reading a Riot: The "Reading Formation" of Synge's Abbey Audience', *Literature and History*, 13/2 (Autumn 1987), 219–37. See also Maria Shevtsova, *Theatre and Cultural Interaction* (Sydney, 1993), p. viii.

[15] ' "The Playboy of the West" and the Abbey Peasant: A Curious Development and its Inner History', *Evening Telegraph*, 13 May 1911.

was one that received its impetus from expectation, not acquiescence. It took its place in the vogue of critical realism that had pride of place at the Abbey, the stature of which must be considered in the light of its potency as an immediate art, with a relevance rooted in topicality.

Dublin's role as putative independent capital focused the energies of all these 'advanced' elements. Parnell's return in 1890 not only effectively reconfigured the politics of culture, pushing literature to the fore; it recharged Dublin as the engine of change. Dublin absorbed the talents of Ireland south, west, north (and east, in London and Paris) to reissue their difference in terms of the competing claims on Irish identity, drawing them to the seething pot of revival politics. Dublin Castle drew forces of opposition as to a siege, and the operations of its power met with those alternatives in a mutual dispersion sharing their source. Parnell's plan worked: Westminster was demoted. The Gaelic Leagues, Clubs, newspapers, theatre groups emanated out contradicting and contradictory possibilities for the reinterpretation of what Ireland had been, was, and could be.

Yet Dublin's authority was also transformed as it was interpreted. The Abbey on tour met with astonishment, apathy, and hostility; and Dublin's dramatic revival inspired projects that transcended mere imitation, in turn adding to the echoes altering Ireland's self-image. Cork's intra-IPP feuding gave form to the advanced sympathies of its dramatic society, and rise to the scornful craft of its native realists. In Belfast, the ULT very quickly evolved a distinct style that, faced with the profound divisions of North-East Ireland, queried the formal limitations of Dublin's dramatic templates—and tried to take the heat out of them at the same time.

The success of the ULT proved particularly important. It confirmed the potency of the dramatic revival, offered alternatives to the Abbey, and gave new impetus to the Abbey's rivals in the Theatre of Ireland and beyond. And yet it was part of a cultural political dynamic as crucial to the rehabilitation of the Abbey as was realism's increasing currency. It too was a product of marginality. Belfast gave life to the neo-republican Dungannon Clubs that offered an alternative to the Griffithite direction of Sinn Féin and gave new impetus to the IRB. There on the fringe of nationalist consensus a republican vanguard sought to make room between constitutional-party sectarian blocs. Sharing a common origin with the ULT, the Dungannon Clubs were wary of the aesthetic prescriptions that came so readily to their partners in the Sinn Féin Alliance, and argued for a more indulgent reception to the creative interpretations of Ireland's ills that theatre made flesh. The Northern dimension made space for the Abbey.

The issues socialist, feminist, and republican groups took to the theatre question responded to the logic of a literary avant-garde that understood its limited popularity in terms of a predictive sensibility: the taste of taste to come. Shaw's reading of Ibsen and Yeats's Anarchistic interpretation of poetic licence pursued the difference between democracy and populism, interrogating the rationalities of progressive politics. One reason why *The Enemy of the People* remained a popular template was because it had posited this dialectic so expressively. The pursuit of public good despite popular disapprobation and the pursuit of individual integrity at the expense of personal status gave notice of the possibility of righteous minority. Any play drawing on this dynamic was never complete, however, until performance pressured the audience into acting as an advanced jury, reflecting on a popular error and correcting it with a new consensus declaring the anti-hero heroic. The longer the delay in this response, the greater its potency, and the more secure the elevation of its creator from public enemy to visionary. George Sorel, whose *Reflections on Violence* was published in 1906, commented (of Nietszche) that 'Many moral evils would prevent humanity from progressing if some hero of revolt did not force the people to examine its conscience.'[16] Such lessons were scarcely confined to the playhouse.

The concept of organized resistance enduring into an act of national will had sustained the physical-force tradition since Fintan Lalor had observed that forcing an excessively aggressive response was the best means of revealing the coercive nature of British rule:[17] given the right conditions that revelation could propel Irish opinion toward a correspondingly militant resolve. The witnessed history of the theatre contained new proofs of how valid this performative logic could prove. In 1907 the enemy of the Irish people was John Millington Synge, and his greatest work, *The Playboy of the Western World*, remained a subject of popular disapproval. But amongst influential cadres of advanced-nationalist intelligentsia who observed its themes become the currency of social division, that reputation was revised. The promise of that play's modernity proving an eventual vindication of its temporary unconventionality resonated with the concerns of the alert republican mind.

Chief amongst these concerns was an acute sensitivity to Continental politics. The energy Irish cultural development drew from Europe

---

[16] *Reflections on Violence* (Cambridge, 1999), 233.
[17] Charles Townshend, *Political Violence in Ireland: Government and Resistance since 1848* (Oxford, 1983), 239.

became infused with a combative nationalism on the up as war loomed. The constitutional crisis and the delay of Home Rule underlined the ambivalence of Ireland's status as a nation hoping for a post-colonial position at the heart of imperial Europe. Increasingly the possibility of violent change offered both a rejection of the old regime and the satisfaction of embracing the shared view of modernity that system produced—a mutually celebrated world war. The shared experience of arming unionism and nationalism was an early offer to open the Western Front further west than it finally proved to be.

The years of the First World War saw the militarization of Ireland continue apace. From volunteerism to the use of Irish regiments abroad, the Rising and beyond to the extension of martial law in its wake, the introduction of conscription and later the battle-hardened Black and Tans, the pursuit of politics by other means became the norm. In the course of this turbulence, the unalterable shift in Irish opinion toward a more radical form of self-government appeared to vindicate the logic of an insurrectionary van prepared to redirect this culture of violence to inspire revolt and stimulate repression, and thus secure a new consensus. The reassessment of the importation of European aesthetics into the politics of Irish culture naturally took place amongst republicans whose view of those aesthetics became more favourable, as the 'modern' not only appeared less decadent and more stringent, but capable of catalysing the rapid social transformations Ireland needed to generate a sea change in national consciousness.[18]

Ireland's struggle in the nets of Empire and Nationality demands that the polyphony of its voices be seen in the wider context of both colonial and European politics. Yet Yeats, looking back on the Rising, very soon restricted his view to the internal dynamics of influence. A year on, *The Dreaming of the Bones* viewed 1916 in terms of a veteran revisiting a curse upon Diarmuid and Dervorgilla, who as Ireland's original sinners haunt the soldier's Western refuge. Their guilt has kept them in seven centuries of desire and denial, a perpetual agony that may only be broken by reprieve. Watching them dance, the soldier has 'almost yielded and forgiven it all' but can only repeat his judgement as they repeat their penance: 'never, never | Shall Diarmuid and Dervorgilla be forgiven'.[19]

First printed in 1919, this play reversed the dynamics of *Cathleen ni Houlihan*, continuing the retreat from his earlier provocative assumption

---

[18] Joseph Lee, *The Modernisation of Irish Society 1848–1918* (Dublin, 1973), 141–7.
[19] Yeats, *VP*, 775.

of a national audience into an 'unpopular theatre and an audience like a secret society . . . theatre's anti-self'.[20] In the earlier play the protagonist, sent by a mythically militant figure to fight in a historically specific European war that will feed Ireland's need for sacrifice, restores the power of the performative symbol as he does so. In *The Dreaming of the Bones* a soldier returns from the battle to condemn the figures who personify guilt and transgression, but which also ask for a clemency that will feed Ireland's need for forgiveness. This performative symbol discomforts and disturbs but is finally doomed to an ineffective repetition. And here is Yeats's model for his new theatre, wrought from the purgatorial pull between the confidence in a mesmeric adaptation of Noh theatre and a denial of its power to make an audience 'yield': an art that is resignedly, as well as designedly, unpopular.

Part of the powerlessness the play plays with thus lies in its insularity, with the myopia of reference that keeps Continental complication at bay. The play's dance elements evidenced the influence of European symbolism in terms of stylistic continuities, but the threat of the real had been removed.[21] If the French had been at hand in 1789 to aid Cathleen, here was no reference to wider wars. And this would also give form to the function of the Abbey Theatre in Ireland after the Treaty of 1921. Although Yeats warmed to O'Casey's triptych of interrogations into nationalist ideology, he balked at the way the *Silver Tassie* dwarfed Ireland's woes beneath the guns of the Western Front. Yeats's fear of theatre hostile to his own work was a self-fulfilling prophecy. Disguised within an apparent stylistic opposition was a shared proclivity: the Abbey responded to his caricature of the narrowing ground of politics post-partition, and evolved a realism which came to reinforce the conservatism it had once resisted. When Ernest Blythe, as the Free State Minister of Finance, consented to make the Abbey a state theatre in 1925, he reduced box-office anxieties but drew it closer to the restricted purview of the new government. His own revolutionary zeal recast in the civil war, Blythe had become an executor of the Irish Thermidor who dismissed the 'codology and codology and codology'[22] of idealist politics. When after Yeats's death in 1939 he became the dominant force in the Abbey that restriction of possibility

---

[20] Yeats, 'A People's Theatre', *Explorations* (New York, 1962), 257. First published in the *Irish Statesman* (Autumn 1919).

[21] For the European dimension of *The Dreaming of the Bones*, see Katherine Worth, *The Irish Drama of Europe from Yeats to Beckett* (London, 1978) ('Drama of the Interior'), 170–4.

[22] John M. Regan, *The Irish Counter-Revolution 1921–1936* (Dublin, 1999), 256.

came to characterize the theatre too. As Chris Morash has noted, Tomas MacAnna put it in a nutshell: 'His attitude was that . . . our stage had to reflect its natural image and never exaggerate it; indeed it was preferable to diminish it.'[23]

The Abbey was never Irish theatre alone, however; just as regional imitators and local alternatives gave width to the dramatic revival, the desire to take on European experiment that had kept future rebels busy at the Hardwicke Street Theatre went on to generate the Dublin Drama League (1918), the Gate Theatre (1928), and the Pike (1953). Denis Johnson famously renamed his Robert Emmet montage-drama *The Old Lady Says No!* to celebrate its rejection by the Abbey (although it was Yeats's rather than, as the title implied, Lady Gregory's decision)[24] and the play went on to make the Gate's reputation at its debut in 1929. The title also tellingly referred to his aged crone who can only recite bits of *Cathleen ni Houlihan*, the latest incarnation of an Ireland that was closing down the range of possibilities. The irony was that republican intellectuals had been drawn to the Hardwicke Street Theatre for the same reason: looking for impulse and ideas outside Ireland to revivify what they perceived to be an insular, stale, and self-satisfied generation.

But there are deeper ironies to conclude with. The works of O'Casey and Johnson were disdained by nationalists—and particularly republicans—for their attack on the ideals of 1916. But it was these playwrights' attempts to expose the limitations of the revolution that gave their work breath. Whereas post-civil war, republicans resisted the Treaty for its compromise of Irish independence and geographical definition, these plays returned to the energy of those emerging radical agendas which had, however obliquely, fuelled republican thinking in the pre-revolutionary period. What Nicholas Grene has called the 'multi-inhabited plurality'[25] of such treatments may have offended the single-mindedness of those who saw the sacrifice of the Easter rebels as the surest guide to the ethics of resistance, but they did so through an attempt to revisit options lost in the struggle—and to remind those who cared that more than one star had been sewn above the plough.

---

[23] Quoted by Chris Morash, ' "Something's Missing": Theatre and the Republic of Ireland Act', in Ray Ryan (ed.), *Writing in the Irish Republic: Literature, Culture, Politics 1949–1999* (London, 2000), 75.

[24] Christopher Murray, *Twentieth Century Irish Drama: Mirror up to Nation* (Manchester, 1997), 121.

[25] *The Politics of Irish Drama: Plays in Context from Boucicault to Friel* (Cambridge, 1999), 145.

James Connolly committed himself and the Irish Citizen Army to insurrection in an attempt to reinsert the working class into the equation of national identity as it responded to the First World War. In 1914 he famously suggested that partition, if it took place, would create 'a carnival of reaction'[26] in which the already sectarian division of labour in the North would become entrenched and the conservative instincts of Catholic social teaching would become a defining characteristic. Less a prediction than an observation of events already in train, his analysis was a recognition of the failure of radical alternatives to provide an agenda for unity. In finally subordinating socialist to republican objectives, however, he inevitably resigned the agenda of the radical—economic as well as political—democracy he had championed since the days of the *Worker's Republic*, and with it the possibility of mobilizing against the conservative nationalism he had long resisted. Perhaps Connolly had also imagined an audience response characterized by the turmoil of crisis, and that his compromise would find validation in a new dispensation. Nevertheless it was, by his own admission, more likely to involve a process whereby the expanding multivalency of cultural politics would become re-pressed into the two-dimensionalities of post-colonial cartography.

In that process can also be traced differing readings of Synge's great play. What Pearse first condemned as 'the gospel of animalism, of revolt'[27] and came to recommend as visionary, Ireland's own manifestation of *élan vital*, of the Sorelian impulse seen in its broadest spectacular category as an event, was the apparent heroism of Synge's provocation. 'It makes people think, makes them angry, sends them to find their tempers and their profanity', P. S. O'Hegarty commented approvingly in 1912.[28] The dirty story could inspire the gallous deed.

Yet the victory of the the *Playboy* paradoxically lay in open anxiety rather than closed confidence. Given the particularly public quality of theatre it was unsurprising that national drama should combine the lines of friction of pre-revolutionary Ireland and produce plays capable of responding to a wealth of conflict. The reason that conflict was nowhere more palpably staged than in the *Playboy* was that it drew into its ambit that broader drama of criticism as an element of its own energy. The 'reaction of carnival' Synge provoked fulfilled his study of the separation between community and artist-individual with an admixture of debate

---

[26] Connolly, 'Labour and the Proposed Partition of Ireland', *Irish Worker*, 14 Mar. 1914; repr. in *Collected Works*, i. (Dublin, 1987), 393.

[27] *ACS*, 9 Feb. 1907.

[28] 'Art and the Nation IV', *Irish Freedom*, May 1912.

and complaint that gave form to the divided society in which he wrote, and it is only by attempting to apprehend its complex history that it becomes apparent as a celebration of the incapacities and potential of the national drama. Synge's masterpiece may indeed have appeared an assertion of the artist as visionary, and a conduit of revolt that lent politics the possibility of being equally creative. But the essence of the *Playboy* as an event was a system's immanent self-criticism expressed through the medium of the theatre as a whole. For all Yeats's fearful pride, we may acquit him from the charge—or divest him of the honour—of being the primary theatrical provocateur in revived Ireland. But nor should we demote him in favour of John Millington Synge or any other single author. If the *Playboy* had produced an explosion of possibility, it was an outrage displaying a panoply of revolts. Republicanism sought to contain that diversity, directing and reducing the multivalency of its riotous discharge, and returning its singular echo in the act of insurrection. *Cathleen ni Houlihan* may have provided the impulse: but if Pearse did summon Cuchulain to his side, what stalked through the Post Office was the shade of Christy Mahon.

BIBLIOGRAPHY

I MANUSCRIPTS

British Library

Lord Chamberlain's Plays and Correspondence
O'Grady, Hubert, *The Eviction*, MS 53226D.
Shaw, G. B., *The Shewing Up of Blanco Posnet*, MS 1916/91.
Todhunter, John, *The Poison Flower*, MS 53476K.
—— *The Comedy of Sighs*, MS 53545.
Whitbread, J. W., *The Irishman*, Add. MS 53437.
—— *Sarsfield*, MS 1905/180.
Wilson, A. P., *The Slough*, Add. MS 1914/35.

National Library of Ireland

Celtic Literary Society Minutes
James Connolly, *Under Which Flag?* MS 13945.
Frank Fay Papers
T. P. Gill Papers
Bulmer Hobson Papers
Joseph Holloway Papers
Irish National Theatre Society Minutes
Irish Socialist Republican Party Minutes
Joseph McGarrity Papers
William O'Brien Papers
Sheehy-Skeffington Papers
Theatre of Ireland Minutes

New York Public Library

Henry W. and Albert A. Berg Collection

University College, Dublin

Terence MacSwiney Papers
   The Holocaust, P48b/296
   The Dreamers, P48b/297
   The Wooing of Emer, P48b/298
W. P. Ryan Papers

2 PRINTED SOURCES

(a) Newspapers and Periodicals

All Ireland Review; An Claidheamh Soluis; Arrow; Beltaine; Catholic Bulletin; Daily Chronicle; Daily News; Dana; Dublin Daily Express; Evening Herald; Evening Mail; Evening Telegraph; Eye Witness; Forum; Freeman's Journal; Harp; Irish Catholic; Irish Citizen; Irish Freedom; Irish Independent; Irish Nation and Peasant; Irish Peasant; Irish Review; Irish Times; Irish Volunteer; Irish Worker; Leader; Lyceum; National Democrat; Nationist; New Ireland Review; Peasant and Irish Ireland; Republic; Samhain; Scissors and Paste; Shanachie; Shan Van Vocht; Sinn Féin; Sinn Féin (Daily); Spark; Uladh; United Ireland; United Irishman; Westminster Review; Worker's Republic.

(b) Plays

AE (Russell, George), *Deirdre* (Dublin, 1907).

Birmingham, George A., *General John Regan* (London, 1933).

Boucicault, Dion, *Selected Plays of Dion Boucicault*, ed. Andrew Parkin (Gerrards Cross, 1987).

Bourke, P. J., *When Wexford Rose* and *For the Land She Loved*, in Cheryl Herr, *For the Land They Loved: Irish Political Melodramas 1890–1925* (Syracuse, 1991).

Boyle, William, *The Building Fund* (Dublin, 1905).

—— *The Mineral Workers* (Dublin, 1910).

—— *The Eloquent Dempsey* (Dublin, 1912).

—— *Family Failing* (Dublin, 1912).

Campbell, Joseph, *Judgement* (Dublin, 1912).

Chekhov, Anton, *The Seagull, in a new version by Thomas Kilroy* (London, 1981).

Christie, R. A., *The Dark Hour* (Belfast, 1950).

Colum, Padraic, *The Saxon Shillin'*, *United Irishman*, 15 Nov. 1902.

—— *The Land* (Dublin, 1905).

—— *The Land and The Fiddler's House* (Dublin, 1909).

—— *Thomas Muskerry* (Dublin, 1910).

Corkery, Daniel, *The Embers* and *Onus of Ownership*, in Richard Burnham and Robert Hogan (eds.), *Lost Plays of the Irish Renaissance*, iii. *The Cork Dramatic Society* (Newark, Del., 1984).

Dunsany, Lord (E. J. M. D. Plunkett), *Five Plays* (London, 1914).

Ervine, St John G., *Mixed Marriage* (Dublin, 1911).

—— *Four Irish Plays* (Dublin, 1914).

—— *Selected Plays* (Gerrards Cross, 1988).

Feeney, W. J. (ed.), *Lost Plays of the Irish Renaissance*, ii. *Edward Martyn's Irish Theatre* (Newark, Del., 1980).

Fitzmaurice, George, *Five Plays* (Dublin, 1914).

—— *The Plays of George Fitzmaurice: Dramatic Fantasies* (Dublin, 1967).

Galsworthy, John, *Five Plays* (London, 1984).

Gregory, Lady Augusta, *Seven Short Plays* (Dublin, 1909).

—— *The Collected Plays*, ed. Ann Saddlemyer, vols. i–iv (*The Coole Edition of the Works of Lady Gregory*, ed. T. R. Henn and Colin Smythe; Gerrards Cross, 1970).

Guinan, John, *The Cuckoo's Nest* (Dublin, 1933).

Hobson, Bulmer, *Brian of Banba*, United Irishman, 2 Aug. 1902.

Hogan, Robert, and Kilroy, James (eds.), *Lost Plays of the Irish Renaissance*, i. *The Abbey Theatre* (Newark, Del., 1970).

—— and Burnham, Richard (eds.), *Lost Plays of the Irish Renaissance*, iii. *The Cork Dramatic Society* (Newark, Del., 1984).

Hyde, Douglas, *Casadh an tSugáin or The Twisting of the Rope*, trans. Lady Gregory, *Samhain*, 1 (Oct. 1901), 20–38.

—— *Pleúsgadh na Bulgóidhe or The Bursting of the Bubble*, trans. Lady Gregory (Dublin, 1903).

—— *Selected Plays of Douglas Hyde*, ed. Gareth W. Dunleavy and Janet Egleson Dunleavy (Gerrards Cross, 1991).

MacCarthy, J. Bernard, *Wrecked* (Dublin, 1922).

—— *Kinship* (Dublin, 1936).

MacDonagh, Thomas, *When the Dawn is Come: A Tragedy in Three Acts* (Dublin, 1908).

—— *Metempsychosis*, Irish Review (Jan. 1912).

—— *Pagans: A Modern Play in Two Conversations* (Dublin, 1920).

MacManus, Seumas, *The Hard Hearted Man* (Dublin, 1905).

—— *The Lad from Largymore* (Mount Charles, n.d.).

—— *Orange and Green* (Mount Charles, n.d.).

—— *The Townland of Tamney* (Mount Charles, n.d.).

MacNamara, Gerald, *Suzanne and The Sovereigns* in Kathleen Danaher (ed.), 'The Plays of Gerald MacNamara', *Journal of Irish Literature*, 17/2–3 (May–Sept. 1988).

—— *The Mist That Does Be On The Bog*, in Danaher (ed.), 'Plays of Mac-Namara'.

—— *Thompson in Tir-na-n-og* (Dublin, n.d.).

McNulty, Edward, *The Lord Mayor* (Dublin, 1917).

MacSwiney, Terence, *The Revolutionist* (Dublin, 1914).

—— *The Last Warriors of Coole*, in Robert Hogan and Richard Burnham (eds.), *Lost Plays of the Irish Renaissance*, iii. *The Cork Dramatic Society* (Newark, Del., 1984).

Martyn, Edward, *The Heather Field and Maeve* (London, 1899).

—— *The Place-Hunters*, Leader, 26 July 1902.

—— *The Tale of A Town and An Enchanted Sea* (London, 1902).

Martyn, Edward, *Grangecolman* (Dublin, 1912).

—— *The Dream Physician* (Dublin, 1914).

—— *Romulus and Remus, or The Makers of Delights*, in W. J. Feeney (ed.), *Lost Plays of the Irish Renaissance*, ii. *Edward Martyn's Irish Theatre* (Newark, Del., 1980).

—— *Selected Plays of George Moore and Edward Martyn*, ed. David B. Eakin and Michael Case (Gerrards Cross, 1995).

Mayne, Rutherford, *The Drone and Other Plays* (Dublin, 1912).

—— *Selected Plays*, ed. John Killen (Belfast, 1997).

Murray, T. C., *Birthright* (Dublin, 1911).

—— *Spring and Other Plays* (Dublin, 1917).

—— *Maurice Harte and A Stag At Bay* (London, 1934).

O'Brien, Seumus, *Duty and Other Irish Comedies* (Boston, 1916).

O'Casey, Sean, *Plays One* (London 1998).

—— *Plays Two* (London, 1998).

O'Duffy, Eimar, *The Walls of Athens*, *Irish Review*, 4/40 (June 1914).

—— *The Phoenix on the Roof*, *Irish Review*, NS 1/20 (Jan. 1923).

O'Farrell, P. J., *Ireland's English Question* (London, 1971).

O'Grady, Hubert, *Emigration*, ed. Stephen Watt, *Journal of Irish Literature*, 14/1 (Jan, 1985).

—— *The Famine*, ed. Stephen Watt, *Journal of Irish Literature*, 14/1 (Jan. 1985).

O'Kelly, Seumas, *The Shuiler's Child* (Dublin, 1909).

—— *The Bribe* (Dublin, 1911).

O'Riordan, Conal (Norrey's Connell), *Shakespeare's End (and Other Irish Plays)* (London, 1912).

Pearse, Patrick H., *Collected Works of Padraic H. Pearse: Plays, Stories, Poems* (Dublin, 1917).

Purcell, Lewis, *The Enthusiast*, *Uladh*, 3 (May 1903).

—— *The Pagan* (Dublin, 1907).

Robinson, E. S. Lennox, *The Cross Roads* (Dublin, 1910).

—— *Two Plays: Harvest; The Clancy Name* (Dublin, 1911).

—— *Patriots* (Dublin, 1912).

—— *The Dreamers* (Dublin, 1915).

Redmond, Joanna, *Falsely True* (Dublin, 1911).

Russell, George, *Deirdre* (Dublin, 1907).

Ryan, Frederick, *The Laying of the Foundations*, in Robert Hogan and James Kilroy (eds.), *Lost Plays of the Irish Renaissance*, i. *The Abbey Theatre* (Newark, Del., 1970).

Shaw, G. Bernard, *The Complete Plays of Bernard Shaw* (London, 1934).

Stephens, James, *Julia Elizabeth* (New York, 1929).

Strindberg, August, *There are Crimes and Crimes*, trans. Edwin Björkman (London, 1912).

—— *Miss Julia, The Stronger*, trans. Edwin Björkman (London, 1912).

Synge, J. M., *The Plays and Poems of J. M. Synge*, ed. T. R. Henn (London, 1963).
—— *Collected Works* ed. Alan Price, 4 vols. (London, 1966).
Tagore, Rabindranath, *The Post Office*, trans. Devabrata Mukerja (London, 1914).
Todhunter, John, *A Sicilian Idyll* (London, 1890).
Whitbread, J. W., *The Nationalist* (Dublin, 1892).
—— *Lord Edward, or '98*, and *Wolfe Tone*, in Cherly Herr (ed.), *For the Land They Loved: Irish Political Melodramas 1890–1925* (Syracuse, 1991).
Wilson, Andrew Patrick, *Victims and Poached* (Liberty Hall Plays no. 1, Dublin, n.d.).
Yeats, W. B., *The Variorum Edition of the Plays of W. B. Yeats*, ed. Russell K. Alspach, assisted by Catherine C. Alspach (London, 1966).

(c) Books, Articles, and Essays

Anderson, R. A., *With Plunkett in Ireland: The Co-Op Organiser's Story* (London, 1983).
Archer, William, *The Theatrical 'World' of 1893* (London, n.d. [1894]).
Augusteijn, Joost, *From Public Defiance to Guerilla Warfare* (Dublin, 1996).
Bell, Sam Hanna, *The Theatre in Ulster* (Dublin, 1972).
Benson, Eugene, *J. M. Synge* (Dublin, 1982).
Bew, Paul, *Conflict and Conciliation in Ireland 1890–1910: Parnellites and Radical Agrarians* (Oxford, 1987).
—— *Ideology and the Irish Question: Ulster Unionism and Irish Nationalism, 1913–1916* (Oxford, 1994).
Bhabha, Homi K., (ed.) *Nation and Narration* (London, 1990).
—— *The Location of Culture* (London, 1994).
Bloom, Harold, *The Anxiety of Influence: A Theory of Poetry* (Oxford, 1973).
Bohlmann, Otto, *Yeats and Nietzsche: An Exploration of Major Nietzschean Echoes in the Writings of William Butler Yeats* (London, 1982).
Bowen, Zack, *Padraic Colum: A Biographical-Critical Introduction* (Carbondale, Ill., 1970).
Boyd, E. A., *Ireland's Literary Renaissance* (Dublin, 1916).
Boyle, John W., *The Irish Labour Movement in the Nineteenth Century* (Washington, 1988).
Brotherton, George, 'A Carnival Christy and a Playboy for All Ages', in Daniel J. Casey (ed.), *Critical Essays on John Millington Synge* (New York, 1994).
Brown, Malcolm, *The Politics of Irish Literature, from Davis to W. B. Yeats* (London, 1972).
Brown, Terence, *Ireland: A Social and Cultural History 1922–1985* (Dublin, 1986).
Brustein, Robert, *The Theatre of Revolt* (London, 1965).
Bull, Philip, 'The Significance of the Nationalist Response to the Irish Land Act of 1903', *Irish Historical Studies* (May 1993).

Bull, Philip, *Land, Politics and Nationalism: A Study of the Irish Land Question* (Dublin, 1996).

de Burca, Seumus, *The Queen's Royal Theatre Dublin, 1829–1969* (Dublin, 1983).

Bürger, Peter, *Theory of the Avant-Garde* (Manchester, 1984).

Butler, Hubert, *The Sub-Prefect Should Have Held His Tongue, and Other Essays*, ed. R. F. Foster (London, 1990).

Cairns, David, and Richards, Shaun, 'Reading a Riot: The "Reading Formation" of Synge's Abbey Audience', *Literature and History*, 13/2 (Autumn 1987), 219–37.

—— *Writing Ireland: Colonialism, Nationalism and Culture* (Manchester, 1988).

Callanan, Frank, *The Parnellite Split 1890–1891* (Cork, 1992).

Chapman, W. K., and Helyar, James, 'P. S. O'Hegarty and the Yeats Collection at the University of Kansas', *Yeats Annual*, 10 (1993).

Colum, Padraic, *The Road round Ireland* (New York, 1926).

—— *Arthur Griffith* (Dublin, 1959).

Connolly, James, *Collected Works*, vols. i and ii (Dublin, 1987–8).

Corkery, Daniel, *Synge and Ango-Irish Literature* (Cork, 1931).

Costello, Francis J., *Enduring the Most: The Life and Death of Terence MacSwiney* (Dingle, 1995).

Costello, Peter, *The Heart Grown Brutal: The Irish Revolution in Literature from Parnell to the Death of Yeats, 1891–1939* (Dublin, 1977).

—— *James Joyce: The Years of Growth: 1882–1915* (New York, 1993).

Coxhead, Elizabeth, *J. M. Synge and Lady Gregory* (London, 1962).

Cullingford, Elizabeth Butler, *Yeats, Ireland and Fascism* (London, 1981).

Dangerfield, George, *The Strange Death of Liberal England, 1910–1914* (London, 1935).

Davis, Richard P., *Arthur Griffith and Non-Violent Sinn Féin* (Dublin, 1974).

Davis, Tracy C., *George Bernard Shaw and the Socialist Theatre* (Westport, Conn., 1994).

Davitt, Michael, *Within the Pale: The True Story of Anti-Semitic Persecutions in Russia* (London, 1903).

Deane, Seamus, *Celtic Revivals: Essays in Modern Irish Literature, 1880–1980* (London, 1985).

—— *A Short History of Irish Literature* (London, 1986).

—— (ed.) *The Field Day Anthology of Irish Writing*, 3 vols. (Derry, 1991).

—— *Strange Country: Modernity and Nationhood in Irish Writing since 1790* (Oxford, 1997).

Dhuibhne-Almqvist, Éilís Ní, 'Synge's Use of Popular Material in *The Shadow of the Glen*', *Béaloideas*, 58 (1990).

Digby, Margaret, *An Anglo-American Irishman* (Oxford, 1949).

Donaldson, Ian, 'A Transplanted Doll's House: Ibsenism, Feminism and Socialism in Late-Victorian and Edwardian England', in id. (ed.), *Transformations in Modern Irish Drama* (London, 1983).

Dudley Edwards, Ruth, *Patrick Pearse: The Triumph of Failure* (London, 1977).

Dunleavy, J. E., and Dunleavy, G. W., *Douglas Hyde: A Maker of Modern Ireland* (Berkeley and Los Angeles, 1991).

Dunne, Tom, 'A Polemical Introduction: Literature, Literary Theory and the Historian', in id. (ed.), *The Writer as Witness: Literature as Historical Evidence* (Cork, 1987).

Dunsany, Lord, *Selections from the Writings of Lord Dunsany, with an Introduction by W. B. Yeats* (Dundrum, 1912).

Eagleton, Terry, *Nationalism: Irony and Commitment* (Derry, 1988).

—— *Heathcliff and the Great Hunger: Studies in Irish Culture* (London, 1995).

—— 'The Ideology of Irish Studies', *Bullán*, 3/1 (Spring 1997).

—— *Crazy John and the Bishop, and Other Essays on Irish Culture* (Cork, 1998).

Eksteins, Modris, *Rites of Spring: The Great War and the Birth of the Modern Age* (London, 1989).

Ellis-Fermor, Una, *The Irish Dramatic Movement* (London, 1958).

Ellmann, Richard, *James Joyce* (rev. edn. Oxford, 1982).

—— *Oscar Wilde* (London, 1987).

English, Richard, 'Green on Red: Two Case Studies in Early Twentieth Century Irish Republican Thought', in D. G. Boyce, R. Eccleshall, and V. Geoghegan (eds.), *Political Thought in Ireland since the Seventeenth Century* (London, 1993).

—— *Radicals and the Republic, Socialist Republicanism in the Irish Free State 1925–1937* (Oxford, 1994).

Ervine, St John, *Sir Edward Carson and the Ulster Movement* (Dublin, 1915).

Fay, Frank J., *Towards a National Theatre: The Dramatic Criticism of Frank J. Fay*, ed. Robert Hogan (Dublin, 1970).

Fay, Gerard, *The Abbey Theatre: Cradle of Genius* (London, 1958).

Fay, W. G., and Carswell, Catherine, *The Fays of the Abbey Theatre: An Auto-biographical Record* (London, 1935).

Feeney, W. J., *Drama in Hardwicke St: A History of the Irish Theatre Company* (London, 1984).

Flannery, James W., *W. B. Yeats and the Idea of a Theatre: The Early Abbey Theatre in Theory and Practice* (Yale, 1976).

Foster, John Wilson, *Colonial Consequences: Essays in Irish Literature and Culture* (London, 1988).

Foster, R. F., *Modern Ireland, 1600–1972* (London, 1988).

—— *Paddy and Mr Punch: Connections in Irish and English History* (London, 1993).

—— *The Story of Ireland: An Inaugural Lecture delivered before the University of Oxford on 1 December 1994* (Oxford, 1995).

—— *W. B. Yeats: A Life*, i. *The Apprentice Mage, 1865–1914* (Oxford, 1997).

Frazier, Adrian, *Behind the Scenes: Yeats, Horniman and the Struggle for the Abbey Theatre* (Berkeley and Los Angeles, 1990).

—— *George Moore, 1852–1933* (New Haven, 2000).

Gailey, Andrew, *Ireland and the Death of Kindness: The Experience of Constructive Unionism 1890–1905* (Cork, 1987).

Garvin, Tom, 'Great Hatred, Little Room, Social Background and Political Sentiment Among Revolutionary Activists in Ireland, 1890–1922', in D. B. Boyce (ed.), *The Revolution in Ireland, 1879–1923* (London, 1988).

—— *Nationalist Revolutionaries in Ireland 1858–1928* (Oxford, 1988).

Gibbons, Luke, *Transformations in Irish Culture* (Cork, 1996).

Glandon, Virginia E., *Arthur Griffith and the Advanced Nationalist Press, 1900–1922* (New York, 1985).

Gonne MacBride, Maud, *A Servant of the Queen: Reminiscences* (1938: London, 1974).

—— and Yeats, W. B., *The Gonne–Yeats Letters 1893–1938: Always Your Friend*, ed. Anna MacBride White and A. Norman Jeffares (London, 1992).

Gramsci, Antonio, *Selections from the Prison Notebooks* (London, 1971).

Gray, John, *City in Revolt: James Larkin and the Belfast Dock Strike of 1907* (Belfast, 1985).

Greaves, C. Desmond, *The Life and Times of James Connolly* (London, 1961).

—— *Sean O'Casey, Politics and Art* (London, 1979).

—— *The Irish Transport and General Workers' Union: The Formative Years 1909–1923* (Dublin, 1982).

Greene, David H., and Stephens, Edward M., *J. M. Synge 1871–1909* (rev. edn. New York, 1989).

Gregory, Lady Augusta, (ed.), *Ideals in Ireland* (London, 1901).

—— *Our Irish Theatre* (London, 1913).

—— *Lady Gregory's Diaries, 1892–1902*, ed. James L. Pethica (Gerrards Cross, 1996).

Grene, Nicholas, *Synge: A Critical Study of the Plays* (London, 1975).

—— *The Politics of Irish Drama: Plays in Context from Boucicault to Friel* (Cambridge, 1999).

Griffith, Arthur, *The Resurrection of Hungary: A Parallel for Ireland* (Dublin, 1904).

—— *The Sinn Féin Policy* (Dublin, 1905).

Gwynn, Denis, *Edward Martyn and the Irish Revival* (London, 1930).

Hart, Peter, *The I. R. A. and its Enemies: Violence and Community in Cork, 1916–1923* (Oxford, 1998).

Hays, Michael, 'Theatrical Texts and Social Context', *Theater* (Winter 1983).

Herr, Cheryl, *For the Land They Loved: Irish Political Melodramas 1890–1925* (Syracuse, 1991).

Hobson, Bulmer, *Ireland Yesterday and Tomorrow* (Tralee, 1968).

Hogan, Robert, *Eimar O'Duffy* (Newark, Del., 1971).

—— and Kilroy, James, *A History of Modern Irish Drama*, i. *The Irish Literary Theatre, 1899–1901* (Dublin, 1975).

—— *A History of Modern Irish Drama*, ii. *Laying the Foundations, 1902–1904* (Dublin, 1976).

—— —— *A History of Modern Irish Drama*, iii. *The Years of Synge, 1905–1909* (Dublin, 1978).

—— —— Burnham, Richard, and Poteet, Daniel D., *A History of Modern Irish Drama*, iv. *The Rise of the Realists 1910–1915* (Dublin, 1979).

—— —— *A History of Modern Irish Drama*, v. *The Art of the Amateur 1916–1920* (Gerrards Cross, 1984).

—— —— *A History of Modern Irish Drama*, vi. *The Years of O'Casey 1921–1926* (Gerrards Cross, 1992).

Holloway, Joseph, *Joseph Holloway's Abbey Theatre: A Selection from his Unpublished Journal Impressions of a Dublin Playgoer*, ed. Robert Hogan and Michael J. O'Neill (Carbondale, Ill., 1967).

Holroyd, Michael, *George Bernard Shaw*, 4 vols. (London, 1988–92).

Howe, Stephen, *Ireland and Empire* (Oxford, 2000).

Hutchinson, David, *The Modern Scottish Theatre* (Glasgow, 1977).

Hutchinson, John, *The Dynamics of Cultural Nationalism: The Gaelic Revival and the Creation of the Irish Nation State* (London, 1987).

Hyde, Douglas, 'The Necessity for De-Anglicising Ireland', in *The Revival of Irish Literature: Addresses by Sir Charles Gavan Duffy, KCMG, Dr George Sigerson, and Dr Douglas Hyde* (London, 1894).

Hyman, Louis, *The Jews of Ireland* (Shannon, 1972).

Hywel, Elin Ap, 'Elise and the Great Queens of Ireland: "Femininity" as constructed by Sinn Féin and the Abbey Theatre, 1901–1907', in Toni O'Brien Johnson and David Cairns (eds.), *Gender in Irish Writing* (Milton Keynes, 1991).

Innes, Christopher, *Avant–Garde Theatre 1892–1992* (London, 1993).

Joyce, James, *The Critical Writings of James Joyce*, ed. Richard Ellman (New York, 1959).

—— *A Portrait of the Artist as a Young Man*, ed. Chester Anderson and R. Ellmann (London, 1964).

—— *The Essential James Joyce*, ed. Harry Levin (London, 1977).

Kain, Richard M., 'The Playboy Riots', in Suheil B. Bushrui (ed.), *Sunshine and the Moon's Delight: A Centenary Tribute to John Millington Synge 1871–1909* (Gerrards Cross, 1972).

Kee, Robert, *The Laurel and the Ivy: The Story of Charles Stuart Parnell and Irish Nationalism* (London, 1993).

Kelly, John, 'The Fall of Parnell and the Rise of Irish Literature: An Investigation', *Anglo-Irish Studies*, 2 (1976).

Kennedy, David, 'The Ulster Region and the Theatre', *Lagan*, 1/2 (1946).

Kenny, Patrick D., *The Sorrows of Ireland* (London, 1907).

Keogh, Dermot, *The Rise of the Irish Working Class: The Dublin Trade Union Movement and Labour Leadership 1890–1914* (Belfast, 1982).

—— *Jews in Twentieth-Century Ireland: Refugees, Anti-Semitism and the Holocaust* (Cork, 1998).

Kettle, T. M., *The Day's Burden* (Dublin, 1910).
—— *The Open Secret of Ireland* (London, 1912).
Kiberd, Declan, *Synge and the Irish Language* (London, 1979).
—— *Inventing Ireland* (London, 1995).
—— *Irish Classics* (London, 2000).
Kilroy, James, *The Playboy Riots* (Dublin, 1971).
King, Mary C., *The Drama of J. M. Synge* (London, 1985).
Kohfeldt, Mary Lou, *Lady Gregory: The Woman behind the Irish Renaissance* (London, 1985).
Kuch, Peter, *Yeats and AE: 'The antagonism that unites dear friends'* (Gerrards Cross, 1986).
Laclau, Ernesto, and Mouffe, Chantal, *Hegemony and Socialist Strategy: Towards a Radical Democratic Politics* (London, 1985).
Laffan, Michael, *The Resurrection of Ireland: The Sinn Féin Party 1916–1923* (Cambridge, 1999).
Larkin, Emmet, *James Larkin: Irish Labour Leader 1867–1947* (London, 1989).
Laurence, D. H., and Grene, Nicholas, *Shaw, Lady Gregory and the Abbey: A Correspondence and Record* (Gerrards Cross, 1993).
Lee, Joseph, *The Modernisation of Irish Society 1848–1918* (Dublin, 1973).
—— *Ireland 1912–1985* (Cambridge, 1989).
Leerssen, Joep, *Mere Irish and Fíor-Ghael: Studies in the Idea of Irish Nationality, its Development and Literary Expression prior to the Nineteenth Century* (2nd edn., Cork, 1996).
—— *Remembrance and Imagination: Patterns in the Historical and Literary Representation of Ireland in the Nineteenth Century* (Cork, 1996).
Levenson, Leah, *With Wooden Sword: A Portrait of Francis Sheehy-Skeffington, Militant Pacifist* (Boston, 1983).
Lloyd, David, *Anomalous States: Irish Writing and the Post-Colonial Moment* (Durham, 1993).
—— *Ireland after History* (Cork, 1999).
Longenbach, James, 'The Conditions of Music: Yeats, Symons and the Politics of Symbolism', *Yeats Annual*, 8 (1990).
Lukács, George, 'The Sociology of Modern Drama', in Eric Bentley (ed.), *The Theory of the Modern Stage* (rev. edn., London, 1976).
Lynd, Robert, *Irish and English Portraits and Impressions* (London, 1908).
Lyons, F. S. L., *Ireland since the Famine* (London, 1971).
—— *Culture and Anarchy in Ireland, 1890–1939* (Oxford, 1979).
Lyons, J. B., *The Enigma of Tom Kettle: Irish Patriot, Essayist, Poet, British Soldier, 1880–1916* (Dublin, 1983).
McBride, Lawrence W., *The Greening of Dublin Castle: The Transformation of Bureaucratic and Judicial Personnel in Ireland 1892–1922* (Washington, 1991).
McCormack, W. J., *From Burke to Beckett: Ascendancy, Tradition and Betrayal in Literary History* (Cork, 1994).

—— *Fool of the Family: A Life of J. M. Synge* (London, 2000).

McCracken, Donal P., *The Irish Pro-Boers, 1877–1902* (Johannesburg, 1989).

McDiarmid, Lucy, 'Augusta Gregory, Bernard Shaw, and the Shewing-Up of Dublin Castle', *PMLA* 109/1 (Jan. 1994).

MacDonagh, Thomas, *Literature in Ireland: Studies in Irish and Anglo-Irish* (Dublin, 1916).

Malone, Andrew E., 'The Rise in the Realistic Movement', in Lennox Robinson (ed.), *The Irish Theatre: Lectures delivered during the Abbey Theatre Festival in Dublin in August 1939* (London, 1939).

Martin, F. X., *The Irish Volunteers 1913–1915: Recollections and Documents* (Dublin, 1963).

Maume, Patrick, *'Life that is Exile': Daniel Corkery and the Search for Irish Ireland* (Belfast, 1993).

—— *D. P. Moran* (Dundalk, 1995).

—— 'Nationalism and Partition: The Political Thought of Arthur Clery', *Irish Historical Studies* (Nov. 1998).

—— 'Young Ireland, Arthur Griffith and Republican Ideology: The Question of Continuity', *Éire-Ireland* (Autumn 1999).

—— *The Long Gestation: Irish National Life 1891–1918* (Dublin, 1999).

Maxwell, D. E. S., *A Critical History of Modern Irish Drama 1891–1980* (Cambridge, 1984).

Maye, Brian, *Arthur Griffith* (Dublin, 1997).

Mayne, Rutherford, 'The Ulster Literary Theatre', *Dublin Magazine*, NS, 31 (Apr.–June 1955).

Mengel, Hagal, *Sam Thompson and Modern Drama in Ulster* (Frankfurt on Main, 1986).

Mikhail, E. H. (ed.), *J. M. Synge: Interviews and Recollections* (London, 1977).

—— *W. B. Yeats: Interviews and Recollections*, vol. i (London, 1977).

Miller, David W., *Church, State and Nation in Ireland 1898–1921* (Dublin, 1973).

Moore, George, *Parnell and his Island* (London, 1887).

—— *Hail and Fairwell: Ave, Salve, Vale* (Gerrards Cross, 1976).

Moran, D. P., *The Philosophy of Irish Ireland* (Dublin, 1905).

Moran, Sean Farrell, *Patrick Pearse and the Politics of Redemption: The Mind of the Easter Rising, 1916* (Washington, 1994).

Morash, Chris, 'Sinking Down into the Dark: The Famine on Stage', *Bullán*, 3/1 (Spring 1997).

—— ' "Something's Missing": Theatre and the Republic of Ireland Act', in Ray Ryan (ed.), *Writing in the Irish Republic: Literature, Culture, Politics 1949–1999* (London, 2000).

Morgan, Austen, *Labour and Partition: The Belfast Working Class 1905–1923* (London, 1991).

Murphy, Cliona, *The Women's Movement and Irish Society in the Early Twentieth Century* (Hemel Hempstead, 1989).

Murphy, William M., *Prodigal Father: The Life of John Butler Yeats 1839–1922* (New York, 1978).

Murphy, William Martin, *The Story of a Newspaper* (Dublin, 1909).

Murray, Christopher, *Twentieth-Century Irish Drama: Mirror up to Nation* (Manchester, 1997).

Nevin, Donal (ed.), *Trade Union Century* (Cork, 1994).

Ni Dhonnchadha, Máirín, and Dorgan, Theo (eds.), *Revising the Rising* (Derry, 1991).

Nic Shiublaigh, Maire, and Kenny, Edward, *The Splendid Years* (Dublin, 1955).

Norstedt, Johann A., *Thomas MacDonagh: A Critical Biography* (Charlottesville Va., 1980).

O'Brien, Conor Cruise, 'Passion and Cunning: An Essay on the Politics of W. B. Yeats', in A. Norman Jeffares and K. G. W. Cross (eds.), *In Excited Reverie: A Centenary Tribute to W. B. Yeats, 1865–1939* (New York, 1965).

——— *Ancestral Voices: Religion and Nationalism in Ireland* (Dublin, 1994).

Ó Broin, Leon, *The Chief Secretary: Augustine Birrell in Ireland* (London, 1969).

——— *Revolutionary Underground: The Story of the Irish Republican Brotherhood 1858–1924* (Dublin, 1976).

O'Connor, Gary, *Sean O'Casey, A Life* (New York, 1988).

O'Donnell, Frank Hugh, *Souls for Gold! Pseudo-Celtic Drama in Dublin* (London, 1899).

——— *The Stage Irishman of the Pseudo-Celtic Drama* (London, 1904).

O'Driscoll, Robert, (ed.) *Theatre and Nationalism in Twentieth-Century Ireland* (London, 1971).

O'Duffy, Eimar, *Printer's Errors* (Dublin, 1922).

O Duibhir, Ciarán, *Sinn Féin: The First Election 1908* (Manorhamilton, 1993).

O'Farrell, P. J., *Ireland's English Question* (London, 1971).

Ó Gráda, Cormac, *Ireland: A New Economic History 1780–1939* (Oxford, 1994).

O'Grady, Standish, *The Crisis in Ireland* (Dublin, 1882).

——— *The History of Ireland: The Heroic Period* (London, 1878).

O'Hegarty, P. S., *The Victory of Sinn Féin* (Dublin, 1924).

O'Leary, Philip, *The Prose Literature of the Gaelic Revival, 1881–1921: Ideology and Innovation* (University Park, Pa., 1995).

O'Riordan, Manus, 'Sinn Féin and the Jews', *Irish Communist*, 171–8 (Mar.–Nov. 1980).

——— Feeley, Pat, and Kenny, Jim, *The Rise and Fall of Irish Anti-Semitism* (Dublin, 1984).

Owen, Rosemary Cullen, *Smashing Times: A History of the Irish Women's Suffrage Movement 1889–1922* (Dublin, 1984).

Parks, E. W., and Parks, A. W., *Thomas MacDonagh: The Man, the Patriot, the Writer* (Athens, Oh., 1967).

Paseta, Senia, *Before the Revolution: Nationalism, Social Change and Ireland's Catholic Élite 1879–1922* (Cork, 1999).

—— 'Nationalist Responses to Two Royal Visits to Ireland, 1900 and 1903', *Irish Historical Studies*, 21/124 (Nov. 1999).

Patterson, Henry, *Class Conflict and Sectarianism: The Protestant Working Class and the Belfast Labour Movement 1868–1920* (Belfast, 1980).

Pearse, Patrick, *Collected Works of Padraic H. Pearse* (Dublin, 1922).

—— *The Letters of P. H. Pearse*, ed. Séamus Ó Buachalla (Gerrards Cross, 1980).

Pethica, James, ' "Our Kathleen": Yeats's Collaboration with Lady Gregory in the Writing of Cathleen ni Houlihan', in Deirdre Toomey (ed.), *Yeats and Women* (2nd edn. Basingstoke, 1997).

Pilkington, Lionel, ' "Every Crossing Sweeper Thinks Himself a Moralist": The Critical Role of Audiences in Irish Theatre History', *Irish University Review*, 27/1 (Spring–Summer 1997).

Plunkett, Horace, *Ireland in the New Century* (London, 1904).

—— *Noblesse Oblige: An Irish Rendering* (Dublin, 1908).

Rafoidi, Patrick, Popot, R., and Parker, W., *Aspects of Irish Literature* (Paris, n.d.).

Regan, John M., *The Irish Counter-Revolution 1921–1936* (Dublin, 1999).

Regan, Stephen, 'W. B. Yeats and Irish Cultural Politics in the 1890s', in Sally Ledger and Scott McCracken (eds.), *Cultural Politics at the Fin de Siècle* (Cambridge, 1995).

Robinson, E. S. Lennox, *Curtain Up: An Autobiography* (London, 1942).

—— *Ireland's Abbey Theatre: A History, 1899–1951* (London, 1951).

Rolleston, C. H., *Portrait of An Irishman: A Biographical Sketch of T. W. Rolleston* (London, 1939).

Rolleston, T. W., *Ireland, the Empire and the War* (Dublin, 1900).

Rumpf, E., and Hepburn, A., *Nationalism and Socialism in Twentieth-Century Ireland* (Liverpool, 1977).

Ryan, Frederick, *Criticism and Courage* (Dublin, 1906).

—— *Articles by Frederick Ryan*, ed. Manus O'Riordan (Dublin, 1984).

—— *Socialism, Democracy and the Church*, ed. Manus O'Riordan (Dublin, 1984).

Ryan, Louise, 'Traditions and Double Standards: The Irish Suffragists' Critique of Nationalism', *Women's History Review*, 4/4 (1995).

Ryan, W. P., *The Heart of Tipperary* (London, 1893).

—— *The Irish Literary Revival* (London, 1894).

—— *The Plough and The Cross* (Dublin, 1910).

—— *The Pope's Green Island* (London, 1912).

—— *The Labour Revolt and Larkinism* (London, 1913).

Saddlemyer, Ann (ed.), *Theatre Business: The Correspondence of the First Abbey Theatre Directors: W. B. Yeats, Lady Gregory and J. M. Synge* (Gerrards Cross, 1982).

Said, Edward W., *Culture and Imperialism* (London, 1993).

Samuel, Raphael, 'Theatre and Socialism in Britain 1880–1935', in Raphael Samuel, Ewen MacColl, and Stuart Cosgrove (eds.), *Theatres of the Left 1880–1935: Worker's Theatre Movements in Britain and America* (London, 1985).

Schuchard, Ronald, 'W. B. Yeats and the London Theatre Societies, 1901–1904', *Review of English Studies*, NS 29/116 (1978).

Setterquist, Jan, *Ibsen and the Beginnings of Anglo-Irish Drama*, i. *J. M. Synge* (Uppsala, 1951).

—— *Ibsen and the Beginnings of Anglo-Irish Drama*, ii. *Edward Martyn* (Uppsala, 1960).

Shaw, G. B., *The Quintessence of Ibsenism* (London, 1891).

—— *Prefaces* (London, 1938).

Shevtsova, Maria, *Theatre and Cultural Interaction* (Sydney, 1993).

Sorel, George, *Reflections on Violence* (Cambridge, 1999).

Synge, J. M., *The Plays and Poems of J. M. Synge*, ed. T. R. Henn (London, 1963).

—— *Collected Works*, ed. Alan Price, 4 vols. (London, 1966).

—— *The Aran Islands* (Oxford, 1979).

—— *The Collected Letters of J. M. Synge*, ed. Ann Saddlemyer i. 1871–1907; ii. 1907–1909 (Oxford, 1983–4).

Thompson, William Irwin, *The Imagination of an Insurrection—Dublin, Easter 1916: A Study of An Ideological Movement* (Oxford, 1967).

Toomey, Deirdre, 'Labyrinths: Yeats and Maud Gonne', *Yeats Annual*, 9 (1992).

Townsend, Charles, *Political Violence in Ireland: Government and Resistance since 1848* (Oxford, 1983).

Tymoczko, Maria, 'Amateur Political Theatricals, Tableaux Vivants and Cathleen ni Houlihan', *Yeats Annual*, 10 (1993).

Ure, Peter, *Yeats the Playwright* (London, 1963).

Valente, Joseph, 'The Myth of Sovereignty: Gender in the Literature of Irish Nationalism', *ELH* 61/1 (Spring 1994).

Vance, Norman, *Irish Literature: A Social History: Tradition, Identity and Difference* (Oxford, 1990).

Ward, Margaret, *Unmanageable Revolutionaries: Women and Irish Nationalism* (London, 1983).

Watson, G. J., *Irish Identity and the Literary Revival: Synge, Yeats, Joyce and O'Casey* (Washington, 1984).

Watt, Stephen, *Joyce, O'Casey and the Irish Popular Theater* (Syracuse, 1991).

Welch, Robert, *The Abbey Theatre 1899–1999: Form and Pressure* (Oxford, 1999).

West, Trevor, *Horace Plunkett: Co-Operation and Politics, An Irish Biography* (Gerrards Cross, 1986).

Weygandt, Cornelius, *Irish Plays and Playwrights* (London, 1913).

Wilde, Oscar, *De Profundis and Other Writings* (London, 1954).

Williams, Raymond, *Drama from Ibsen to Brecht* (London, 1958).

—— *The Long Revolution* (London, 1961).

—— *Modern Tragedy* (London, 1966).

—— *Politics and Letters: Interviews with New Left Review* (London, 1979).

Wilson, Stephen, *Ideology and Experience: Antisemitism in France at the Time of the Dreyfus Affair* (Rutherford, 1982).

Wolfe, Francis R., *Theatres in Ireland* (Dublin, 1898).

Worth, Katherine, *The Irish Drama of Europe from Yeats to Beckett* (London, 1978).

Yeates, Pádraig, *Lockout: Dublin 1913* (Dublin, 2000).

Yeats, W. B., *The Letters of W. B. Yeats*, ed. Allen Wade (London, 1954).

—— *Autobiographies* (London, 1955).

—— *Essays and Introductions* (London, 1961).

—— *Uncollected Prose by W. B. Yeats*, ed. John P. Frayne and Colton Johnston, 2 vols. (London, 1970).

—— *The Collected Works of W. B. Yeats*, i. *The Poems*, ed. Richard J. Finneran, (rev. edn. London, 1991).

—— *Where There is Nothing: The Unicorn from the Stars*, ed. Katherine Worth (Washington, 1987).

—— *The Collected Letters of W. B. Yeats*, i. *1865–1895*, ed. John Kelly (Oxford, 1986).

—— *The Collected Letters of W. B. Yeats*, iii. *1901–1904*, ed. John Kelly and Ron Schuhard (Oxford, 1994).

—— *The Collected Letters of W. B. Yeats*, ii. *1896–1900*, ed. Warwick Gould, John Kelly, and Deirdre Toomey (Oxford, 1997).

(d) Theses

Kelly, John S., 'The Political, Intellectual and Social Background to the Irish Literary Revival to 1901', Ph.D. thesis (Cambridge, 1972).

Marshalsay, Karen Anne, 'The Scottish National Players: In the Nature of an Experiment 1913–1934', Ph.D. thesis (Glasgow, 1991).

Novick, Benjamin Zvi, 'Ireland's Revolutionary War?: Nationalist Propaganda, the Great War, and the Construction of Irish Identity', D.Phil. thesis (Oxford, 2000).

O'Neill, Shane, 'The Politics of Culture in Ireland 1899–1910', D.Phil. thesis (Oxford, 1982).

Parks, Kathleen Danaher, 'Gerald MacNamara: Ulster Playwright', D.Phil. thesis (Delaware, 1984).

Pethica, James L., 'Dialogue of Self and Service: Lady Gregory's Emergence as an Irish Writer and Partnership with W. B. Yeats', D.Phil. thesis (Oxford, 1987).

INDEX

Abbey Theatre 105–6, 165, 215, 239–40
   Blanco Posnet controversy 168–73
   directorship of 143, 190, 230
   and Gaelic League 103–4, 180–1
   finances 141 n 14, 217, 221
   and *Irish Worker* 196–7
   and lockout 207–8
   first opens 93
   Playboy riots 127–34
   post-*Playboy* 150–1, 156–9, 174–5
   splits 101–3
   stylistic change in 187–8, 192–4,
      199
   and Theatre of Ireland 160–1
   and ULT 138–40, 167–8, 236
   in War climate 220–1
   see also Irish National Theatre Society;
      National Theatre Society
Aberdeen, Lord 169–70
AE, *see* Russell, George
All Ireland Review 41, 67
Allgood, Molly 115, 125
An Claidheamh Soluis 41, 99–100, 160,
   180–1, 201
   attacks ILT 49–50
   Playboy controversy 131
   supports Yeats 104
   and volunteer movement 201
Ancient Order of Hibernians (AOH) 110,
   132, 152, 177, 186, 192, 203, 206
anti-Semitism 31, 89–92, 231
   see also Dreyfus Affair
Archer, William 33
Ardilaun, Lord 42
Arrow 111, 142
Atkinson, Robert 51

Bailey, W. F. 220
Bean na hÉireann 162, 194
Béaslaí, Piaras 128, 181
Beerbohm Tree, Herbert 27
Beltaine 45
Benjamin, Walter 230
Birmingham, George 109–10, 147, 207
Blunt, Wilfred Scawen 189
Blythe, Ernest 177, 239
Boer War 51–5, 59, 72, 74, 211, 230
Boucicault, Dion 15, 18–19

   Robert Emmet 25
Bourke, P. J. 19, 207
   For The Land She Loved 220–1
Boyd, Ernest 187
Boyle, William 101, 113, 184, 190
   Eloquent Dempsey 111–12
   Mineral Workers 112

Cairns, David 234
Casement, Roger 211
Casey, W. F. 151
Catholic Truth Society 189–90
Celtic Literary Society 23
Celticism 81, 86
Chekhov, Anton 40, 215
Christie, R. A. 217
Clarke, Tom 175, 222
Clery, Arthur 44, 80, 163
Colum, Mary 214
Colum, Padriac 99, 117, 121, 130, 190,
   193–4
   Broken Soil 92–4
   Fiddler's House 160
   Land 94–6, 164
   Saxon Shillin' 78
   and Theatre of Ireland 101–2
   Thomas Muskerry 183
Connell, Norreys 149
   Piper 149–50, 160
Connolly James 154–5, 181, 202, 241
   anti-racist 54
   edits *Worker's Republic* 38
   influence of 35, 232
   and Irish Citizen Army 219–20
   and ITGWU 185–6
   and Socialist Party of Ireland 175
   Under Which Flag? 225
Cork Dramatic Society (CDS) 175–6, 222,
   236
Corkery, Daniel 119, 126, 150, 159
   Embers 175
Cousins, James 70, 102
   Racing Lug 77, 217
   Sold 77–8
Cousins, Margaret 87, 163
Craig, Gordon 191
Crawford, Lindsay 109, 146
Creagh, Fr. John 90

Cumann na nGaedheal 60, 78, 138
Cumann na nGaedheal Theatre Co. 81,
        95

Daily Express (Dublin) 37–8, 60
Daly, P. T. 175
Dana 99–100, 134, 138
Davis, Thomas 16, 234
    literary influence 60–1
Davitt, Michael 31, 90
Dawson, William 150–1
Devlin, Joseph 110
Digges, Dudley 77
Dillon, John 42
Dineen, Fr. Patrick 103–4, 142–3
Dolan, C. J. 152
Dougherty, Sir James 170
Dowden, Edward 39
Dreyfus Affair 53–4, 88
    see also anti-Semitism
Drumont, Edouard 53
Dublin Corporation 81, 87
Dublin Drama League 240
Dublin Metropolitan Police 132
Dublin Repertory Theatre 203
Dublin Trades Council 204
Dungannon Clubs 110, 138, 174, 236
Dunsany, Lord Edward 191–2

Eagleton, Terry 233
Edward VII, King 81
Eglinton, John 39, 73, 98–100
Employers' Federation 204
Ervine, St John 218, 221, 235
    Critics 208
    Magnanimous Lover 197
    Mixed Marriage 186–7, 194, 219
Eygpt 189

Fay, Frank, 27, 58, 64, 78, 149–50, 161,
        228
Fay, William G. 27, 64, 78, 101, 115, 149,
        228
Fianna Éireann 207
Finlay, Thomas 26
First World War 238
Fitzmaurice, George:
    Country Dressmaker 148–50
    Dandy Dolls 200
    Magic Glasses 200
    Pie-Dish 165
Fort, Paul 24
Frazier, Adrian 230

Freeman's Journal, 9–10, 37, 42, 44, 158–9
    on ILT 62
    and literary establishment 17, 28
    on *Playboy* 124, 129
Fullerton, Revd R. 189

Gaelic Athletic Association 150
Gaelic League 58, 70, 90, 236
    and Abbey 103–4, 112, 180
    and education 179
    founding of 14
    and ILT 49–51, 61
    and *Playboy* controversy 120
    and Sinn Féin 99–100
Gaiety Theatre 15, 27
Gate Theatre 240
Gill, T. P. 37–8
Gogarty, St John 99
Gonne Maud 38, 54–5, 65, 84, 95
    in *Cathleen ni Houlihan* 66–8, 125, 228
    marriage of 78–80, 87
Good, J. W. 108, 168
Gregory, Lady Augusta 168–9, 174, 183–5,
        189, 213–14
    and *Blanco Posnet* controversy 169–73
    Bogie Men 190
    Canavans 106, 112
    Cathleen ni Houlihan (with W. B. Yeats)
        66–8, 71, 78, 83, 148, 221, 228, 238,
        240, 242
    Dama's Gold Deliverer 190–1
    Dervorgilla 143–4
    diplomatic skills of 107, 141–3, 230
    Gaol Gate 113, 141, 162
    Hyacinth Halvey 105, 141–2
    and ILT 35, 62, 65
    Jackdaw 141–2
    Kincora 106–7
    McDarragh's Wife 190
    and *Playboy* 115, 117, 124
    Pot of Broth (with W. B. Yeats) 70
    as propagandist 101, 105–6
    Rising of the Moon 141, 160
    Spreading the News 105–6, 142
    translated 181
    Twenty-Five 77
    Unicorn from the Stars 148
    White Cockade 106–7, 141
    and Yeats 45, 66, 73, 150, 174, 213
Grene, Nicholas 240
Griffith, Arthur 33, 37, 47, 75, 77, 117,
        161, 211, 231, 233
    anti-semitic 89–91

anti-trade union 145, 209
and *Blanco Posnet* controversy 172
corporatism 98, 112
economics 97, 153
German militarism 97
on Hungary 81, 96–7
on ILT 45–6, 58–60, 64
on *Playboy* 121, 127
pragmatism of 97
praises *Cathleen ni Houlihan* 66
on suffragist tactics 162
supports Gonne 65
on Synge 84–5, 87
republicans criticize188
Resurrection of Hungary 97–8
see also *United Irishman*; Sinn Féin;
    Sinn Féin
Gunning, G. Hamilton 187
Gwynn, Stephen 99, 102, 112

Harp 175
Hauptmann, Gerhart 214
Healy, Timothy 11, 42
Hobson, Bulmer 131, 138, 192, 217, 222
edits *Irish Freedom* 188, 198
founds ULT 71, 108–9
Horniman, Annie E. F. 73, 81, 149, 161,
    183
Hyde, Douglas 13, 17, 45, 117, 141, 181
Cásadh an tSúgáin 27, 61, 64
Tinéar agus an tSídheog 70

Ibsen, Henrik 10, 24, 76
A Doll's House 87, 162
An Enemy of the People 10, 27, 57, 108,
    237
Brand 113
Ghosts 10, 226
influence of 32, 50, 68, 122
Independent Orange Order 109, 146
Independent Theatre Society 24
Inghinidhe na hÉireann 61, 64, 78, 162,
    228, 232
Irish Citizen 194, 197, 204, 232
Irish Citizen Army 219, 225
Irish Freedom 178, 185, 188, 197, 211, 216,
    220
Irish Independent 203–4, 208
Irish Literary Society 11
Irish Literary Theatre (ILT) 14, 27, 48, 55,
    184, 215
formed 35–6
and Gaelic League 61, 64

manifesto 36, 230
radicalized 51–2, 60
splits 62, 65–6
uses English actors 58–9
Irish Nation and Peasant 168, 173–4
Irish National Alliance (INA) 35, 38
Irish National Dramatic Company (INDC)
    66, 68, 70
Irish National Theatre Society (INTS) 77,
    87, 89, 95, 99
and Abbey 93
becomes professional 96
democratic instincts of 230
resilience of 92
splits 81, 96, 101–2
see also Abbey Theatre; National
    Theatre Society
Irish Parliamentary Party (IPP) 55, 60,
    101, 196, 233
and Boer War 60
Cork factionalism 164–5,175, 177
and fall of Parnell 9–12, 28
and Liberal alliance 178–9
resistence to suffragism 194
and Sinn Féin 147, 152–3, 185
Irish Republican Brotherhood (IRB) 38, 65
    153, 185, 212
anti-clericalism of 30, 91
and Dungannon Clubs 157, 174–5, 236
and Easter Rising 222–5
and '98 movement 60
and Sinn Féin 185
response to War 216–17
Irish Review 187, 214
Irish Socialist Republican Party (ISRP) 34,
    38, 54–5, 232
Irish Theatre 215, 217, 223
Irish Times 219
Irish Transport and General Worker's
    Union (ITGWU) 145–7, 185–6,
    194, 203, 232
Irish Volunteer 220, 223, 225
Irish Volunteers 215, 222–3
Irish Women's Franchise League (IWFL)
    87, 145, 163, 189, 232
Irish Worker 185, 197, 202–3, 220, 235
Irlande Libre 54

Jaurés, Jean 101
Jauss, Hans Robert 234
Johnson, Lionel 50
Johnston, Denis 240
Joy, Maurice 9, 102

Joyce, James 44, 61–2, 88, 99, 105, 234
Jubainville, Henri d'Arbois de 119

Kennedy, David 167
Kenny, Patrick 134, 138, 175
Kettle, Thomas 44, 100–2, 152, 178, 198
Koehler, Thomas 102, 135
Kropotkin, Prince Pyotr 75

Laclau, Ernesto 228
Land Conference 81
Lane, Hugh 204
Larkin, James 185, 203, 218–9, 232
    Abbeygoer 202
    impact of 145–7
    and Socialist Party of Ireland 175
    see also Irish Transport and General
        Worker's Union; *Irish Worker*
Lawrence, W. J. 134, 161
Leader 41, 63, 72, 230
    anti-socialist 189
    isolated 99–100
    moves mainstream 150–3
    sectarian 76–7
    see also Moran, D. P.
Leamy, Edmund 12
Lecky, W. E. H. 38, 42
Limerick Pogrom 89–92
Literary and Historical Society 44
Local Government Bill (1898) 38
Lyceum 26, 31
Lynd, Robert 168, 185

MacBride, John 59, 78,
McCartan, Patrick 110
McCarthy, J. Bernard 217
McCarthy, Justin 11
MacDermott, Sean 222
MacDonagh, Thomas 163, 222
    Metempsychosis 214
    Pagans 215–16
    When the Dawn is Come 157–60, 215
McGarrity, Joseph 110, 139, 192
McGinley, P. T. 185
McGrath, John 12, 16, 36
MacManus, Seumas 95–7
MacNamara, Gerald (Harry Morrow)
    165
    Mist That Does Be On The Bog 167–8
    Suzanne and the Sovereigns (with Lewis
        Purcell) 166–7
    Thompson in Tir-na-n-og 200–2
MacNeill, Eoin 201, 222

McNulty, Edward 210
    Lord Mayor 210–11, 217, 219
MacSweeney, Terence 153, 198, 235
    Dreamers 222
    Holocaust 176
    Last Warriors of Coole 175
    Revolutionist 222
Maeterlinck, Maurice 30
Magee, William K., *see* Eglington, John
Mahaffy, John 42, 51
Markievicz, Constance, Countess 102, 162,
    207
Markievicz, Count 203, 207
Martyn, Edward 33, 62, 65, 102, 214–5
    Dream Physician 215
    Heather Field 33, 46–8, 112, 182
    Maeve 57, 160
    Placehunters 70
    Tale of a Town 56
Marx, Karl 119
Mayne, Rutherford 108, 160, 165–6, 200
melodrama 15, 18–26, 58, 207
Millevoye, Lucien 53
Milligan, Alice 24, 70, 129, 141
    Last Feast of the Fianna 57, 160
Mitchel, John 16
Molière, 142
Monck, Nugent 192
Moore, George 32, 45, 65, 99
    Bending of the Bough 55–6, 59
    Diarmuid and Grania 56, 61–4, 68
    Hail and Fairwell 143, 215
Moran, D. P. 32, 38, 58, 60, 70, 98, 144,
    203
    attacks Abbey 93
    defends ILT 46
    Dublin lockout 205–6
    edits *Leader* 41, 231
    fatigued 150–1, 233
    and industrialization 47
    Playboy controversy 130
    sectarian 76
    racism and anti-semitism 63, 89–90
    on suffragism 163, 189
    see also Leader
Morash, Christopher 240
Morrow, Frederick 139
Morrow, Harry, *see* MacNamara, Gerald
Morrow, Jack 139
Mouffe, Chantal 228
Murphy, William Martin 42, 203–4, 207,
    209
Murray, Thomas C. 176

Birthright 182
  Maurice Harte 195, 199–200

Narodniki 76
Nation 234
National Democrat 134–5, 138
National Literary Society (NLS) 13
  National Council 81, 138, 147
National Players Society 95, 160
National Theatre Society (NTS) 102, 111,
  160–1, 173
  expansion of 184
  and Gaelic League 180–1
  and ULT 139–40
  see also Abbey Theatre
National Union of Dock Labourers 145
National Volunteers 215, 217
Nationist 100–3, 134, 152
Neitzsche, Friedrich 73, 75, 77, 80–2,
  98–9, 237
New Ireland Review 26, 31–2, 44

O'Brien, Francis Cruise 152, 163
O'Brien, Seamus 207
O'Brien, William (labour leader) 185
O'Brien, William (MP) 16, 28, 35, 174
O'Casey, Sean 105, 235, 240
  Plough and the Stars 220
  Silver Tassie 239
O'Connell, J. J. 223
O'Donnell, Frank Hugh 32, 38, 48, 58
  anti-Semitism of 31, 54–5, 89
  attacks Yeats 42–3
O'Donoghue, D. J., 13, 129
O'Duffy, Eimar 215
  Pheonix on the Roof 223
  Walls of Athens 223–4
O'Grady, Hubert 15, 18
  Emigration 21
  Eviction 19–21
  Famine 21–2
O'Grady, Standish 32, 41, 58, 69, 99
  defends Jews 91
  rural radicalism of 155, 202
O'Hegarty, P. S. 153–4, 156, 159–61, 185,
  198, 211–12, 241
O'Kelly, Seumas 160
  Bribe 208–9, 219
  Shuiler's Child 161–2, 164, 183, 208
O'Leary, John 30, 76
O'Neill, Revd George 44
O'Riordan, Connell, *see* Norreys Connell
O'Shea, John Augustus 18

O'Toole, J. J. 76
Orange Order 132, 186

Pankhurst, Christabel 162
Pankhurst, Emmeline 87
Parkhill, David, *see* Lewis Purcell
Parnell, Charles Stewart 31, 62, 69, 204,
  236
  canonization of 178, 190, 192
  fall of 9–14, 226, 229
  compared to Synge 193
Payne, Ben Iden 143
Pearse, Patrick 192, 198, 241
  admires Gregory 106
  An Rí 212–13
  'The Coming Revolution' 201
  and Easter Rising 224–6
  and education 179, 181, 212
  funeral oration 222–3
  Ghosts 226
  and ILT 49
  and IRB 212, 216
  Isoagán 212
  Master 224
  Singer 224
  and Synge 213
  and Theatre of Ireland 102–3
Peasant and Irish Ireland 137–40, 156, 159,
  235
  see also *Irish Nation and Peasant*
Pike Theatre 240
Plunkett, Joseph 214, 216, 222
Plunkett, Sir Horace 38, 45, 100, 138
Purcell, Lewis 108, 165
  Enthusiast 108–11
  Suzanne and the Sovereigns (with
    Gerald MacNamara) 166–7

Queen's Royal Theatre 15, 58, 60, 102,
  207, 221
Quinn, Maire 77

Ray, R. J. 183
Redmond, John 42, 93, 154, 190, 194, 215
Republic 131, 138–9
Richards, Shaun 234
Roberts, George 102, 136
Robinson, E. S. Lennox 176
  Clancy Name 158–9
  Cross Roads 164, 183, 197
  Dreamers 221–2
  Harvest 182–3
  Patriots 195–7

Rolleston, T. W. 13, 45, 53
Rooney, William 23–4, 33, 37, 51
Royal Irish Constabulary 207–8
Russell, George 37–41, 47, 99–100, 102
   Deirdre 68–70, 160
   'To the Masters of Dublin' 204
Russell, T. W. 109
Ryan, Frederick 65, 175, 185, 189–90, 219, 325
   attacks anti-Semitism 54–5, 89–92
   criticizes Theatre of Ireland 103
   edits *Dana* 99–101
   edits *National Democrat* 134–5
   on Ibsen 33–4
   Laying of the Foundations 71–2
   on *Mixed Marriage* 194
   on *Playboy* 127, 193
Ryan, William Patrick 16, 160, 175–6, 185, 202
   attacks Sinn Féin 154
   edits *Peasant* 137–8
   on George Birmingham 147
   Irish Literary Revival 28
   on Synge 193

Sagnier, Marc 101
Samhain 104, 151
Scissors and Paste 220
Shan Van Vocht 35
Shanachie 136
Shaw, George Bernard 10, 17, 28, 40, 237
   Arms and the Man 29
   John Bull's Other Island 103
   O'Flaherty V.C. 220
   Quintessence of Ibsenism 10–11, 32
   Shewing-Up of Blanco Posnet 169–73, 207, 220
Shawe-Taylor, John 81
Sheehan, Daniel 134
Sheehy-Skeffington, Francis 44, 88–9, 100, 134, 152, 163, 185
   'Dialogues of the Day' 144–5, 229
Sheehy-Skeffington, Hanna 87, 163, 232
Shiublaigh, Maire Nic 121
Sinn Féin (Daily) 172, 174
Sinn Féin 97, 148, 185, 211
   and Dublin lockout 209
   and *Peasant* 154
   and *Playboy* controversy 127
   proscribed 220
   republicans criticise 153, 188
   supports Theatre of Ireland 154

Sinn Féin 97–9, 141, 159, 233
   founded 138
   and IPP 152, 165
   and ITGWU 147
   left criticism of 154
   splits 174, 177, 188
Sloan, Thomas 109, 146
Socialist Party of Ireland 175, 232
Sorel, George 237, 241
Starkey, J. S. 102
Stephens, James 197, 202, 206
Stepniak, Sergius 75
Strindberg, August 214–15
   There Are Crimes and Crimes 214
   Easter 215
Sudermann, Hermann 142, 213
Sweetman, John 153–4
Symons, Arthur 62
Synge, John Millington 30, 69, 74, 95, 142, 230
   Aran Islands 83
   Deirdre of the Sorrows 184
   and Dreyfus Affair 88
   European sensibility of 119–20
   and Gaelic League 83, 120
   In the Shadow of the Glen 75, 81–5, 104, 112, 125, 127, 164, 197
   nationalism of 83
   Playboy of the Western World 113–37, 139, 155, 172–7, 182, 192, 197, 234–5, 237, 241–2
   praised by Pearse 213, 224
   and unconventionality 82–3, 105
   upbringing of 119
   radicals' reassessment of 174–7
   Riders to the Sea 92–3, 176
   socialism of 83, 88, 119–20
   Tinker's Wedding 105
   on W. Boyle 111
   Well of the Saints 104

Tagore, Rabindranath 213
   Post Office 214
Theatre of Ireland 102, 140, 160, 236
Theatre Royal 15
Todhunter, John 17–18

Uladh 108–9
Ulster Literary Theatre (ULT) 71, 108–111, 132, 138–40, 165–8, 200–2, 236
United Ireland 12–15, 34–6, 38
   opposing *Leader* 52

United Irish League (UIL) 55, 163, 175, 177
  Young Ireland Branch of 101, 152
United Irishman 35, 41, 48, 90, 94, 137
  and censorship 64, 72
  literary platform 70–2, 77
University College, Dublin 44

Vigilance Committees 189–90

Wagner, 24, 40
Walker, Maire, *see* Maire Nic Shiublaigh
Weygandt, Cornelius 70
Whitbread, James W. 15, 18, 27
  Lord Edward 25
  Nationalist, 22–3
  Wolfe Tone 25
Wilde, Oscar 10, 15, 31, 64
Williams, Raymond 228
Wilson, Andrew Patrick 203, 210, 217, 235
  Call to Arms 219
  Slough 211, 218–19
  Victims 202
Women's Social and Political Union 87
Worker's Republic (1898–1903) 38, 67, 72, 241
Worker's Republic (1914–16) 220

Yeats, John Butler 76, 83–4, 130, 134
Yeats, William Butler 95, 117, 143, 230, 234
  and anarchism 237
  alienation 168–9, 190
  and *Blanco Posnet* controversy 169–73
  Cathleen ni Houlihan (with Lady Gregory) 66–8, 71, 78, 83, 148, 221, 228, 238, 240, 242
  cosmopolitanism 39–40, 67, 113

Countess Cathleen 14, 17, 42–5, 48
'Crucifixion of the Outcast' 30
Diarmuid and Grania 56, 61–4, 68
Deirdre 69, 112, 155
Dreaming of the Bones 238–9
  and Dublin lockout 206, 208
  on Easter Rising 227–9
King's Threshold 79
Golden Helmet 151
  and Gonne 65, 79–81
Green Helmet 180, 191
  and Gregory 45, 66, 73, 150, 174, 213
  and Griffith 60, 97–8
Hourglass 79–80, 191
  and National Literary Society 13
  influence of Morris on 72, 75, 82
  influence of Nietzsche on 73, 75, 77, 80–82
  and Irish language 14, 103–4, 180
  and Irish Literary Society 11
  and Irish Literary Theatre 57
  and Irish National Dramatic Company 68
Land of Heart's Desire 29–30
Last Poems 227–8
  literary elitism 48–9, 73
  on realists 185
On Baile's Strand 79–80
  on Parnell 9
Playboy controversy 115, 127–35, 156
Pot of Broth (with Lady Gregory) 70
  praised by Connolly 156
Shadowy Waters 30, 112
  and Synge 75–7, 82, 104–5, 176–7
Unicorn from the Stars 148
Where There is Nothing 72–3

Zola, Émile 122